The Media in Africa
and
Africa in the Media:
An Annotated Bibliography

Some Hans Zell titles of related interest:

Publishing and Development in the Third World
Edited by PHILIP G. ALTBACH
(Hans Zell Studies on Publishing, 1)

**Publishing and Book Development in Sub-Saharan Africa:
An Annotated Bibliography**
HANS M. ZELL & CECILE LOMER
(Hans Zell Studies on Publishing, 3)

The Media in Africa
and
Africa in the Media:
An Annotated Bibliography

Gretchen Walsh
Mugar Memorial Library, Boston University

With an introductory essay by Keyan G. Tomaselli

HANS ZELL PUBLISHERS
London • Melbourne • Munich • New Providence • 1996

© Gretchen Walsh 1996

All rights reserved. No part of this publication may be reproduced or transmitted in any form or by any means (including photocopying and recording) without the written permission of the copyright holder except in accordance with the provisions of the Copyright, Designs and Patents Act 1988 or under the terms of a licence issued by the Copyright Licensing Agency, 90 Tottenham Court Road, London, W1P 9HE. The written permission of the copyright holder must also be obtained before any part of this publication is stored in a retrieval system of any nature. Applications for the copyright holder's written permission to reproduce, transmit or store in a retrieval system any part of this publication should be addressed to the publisher.

Warning: The doing of any unauthorised act in relation to a copyright work may result in both a civil claim for damages and criminal prosecution.

British Library Cataloguing in Publication Data

Walsh, Gretchen
    The media in Africa and Africa in the media: an annotated bibliography
    1. Mass media - Africa - Bibliography   2. Africa in mass media - Bibliography
    I. Title
    016'.3'0223'096

    ISBN 1-873836-81-3

Library of Congress Cataloging-in-Publication Data

Walsh, Gretchen
    The media in Africa and Africa in the media : an annotated bibliography /
    Gretchen Walsh : with an introduction by Keyan G. Tomaselli.
    318pp 24cm.
    Includes bibliographical references and indexes.
    ISBN 1-873836-81-3
    1. Mass media -- Africa -- Bibliography. 2. Africa in mass media -- Bibliography.
    I. Title.
    Z5634.A4W35 1996
    [P92.A4]
    016.30223'096 -- DC20   96-34610
                                                                      CIP

Published by Hans Zell Publishers, an imprint of Bowker-Saur, a division of
Reed Elsevier (UK) Limited, Maypole House, Maypole Road, East Grinstead,
West Sussex RH19 1HU, United Kingdom
Tel: +44 (0) 1342 330100   Fax: +44 (0) 1342 330191
email: lis@bowker-saur.co.uk
WWW: http://www.bowker-saur.co.uk/service

Bowker-Saur is a part of REED REFERENCE PUBLISHING.

Cover design by Robin Caira

Printed on acid-free paper.
Printed and bound in Great Britain
by Antony Rowe Ltd., Chippenham, Wiltshire.

Table of Contents

African Mediascapes:
    A Continent Swept by More Winds Than One   vii

Introduction   xix

List of Journals Consulted   xxiii

The Press   1

Broadcasting   83

Film   123

General   179

Author Index   257

Subject and Geographical Index   275

African Mediascapes:
A Continent Swept by More Winds Than One

By Keyan G. Tomaselli
Director, Centre for Cultural and Media Studies, University of Natal

The winds of change have swept across African following the end of the Cold War. These changes, which have characterized the 1990s, have also been further catalysed by South Africa's attainment of a democratic order. Related to these events has been the demise, and contestation, in many other countries, of the power of the neo-colonial elites which took over in the immediate post-independence era.

Globalizing Africa

While the attitudes of many new African governments towards the press are little different to their authoritarian predecessors, the political conditions which led to their ascent to power locate this authority within global relations of an order not previously experienced at the local level of individual countries. The US victory of the Cold War fundamentally altered local-global relations in Africa. Altered too, are the solutions which African nations are now expected to pursue by the major global institutions such as the World Bank, the World Trade Organisation, the International Monetary Fund, and the host of United Nations agencies. The freedom of the press (as a watchdog for capitalism) is amongst the new conditions within which governments now have to conduct themselves.

The recent emergence of new democratically elected governments during the 1990s situates African media in transformed global, regional and local contexts. This pertains notwithstanding attempts by some new governments, like Zambia's, under President Frederick Chiluba who has since 1992 reverted to muzzling the press and harassing journalists. These attacks have occurred simply because certain independent newspapers and editors have used the space afforded by the fledgling Zambian democracy to report in ways and on topics which may be challenging to social and political taboos. There are some taboos, established by the previous Kaunda regime, which the new government prefers to retain.

Access, Power and Critical Practice

Studies of the African media by African scholars are often difficult for Westerners to come by. They do exist, and their academic rigour is improving all the time. They exist in journals published in Africa, such as *Africa Media Review* published by the African Council for Communication Education, based in Nairobi. the Council also publishes books, bibliographies and monographs. There is also the work of numerous individual publishing houses in various African countries, and there are, of course, the occasionally African published articles in the flagship disciplinary journals published in the West. Though publication in such flagship journals confers a prestigious aura on such African authors, some of these journals do the cause of African academia little good when they knowingly publish ill-conceived, uncritical and thin analyses. This mainly occurs because of inadequate, often incompetent, refereeing by journal editors who may know nothing about Africa. Further, the simple wish to fill pages, or to provide adequate representation (i.e.. quantity rather than quality) to authors in regions which have failed to ensure themselves a visible presence, is an exacerbating factor. The result is to boost egos beyond competence, and to elevate such writers to continental guru status, which then links them into international funding networks. The benefits of this individual status rarely, it seems, filter down to the community of scholars who form the backbone of the teaching components at African universities. Solutions to this problem need to be found.

Most widely known, however, are books and journal articles published in North America by North American scholars for their students, often based on brief research field trips to Africa. This work tends to assume US perspectives, US conceptions of freedom of the press and freedom of speech, and US practices and solutions. There is nothing wrong with this US-centrism - and without these publications it is unlikely that the African media would get much coverage. This orientation, however, becomes a problem when these publications impose US perspectives on Africans in Africa: it excludes the corresponding debate from African media scholars and practitioners themselves.

The result, therefore, tends to be a one-sided perspective which a) ignores African-authored work on the same topics; b) belittles African media and studies; c) perpetuates an incestuous circle of discussion in which US and European African studies scholars reference themselves only; and d) appropriates African-authored work without adequate citation. In all these instances, the most conspicuous scholarship on African media fails to engage African scholars, or expose their work to students more broadly. Thus, Africa is studied by Americans in America from American authored texts in an American context. Africa becomes a site for academic research, but its own academics do not themselves necessarily contribute to the debates which shape that activity and its conclusions about African media.

African students at many European universities are occasionally permitted to register research dissertations on African media topics. It is always surprising how little these students' supervisors know about Africa, and even about the key studies on African media available in their own cities, published or distributed by European companies. This is careless practice and perpetuates the cycle of ignorance described in the above paragraph. Alternatively, academics who have `escaped' Africa and its traumas through emigration sometimes use their now more central location in the West to cynically berate those who continue struggling for freedom of speech and democracy from inside their societies in an attempt to negotiate the structures of oppression in which they find themselves. Such critique is vital, but it must be offered from an empirically informed position. Bibliographies such as this one by Gretchen Walsh remove any excuse for this kind of shoddy and/or opportunistic research practice.

There are, of course, exceptions. Highly nuanced and deeply textual studies have been produced by some US, Canadian and European scholars. These researchers tend to be more interdisciplinary in their training, theoretical perspectives and research methodologies. This transdisciplinarity enables them to pursue a more contextual approach to African media studies. These are the people who have spent considerable periods working in Africa in the contexts of national, continental and international discourses about media, media and society, and media and politics. Debates on media and training cannot occur outside these broader ideological issues. And nowhere is criticism of these issues more vigorous than in Africa itself. A study of articles published in *Africa Media Review*, for example, is merciless in its questioning of the quality of work it publishes (Edeani 1995). This kind of self-evaluation is rarely found in journals elsewhere (see also *Critical Arts' Retrospective,* 1983) and indicates not only academic security, but an enormous dialectical potential within the African media studies community.

This kind of critical practice, however, is often negated when university departments in African universities prescribe for their students the US or European textbook over equally and perhaps even more appropriate indigenous publications, which are cheaper and, more importantly, offer highly textured analyses of local conditions not found in the text books published in the First World. Thus, students located in Africa get fed the US and/or European perspectives on their own media. They don't get to study their media also from the perspectives of indigenous scholarship. Such imported frameworks may or may not be pertinent to the micro issues of specific media in particular countries or regions.

Why does this happen?

When First World methods, theories, and ideas are imported directly and without adaptation into Africa, some problems arise. Importantly, these methods and theories assume that conditions - like `modernity' and `the post-modern'- necessarily exist in Africa or South Africa in exactly the same ways they do in the US. The insistence on the application of the post-Freudian psychoanalysis of Jacques Lacan to cinema studies, for example, is seen by some African scholars - and most African film directors - as relatively inappropriate. This approach is even considered by some as a conceptually imperialist imposition on societies which remain very much enmeshed in a disjointed set of non-industrial/industrial ontologies, which integrate orality and literacy, the traditional and modern, and the spiritual and the material. Those Western ideas which assume a Cartesian derived ontological division of Subject and Object often cannot easily account for ways in which African and Western/Eastern forms of expression have meshed, or for indigenous ways of knowing and making sense. What is needed are theories which can account for the various, often widely different and original African applications of imaging and recording technologies. The resulting aesthetics, and how these in turn are encountered and made sense of in radically different contexts and societies, needs study.

Indigenizing Theory

Indigenization of theory is occurring most noticeably in cinema and television analysis, in which issues of cosmology are so prevalent. Journals such as *Research in African Literatures, Iris, Oral Tradition* in the US, and *Critical Arts* in South Africa, together with publications emanating from the Federation of Pan African Filmmakers, based in Ouagadougou, Burkina Faso, and the British Film Institute, have begun to explore a different - indigenous - set of assumptions about African cinema. Much of this pioneering work is also produced by expatriates or non-Africans. The bibliographies of Nancy Schmidt and others, for instance, have paved the way for some knowledge of African-authored studies. Access to these works, however, is often hampered by difficult conditions which make the continent itself difficult to traverse and within which to communicate. This is one reason why non-African-authored books and publications prevail over continentally produced works. The rapid development of Internet and the World Wide Web, however, reduces any unbridgeable excuse for the gaps and omissions in the First World. But it is up to African scholars themselves to write their presence into the Web in particular. When I checked the Web in May 1996 for a listing of African departments of communication and journalism, I found only three, all located in South Africa.

Another explanation for the importation of unreconstituted theory is to be found in the traveling patterns of some African academics. They produce their work in locations where scholarships are tenable and employment is found, and this tenure is sometimes determined by the political preferences of those who teach about African media to non-African students. These lecturers tend to owe their professional and theoretical allegiances to the commercial domain, and have often studied in the USA and elsewhere where there may be little interest in or knowledge of African issues. Frequently, such programmes and scholars may take for granted the practices of American journalism and scholarship, but without testing the applicability of these ethical codes in political and social environments. For whom are African media studies being produced?

Is this constituency being served? These are basic questions which need critical engagement, especially as far as Africa is concerned.

Scholarly practice is also partly guided by career considerations, which complement the need for academics to equip their students with practices, theories and solutions applicable to the needs of a continent which finds itself in a scrambled historical state of various kinds of development. As Valentine Mudimbe might say, African scholars and students are thus often directed into an uncritical embrace of studies by the Western Same of the indigenous Other. This poses a serious problem for scholars who are trying to develop situationally-adequate intellectual responses within the political, ideological and ontological contexts that make up Africa. This relates to debates about the constitution and perception of Africa as a single 'culture' or 'geographical entity', and whether there is actually a single identity for all the peoples of the continent.

The pre-eminence ascribed to overseas text books by so many African scholars also reflects both the lack of appropriate introductory readers in Africa itself, and the extreme difficulties involved in getting such texts published. Achieving publication in the USA is also a problem: some US publishers tend to want to see their ideology reflected in such work, or their referees seem not to understand that other perspectives do, in fact, exist.

The inverse occurs with some African-oriented publishers in the US, who are persuaded to publish books which appeal to oppositional political constituencies in the US. More often than not, the outcome is the reinforcement of romantic myths about Africa. While these may have legitimate ideological purchase within the identity politics of these US-based constituencies, they are distracting and perhaps even questionable as far as Africa itself is concerned.

But these are the books which get published, prescribed and read by US students - often, as I have argued, to the exclusion of consideration of publications emanating from within Africa itself. This is not to say that African-authored work is itself free from flaws or that it should be free of criticism. On the contrary. African scholars tend to publish less, tend to be difficult to cultivate as far as publication and editing is concerned, and are impeded by poor communications, inadequate research funding and unpredictable political conditions. Notwithstanding these problems, some impressive work has emerged, and African journal and book publishers continue to contribute important studies to the field. Gretchen Walsh's book will no doubt have a major impact in making more of this work accessible.

The Power of Media Theory

The power of critical media theory is its ability to explain events, conditions and positions in terms of different political contexts. The recognition of the postmodern world, which is increasingly infiltrating African modernism, means that the power of elites to define reality in their political terms only is fast coming to an end. Despite this global process, some insecure and politically immature governments seem to be just as tempted today to repeat the universalistic impositions of order as were those who ruled prior to 1990.

Given these conditions, it is not surprising that some of the best studies on African media come from political scientists and transdisciplinary scholars not directly located within the field of media, communication or journalism studies. Studies of African media mostly focus on journalistic practice, state interference and censorship; they are insufficiently balanced by work on political economy - the contextual and historical dynamics within which African media systems operate.

These systems have to face processes of restriction, shielding, intimidation, discursive proscriptions, legislative impediments on the free flow of information, open communication, criticism and information. These conditions seem to apply quite generally across Africa at the present time, no matter the ideological leanings of particular governments. Yet, while the processes of controlling the media remain the same, current African moves to domesticate media for partisan political purposes seem to demonstrate a different cause from those found in previous periods in Africa's history.

The new political elites wanting to retain authoritarian media control may have succeeded the previously authoritarian countries, but new technologies such as faxes, Internet and satellites provide influential mechanisms to monitor, mobilise and campaign internationally around local attacks on media and journalists. The Media Institute of Southern Africa (MISA), based in Windhoek, Namibia, for example, transmits on e-mail news of infringements on press freedom almost as they happen. One item received on 10 June 1996, contained the following paragraph in its *Action Alert* on Zimbabwe:

> Reuters bureau chief in Zimbabwe, Chris Chinaka, says he has been warned that he would be killed if he continued to "write reports critical of President Mugabe". Chinaka says he was attending a government reception on March 27 when he was called over by the Secretary-General of the Indigenous Business Development Centre (IBDC), Enoch Kamushinda. "You should have been killed for writing reports critical of President Robert Mugabe,'" Chinaka reports

Kamushinda as saying. "'I am warning you to stop writing reports against President Mugabe. Stop everything you are writing on Mugabe."

This is chilling commentary of the continuing character of media-state relations in many parts of Africa. MISA transmits such Action Alerts on a daily, and even an hourly, basis. Repressive African governments thus have fewer places to hide - at least they cannot conceal their actions as easily as was the case prior to 1990.

Democratizing Tendencies

Some governments, however, are moving in the opposite direction to the Zimbabwean case. The Botswana High Commission in Namibia, for example, was the first African government to provide financial support to MISA and its work in promoting media freedom and diversity in the Southern Africa Development Community (SADC) region. Botswana's High Commissioner to Namibia, Tuelonyane Oliphant, stated that freedom of expression through the media is one way of ensuring that the citizenry is accorded means to express their independent and diverse opinions on important issues and thereby contribute to the overall democratic process and development.

Oliphant further argued that a responsible and pluralistic press should be regarded as a partner in the development of any nation. "As partners in development, media practitioners hold in their hands a powerful weapon which can be used to effect changes in our societies as well as to bring certain injustices to the attention of the world" (Statement issued by MISA, 10 June 1996). This noble support for MISA notwithstanding, the Botswana government has itself been known, on occasion, to lean on its press.

The 1990s saw media in Africa flexing their muscles in ways not previously possible. Attempts to bring them under direct state control can only be temporary last gasps on the part of governments unused to, or frightened of, being held accountable by news media and their readers/listeners. This realisation, of course, raises the thorny question of exactly whose interests the different sectors of the media serve. Each has its own constituency, and each tries to mask this by claiming universal validity and by representing its sectoral interests as the interests of the entire nation. Thus, `development journalism' came to represent the interest of the state, while the libertarian philosophy assumes that capitalism is in the interests of all classes, even the working class and the lumpenproletariat. In between these poles are a variety of other groupings and perspectives all jostling for the access and the power to define meanings and solutions.

Ideology is shaped by class position, rank and mobility within hierarchies, and the expectations that accompany these. Newly-elected parliaments and administrations are now staffed by members drawn from the liberation movements or previously suppressed opposition parties. They now manage state institutions which frequently replicate those previously constituted around the technocratic and largely secretive business of maintaining structures of oppression and patronage. Critical media studies therefore necessarily confronts political and administrative institutions; where these were once the perfected tools of patronage and oppression, as under apartheid for example, critical theory sought to expose the mechanisms of inequity entrenched in them.

Today's *institutions* are essentially those that existed previously, but now their incumbents face a contradictory task. On the one hand, they are employed in technocratic, secretive positions perfected by generations of institutionalized oppression in isolated local conditions. It is remarkable how easily and quickly the new incumbents adopt, and fit into, the old top-down assumptions. On the other hand, the new apparatchiks have to re*constitute* these around the achievement of democratic conditions in a global environment. In these circumstances, critical media theory once again needs to engage the political nature of transformation in an institutional arena.

Where imported theories would tend to focus on individuals and how their activities represent misuse of patronage (the `gravy train'), they take political issues to be a question of the status quo and not one of inheritance. The question underlining this issue is why some media systems are researched to the exclusion of others; and why media in the smaller countries are almost totally ignored. Why do the new elites make the same mistakes as the old ones? And whose interests does it serve to mask the continuation of the status quo under discourses such as `transformation' and `revolutionary change'? Research dissertations on these issues and countries do exist, but they are difficult to access as they are rarely published. Yet they can be of crucial importance in beginning to understand how and why internecine conflicts occur in Africa, and why the use of radio in hate speech, for example, was used to fan the genocide of Hutus in Rwanda (Gatwa 1995). Yet radio remains the least studied aspect of media in Africa, though it is without doubt the most politically and socially influential, especially in societies where TV signals are sparse and literacy levels are low.

Political analyst Hannah Arendt's distinction between institutions and constitutions is crucial: the former are *maintained* as part of a world, while the latter *begin* something new. Broadcasting corporations, for example, might be state institutions, but through rather constituting themselves as public service facilities, they redefine their relation to the state. This is the struggle facing the South African Broadcasting Corporation (SABC) in the post-apartheid era (Teer-Tomaselli, 1994). To follow Arendt further, institutions are familiar in our *social* context, while constitutions always generate actions, the consequences of which are *unpredictable*. Will the SABC be able to ensure its independence from state interference, for example? The role of the critical media practitioner, therefore, has to be to delineate the social - the realm in which familiar everyday life goes on - from the political, the realm in which consequences are taken on trust.

Parts of Africa may now well be on a different, if tortuous path, one in which the media more than ever have roles to play. And these will be crucial. In South Africa, and the rest of much of the so-called Third World, the winds of change have indeed swept through the constitutional world of politics; actions have been set in motion, but the consequences are located in the indeterminate future. The critical media theorist has now to unpack the disparities of conduct between the political realm, which has begun to transform, and the social realm, which is still in the form of institutions and inherited practices derived from the past. Critical media theory, in other words, also has an ethical dimension as well in an era after resistance.

Debate, dissent, argument, disagreement and criticism are the motors of constructive and democratic progress and development. The Frankfurt School which tried to explain the success of Nazism taught that to the kill the social dialectic (debate, critique and dialogue) in any society is to terminate democracy, reason, justice and development. Authoritarianism results. Democracy and justice, fought for over generations, even centuries, dies in a moment.

We can then look at Walsh's book as a beginning in Arendt's sense, of a task which has to be taken up and run with by African scholars at their own risk. New winds, new tasks, and new challenges: journalists and academics in Africa have dangerous professions. As these individuals, especially the outspoken ones, are usually in leadership positions, and therefore easily visible, they are easily identified and targeted. Apart from career reasons, this is another reason why so many have left Africa for safer climes on other continents.

Negotiating Cosmologies and Superpower Rivalry

The books and journal articles listed in this Bibliography - written by both insiders and outsiders to Africa, and insiders and outsiders to the media - reveal totally different epistemologies, even cosmologies, in making sense of media in Africa and media reports on Africa. This results in different paradigms, different styles of writing, and different ways of accessing knowledge. These range from the development of explicit theories to the conferring of significance to anecdotes as illustrations of experience and process. The field is wide open and the examples discussed here will hopefully generate further analyses, especially from African-based scholars whose work needs to be made more accessible to First World academia.

Gretchen Walsh's Bibliography also cites studies on the image of Africa in the media. The Western gaze on Africa is balanced with Africa's analysis of its image in the West. Where stereotypes of Africa and its societies abound, Western foreign policy and development projects will fail, as did those of the communist bloc. Africa became the battleground for opposing capitalist and communist ideologies, a battle fought to the death in Africa - witness the appalling atrocities committed by the South African proxy troops in Angola and Mozambique, and the opportunistic propping up by both superpower blocs of repressive governments all over Africa whose policies resulted in famine, war, and pestilence. Africa as victim of international power relations is then blamed for the result. Films and TV programmes on the horrific social consequences of these wars often image Africans as victims - as helpless people waiting to die - the only unpredictability being the cause of death. Few such programmes deal with the extraordinary courage and determination by which ordinary people survive and cope, overcome their personal impediments and get on with life as they find it.

African interpretations of Western media, their appropriation into different African contexts, and theoretical mixes which acknowledge the impact of traveling theories on our analytical tools, similarly need explanation and development. This is one way in which African countries might critically negotiate being again sandwiched between superpower rivalries. Indigenizing theory and practices is also a way empowering ordinary people in relation to national institutions which are often at the interface between the local and the global.

Walsh's bibliography lists publications available in US and European libraries. There are probably many more important works, especially unpublished dissertations, which remain outside this ambit. These need to be found, indexed and made available both within and without Africa itself. But this will be a project for another compendium.

In sum, I hope that Walsh's Bibliography will:
treat Africa as dynamic rather than static, as heterogeneous rather than singular, as always in question rather than always having been known, as known only through global comparisons, as living rather than mortified or naturalized, and therefore as incomplete and imperfect rather than either inferior or idealized (Herwitz et al 1996).

Acknowledgements

Thanks to Arnold Shepperson for his comments and additions, especially those relating to my discussion of Arendt; to James Zaffiro for his most helpful suggestions; and Belinda Jeursen for copy editing.

References

Arendt, H. 1958: *The Human Condition* Chicago: University of Chicago Press.

Edeani, D.O. 1995: "Role of *Africa Media Review* in the Sustainable Development of African Communication Research", *Africa Media Review* 9(1), 24-52.

Gatwa, T. 1995: "Ethnic Conflict and the Media: the Case of Rwanda", *Media Development*, 42(3), 18-20

Herwitz, D. in consultation with Shepperson, A., Tomaselli, K.G., Brown, D. and Chapman, M. 1996: African Studies project: A Working Report. Mimeo, University of Natal.

Teer-Tomaselli, R.E. 1994: "The Mediazation of Culture: John Thompson and the Vision of Public Service Broadcasting", *South African Journal of Philosophy*, 13(3), 124-132.

Introduction

How have the *media in Africa* developed and how are they used? How do images of *Africa in the media* shape outsiders' views of the continent and its peoples? A great deal has been written about these questions, as this bibliography illustrates. Within each of its sections, **Press, Broadcasting, Film, and General** (comprising works dealing with more than one medium as well as works on mass communications and theoretical issues), certain themes in the literature can be discerned.

Books and articles dealing with the press in Africa focus strongly on questions of press freedom, whether discussing the role of the press during the colonial era, in independence movements, or in the current independent nations. "Development Journalism" is a recurrent theme. The definition is seldom given in precise and concrete terms, but its main idea is that the responsibility of the press in a developing nation is to further national development, and not to play the role of free-spoken gadfly. Works dealing with Africa in the press of the rest of the world center primarily on questions of coverage and tone. Generally speaking the selection of stories published on Africa emphasizes negative aspects: war, famine, corruption. Even those sensational negative stories occupy news pages briefly. Another thread of interest is research on the effect of news stories on readers' opinions. Research has been done both in Africa and in the west, sometimes with surprising results.

Broadcasting is a much younger medium than the press, and different sets of questions are explored in the literature. The educational use of radio and television is an important theme. Press freedom, censorship and political control are explored in depth. South Africa's refusal to allow television in the country until 1976, and the consequences of its introduction make an interesting sub-theme. Much concern is expressed over the pervasive importation of foreign programs at the expense of developing local fare, with the attendant danger of losing national and ethnic identity. Identity itself is an important issue; many items explore the influence of radio and television on national unity and identity. Africa in the broadcast media in the West and the rest of the world is largely explored in terms of image presented and the nature and amount of news coverage. The television series *Roots*, and to a lesser extent *The Africans* and a few other specials, inspired a great deal of research into audience response.

Literature on Africa and film runs a broad gamut. Histories of filmmaking in the colonial era center on film's use in education and to some extent propaganda within Africa. The Boer war was the first covered by motion picture cameras. Films made in Africa by African filmmakers have become an important feature of the cinema world, although that industry is plagued by lack of money and infrastructure as well as philosophical and artistic questions of how best to portray the African experience on film. The image of Africa in Western films is a theme that has been examined to a

Introduction

great extent. The effect of images in films such as the Tarzan series has been incalculably damaging to Africa.

The section called General is by nature a catch-all for whatever didn't fit into other categories. In this section, for instance, I have clustered the extensive writing on the South African propaganda machine, and Muldergate, the scandal resulting from the clandestine activities and questionable financial transactions of the Department of Information in the 1970s and 1980s.

Why bother with a printed bibliography when bibliographic and full text databases are available electronically? For Africa the most important reason is that few African publications are indexed electronically -- or in print form, for that matter -- and African information published anywhere in the world is poorly covered in the major subject-based indexes. The bibliographer of African subjects is thus doing a real service, not just reformatting information otherwise available easily enough.

A printed bibliography differs from broad electronic index resources in the selectivity and focus that shape it. The first version of this work was a "Working Bibliography" on the theme of the 1979 African Studies Association meeting, "Media in Africa; Africa in the Media." (Boston University African Studies Center, *Working Paper* no. 17, 1979) This small work only scratched the surface of the subject, but provided some fascinating insights into what is written about the development and use of media in Africa, and about the image of Africa in western and worldwide media. Interest in the media has remained high in the African Studies Association and other organizations. At the 1995 ASA meeting in Orlando, Florida, five panel and roundtables focused on media issues, including coverage of Africa in U.S. news media, African filmmaking, griots and technology, and media's influence on African identity. The theme of the 1996 London meeting of the Standing Committee on Library Materials from Africa (SCOLMA) was "Sight and Sound: Africa on Film and Tape". As the bibliography demonstrates, writing on the media and Africa is broadly interdisciplinary.

It was quickly apparent in the process of compiling this bibliography that a firm selection process had to be employed. The rule of thumb was to limit to works which, whether or not they were scholarly in nature themselves, were of a size and substance to be of use in scholarly research. This eliminated newspaper articles for the most part, short reviews and brief articles in news and other popular magazines. Exceptions were made to this rule if a brief article made a particularly interesting point or was of key importance and widely cited in other sources.

Care was taken not to needlessly duplicate good bibliographies already existing, such as Nancy Schmidt's works on film and filmmakers.

Introduction

A subject bibliography is, however, as much an organic whole as a scholarly treatise, and some duplication is needed to cover the subject satisfactorily.

The cutoff date for entries is May 1996. Film and broadcast media are by definition largely 20th century phenomena, and the print media in Africa are basically limited to the 19th and 20th centuries, so the beginning of the date range was self-selecting.

Selection criteria aside, no bibliography is ever complete. New publications appear - inevitably - just as the manuscript is delivered to the printer. More frustrating are the citations that come to light too late because they were obscure, unindexed, unreferenced - or, maddeningly, simply overlooked. Even with a wealth of research libraries nearby, some journals are just not available for scanning. There's more information out there, waiting to be found for a supplementary volume.

There are two large areas which do need to be addressed in future works. First, although a major portion of this bibliography cites works written by Africans and/or published in Africa, a criterion for inclusion was availability at a U.S. or European library. That leaves a body of writing, potentially immense, that is unavailable in the U.S., unverifiable except for references in other works, possibly unpublished. Nancy Schmidt, in the introduction to one of her own exhaustive bibliographies on Sub-Saharan African film, says that the field will not be fully covered until film reviews and commentary in African newspapers and magazines are fully indexed and made more generally available. In his introduction to this work, Keyan Tomaselli draws attention to dissertations, particularly those done in Africa. There are other genres, such as working papers, papers from conferences and symposia and the like, that may elude the bibliographer, and if they are cited, will most likely elude the researcher who wants to read them. Hopefully African scholars will compile bibliographies and guides to this material, and African librarians in concert with their colleagues in other nations will find ways of making the material itself more widely available for researchers.

Besides this body of conventional literature that proves difficult to bring under bibliographic control for the moment, there is a growing body of electronic information that defies any attempt at imposing order: the Internet and World Wide Web. A reference guide to these resources will need another approach and another format to be completely useful. For the moment, however, some mention must be made of this incredibly rich, albeit amorphous and chaotic resource.

The Internet is both a medium and a source of information about media. The two functions are not completely separable. The following is only a sampling.

Introduction

    A number of news services are available on the Internet, some free, some accessible only to subscribers. One of the Africa-focused free sources is provided by the Africa Policy Information Center (apic@igc.apc.org), which operates a mailing list and a web site:
    (http://www.igc.apc.org/apic/index.html).
A recent posting on this site included Zambia Press Freedom Alerts from the Committee to Protect Journalists (http://www.cpj.org), Amnesty International (amnesty-info@igc.apc.org), and the Media Institute of Southern Africa (leep@ingrid.misa.org.na). The articles describe the banning of the *Post*, which is itself available at:
    http://www.zamnet.zm/zamnet/post/post.html
Selected articles from the *Post* are available at:
    http://www.afnews.org/ans/central/ANScentral.html.
    Listservs are discussion groups in which information supplied can be accurate and authoritative or simply the opinion or imagining of the sender. Two lively and reasonably reliable groups are the African Cinema Conference (african-cinema-conference@XC.org) and H-Africa (H-Africa@msu.edu). African Cinema Conference members post notices of film festivals and publications as well as queries and discussion of African films. H-Africa is broader based, covering all humanities, particularly history, but carries relevant book reviews, a table of contents service for many Africanist journals, notices, and moderated discussion, frequently on media topics.
    Information on the Internet is ephemeral; unless you download or print it when you come across it, you may never find it again. The origin and authenticity of information found in cyberspace cannot always be verified. It's an important resource, but needs more than this sampling as a guide.
    In this bibliography of print sources, most of the works cited have been examined and annotated. Those not annotated were not available for examination, but have been verified. Authors' names have been standardized in the bibliography, usually using Library of Congress authority records or choosing the most common and most complete form of the name. Cross references in the index are given for known name changes.
    I gratefully acknowledge the invaluable and always cheerful assistance of Mugar Library's Interlibrary Loan Staff, particularly Traci Turner. The staff of the African Studies Library is to be commended for ably "holding the fort" while this work was in progress. Jill Young Coelho and Greg Finnegan, at Harvard's Widener and Tozzer Libraries respectively, were extremely generous with their time, help, and advice. Special thanks to Dan Walsh, who skillfully proofread and copy edited the seemingly unending pages of annotations and provided much needed encouragement in this long process.

Journals Consulted

Africa (Sao Paulo)
Africa 2000
Africa Media Review
Africa News
Africa Now
Africa Quarterly
Africa Report
Africa Today
Africa: An International Business, Economic and Political Monthly
African Affairs
African Book Publishing Record
African Business
African Commentary
African Communist
African Forum
African Freedom Annual
African Journal of International and Comparative Law
African Research and Documentation
African Review
African Studies Review
Africana Journal
Africana Library Journal
Afrika Spektrum
Afrique Contemporaine
Afrique et l'Asie Modernes
Afrique Littéraire (formerly Afrique Littéraire et Artistique)
AfterImage
ALA Bulletin
American Anthropologist
American Behavioral Scientist
American Film
American Journalism
ASBU Review: The Quarterly Publication of the Arab States Broadcasting Union
Atlantic Monthly
Atlas World Press Review
Ba Shiru
Black American Literary Forum
Black Film Review
Black Scholar
Boston College Third World Law Journal
Bulletin de l'Institut Français d'Afrique Noire, Série B: Sciences Humaines
Cahiers d'Études Africaines
Censorship News
Cinéaste
Cinema Canada
Cinema Journal
Columbia Journalism Review
Communications in Africa
Comparative Studies in Society and History
Con-Text
Congo-Afrique
Connecticut Journal of International Law
Covert Action
Critical Arts
Cultural Critique
Cultures
Current Research on Peace and Violence
Democratic Journalist
Discourse and Society
East Africa Journal
East African Report on Trade and Industry
Educational Media International
Encounter
Evergreen Review
Film and History
Film Library Quarterly
Film Quarterly
Fletcher Forum
Frontline
Gazette
Grands Lacs
Harpers
Historical Journal of Film, Radio and Television

Journals Consulted

History in Africa
Howard Journal of
  Communication
IDOC Internazionale
Index on Censorship
Indicator SA
Inspan
Intermedia
International Affairs
International Affairs Bulletin
International Journal of African
  Historical Studies
International Journal of
  Intercultural Relations
International Third World
  Studies and Review
Issue
Jeune Afrique
Journal of African
  Communications
Journal of African History
Journal of African Studies
Journal of Black Studies
Journal of Broadcasting
Journal of Broadcasting and
  Electronic Media
Journal of Commonwealth
  Political Studies
Journal of Communication
Journal of Communication Inquiry
Journal of Democracy
Journal of Development
  Communication
Journal of Mass Media Ethics
Journal of Media Law and
  Practice
Journal of Modern African Studies
Journal of Social Development in
  Africa
Journal of Southern African
  Studies
Journal of the Royal African
  Society

Journal of the University Film
  and Video Association
Journal of the University Film
  Association
Journal of Third World Studies
Journalism Quarterly
Jump Cut
Kroniek van Afrika
Liberia-Forum
Library Notes
Marang
Media Development
Media Studies Journal
Media, Culture and Society
Médiaspouvoirs
Mondes en Développement
Monthly Film Bulletin
Nairobi Law Monthly
Nation
New African
New American
New Republic
New York Review of Books
New York Times Magazine
New Yorker
Nieman Reports
Nigeria Magazine
Nigerian Journal of Economic and
  Social Studies
Nigerian Theatre Journal
Northeast African Studies
Oral Tradition
Passages: A Chronicle of the
  Humanities
Peace Research
Peuples Noirs, Peuples Africains
Planned Parenthood Challenges
Plural Societies
Political Communication and
  Persuasion
Politikon: The South African
  Journal of Political Studies
Politique Africaine

Journals Consulted

Popular Music and Society
Presénce Africaine
Progressive
Public Culture
Public Relations Journal
Quarterly Review of Film Studies
Quest Philosophical Discussions: An International African Journal of Philosophy
Quill
Race and Class
Radical America
Reality
Research in African Literatures
Revue Française d'Études Politiques Africaines
Round Table
Rural Africana
Screen
Sechaba
Sierra Leone Studies
Sight and Sound
Social Dynamics
Social Forces
Social Justice
Social Science Quarterly
South Africa Outlook
South African Geographical Journal
South African Historical Journal
South African Journal on Human Rights
South African Law Journal
South African Review
South African Theatre Journal
Southern Africa
Southern Africa Report
Studies in Third World Societies
Studies in Twentieth Century Literature
Taamuli: A Political Science Forum
Tempo
Temps Modernes
Texas Studies in Literature and Language
Text and Performance Quarterly
Third World Affairs
TransAfrica Forum
Transition
TV Guide
Ufahamu
UNESCO Courier
Vie Africaine
Visual Anthropology
Voices From Africa
Voices of the African Diaspora
Washington Journalism Review
West Africa
Western Journal of Black Studies
Wide Angle
Work in Progress
World Communication
Zimbabwe Law Review

The Press

1
Abdel Rahman, Awatef. "Main Trends of Press Research in Egypt: 1950-1980." *Communication Research in Africa: Issues and Perspectives*, 27-38. Edited by S. T. Kwame Boafo and Nancy A. George. Nairobi: African Council on Communication Education, 1992.
> A survey of research on the Egyptian press carried out at Cairo University, with analysis of trends.

2
Abuoga, John Baptist, and Absalom Aggrey Mutere. *The History of the Press in Kenya*. Nairobi: African Council on Communication Education, 1988. 116pp.
> Historical overview of the press in Kenya from 1895 to the late 1980s, covering the early settler press, the rise of African nationalism, the Emergency (Mau Mau), and the post-Independence era.

3
Acker, Vincent. "La Presse au Nigéria et au Ghana." *Revue Française d'Études Politiques Africaines*, no. 84 (December 1972): 72-94.
> An overview of the press in Nigeria and Ghana with a brief history and notes on current newspapers and newsmagazines.

4
Adeyemi, Adeyinka. *The Nigerian Press Under the Military: Persecution, Resilience and Political Crisis (1983-1993)*. Cambridge, MA: Harvard University, John F. Kennedy School of Government, 1995. 29pp.
> An examination of relations between the press and three successive military regimes in Nigeria, noting those governments' superficial support of freedom of expression and documenting their actual policies and actions.

5
"Africa's Press Breaks Free." *New African*, no. 294 (March 1992): 8-13.
> The cover story on "the new wind of press freedom" provides short reports on the press in Kenya, Zambia, Ghana, Botswana, Côte d'Ivoire and South Africa.

6
Africa's Trade Union Press: a Discussion of Its Current Status and Future Prospects. Lomé: Regional Economic Research and Documentation Center, 1976. Special issue of *Labor and Development*. 48pp.
> Papers from the Pan-African Colloquium on the Trade Union Press, December 1975, Lomé, Togo. Contains press clippings, lists of participants and trade union publications.

7
Agbaje, Adigun. "Beyond the State: Civil Society and the Nigerian Press Under Military Rule." *Media, Culture and Society* 15, no. 3 (1993): 455-472.
> A discussion of attempts of military governments in Nigeria to control the press, which has proven irrepressible.

8

---. "Freedom of the Press and Party Politics in Nigeria: Precepts, Retrospect and Prospects." *African Affairs* 89, no. 355 (April 1990): 205-226.
> A discussion of references to press freedom in the 1988 report of Nigeria's Constitutional Review Committee, with an historical overview of relations of press and government during the Second Republic, 1979-1983, when press freedom was not specifically guaranteed.

9

---. *The Nigerian Press: Hegemony and Social Construction of Legitimacy.* Lewiston, NY: Edwin Mellen, 1992. 333pp.
> An examination of the relation of the press in Nigeria to both civilian and military governments, and the role that it has played in social and political events. Appendices include a list of Nigerian court cases involving the press and the Nigerian Press Organization's *Code of Conduct*. 18 page bibliography. Index.

10

Agbese, Pius Ogbaba, and Chris W. Ogbondah. "The U.S. Press and Political Change in the Third World: The Coverage of Military Coups." *Political Communication and Persuasion* 5, no. 1 (1988): 33-47.
> An analysis of U.S. press coverage of the Nigerian military coup of December 1983, when the civilian regime of President Shehu Shagari was overturned and Major-General Mohammed Buhari became Head of State, and the coup of August 1985, when Buhari was ousted by Major-General Ibrahim Babangida.

11

Agbu, Chike. *I Am an Ex-Prisoner.* Yaba: n.p.,1958. 118pp.
> Autobiographical account by the editor of the Nigerian newspaper *West African Pilot* describing his imprisonment in 1958 for an editorial he had written concerning Nigeria's Justice Department.

12

Ainslie, Rosalynde. *The Press in Africa: Communications Past and Present.* London: Gollancz, 1966. 256pp.
> A region-by-region overview of the press in Africa, with comments on radio and television. List of African broadcasting stations, news agencies and daily newspapers as of December 1965, with additional information on population and literacy. Index.

13

Akahenda, Elijah F. "The Imperative of National Unity and the Concept of Press Freedom: the Case of East Africa." *Gazette* 31, no. 2 (1983): 89-98.
> A synthesis of studies and theories concerning national integration and its relationship to press freedom in Kenya, Tanzania, and Uganda.

14

Akhalwaya, Ameen. "The Role of the Alternative Press." *Nieman Reports* 42, no. 4 (December 1988): 14-18.

A discussion of the difficulties facing alternative newspapers in South Africa, beginning with the problem of defining "alternative", which has important implications for the kind and amount of support the papers receive.

15
---. "Through the Loopholes." *Index on Censorship* 17, no. 3 (1988): 24-26.
The editor of the South African alternative newspaper *The Indicator* describes the difficulties such newspapers encountered during the apartheid regime.

16
Akhalwaya, Ameen, and Les Payne. "Remembering Percy Qoboza." *Africa Report* 33, no. 2 (March 1988): 32-34.
A South African editor and an American journalist pay tribute to the late South African editor of *The World*.

17
Akinfeleye, Ralph A. *Essentials of Modern African Journalism: A Premier (sic)*. Lagos: Miral Printing Press, 1987. 164pp.
A textbook on journalism with a survey of training available for journalists in Africa.

18
Akinjide, Olajumoke. *The Press in Nigeria*. 1981. 75pp.

19
Akinyemi, A. Bolaji. "The American Press and the Nigerian Civil War." *Nigerian Journal of Economic and Social Studies* 13, no. 2 (1971): 241-259.
A critique of coverage of the Nigerian Civil War in the *New York Times*, the *Christian Science Monitor*, and *Time Magazine*, finding biased and sensationalist reporting.

20
---. "The British Press and the Nigerian Civil War." *African Affairs* 71, no. 285 (October 1972): 408-426.
An analysis of the accuracy of coverage of the Nigerian Civil War (1967-1970) by major British newspapers.

21
---. *The British Press and the Nigerian Civil War: the Godfather Complex*. Ibadan, Nigeria: University Press, 1979. NIAA Monograph Series no. 2. 102pp.
Assessment of the coverage by the British press of the Biafran secession and the subsequent civil war in Nigeria, with commentary on the relationship of press coverage and public sentiment in England. 18 page bibliography of newspaper articles covering the war.

The Press

22

Almaney, Adnan. "Government Control of the Press in the United Arab Republic, 1952-1970." *Journalism Quarterly* 49 (June 1972): 340-348.

23

Alot, Magaga. *People and Communication in Kenya*. Nairobi: Kenya Literature Bureau, 1982. 221pp.
   Historical overview of the press in Kenya, with suggestions for increasing its relevance and utility.

24

Amatokwu, F. Nwaokedi. *Journalism Profession in Nigeria*. Lagos: Citadel Resources for Taorgan, 1989. 182pp.
   A discussion of the Nigerian Media Council Decree of 1988 and conditions for journalists in that country.

25

Amin, Mustafa. "If It Makes the President Happy..." *Index on Censorship* 14, no. 5 (October 1985): 18-21.
   An interview with the editor of the Egyptian newspaper *Akhbar al-Youm* discussing press freedom in Egypt over the last fifty years.

26

Analyzing the Press. Stanford: Leland Stanford Junior University, 1985. 61pp.
   An exercise developed by the Africa Project of the Stanford Program on International and Cross-Cultural Education, aimed at teaching American students how to distinguish fact from opinion in African news coverage.

27

Anamaleze, John. *The Nigerian Press: The People's Conscience?* New York: Vantage Press, 1979. 142pp.
   An overview of the history of the press in Nigeria and its role in political and social affairs. 2 page bibliography, mostly Nigerian newspaper articles. Index.

28

Ankomah, Baffour. "Cameroon's Forbidden Topics." *Index on Censorship* 17, no. 2 (February 1988): 22-24.
   Report on censorship in Cameroon, which is carried to such lengths and is so harsh that the author sums up by suggesting that South Africa might be a more humane place for journalists.

29

---. "Ghana's Culture of Silence." *Index on Censorship* 16, no. 10 (November 1987): 17-19.
   A former editor of *The Pioneer* calls upon Jerry Rawlings to call off attacks on the press and live up to his promise of *glasnost*.

30
---. "Where Truth Is on Holiday." *Index on Censorship* 15, no. 4 (April 1986): 33-36.
   A discussion of self-censorship among Ghanaian journalists in response to government repression of press freedom.

31
Anokwa, Kwadwo, and Michael B. Salwen. "Newspaper Agenda-Setting Among Elites and Non-Elites in Ghana." *Gazette* 41, no. 3 (1988): 201-214.
   Report of a survey conducted by the University of Ghana's School of Journalism and Communication to determine readership of Ghanaian newspapers, to identify the issues deemed most important by those surveyed, and to correlate these factors with the socio-economic profile of the survey group.

32
Anonymous. "Tightening the Grip." *Index on Censorship* 15, no. 5 (May 1986): 30-32, 37.
   A report on repression of the press in Cameroon, described as a country where journalism is "synonymous with detentions, harassment and...going for months without pay".

33
Ansah, Paul A. V. "Blueprint for Freedom." *Index on Censorship* 20, no. 9 (October 1991): 3-8.
   A proposal for the legal and political framework for a free and pluralistic press in Africa.

34
---. *Rural Journalism in Africa*. Paris: Unesco, 1981. 35pp.
   A brief overview of rural newspapers and available resources for training journalists in Africa.

35
Anyadike, Nnamdi. "What Price Press Freedom." *Index on Censorship* 14, no. 2 (April 1985): 39-42.
   A report on Nigeria's 'Decree 4', which prohibits publication of any information that is false or that brings the Government or individual officials into ridicule or disrepute.

36
Aouchar, Amina. *La Presse Marocaine dans la Lutte pour l'Indépendance (1933-1956)*. Casablanca: Wallada, 1990. 160pp.
   History of the political involvement of the press in Moroccan independence.

37
Asaju, Michael. "Assessing Nigeria's Newspapers." *West Africa*, no. 3287 (21 July 1980): 1337-1339.

The Press

The text of a speech by the President of the Nigerian Union of Journalists to students of the Nigerian Institute of Journalism, commenting on the quality of the country's journalists and media.

38

Asante, Clement E. *The Press in Ghana: Problems and Prospects.* Lanham, MD: University Press of America, 1996. 196pp.

39

"*Atlas* Report: Change in South Africa." *Atlas World Press Review* 26, no. 5 (May 1979): 35-40.
A sampling of articles in the French newspaper *Le Point*, the Gemini News Service of London, and several South African newspapers on events in South Africa.

40

Attacks on the Press. New York: Committee to Protect Journalists, Annual.
An annual publication of the Committee to Protect Journalists reporting all known incidents of suppression of the press and oppression of journalists.

41

Ayodele, Olumuyiwa. "African Print Media Misuse of the English Definite Article "The": A Content Analysis of Seven Nigerian Newspapers' Lead Items." *Africa Media Review* 2, no. 3 (1988): 92-109.
A survey of seven Nigerian newspapers for typographical and linguistic errors, focusing on the misuse of "the", linking that misuse to difference in mother tongue structures.

42

Azikiwe, Nnamdi. *Suppression of the Press in British West Africa.* Onitsha: African Book Company, 1945. 15pp.
A description of the suppression of two Nigerian papers, the *West African Pilot* and the *Daily Comet*, during the general strike in Nigeria in June 1945, by the leading Nigerian statesman, who was also chairman of the Comet Press.

43

Babiker, Mahjoub Abd al-Malik. *Press and Politics in the Sudan.* Khartoum: University of Khartoum, 1985. *Graduate College Publications* no. 14. 139pp.
History of the press in Sudan. Contains copies of ordinances and other documents pertaining to the press. 5 page bibliography.

44

Badibanga, André. "La Presse Africaine et le Culte de la Personalité." *Revue Française d'Études Politiques Africaines*, no. 159 (March 1979): 40-57.
An examination of Francophone African newspapers to determine how their local news coverage affects the careers of local politicians and leaders.

45
Baesjou, René, Rudo Niemeijer, and Rob Buijtenhuijs. "Africa in the Dutch Press, an Exploration." *Kroniek van Afrika* , no. 3 (1993): 317-346.
   A content analysis of seven Dutch daily newspapers in 1972 to determine their coverage of Africa.

46
Baldwin, Fletcher N., and W. Edward McLeod. "Press Freedoms During Times of Emergency: An Examination of South Africa and the United States." *Connecticut Journal of International Law* 8, no. 1 (September 1992): 109-173.
   A comparison of regulation of the press in South Africa during the last years of apartheid and in the United States during periods of war from World War I to Desert Storm.

47
Balikowa, David Ouma. "Media Marketing: An Essential Part of a Free Press for Africa." *Media, Culture and Society* 17, no. 4 (October 1995): 603-613.
   Citing his own experiences in Uganda, the author discusses the sometimes overlooked fact that a newspaper must be financially successful if it is to be able to play a significant role in conveying information and shaping opinion.

48
Bamisaiye, Adepitan. "The Nigerian Civil War in the International Press." *Transition* 9, no. 44 (1974): 30-35.
   A critical review of coverage of the Nigerian Civil War which the author contends was inaccurate, biased, and condescending.

49
Barton, Frank. *African Assignment: The Story of IPI's Six Year Training Programme in Tropical Africa*. Zurich: International Press Inst., 1969. 75pp.
   A personal account of the program instituted by the International Press Institute shortly after the first wave of independence in Africa to prepare a corps of African journalists from all over the continent to take on the daunting task of establishing and maintaining a responsible press in their homelands.

50
---. *The Press in Africa*. Nairobi: East African Publishing House, 1966. 80pp.
   Brief overview of journalism and the press in Africa.

51
---. *The Press of Africa: Persecution and Perseverance*. New York: Africana, 1979. 304pp.
   A region-by-region overview of the press in Africa, with emphasis on freedom of the press. 3 page bibliography. Index.

The Press

52

Bayart, Jean-François. "Presse Écrite et Développement Politique au Cameroun." *Revue Française d'Études Politiques Africaines*, no. 88 (April 1973): 48-63.
 An exploration of the role of the press in political development in Cameroon, noting the economic problems encountered by newspapers.

53

Bayemi, Jean Paul. *L'Effort Camerounais ou la Tentations d'une Presse Libre*. Paris: Harmattan, 1989. 170pp.

54

The Beat of Drum: The Story of a Magazine That Documented the Rise of Africa as Told by Drum's Publisher, Editors, Contributors and Photographers. Nairobi: Drum, 1988. 168pp.
 Essays and extracts from past issues of the magazine combine to tell its story and history.

55

Beckett, Denis. "The MWASA Strike: Beneath the Surface Lie Bottomless Depths." *Frontline* 1, no. 7 (December 1980): 4-7, 37-38.
 A report of the first production-stopping strike in South African publishing history, when the Media Workers of South Africa, a small Blacks-only trade union, took on the major newspapers, demanding not only pay increases but a share in decision-making. The strike galvanized sympathy across the country.

56

Behn, Hans Ulrich. *Die Presse in Westafrika*. Hamburg: Deutsches Institut for Afrika-Forschung, 1968. *Hamburger Beitrage zur Afrika-Kunde*, Band 8. 267pp.
 An overview of the press in West Africa, with emphasis on problems of press freedom and the relationship of the press to national governments. Appendices list newspapers and magazines, with circulation and price information. 6 page bibliography.

57

Benson, Ivor. *The Opinion Makers*. Pretoria: Dolphin Press, 1967. 177pp.
 A collection of essays advancing the idea that the "Leftist" press misrepresents, through exaggeration and distortion, the behavior and activities of Whites in South Africa and Rhodesia.

58

Berger, Guy. "New Barons of the Press." *Index on Censorship* 24, no. 3 (May 1995): 125-133.
 Despite the new democracy in South Africa, alternative newspapers still face severe economic problems. Many are folding, while mainstream newspapers are being bought by foreigners and experiencing new kinds of control.

59
Bernstein, Peter. "Reporting in Pretoria." *Index on Censorship* 4, no. 3 (1975): 44-48.
   Personal account of an American who spent six months as a reporter in South Africa, summarizing the legal and social restraints on journalists.

60
Bertelsen, Eve. "The Unspeakable in Pursuit of the Unbeatable: The Press, UCT and the O'Brien Affair." *Critical Arts* 5, no. 4 (1991): 116-132.
   An analysis of local media coverage of a 1986 incident at the University of Cape Town in which a student protest over a lecture by Conor Cruise O'Brien, whose visit was breaking the international cultural boycott of South Africa, was violently subdued by police.

61
Blackwell, Leslie. *Newspaper Law of South Africa*. Cape Town: Juta, 1963. 112pp.

62
Blay-Amihere, Kabral. "Ghana's *Free Press*." *Index on Censorship* 16, no. 1 (January 1987): 21-23.
   The editor of the *Free Press* explains why he decided to close down his newspaper following the banning of other independent newspapers by the government and a campaign of harassment against his own paper.

63
Boafo, S. T. Kwame. "Ghana's Press Under the PNDC: Performance Under Confinement." *Gazette* 35, no. 2 (1985): 73-82.
   Using a theoretical framework developed from several studies of the press in other authoritarian regimes, the author outlines the press control practiced by Jerry Rawlings since the coup which brought him to power in 1981.

64
---. "Journalism Profession and Training in Sub-Saharan Africa: A Case Study of Ghana." *Africa Media Review* 2, no. 3 (1988): 56-74.
   Overview of journalists in Ghana, their training and career prospects.

65
Bodie, Charles Alvis. "The Images of Africa in the Black American Press, 1890-1930." Ph.D. diss., Indiana University, 1975. 224pp.
   A study of the development of the Black press in America following the Civil War and the relationship of the coverage that these newspapers gave to Africa to local agendas of civil rights, economic advancement and political militancy.

66
Journalism and Society, edited by Dokun Bojuwade. Ibadan: Evans Brothers, 1987. 171pp.

The Press

A collection of the Guest Lectures of the Nigerian Institute of Journalism, covering press freedom, government control and professional responsibility.

67
Bolela, Albert Oscar. "Un Aperçu de la Presse Congolaise Écrite par les Noirs de 1885 à 1960." *Congo-Afrique* 11, no. 51 (January 1971): 5-23.
An overview of newspapers and journalists in Zaire during the colonial era.

68
Bosompra, Kwadwo. "African News in the World Press: Comparative Content Analysis of a North and a South Newspaper." *Africa Media Review* 3, no. 3 (1989): 58-69.

69
Boulegue, Marguerite. "La Presse au Senegal avant 1939: Bibliographie." *Bulletin de l'Institut Français d'Afrique Noire, Série B: Sciences Humaines* 27, no. 1/2 (January 1965): 715-754.
A list of newspapers and journals published in Senegal before 1939, with publication information, and holdings in libraries and archives.

70
Bourgault, Louise M. "The Oral Tradition in the Nigerian Press." *World Communication* 16, no. 2 (1987): 211-235.

71
Brice, K. "Muzzling the Press." *Africa Report* 37 (July 1992): 49-51.
A brief report summarizing the 1991 report of the Committee to Protect Journalists, published as *Attacks on the Press*, giving a grim picture of press freedom in Africa.

72
Brookes, Heather Jean. "Suit, Tie and a Touch of Juju - the Ideological Construction of Africa: A Critical Discourse Analysis of News on Africa in the British Press." *Discourse and Society* 6, no. 4 (October 1995): 461-494.
A discourse analysis of the terminology used in coverage of Africa by the British press. The beginning phrase of the title is a quote from the headline of an article on Liberia in the British *Daily Telegraph*, exemplifying the overall tone of much of the coverage examined.

73
Broughton, Morris. *Press and Politics of South Africa*. Cape Town: Purnell and Sons, 1961. 306pp.
A history of journalism and its relation to politics in South Africa. Appendix gives circulation of newspapers in 1959. Index.

74
Brown, Trevor. "Did Anyone Know his Name? U. S. Press Coverage of Biko." *Journalism Quarterly* (March 1980): 31-38.

75
---. "Free Press Fair Game of South Africa's Government." *Journalism Quarterly* 48, no. 1 (March 1971): 120-127.
> Discussion of the press in South Africa, which was strenuously repressed and described by a National Party member of Parliament as "the opposition".

76
Brush, Michael. "Press Content as a Key to a Country's Alignment: The Case of Ethiopia." *Political Communication and Persuasion* 5, no. 2 (1988): 93-100.
> A content analysis of the *Ethiopian Herald* over two ten-year periods, one before and one after the 1974 overthrow of Emperor Haile Selassie by Mengistu Haile Mariam and installation of a socialist regime. The study showed a dramatic shift in the nature of coverage from pro-U.S. before the coup to pro-Soviet Union afterward.

77
Buijtenhuijs, Rob, and Rene Baesjou. "Center and Periphery News in Two African Dailies: Testing Some Hypotheses on Cultural Dominance." *Kroniek van Afrika*, no. 3 (1993): 243-271.
> The authors test the theories of Norwegian scholar Johan Galtung regarding the role of news communication in imperialism by comparing home and foreign news coverage of Senegal's *Le Soleil* and Kenya's *Daily Nation*. 1 page bibliography and response by Johan Galtung.

78
Bunting, Brian. *Who Runs our Newspapers: the Story Behind the Non-White Press*. Cape Town: New Age, 1960. 9pp.
> Reprint of an article from *New Age*, an independent weekly, reviewing the newspapers for and by Black Africans in South Africa.

79
Burchell, Jonathan. "Contempt of Court by the Media: Another Opportunity to Extend Press Freedom is Lost: *S v Harber* 1988 (3) SA 396 (A)." *South African Journal on Human Rights* 4, no. 3 (November 1988): 375-391.
> Discussion of the practice of using contempt of court to control media, with commentary on the trial of staff of the *Weekly Mail* for publishing articles on the proceedings of the Delmas Treason Trial in May 1986.

80
Burkhart, Ford. "Nigeria: Tribalism Fosters Free-Press Values in US-Style System." *Quill* 71, no. 3 (March 1983): 6-12.

The Press

An optimistic assessment of Nigeria's press in the early 1980s, when democratic elections were planned and press freedom flourished.

81
Byrne, Eileen. "Dialogue Suspended." *Index on Censorship* 22, no. 2 (February 1993): 21-23.
A report on independent newspapers in Algeria whose attempts to further democracy through free speech were met with repression.

82
Cameroon: The Press in Trouble. London: Article 19, 1993. 15pp.
A report by the International Centre Against Censorship (Article 19) on the restriction of press freedom in Cameroon. A summary of events in 1992 and 1993 is followed by a memorandum addressed to Cameroon's National Commission on Human Rights and Freedoms objecting to the laws which permit those restrictions.

83
Campion-Vincent, Véronique. "L'Image du Dahomey dans la Presse Française (1890-1895): Les Sacrifices Humains." *Cahiers d'Études Africaines* 7, no. 1 (1967): 27-58.
A discussion of reports in the French press of human sacrifices in Dahomey (now Benin), focusing on the motivations for the sensationalism and the degree of exaggeration and misrepresentation. Reproductions of illustrations from newspaper articles.

84
Carter, Felice. "The Asian Press in Kenya." *East Africa Journal* 6, no. 10 (October 1969): 30-34.
An overview of the newspapers published by and for the Asian community in Kenya, pointing out that besides their own papers, Asian publishers frequently did the printing for African newspapers in Kenya.

85
---. "The Press in Kenya." *Gazette* 14, no. 2 (1968): 85-88.
A brief overview of press ownership and activities in Kenya.

86
Carver, Richard. "How the *Chronicle* Lost Two Editors." *Index on Censorship* 18, no. 9 (October 1989): 20-23.
After exposing major government corruption, two editors of a Zimbabwean newspaper were "kicked upstairs" to isolated posts and the newspaper was placed in the hands of an editor more cooperative with the government.

87
Cerullo, Margaret, and Evelynn Hammonds. "AIDS and Africa: The Western Imagination and the Dark Continent." *Radical America* 21, no. 2/3 (March 1988): 17-23.

An examination of reporting on AIDS in Africa in the popular and professional medical press, emphasizing the attitudes that are consciously or unconsciously expressed.

88

Charles, Jeff, Larry Shore, and Rusty Todd. "The *New York Times* Coverage of Equatorial and Lower Africa." *Journal of Communication* 29, no. 2 (March 1979): 148-155.
    A content analysis of a sampling of the *New York Times* using the first six months of 1960, 1965, 1970, and 1975 to determine what countries in Africa were covered and what kinds of stories were reported.

89

Chick, John D. "The *Ashanti Times*: A Footnote to Ghanaian Press History." *African Affairs* 76, no. 302 (January 1977): 80-94.
    An account of the establishment, life, and demise of a Ghanaian newspaper which began as a house organ of the Ashanti Goldfields mining company and opposed Nkrumah's policies and ideas.

90

---. "The Nigerian Press and National Integration." *Journal of Commonwealth Political Studies* 9, no. 2 (1971): 115-133.
    A discussion of the role of the press in political and social national identity.

91

Chinje, Eric. "The Media in Emerging African Democracies: Power Politics and the Role of the Press." *The Fletcher Forum* 17, no. 1 (December 1993): 49-66.
    A discussion focusing on censorship as an instrument of power and the ways that governments in Africa are using that power as they go through a period of dynamic change.

92

Cohen, Roberta. "Censorship Costs Lives." *Index on Censorship* 16, no. 5 (May 1987): 15-18.
    A former officer in the U.S. embassy in Addis Ababa reports on the restrictions placed on Western and local journalists which inhibited reporting of famine in Ethiopia in 1983, two years before headlines triggered an outpouring of international aid. The suppression of the story may have allowed suffering that could have been prevented.

93

Coker, Increase H. E. *Landmarks of the Nigerian Press: an Outline of the Origins and Development of the Newspaper Press in Nigeria, 1859 to 1955.* Apapa, Lagos, Nigeria: Nigerian National Press, 1968. 126pp.
    A history of the press in Nigeria, with a retrospective list of newspapers. 2 page bibliography.

The Press

94

Committee on Inter-African Relations. *Press and Progress in the New West Africa*. Dakar: 1960. Various pagings.
  More papers from the conference (See also Item # 95).

95

---. *Report on the Press in West Africa*, prepared for the International Seminar on "Press and Progress in West Africa", University of Dakar, May 31 to June 4, 1960. Ibadan, Nigeria: Distributed by Director, Dept. of Extra-Mural Studies, University College, 1960.
  Introductions and five papers from the seminar, covering the press in French-speaking West Africa, Ghana, Liberia and Nigeria. (See also #94).

96

Comptes-Rendu Intégral de la Réunion Responsables-Enseignants: Paris, 19-21 Septembre, 1973. Paris: Université de Droit, d'Économie, et de Sciences Sociales de Paris 2, Institut Français de Presse et des Sciences de l'Information, Département des Études Sur l'Information dans les Pays du Tiers-Monde, 1973. 153pp.
  Proceedings of a seminar of faculties of journalism and communications from Senegal, Cameroon, France, and Canada.

97

Condon, John. "Nation Building and Image Building in the Tanzania Press." *Journal of Modern African Studies* 5, no. 3 (1967): 335-354.
  A content analysis of four daily newspapers in Tanzania, *The Standard, Ngurumo, Uhuru,* and *The Nationalist*, to determine coverage of events in Tanzania, the rest of Africa, and the world.

98

Connell, Dan. "Correspondent's Report: Return of the Ugly American." *Africa Today* 29, no. 4 (1982): 17-23.
  A critique of the attitudes and behavior of "globe-trotting journalists" in Africa which color and shape their presentation of events, often leading to distortions and misrepresentation.

99

Couzens, Tim. *The New African: A Study of the Life and Work of H. I. E. Dhlomo*. Johannesburg: Ravan, 1985. 382pp.
  Biography of a noted South African writer journalist. Index.

100

---. "A Short History of *The World* and Other Black South African Newspapers." *Inspan* 1, no. 1 (June 1978): 69-72.

101

Cross River State, Nigeria. Select Committee. *Report of the Enquiry into the Problems of the Cross River State Newspaper Corporation.* Calabar, Nigeria: Government Printer, 1981. 43pp.
   Investigation into possible irregularities in the procurement of newsprint and other questionable uses of funds by the Corporation.

102

Cuddy, Robert. "The Good Guys and the Bad and Other Myths: An Analysis of *Los Angeles Times* coverage of the Shaba "Invasion", 1978." *Ufahamu* 9, no. 1 (1979): 6-55.
   An examination of the coverage of the incidents in Shaba (formerly Katanga) province of Zaire in 1978. The *Los Angeles Times* stories described these events as Communist-inspired attacks by Angola aided by Cuban troops, and gave a disparaging view of all Africans.

103

Cutten, Theo E. G. *A History of the Press in South Africa.* Cape Town: National Union of South African Students, 1935. 160pp.
   An abridged version of the author's M.A. thesis, this work covers the early years of South Africa's press, beginning with the first printing press in 1800 through the early 1930s.

104

Dare, Olatunji. "Nigeria: the Polarized Press." *Nieman Reports* 50, no. 1 (March 1996): 50-53.
   The former Editorial Chairman of the Guardian Newspapers in Nigeria, who was forced out of his position for criticizing the Nigerian government, discusses the state of the press in Nigeria today.

105

Davidson, Joe. "The Price of African Press Freedom." *Media Studies Journal* 9, no. 3 (June 1995): 53-61.
   An assessment of press freedom in Africa, with anecdotes from Mozambique, Zambia and Namibia.

106

de Kock, Wessel. *A Manner of Speaking: the Origins of the Press in South Africa.* Cape Town: Saayman and Weber, 1982. 150pp.
   A history of the European press in South Africa beginning in 1824 when the *South African Journal* defied colonial government restrictions on non-official newspapers. The appendix contains documents and articles pertaining to that early paper and the later founding of the Newspaper Press Union. 3 page bibliography. Index.

107

de St. Jorre, John. "Nigerian Civil War Notebook." *Transition* 8, no. 38 (1971): 36-41.
   Informal notes by a journalist who covered the Nigerian Civil War.

The Press

108

Deguine, Hervé, and Menard Robert. "Are There Any Journalists Left in Rwanda?" *Index on Censorship* 23, no. 6 (November 1994): 55-59.
> A report on the activities and mortality rate of Rwandan journalists during the massacres.

109

Dekou, Abotsi. "L'Utilisation des Langues Maternelles dans la Presse Africaine." *L'Afrique Littéraire et Artistique* , no. 33 (1974): 9-12.
> A survey of newspapers in Togo published wholly or partly in Ewe, with notes on use of local languages in Nigerian and Cameroonian newspapers, and the Swahili press in Kenya and Tanzania.

110

Delarbre, Anne. "Les Agences de Presse Internationales en Afrique." *Mondes en Développement* 19, no. 73 (1991): 21-34.
> A comparative study of Agence France Press and Reuters in Africa with a content analysis of dispatches about Senegal in 1987 and 1988 and Kenya in 1987 to assess AFP's image of Africa.

111

Deveneaux, Gustav Kashope. "Public Opinion and Colonial Policy in Nineteenth-Century Sierra Leone." *International Journal of African Historical Studies* 9, no. 1 (1976): 45-67.
> A discussion of public opinion in Sierra Leone with commentary on newspapers as a major means of influencing that opinion.

112

Dias, Raul Neves. *A Imprensa Periodica em Moçambique, 1854-1954.* Lourenço Marques: Imprensa Nacional de Moçambique, 1956. 110pp.
> A history of popular magazines and newspapers in Mozambique. Photographs and facsimiles of pages.

113

Diop, Babacar et al. *L'Impact des Journaux en Langues Nationales sur les Populations Sénégalaises.* Dakar: Association des Chercheurs Sénégalais, 1990. 109pp.
> Discussion of the need for newspapers in local languages as vehicles for raising literacy rates.

114

Doherty, Christo. "The Wits-Koornfoh Debate: Is There Really a Difference Between the English and Afrikaans Presses?" *Critical Arts* 2, no. 2 (1981): 39-49.
> A comparison of the coverage in three newspapers, *Cape Times, Weekend Argus*, and *Die Burger*, of an incident at the University of the Witswatersrand in which a group of protesting students disrupted a speech by South Africa's Minister of Co-operation

and Development. Despite ideological differences among the papers, they all took the same approach to the story.

115
Domatob, Jerry Komia. "Coverage of Africa in American Popular Magazines." *Issue* 22, no. 1 (March 1994): 24-29.
    A content analysis comparing the coverage of Africa in *Time* and *Newsweek* from 1989 to 1991, with graphs illustrating what types of stories appeared and text supplying details on those stories.

116
Domisse, Ebbe. "The Changing Role of the Afrikaans Press." *The Afrikaners*, 95-106. Edited by Edwin S. Munger. Cape Town: Tafelberg Publishers, 1979.
    An overview of the Afrikaans press of South Africa, claiming that it had begun promoting an inclusive nationalism.

117
Dumbia, Therese. "The "Second Wave" Press in Tropical Africa." *The Democratic Journalist* 38, no. 7 (July 1991): 16-17.
    An assessment of the role of the press in the "Second Wave of Independence", the growing movement in favor of political pluralism. The article examines newly established newspapers in Zaire and Mali.

118
Duodu, Cameron. "*Cape Times*." *Index on Censorship* 15, no. 1 (January 1986): 8-10.
    A report on the arrest of Anthony Heard, editor of the *Cape Times*, following his publication of an interview with Oliver Tambo, banned president of the ANC. An inset on page 9 of the article reports on crackdowns on foreign journalists.

119
Durieux, A. *De la Liberté de la Presse en Droit Belge Colonial.* Brussels: Établissements Emile Bruylant, 1958. 55pp.
    An overview of press freedom in Belgian colonial Africa, including Ruanda-Urundi and the Belgian Congo (Rwanda, Burundi and Zaire). One chapter outlines the relevant statutes.

120
Duyile, Dayo. *Makers of Nigerian Press: An Historical Analysis of Newspaper Development, the Pioneer Heroes, the Modern Press Barons from 1859-1987.* Lagos: Gong Communications, 1987. 726pp.
    History of the press in Nigeria, focusing on specific newspapers, editors, publishers and writers.

121
Eapen, K. E. "ZANA, an African News Agency." *Gazette* 18, no. 4 (1972): 193-207.

The Press

History and description of the Zambia News Agency with a critique of its coverage of news from neighboring countries.

122
Ebo, Boshah L. "The Ethical Dilemma of African Journalists: a Nigerian Perspective." *Journal of Mass Media Ethics* 9, no. 2 (1994): 84-93.
Explores the conflicting obligations of Nigerian journalists: professional ethics versus political and social pressures.

123
Edeani, David O. "Nigerian Mass Media Handling of Conflict Situations in the West African Sub-Region." *Africa Media Review* 8, no. 1 (1994): 25-46.
Analysis of the coverage of conflicts in West Africa by three major Nigerian daily newspapers and three leading Nigerian weekly news magazines. 1 page bibliography.

124
---. "Ownership and Control of the Press in Africa." *Gazette* 16, no. 1 (1970): 55-66.
Survey of religious, political party, private, and government ownership of the press in Africa with commentary on differing levels of control.

125
---. "Value Orientations in Press Coverage of a National Mobilization Campaign." *Africa Media Review* 2, no. 2 (1988): 65-84.

126
Edoga-Ugwuoju, Dympna. "Ownership Patterns of Nigerian Newspapers." *Gazette* 33, no. 3 (1984): 193-201.
A survey of newspapers run by federal and state government agencies and private firms, and the respective effects of each type of ownership.

127
Edwards, Peter. "Press Purge in Malawi." *Index on Censorship* 2, no. 4 (December 1973): 53-57.
A report of President Hastings Banda's suppression of the press and intimidation of journalists, with sharp criticism for the failure of the British press to react strongly to these actions. (See Item #342)

128
Egypt. Ministry of Information. State Information Service. *The Press in Egypt: Laws and Regulations.* Cairo: The Ministry, 1985. 37pp.
An overview of the legal structure for press operations and press freedom in Egypt. Includes transcripts of speeches by Hosni Mubarak and texts of relevant laws.

129
Egyptian Organization for Human Rights. *Freedom of Opinion and Expression in Egypt: A Report*. New York: Lawyers Committee for Human Rights, 1990. 33pp.

130
Eilers, Franz-Josef. *Christliche Publizistik in Afrika: eine Erste Erkundung*. St. Augustin: Styler Verlag, 1964. 103pp.
   An overview of church-based newspapers and other publishing in Africa. 9 pages of photographs. 3 page bibliography. Index.

131
Ekpu, Ray. "Nigeria's Embattled Fourth Estate." *Journal of Democracy* 1, no. 2 (1990): 106-116.
   The editor-in-chief of Nigeria's *Newswatch* magazine draws on his experience with government censorship and oppression to illustrate the state of press freedom in Nigeria.

132
Ekwelie, Sylvanus A. "The Genesis of Press Control in Ghana." *Gazette* 24, no. 3 (1978): 196-206.
   An historical outline of socio-political events which resulted in a series of government actions and legislation to control the activities of the press in Ghana.

133
---. "The Nigerian Press in Cultural Development: Promises Versus Performances." *Nigeria Magazine* , no. 142 (1982): 40-47.
   Analysis of the potential of the Nigerian press for contributing to improvement of Nigerian society, with commentary on how it fulfills that potential in terms of its educational, economic, opinion-shaping and entertainment functions, as well as its news coverage, pointing out some of its shortcomings.

134
---. "The Nigerian Press Under Civilian Rule." *Journalism Quarterly* 63 (March 1986): 98-105,149.

135
---. "The Nigerian Press Under Military Rule." *Gazette* 25, no. 4 (1979): 219-232.
   An historical overview of the growth of the press in Nigeria during the years since independence, with an analysis of the special constraints placed on it by successive military regimes.

136
Ekwelie, Sylvanus A., and Dympna Edoga-Ugwuoju. "Ownership Patterns of Ghanaian Newspapers: An Historical Perspective." *Gazette* 35, no. 1 (1985): 49-59.

An historical overview of the newspaper industry in Ghana, noting that in terms of diversity of voice the country has gone from a single publisher in 1857 to full government monopoly during the Nkrumah years.

137

Emenyeonu, Bernard Nnamdi. "Africa's Image in the Local Press: An Analysis of African News in Some Nigerian Newspapers." *Africa Media Review* 9, no. 2 (1995): 82-104.

A content analysis of four Nigerian newspapers, *The Daily Times*, *The Guardian*, *The Vanguard*, and *The National Concord*, for the period May 1, 1991, through May 1, 1992, to determine the extent and nature of coverage of African events. The author found that the Nigerian newspapers used the same negative images for which the Western press is often criticized.

138

Engelbrecht, Johannes Cornelius Rudolph. *Die Pers as Masskommunikasiemedium*. Pretoria: Raad vir Geesteswetenskaplike Navorsing, 1972. 74pp.

A study of the press and other forms of mass communication in South Africa.

139

Epule, Kome. *Challenge of Responsibility: An Analysis of the Role and Prospects of the African Press*. Buea, Cameroon: Kome Epule, 1978. 165pp.

An overview of the interaction of the press in Africa with social and political events, and its importance in shaping public opinion.

140

Eribo, Festus. "Coverage of Africa South of the Sahara by *Pravda*, *Izvestia*, *Trud* and *Selskaya Zhizn*, 1979-1987: A Content Analysis." *The Journalism Quarterly* 70, no. 1 (March 1993): 51-57.

Report of a content analysis of four Moscow daily newspapers for three one-year periods: 1979, 1983 and 1987.

141

---. "Russian Newspaper Coverage of Somalia and the Former Yugoslavia." *Issue* 22, no. 1 (March 1994): 30-34.

A content analysis of *Pravda* and *Izvestia* in December 1992, during Project Restore Hope.

142

Essoulami, Said. "Attacks on the Press and Journalists." *Index on Censorship* 23, no. 4/5 (September 1994): 141-146.

Report on the restrictions and attacks on the press of the Front Islamique du Salut, Algeria's Islamic fundamentalist party.

143
---. "Attacks on the Press and Journalists." *Africans on Africa Series* #1, Supplement to *IDOC Internazionale* 26, no. 1 (January 1995): 41-44.

144
Eswara, H. S. "Flow of News Between India and Africa During Times of 'Crisis'." *Africa Quarterly* 9, no. 1 (April 1969): 15-22.
 Content analysis for two weeks in January 1966 of four newspapers: *The Statesman* from India, *West African Pilot* from Nigeria, *East African Standard* from Kenya, and *The Cape Times* from South Africa to determine the amount and composition of news about each of those countries.

145
Evert, J. B. "Freedom of the Press in Africa." *African Freedom Annual* (1977): 81-123.
 A country-by-country survey of daily and weekly newspapers with commentary on the legal framework of press freedom and government control.

146
---. "Freedom of the Press in Africa." *African Freedom Annual* (1978): 47-83.
 A country-by-country survey of events relating to press freedom in Africa.

147
Ewumbue-Monono, Churchill. *The Pan African News Agency and Regional Integration in Africa*. Yaounde: University of Yaounde, 1986. 123pp.
 A master's thesis (Memoire submitted in partial fulfillment of requirements for a Maitrise in International Relations, University of Yaounde) which examines PANA and competing agencies in the Arab world, Asia and Europe, with commentary on "media imperialism" in Africa.

148
---. "The Right to Inform and the 1990 Press Law in Cameroon." *Africa Media Review* 6, no. 3 (1992): 19-30. (Author's name on article appears as Ewumbue Monono Churchill).
 An examination of the objectives of the 1900 press law in Cameroon.

149
"Eye of the Storm: Reporting Southern Africa." *Africa News* 20, no. 16 (18 April 1983): 5-11.
 Discussion of censorship and freedom of the press in Zimbabwe and South Africa.

150
Ezeh, Peter. "The Censor comes to Nigeria's *Observer*." *Index on Censorship* 17, no. 7 (August 1988): 18-19, 28.
 Report of the suppression of newspapers in Nigeria's Bendel State following an editorial that displeased the military government.

151
Faringer, Gunilla L. *Press Freedom in Africa.* New York: Praeger, 1991. 144pp.
   An overview of the press and press freedom in Africa, beginning with the period prior to World War II, on through the independence movements to the relationship of press and government in modern Africa. Concentrates on Ghana, Nigeria and Kenya. 5 page bibliography. Index.

152
Fawehinmi, Gani. *Nigerian Law of Libel and the Press.* Lagos: Nigerian Law Publications, 1987. 1 vol.

153
---. *Nigerian Law of the Press Under the Constitution and the Criminal Law.* Lagos: Nigerian Law Publications, 1987. 1 vol.

154
"Feisty Weeklies Under Fire." *Africa News* 29, no. 10 (16 May 1988): 1-5.
   Notes on the problems encountered by several weekly news magazines in South Africa, including *South, New Nation,* and *Weekly Mail,* observing that alternative presses provide the best source of news in that country.

155
Feltoe, Graham. *Guide to Press Law in Zimbabwe.* Harare: Legal Resources Foundation, 1993. 50pp.

156
Feuereisen, Fritz, and Ernst Schmacke. *Die Presse in Afrika/The Press in Africa: Ein Handbuch fur Wirtschaft und Werbung/A Handbook for Economics and Advertising.* Munich: Verlag Dokumentation, 1973. 280pp.
   A country-by-country list of newspapers, noting their political affiliations, addresses, circulation statistics, language, frequency, and advertising rates.

157
Finn, Stephen M. *Mass Media and the 1981 Election: an Analysis of the Extent and Bias of Mass Media Coverage of the 1981 South African Election.* Cape Town: Tafelberg, 1982. 39pp.
   Presentation in tables and graphs with some text of coverage of the several political parties by nine South African newspapers.

158
Finnegan, William. *Dateline Soweto: Travels with Black South African Reporters.* New York: Harper and Row, 1988. 244pp.
   Personal account by an American journalist of his experiences working and talking with Black South African journalists in the mid-1980s.

159
Fitzgerald, Mary Anne. "The News Hole: Reporting Africa." *Africa Report* 34, no. 4 (July 1989): 59-61.
   Criticism of the coverage of Africa by the Western press is here rebutted by accounts of restraint and oppression of local and foreign journalists in several African countries.

160
Flather, Horace. *The Way of an Editor*. Cape Town: Purnell and Sons, 1977. 209pp.
   Autobiography of the editor of the *Star* newspaper (South Africa). Several pages of photographs. Index.

161
Fletcher, Richard, and Tony Smart. "The News Manipulators." *Africa Now*, no. 11 (March 1982): 70-73.
   An exposé, giving considerable historical depth, of British Intelligence manipulation of Reuters and control of the flow of news to Africa and other Third World areas.

162
"Focus on South Africa." *Nieman Reports* 29, no. 3/4 (December 1975): 12-35.
   A feature section with brief articles and reprints dealing with the press in South Africa.

163
Foisie, Jack et al. "Update: the Press in South Africa." *Nieman Reports* 36, no. 2 (June 1982): 23-28.
   Discussion by one American and three South African reporters on the status of the press in South Africa and the ramifications of the report of the Steyn Commission of Inquiry.

164
Fontaine, Arlette. *La Presse au Sénégal (1939-1960): Bibliographie*. PhD. Diss., Université de Dakar, 1967. 422pp.

165
Friedgut, A. J. "The Non-European Press." *Handbook on Race Relations in South Africa*, 484-510. Edited by Ellen Hellmen. Cape Town: Oxford University Press, 1949.
   An overview of the 'Bantu', 'Cape Coloured' and 'Asiatic' presses in South Africa beginning in 1884 with *Imvo Zabantsundu* ("Native Opinion"). The section on "Problems and Possibilities" ends with the observation that the non-European press can serve as a model of quality for the European press.

166
Fussell, Paul. "The Smut Hounds of Pretoria." *New Republic* (23 February 1980): 20-23.

167

Fyfe, C. H. "The Sierra Leone Press in the Nineteenth Century." *Sierra Leone Studies* , no. n.s. 8 (June 1957): 226-236.
    A detailed account of the press in Sierra Leone from the first Freetown printing press, in 1794 through the 19th century, when many newspapers flourished.

168

Gadsden, Fay. "The African Press in Kenya, 1945-1952." *Journal of African History* 21, no. 4 (1980): 515-535.
    A discussion of the growth of African-owned newspapers publishing in African languages in Kenya focusing on the political leanings of their editors and the influence the papers had on their readers. An appendix lists African newspapers published during the period studied.

169

Gaillard, Phillippe. "Des Nouvelles pour Chacun." *Jeune Afrique* , no. 989 (December 1979): 76-79.
    A profile of the major French news agency, Agence France Presse, noting its activities in Africa. Includes an interview with its president, Henri Pigeat.

170

Gakosso, Jean. "Nouvelle Problématique de la Presse Africaine." *Médiaspouvoirs* (April 1991): 63-68.
    A discussion of the future of press freedom in Africa in the context of increasing political pluralism.

171

Gallay, Pierre. "The English Missionary Press of East and Central Africa." *Gazette* 14, no. 2 (1968): 129-133.
    A survey of Roman Catholic newspapers and magazines in the Anglophone countries of East and Central Africa.

172

Gathu, Faith W. "Freedom of Expression in Kenya and USA: A Comparison." *Africa Media Review* 9, no. 3 (1995): 76-89.
    Although clauses in the constitutions of both countries seem to guarantee freedom of speech, Kenya's constitution does not specifically mention press freedom. The author finds that this omission permits Kenya's restrictions on the press.

173

Gboyega, Bade. *Journalism in Nigeria: An All Commers (sic) Profession?* Akure: Ajomro Publications, 1989. 59pp.
    A discussion of journalism in Nigeria following the Media Council Decree of 1988.

174

Gendzier, Irene L. *The Practical Visions of Ya'qub Sanu'*. Cambridge, MA: Harvard University Press, 1966. 175pp.

A study of the life and work of Egyptian journalist Ya'qub Sanu' (1839-1912) in the context of the founding of modern Egypt. 9 page bibliography.

175

Gerold-Scheepers, Therese. "Literature on the Press in Africa, Africa in the Press." *Kroniek van Afrika* , no. 3 (1993): 347-366.
A bibliographic essay reviewing the press in Africa before and after independence, and coverage of Africa in the international press. 7 page bibliography.

176

"Ghana -- The Real Story." *Index on Censorship* 16, no. 1 (January 1987): 19-20.
A report stating that conditions in Ghana, described in the foreign press as an "economic miracle", are actually quite dire, and noting the government control of the Ghanaian press and the naiveté of Western reporters.

177

Gibson, Rex, and Allister Sparks. "South Africa After Muldergate." *Atlas World Press Review* 26, no. 8 (August 1979): 17-20.
Gibson, the editor of *Sunday Express,* and Sparks, editor of the *Rand Daily Mail*, both of Johannesburg, respond to questions from *Atlas'* editor on the role of the English language press in South Africa on the uncovering of the Muldergate scandal and the subsequent crackdown on press freedom.

178

Giffard, C. Anthony. "Circulation Trends in South Africa." *Journalism Quarterly* (March 1980): 86-91, 106.

179

Gikaru, Lawrence. "National Interest and the Media: Comparison of Kenyan Elections by the *New York Times* and *The Guardian*." *Africa Media Review* 8, no. 2 (1994): 27-37.
A comparison of U.S. and British coverage of the Kenyan elections of 1993 to determine their differences and the relationship of those differences to their differing foreign policies regarding Kenya.

180

Ginwala, Frene. "The Press in South Africa." *Index on Censorship* 2, no. 3 (1973): 27-43.
A report on the suppression of the press in South Africa, with a summary of laws allowing censorship and a list of journalists who have suffered persecution.

181

Govea, R. "East-West Themes in the Reporting of African Violence." *Social Science Quarterly* 64, no. 1 (1983): 193-199.
A content analysis of articles from *Newsweek* and the State Department *Bulletin* to determine the terms in which violent events in Africa were described. The study found that Cold War frames of reference were prevalent.

182

Hawks and Doves: the Pro- and Anti-Conscription Press in South Africa, edited by Michael Graaf. Durban: Contemporary Cultural Studies Unit, University of Natal, 1988. 90pp.
  Study of the role of the press in the controversy over conscription in South Africa during the Apartheid era.

183

Grant, Marcia A. "Nigerian Newspaper Types." *Journal of Commonwealth Political Studies* 9, no. 2 (1971): 95-114.
  A classification of Nigerian newspapers according to ownership and affiliation with analysis of their readership and effectiveness.

184

Green, George A. L. *An Editor Looks Back: South African and Other Memories, 1883-1946*. Westport, CT: Negro Universities Press, 1970. 288pp.
  Personal memoir of a South African journalist and editor.

185

Greig, G. *Facts Connected With the Stopping of the South African Commercial Advertiser*. Cape Town: Africana Connoisseurs Press, 1963. 29pp.
  A facsimile reproduction of the original handbill, with transcriptions of subsequent postscripts, dealing with the controversial closing of a South African newspaper in 1824.

186

Grogan, John, and Charles Riddle. "South Africa's Press in the Eighties: Darkness Descends." *Gazette* 39, no. 1 (1987): 3-16.
  A description of the legal and economic conditions affecting the press in South Africa during the last years of apartheid.

187

Gueye, Amadou Mactar. "Decolonising the Media on Africa." *West Africa*, no. 3709 (12 September): 1660-1662.
  A report on the activities of the Pan-African News Agency in providing accurate and broad news coverage for Africa, thereby correcting the imbalance in the flow of information.

188

Guiochet, Sylvie. "Sur l'Afrique des Peintres au XIXe Siècle: les Salons et leurs Échos dans la Presse." *Afrique Littéraire*, no. 58 (1981): 36-45.
  A survey of the depiction of Africa in popular illustrated news magazines in France during the 19th century.

189
Gupta, Anirudha. *Reporting Africa*. Delhi: People's Pub. House, 1969. 340pp.
> A collection of articles on Africa written by an Indian journalist during travel throughout the continent during 1965 and 1966.

190
Hachten, William A. "The Black Journalists under Apartheid." *Index on Censorship* 8, no. 3 (May 1979): 43-48.
> Discussion of the problems confronting Black journalists in South Africa, with analysis of the opportunities they have for advancement.

191
---. "Ghana's Press Under the N. R. C.: An Authoritarian Model for Africa." *Journalism Quarterly* 52 (1975):

192
---. "Newspapers in Africa: Change or Decay?" *Africa Report* 15, no. 9 (December 1970): 25-28.
> A review of the status of the press in Africa, focusing on problems of government control and intervention, foreign influences, and the lack of trained journalists and adequate infrastructure.

193
---. "The Press in a One-Party State: Kenya Since Independence." *Journalism Quarterly* 42-43 (March 1965): 262-266.
> A discussion of government control of the press in newly independent Kenya.

194
---. "The Training of African Journalists." *Gazette* 14, no. 2 (1968): 101-110.
> An outline of education and professional training available for African journalists, including established schools and short term programs and workshops.

195
Hachten, William A., and C. Anthony Giffard. *The Press and Apartheid: Repression and Propaganda in South Africa*. Madison, WI: University of Wisconsin Press, 1984. 336pp.
> Analysis and overview of the press and its repression in South Africa from its early history through the 1980s. Covers the Steyn Commission and Muldergate. Glossary. 16 page bibliography. Index.

196
---. *Total Onslaught: the South African Press Under Attack*. Johannesburg: Macmillan, 1984. 336pp.
> "Total onslaught" was a phrase used by South African Prime Minister P. W. Botha to describe the peril of an all-out attack on [White] South Africa, which could be countered by "total strategy", including a supporting and conforming press. This

study examines how that concept turned into a full-scale attack on much of the English language press in South Africa. Includes analysis of the Steyn Commission and Muldergate.

197

Ham, Melinda. "*Post* Independence." *Africa Report* 36, no. 5 (September 1991): 69-71.
Profile of Zambia's first independent weekly newspaper, The *Weekly Post*, whose editorial staff plan investigative journalism to "wage a relentless war on corruption, mismanagement, and all forms of discrimination.".

198

Hamdani, Mariam Mohamed Abudrahman. *Zanzibar Newspapers 1902 to 1974*. Dar es Salaam: Tanzania School of Journalism, 1981. 73pp.
An historical overview of newspapers published in Zanzibar, noting language of publication, descriptive details, intended readership, and kinds of news covered. 4 page list of newspapers with statistical information for each.

199

Harber, Anton. "Finding the Loopholes: How the *Weekly Mail* Carries on Reporting." *Index on Censorship* 16, no. 4 (April 1987): 22-25.
An interview with the co-editor of the *Weekly Mail* on the difficulties of running an opposition newspaper in apartheid South Africa.

200

Harding, Jeremy. "Inroads into Silence." *Index on Censorship* 18, no. 4 (April 1989): 12-13.
Report of the efforts of some Mozambican journalists, despite enormous difficulties, to report on the desperate conditions of people displaced by war and famine.

201

Harrell-Bond, Barbara E. *Freedom of the Press in Nigeria: the Debate.* Hanover, NH: AUFS, 1978. 12pp.
A discussion of the controversy which arose in Nigeria when the Constituent Assembly, drafting a constitution for the planned return to civilian government in 1979, concluded that the press in Nigeria needed no specific guarantees of freedom of expression.

202

Harris, Phil. *Reporting Southern Africa: Western News Agencies Reporting from Southern Africa*. Paris: Unesco, 1981. 168pp.
An overview of problems encountered in covering southern Africa, including both government restraints on the press and the selection of news stories by Western editors.

203

Haule, John James. "International Press Coverage of African Events: the Dilemma and the Future." *Gazette* 33, no. 2 (1984): 107-114.

The author uses one African news event, a speech made by Tanzania's President Julius Nyerere in December 1981, to compare international and local African news coverage. Nyerere believed the speech had received unfavorable coverage in the international press.

204
Fifty Years of Truth: the Story of Gaskiya Corporation, Zaria, 1939-1991, edited by Husaini Hayatu. Zaria, Nigeria: Gaskiya Corporation, 1991. 190pp.
History of a Nigerian publisher specializing in Hausa language materials, including *Gaskiya ta fi kobo (Truth for a Penny)*, a Hausa language newspaper.

205
Hazoume, Guy-Landry et al. *La Vie et l'Oeuvre de Louis Hunkanrin, Suivi de Deux Écrits de Louis Hunkanrin*. Cotonou: Librarie Renaissance, 1977. 249pp.
A collection of essays on the life and work of a politician and journalist in Dahomey (now Benin) during the first part of the 20th century.

206
Head, Sydney W. "The Content of Children's Letters to a Vernacular Newspaper." *Proceedings of the First United States Conference on Ethiopian Studies, Michigan State University, 2 5 May 1973*, 249-250. Edited by Harold G. Marcus. East Lansing, MI: African Studies Center, Michigan State University, 1975.
Content analysis of letters to the children's page of *Addis Zemen*, the major Amharic daily newspaper, to determine trends in subject matter.

207
Heard, Anthony H. "How I Was Fired." *Index on Censorship* 16, no. 10 (November 1987): 9-12.
The former editor of the *Cape Times* discusses his sixteen year career in South African journalism and his dismissal from his newspaper for "non-political" reasons.

208
---. "The Media Blackout." *Africa Report* 31, no. 2 (March 1986): 57-59.
The editor of the *Cape Times*, under arrest for publishing an interview with Oliver Tambo, the banned leader of the ANC, discusses press freedom and the role of the press in South Africa.

209
Heikal, Mohamed H. *The Cairo Documents: The Inside Story of Nasser and His Relationship with World Leaders, Rebels and Statesmen*. New York: Doubleday, 1973. 360pp.
A contemporary history of Egypt written by "the most powerful journalist in the world," as described by Edward R. F. Sheehan in his introduction to Heikal's book.

210
---. "My 'Trial'." *Index on Censorship* 15, no. 6 (June 1986): 19-23.
  Excerpts from an interview published in the Egyptian newspaper *Akhbar al-Youm* in which the noted journalist and author describes the years he was barred from working with the press and comments on political events in Egypt.

211
Hepple, Alexander. *Censorship and Press Control in South Africa.* Johannesburg: 1960. 78pp.
  A collection of essays and commentary on the press in South Africa in the wake of the Cronje report (the Commission of Enquiry in Regard to Undesirable Publications).

212
---. *Press Under Apartheid.* London: International Defense and Aid Fund, 1974. 67pp.
  Discussion of the history of the conflict between successive South African apartheid administrations and the press, with a compilation of relevant legislation.

213
Hobbs, R., and R. Frost. "Comprehension of Transitional Editing Conventions by African Tribal Villages." *Mass Media Effects Across Cultures*, 19-33. Edited by F. Korzenny et al. Newbury Park: Sage, 1993.

214
Hopkinson, Tom. *In the Fiery Continent.* London: Victor Gollancz, 1962. 376pp.
  Personal memoir of an editor of *Drum*.

215
---. "A New Age of Newspapers in Africa?" *Gazette* 14, no. 2 (1968): 79-84.
  A description of the Annual Assembly of the International Press Institute for 1965, when African journalists discussed "The Press in a One-Party State", with such skill and vigor that the assembled international journalists came away with a new appreciation of their African colleagues.

216
---. *Under the Tropic.* London: Hutchinson, 1984. 307pp.
  A personal memoir of a former editor of *Drum*.

217
The Third World and Press Freedom, edited by Philip C. Horton. New York: Praeger, 1978. 253pp.
  A collection of essays by journalists from the West and the Third World on press freedom and the flow of information. 14 page bibliography.

218

Hotz, L. "The Press: Thomas William Mackenzie." *Better Than They Knew*, 32-56. Edited by R. M. de Villiers. Cape Town: Purnell, 1974.
   A biographical sketch of a South African editor and journalist.

219

"How Free is the Press? A Global Sampler." *Atlas World Press Review* (February 1992): 10-15.
   A world-wide summary of press freedom, including sections on Algeria, Cameroon, Ethiopia, Kenya, Nigeria, South Africa, Uganda and Zimbabwe.

220

Howson-Wright, A. E. *The Press and Nigeria*. Lagos: 1969. 37pp.
   A discussion of freedom of the press in the context of government versus private ownership of newspapers, with discussion of the economic aspects of newspaper publishing, and a call for journalists to accept the responsibility for provision of information to the public.

221

Hughes, Anthony J. "Nairobi Press Notebook." *Africa Report* 26, no. 5 (September 1981): 55-57.
   A journalist covering the 1981 OAU Summit meeting in Nairobi comments on the news media in Kenya and the effects upon those media of government controls.

222

Communicating Health for All in Africa: Report on the Training Course of African Communicators on Primary Health Care, edited by Pirjo Huida. Tampere, Finland: University of Tampere, Unit of Peace Research and Development Studies, 1988. 164pp
   Lectures and reports from a training course for African journalists in reporting on health care issues. Appendices include list of participants, the program of the course and facsimiles of newspaper articles on health care and on the course.

223

Hunt, Gary T. "Development News About Africa: A Comparison of the Content of the Pan African News Agency with the *New York Times* and the Associated Press." *World Communication* 21, no. 2 (December 1992): 51-62.
   An analysis of output of the Pan African News Agency (PANA) over a 15 day period in mid 1990, compared to news on Africa published in the *New York Times* and distributed by the Associated Press. PANA distributed 380 stories while the *New York Times* published 15 stories and AP distributed forty one. Besides the difference in output, PANA stories were generally positive and covered a wide range of topics. AP and *New York Times* coverage focused on the war in Liberia, and were generally negative.

The Press

224

Ibelema, Minabere. "Quantitative changes in *Newsweek*'s and *Time*'s Coverage of Sub-Saharan Africa." *Journal of African Communications* 1, no. 1 (March 1996): 71-91.
> A content analysis comparing African coverage in *Time* and *Newsweek* for the first five years of the 1970s and the first five years of the 1980s.

225

Ibie, Nosa Owens. "Press Responsibility and Public Opinion in Political Transition." *Africa Media Review* 8, no. 1 (1994): 69-80.
> A theoretical discussion of the responsibility of journalists for shaping public opinion.

226

Igbarumah, Matthias. *Ideology, the Mass Media and Journalism*. Jos, Nigeria: Jos University Press, 1990. 47pp.
> A short work exploring the relationship of ideology and the mass media, with examples drawn from the author's experience as a journalist in Nigeria.

227

Ihaddaden, Zahir. *Histoire de la Presse Indigène en Algérie des Origines Jusqu'en 1930*. Algiers: ENAL, 1983. 410pp.
> History of the press in Algeria through 1930, with descriptions of each newspaper published to that date.

228

---. *La Presse Musulmane Algérienne de 1830 à 1930*. Algiers: ENAL, 1986. 50pp.
> A brief overview of the Muslim press in Algeria. 19 page bibliography.

229

"Information et Politique: Sécheresse et Solidarité dans *Le Soleil* (Juin 1972-Fevrier 1973)." *Kroniek van Afrika*, no. 3 (1993): 299-316.
> Analysis of a Dakar newspaper's coverage of a severe drought in Senegal, focusing on ways in which that coverage affected the parliamentary and presidential election campaigns during the period.

230

International Organization of Journalists. *The International Organization of Journalists and Africa*. Prague: International Organization of Journalists, 1975. 79pp.
> A description of the organization and its activities, with a 32 page list of its publications.

231
International Organization of Journalists. *South Africa, Apartheid, Mass Media: A Report on the Present State of Official Restrictions and Persecution.* Prague: International Organization of Journalists, 1973. 28pp.
   A discussion and condemnation of censorship and government control of the press in South Africa.

232
Irving, James, and Fred St. Leger. *Report of an Investigation into the Attitudes of a Sample of Male Residents of the City of East London, Cape Province, Towards the Daily Dispatch and Other Newspapers in the Area.* Grahamstown: Rhodes University, Institute of Social and Economic Research, 1967. 161pp.
   The survey correlates factors such as age, gender, education and occupation to newspaper reading habits and preference for particular papers.

233
Isoba, J. C. G. "The Rise and Fall of Uganda's Newspaper Industry, 1900-1976." *Journalism Quarterly* (June 1980): 224-233.

234
Israel, Adrienne M. "The Afrocentric Perspective in African Journalism: A Case Study of the *Ashanti Pioneer, 1939-1957.*" *Journal of Black Studies* 22, no. 3 (March 1992): 411-428.
   An analysis of the trends in coverage and style of the Ghanaian newspaper *Ashanti Pioneer* over an 18 year period.

235
Jackson, Gordon S. *Breaking Story: the South African Press.* Boulder: Westview Press, 1993. 308pp.
   History of the press in South Africa from Soweto (1976) to 1990, including the alternative press, press laws, and the state of emergency. Speculation on the future of the press in South Africa. Includes a glossary, list of abbreviations, and tables showing circulation of newspapers. 15 page bibliography. Index.

236
---. *The "Prison Exposes" and "Muldergate": A Case Study in Changing Government-Press Relations in South Africa.* Bloomington, IN: African Studies Program, Indiana University, 1981. 25pp.

237
Jakande, Lateef Kayode. "The Press and Military Rule." *Nigerian Government and Politics Under Military Rule, 1966-1979*, 110-123. Edited by Oyeleye Oyediran. New York: St Martin's Press, 1979.
   A Nigerian journalist discusses relations between the Nigerian press and the military regime, sounding an optimistic note in his description of the campaign waged

by Nigerian newspapers to achieve justice in the Amakiri case, when a journalist was detained and beaten because one of his columns had displeased a military leader.

238

Jasper, William F. "South Africa/Media Bias: The Rest of the Story." *New American* 10, no. 11 (30 May 1994): 29-33.
   The senior editor of the conservative *New American* complains of pro-ANC bias in American reporting of events in South Africa since Mandela's release from prison in 1990.

239

Johnson, Shaun. "Barometers of the Liberation Movement: A History of South Africa's Alternative Press." *Media Development* 32, no. 3 (June 1985): 18-21.

240

Jones-Quartey, K. A. B. *History, Politics and Early Press in Ghana: the Fictions and the Facts.* Legon, Ghana: University of Ghana School of Journalism and Communications Studies, 1975. 130pp.
   A history of the press in Ghana in which the author attempts to disprove what he asserts are false assumptions. Contains a chronology of newspapers and capsule histories of them, files of newspapers held at various libraries and archives, and notes on principal newspapers and periodicals. Index.

241

---. "Sierra Leone and Ghana: Nineteenth-Century Pioneers in West African Journalism." *Sierra Leone Studies*, no.12 (December 1959): 230-244.
   A detailed history of early newspapers in Sierra Leone and Ghana with numerous quotations from articles and four facsimile photographs of newspaper pages.

242

---. *A Summary History of the Ghana Press, 1822-1960.* Accra: Ghana Information Services Dept.: 1974, 68pp.
   An overview of the Ghanaian press through the 19th and 20th centuries. Contains reproductions of newspaper pages, and an annotated chronology of newspapers. Appendices include major depositories, lists of principal newspapers and a chronology of Anglo-African journals. Index.

243

Jose, Isma'il Babatunde. "Press Freedom in Africa." *African Affairs* 74, no. 296 (July 1975): 255-262.
   An overview of the problems facing the press in Africa by the Managing Director of the *Daily Times* (Nigeria) presented in an address to the Royal African Society.

244

---. *Walking a Tight Rope: Power Play in Daily Times.* Ibadan, Nigeria: University Press, Ltd., 1987. 421pp.

Memoir of a managing director of the *Daily Times* (Nigeria). Foreword by Cecil King. Index.

245
July, Robert W. "The Journalist in West African Thought." *The Origins of Modern African Thought: Its Development in West Africa during the Nineteenth and Twentieth Centuries*, 345-373. Robert W. July. New York: Praeger, 1967.
: An assessment of the role of journalists in the growth of West African nationalism, with biographical sketches of leading journalists and editors.

246
Kabetesi, Kibisu. *Press Law, Information Technology and Freedom of the Press*. Nairobi: Centre for Law Research International, 1994. 60pp.

247
---. *Press Law : Some Home Truth*. Nairobi: Center for Law Research International, 1994. 84pp.

248
Kagan, Rachael. "U.S. Press Cries Tribalism." *Passages: A Chronicle of the Humanities*, no. 4 (1992): 15. Supplement to *Program of African Studies News and Events* (Northwestern University), Early Fall 1992, Vol. 3, no. 1.
: Reprinted from *Lies Of Our Times: A Magazine to Correct the Record.* June 1992, p 5-6. Discussion of the coverage by U.S. newspapers of political events in Kenya, noting the emphasis on violence and the use of terms such as "tribal clashes".

249
Kalemba, Robert. "Life Censor Banda." *Index on Censorship* 18, no. 10 (November 1989): 32-34.
: A report on repression of journalists and other people whose actions are taken to be dissent by Malawi's President Banda. The author, a Malawian journalist now living in exile, graphically describes his detention and torture.

250
Kalter, Joanmarie. "Can Third World Journalism Find a Way?" *Quill* 71, no. 5 (May 1983): 14-18.
: An assessment by an American journalist of press freedom in selected Third World countries, with several African examples.

251
Kalu, Onuka. *Modern Journalism in Africa (A Newspaperman Looks at His Profession)*. Lagos: Kalsam West Africa Publishers, 1989. 240pp.
: An overview of journalism and the press in Africa, covering training, the legal framework and professionalism. Contains reproductions of newspaper pages.

The Press

252
Kamara, Sylviane. "Soif de Lire dans les Campagnes." *Jeune Afrique* , no. 1066 (10 January 1981): 89.
   A report on rural newspapers in Francophone Africa.

253
Kamara, Tom. "The Liberian Press Under Dictatorship, 1980-1990: a Comment." *Liberia-Forum* 5, no. 9 (1989): 62-67.
   A discussion of the tactics used by Samuel Doe and members of his government to suppress and control the press. The author is a former editor of the *Liberian Age* newspaper.

254
Kapuscinski, Ryszard. *Another Day of Life*. San Diego: Harcourt Brace Jovanovich, 1987. 136pp.
   Personal account of a Polish reporter's experiences in Angola just prior to independence.

255
Kareithi, Peter. "The Press in Kenya: Persecution and Perseverance." *Voices of the African Diaspora* 7, no. 3 (September 1991): 28-32.
   An historical overview of the press in Kenya, demonstrating that past accommodations to the political objectives of foreign owners have contributed to the rise of the Moi government which now suppresses journalists so harshly.

256
Kariithi, Nixon K. "The Crisis Facing Development Journalists in Africa." *Africans on Africa Series*. #1, Supplement to IDOC *Internazionale* 26, no. 1 (January 1995): 2-6.

257
Karikari, Kwame. "Africa: The Press and Democracy." *Race and Class* 34, no. 3 (January 1993): 55-66.
   A study of the relationship of political reforms and democratization in Africa to the establishment of new, often outspoken, newspapers.

258
---. "The "Anti-White Press" Campaign: the Opposition of the African Press to the Establishment of the *Daily Graphic* by the British Mirror Newspaper Company in Ghana, 1950." *Gazette* 49, no. 3 (1992): 215-232.
   An discussion of the efforts of the British colonial government to control the pro-Independence press in Ghana by encouraging a British-based transnational media company to publish in Ghana.

259
Journalism Ethics in Africa, edited by Francis P. Kasoma. Nairobi: African Council on Communication Education, 1994. 193pp.

A collection of essays dealing with both theoretical and practical approaches to issues of ethics in journalism.

260

Kasoma, Francis P. *The Press in Zambia: the Development, Role and Control of National Newspapers in Zambia 1906-1983*. Lusaka: Multimedia Publications, 1986. 244pp.
> A history of the press in Zambia from colonial times through independence, including chapters on newspapers for white settlers, government newspapers, and privately owned newspapers for Africans, with discussion of the directions for future development. Contains copies of documents pertaining to the press in Zambia. 5 page bibliography. Index.

261

---. "The Role of the Independent Media in Africa's Change to Democracy." *Media, Culture and Society* 17, no. 4 (October 1995): 537-555.
> The author examines the vital role of independent media in the development and maintenance of democracy in Africa, noting that dictators begin their rule by muzzling the free press to remove effective opposition.

262

---. "The Rural/Community Press in Africa: Grassroots Communication." *Communication and Culture: African Perspectives*, 19-24. Edited by S. T. Kwame Boafo. Nairobi: Africa Church Information Service, 1989.
> A discussion of the need for rural newspapers that are true expressions of the people of the community, not simply local editions of urban papers with urban agendas.

263

Kasoma, Francis P., and Michael Leslie. "The Vernacular Press in Zambia: A Pilot Study of a Provincial Newspaper." *Africa Media Review* 4, no. 2 (1990): 62-78.
> A critical appraisal of Zambia's provincial press in Zambian languages, recommending that the project should be reviewed for utility and appeal to its intended readership.

264

Kaufman, Michael. "Reporting From Africa." *Harpers* (April 1980): 24-30.

265

Kayyem, Juliette. "The New Censors." *New Republic* 206, no. 4 (27 January): 18-19.
> A brief note on continuing problems for reporters of *The Sowetan*, who have conflicts with their readers, the white owners of the newspaper, and the political groups they are covering.

266
Kenney, Keith R. "Images of Africa in News Magazines: Is There a Black Perspective?" *Gazette* 54, no. 1 (1994): 61-85.
> An exploration of racial bias as the basis of poor coverage of Africa in mainstream American news magazines, with a comparison of *Newsweek* and the new Black-owned magazine, *Emerge*. 4 page bibliography.

267
Kenya A Legal Magazine and Its Editor Under Attack -- Again: Gitobu Imanyara and the Nairobi Law Monthly. New York: Lawyers Committee for Human Rights, 1991. 7pp.

268
Kenya: Continued Attacks on the Independent Press. London: Article 19, 1993. *Censorship News* #25. 11pp.
> A report on government control and harassment of journalists in Kenya.

269
Kenya: Recent Threats to Freedom of Expression. London: Article 19, 1992. *Censorship News* #10. 8pp.

270
Kershaw, Richard. "The Problems of Reporting the African Scene." *African Affairs* 67, no. 269 (October 1968): 351-353.
> Address to the Royal African Society on the mistakes that Western reporters are making in writing about Africa.

271
Kirat, M. "Partiality and Biases: the Coverage of the Algerian Liberation War (1954-1962) by *Al-Ahram* and *Le Monde*." *Gazette* 44, no. 3 (1989): 155-175.
> Content analysis of the Egyptian newspaper *Al-Ahram*, and the French paper *Le Monde* to determine bias in coverage confirmed that each paper was predictably biased: *Le Monde* was pro-French and *Al-Ahram* pro-Algeria.

272
The Press in Africa, edited by Helen Kitchen. Washington, DC: Ruth Sloan Associates, 1956. 96pp.
> Country-by-country overview of newspapers in Africa. Introduction by Nigerian journalist, Abiodun Aloba.

273
Kitchen, Helen. "Some Observations on U. S. Media Coverage of South Africa in the 1980s." *International Affairs Bulletin* 4, no. 3 (1980): 10-17.
> A critical assessment of the way that the U.S. press corps covers Africa, noting that a "safari" or "discovery" mentality still predominates. There is no pool of expertise on the region, and little sense of the relevancy of potential stories.

274

Kivikuru, Ullamaija. *Training Course of East African Journalists on Primary Health Care: Phase III, Follow-up Seminar, Dar es Salaam, Tanzania, 13-22.1.1988.* Tampere, Finland: University of Tampere, Unit of Peace Research and Development Studies, 1988. Various pagings.
    The proceedings and documents of a training course for journalists in aspects of health care reporting. The reports include country overviews and lectures on specific aspects of journalism and coverage of health news.

275

Kleu, Sebastiaan J. "The Afrikaans Press: Voice of Nationalism." *Nieman Reports* 15, no. 4 (October 1961): 9-11.
    An attempt to present the Afrikaner press in a positive light.

276

Koné, Hugues. "Circulation de l'Information et Pluralisme: Quels Défies Pour la Presse Africaine?" *Africa Media Review* 6, no. 2 (1992): 1-12.
    An assessment of the potential role for the press in Africa's democratization movements.

277

Kovach, Bill. "Clampdown in Kenya." *Nieman Reports* 44, no. 4 (December 1990): 2, 26.
    A note on the repression of the press, particularly the *Nairobi Law Monthly*, by the Moi government.

278

Kpodoga: an Experiment in the Uses of a Rural Community Newspaper. Legon, Ghana: University of Ghana, Institute of Adult Education, 1982. 40pp.
    A report on a workshop sponsored by Unesco, *Use of a Rural Community Newspaper in the Use of the Mother Tongue in Education and the Preservation of Cultural Identity*. Tsito, August 17-31, 1981. Includes 8 papers and conclusions, proposals to Unesco, and a list of participants in the Workshop.

279

Lacob, Miriam. "How to Find Africa." *Columbia Journalism Review* (January 1991): 17-18.
    A compendium of information sources intended for journalists who excuse their limited coverage of African affairs on lack of information sources in the U.S.

280

---. "South Africa's 'Free' Press." *Columbia Journalism Review* (November 1982): 49-56.
    The author points out the irony of South African newspapers celebrating "The Year of the Press" while in the midst of powerful repression, and discusses the difficulties in reporting Black anger and the government's harsh reaction to it.

The Press

281
Laurence, John. "Censorship by Skin Colour." *Index on Censorship* 6, no. 2 (April 1977): 40-43.
   A commentary on racial bias in the coverage of the uprisings in South Africa's Soweto township in 1976, which led to misinterpretation and misrepresentation.

282
Le Pape, Marc. "Des Journalistes au Rwanda, l'Histoire Immédiate d'un Génocide." *Les Temps Modernes*, no. 583 (July 1995): 161-180.
   The author examines the moral dilemma of journalists in the midst of genocide.

283
Lepine, Richard M. "A Swahili Fiction Serial from the Kenyan Newspaper *Baraza*." *Ba Shiru* 13, no. 1 (March 1987): 61-74.
   A study of a detective thriller published in a Kenyan Swahili language newspaper, with description of the general content of the paper and commentary on the role of newspapers and their serialized fiction offerings in national and linguistic unity.

284
---. *Swahili Newspaper Fiction in Kenya: the Stories of James L. Mwagojo*. Madison, WI: University of Wisconsin, 1988. 655pp.
   A doctoral dissertation examining fiction published in Kenyan newspapers, highlighting one author. 10 page bibliography. Contains lists of fiction in two newspapers and one magazine, copies of interviews with writers and readers and a translation of one story.

285
Lewin Robinson, A. M. *None Daring to Make Us Afraid: a Study of English Periodical Literature in the Cape Colony From its Beginnings in 1824 to 1835*. Cape Town: Maskew Miller Ltd., 1962. 289pp.
   A critical analysis and overview of magazines in early 19th century South Africa.

286
Leymarie, Philippe. "La Presse de l'Ile Maurice et de l'Ile de la Réunion." *Revue Française d'Études Politiques Africaines*, no. 88 (April 1973): 74-89.
   An overview of the press in Mauritius and Reunion, noting the French influence on it.

287
Liberté de la Presse et Démocratie en Afrique. Abidjan, Côte d'Ivoire: INADES-Documentation, 1996. *Bibliographie Commentée* #33. 30pp.
   An annotated bibliography of books and journal articles relating to press freedom in Africa. Arranged by broad category and indexed by author.

288
Lobulu, William. "American Readers' Interests in News About Africa: A Preliminary Report on a Case Study of the Washington Metropolitan Area." *Africa Media Review* 2, no. 3 (1988): 125-144.
   Report of a survey of 200 newspaper readers and 40 journalists in Washington which elicited comments on eight news stories on Africa.

289
Lopo, Julio de Castro. *Para a Historia do Jornalismo de Angola*. Luanda: Museu de Angola, 1952. 30pp.
   A history of the press in Angola, with sample pages from newspapers.

290
Louw, Louis. "South Africa and Unjustified, Counter-Productive Foreign Meddling." *Nieman Reports* 3332, no. 3 (1978): 22-25.
   The Deputy Editor of the South African newspaper *Die Burger* responds to James Thompson's editorial "African Nemesis?" in the Summer/Autumn 1977 issue of *Nieman Reports*.

291
Luthi, Jean-Jeacques. *Aperçu sur la Presse Egyptienne d'Expression Française (1798-1978)*. Alexandria: Éditions de l'Atelier, 1978. 28pp.
   Historical overview of French language newspapers and magazines in Egypt.

292
Lyons, Louis M. "Press Notes from Africa." *Nieman Reports* 16, no. 3 (July 1962): 18-23.
   The curator of the Nieman Fellowships reports on press conditions he observed during a study tour of Africa.

293
Madjri, John. *Introduction à la Presse Rurale Africaine*. Bobo-Dioulasso, Burkina Faso: Centre d'Etudes Economiques, 1978. 63pp.
   Mimeographed essay on the press in rural Africa and Unesco's role in its development.

294
Magnate, Joseph. *Dele Giwa*. Lagos: New Academy Pub., 1987. 190pp.
   Biography of a Nigerian journalist, editor of the *Sunday Concord*, who was murdered by a letter bomb in 1986.

295
Magubane, Peter. *Magubane's South Africa*. New York: Knopf, 1978. 116pp.
   A collection of black and white photographs by this noted South African photographer, with an autobiographical essay recounting his experiences working for *Drum* and the *Rand Daily Mail*.

The Press

296
Maja-Pearce, Adewale. "Battle for Nigeria." *Index on Censorship* 23, no. 4/5 (September 1994): 188-191.
   A commentary on the political situation in Nigeria and the repression of opposition voices, including the closing down of all five newspapers published by the Guardian Newspapers Ltd. following an article reporting on instability in the government.

297
---. "In the Land of the Zombies." *Index on Censorship* 20, no. 9 (October 1991): 9-12.
   A report on press conditions in Malawi, where harsh suppression makes for a cautious and quiet press.

298
---. "Letter From Zambia: Cautionary Tales." *Index on Censorship* 24, no. 4 (July 1995): 159-162.
   A report on the relationship between Zambia's President Frederick Chiluba and the press, noting the case where the editor of *The Post* stretched the concept of press freedom to include publishing untruths. The editor, Fred M'Membe, rebuts this article in a letter in *Index on Censorship* Vol. 25, No. 5, September/October 1995, p. 6-7.

299
---. "The Press in Central and Southern Africa, a special report." *Index on Censorship* 21, no. 4 (April 1992): 42.
   Report on the press in Zimbabwe, Malawi, Zambia, Botswana and Namibia, focusing on press freedom, with anecdotes illustrating conditions, and featuring facsimiles of newspaper pages.

300
---. "The Press in Nigeria." *Index on Censorship* 23, no. 6 (November 1994): 209-227.
   A report on Nigeria, where the military leader, General Sani Abacha has said, "The Nigerian press is one of the freest in the world", but where conditions for journalists and their newspapers belie that claim.

301
---. "The Press in West Africa." *Index on Censorship* 19, no. 6 (June 1990): 44-80.
   A report on press conditions in Gambia, Sierra Leone, Liberia, and Ghana focusing on press freedom and featuring facsimiles of newspaper pages.

302
Maja-Pearce, Adewale, and Dulue Mbachu. *The Press in Nigeria*. London: Article 19, 1995. 32pp.

303

Manoim, Irwin. "The National Press Union and the Steyn Commission: Getting the Press to Do Its Own Dirty Work." *Critical Arts* 2, no. 3 (1982): iv-ix.
 An editorial pointing out the weakness of South Africa's National Press Union in the face of government imposed censorship.

304

Maron, Claude. "L'Hebodomaire *Lumière* (Madagascar) de 1965 à 1972." *Kroniek van Afrika* , no. 3 (1993): 283-298.
 A study of the changes in style and approach following independence of Madagascar's only French language daily newspaper.

305

Marsot, Afaf Lutfi Al-Sayyid. "The Cartoon in Egypt." *Comparative Studies in Society and History* 13 (January 1971): 2-15.
 A history and analysis of press cartoons in Egypt, describing them as modern versions of older forms of satire: the *goha*, or simpleton tale, proverbs, *zajal*, or rhymed prose, and the *nukta*, an elaborate, spontaneous joke based on current events that the author describes as a safety valve in times of crisis.

306

Martin, Louis E. "What Role for the Black Press?" *Africa Report* 29, no. 3 (May 1984): 51-54.
 An historical overview of the coverage of Africa by the Black press in the U.S. beginning with *Freedom's Journal*, the first U.S. Black newspaper, with comments on an incident following Zimbabwe's independence, when Black journalists were barred from a press conference with Robert Mugabe during his visit to the U.S.

307

Mathane, Nomavenda. *Beyond the Headlines: Truths of Soweto Life.* Johannesburg: Southern Book Publishers, 1990. 153pp.
 Collection of articles by a self-taught journalist of the *World, The Voice* and *Frontline*.

308

Matheson, Alastair. *States of Emergency: Reporting Africa for Half a Century*. Nairobi: Media Matters, 1992. 216pp.
 Personal recollections and commentary of a journalist whose experience in Africa spans the half century from the 1940s through the 1990s.

309

Matloff, Judith. "The Legacy of Kevin Carter: Eye on Apartheid." *Columbia Journalism Review* (November 1994): 57-60.
 Brief note on the suicide of Pulitzer Prize winning South Africa photographer Kevin Carter, raising the issue of the ethical and emotional dilemma of covering news stories involving human suffering.

The Press

310

Reaction and Protest in the West African Press: A Collection of Newspaper Articles on Five Nineteenth Century African Leaders, edited by Georgia McGarry. Leiden: Afrika-Studiecentrum, 1978. *African Social Research Documents* v.10. 197pp.
  The articles transcribed here deal with Niger Delta traders JaJa of Opobo and Nana of Benin, Prempeh of Ashante, Samori and Bai Burah of Sierra Leone. The introduction contains an historical overview. 2 page bibliography. Index.

311

McGarry, Richard G. *The Subtle Slant: A Cross-Linguistic Discourse Analysis Model for Evaluating Interethnic Conflict in the Press.* Boone, North Carolina: Parkway Publishers, 1994. 195pp.
  A study of press coverage of the 1993 campaign and elections in Kenya using linguistic analysis to determine bias.

312

McLoughlin, T. O. "Reading Zimbabwean Comic Strips." *Research in African Literatures* 20, no. 2 (June 1989): 217-241.
  A study of comics in newspapers and magazines, exploring their social and political themes.

313

McParland, Kelly. "'Toe the Line or Get Out'." *Index on Censorship* 15, no. 5 (May 1986): 28-29.
  Report on Willie Masarurwa, editor of Zimbabwe's *Sunday Mail*, who was fired for printing articles unfavorable to the government.

314

Mehra, Achal. "The Hero as Villain: Western Media Coverage of the Sadat Crackdown." *Gazette* 29, no. 3 (1982): 137-153.
  Review of coverage in the London *Times, Washington Post,* and *New York Times* of Sadat's suppression of opposition in September 1981, shortly before his assassination, with commentary on the accuracy and effects of that coverage.

315

Meldrum, Andrew. "Fragile Freedom." *Africa Report* 38, no. 5 (September 1993): 54-57.
  Report on the conference "An Update on the Media in a Changing Africa", held in Zimbabwe in July 1983, in which African journalists discussed issues of press freedom and professional responsibility.

316

Meurant, L. H. *Sixty Years Ago: or, Reminiscences of the Struggle for the Freedom of the Press in South Africa and the Establishment of the First Newspaper in the Eastern Province.* Cape Town: Africana Connoisseurs Press, 1963. 107pp

Facsimile reprint of the 1885 publication. Personal recollections of the establishment and early days of the *South African Commercial Advertiser* from its founding in 1824 to 1885, including problems of censorship. Appendix includes list of South African newspapers in 1881. Index.

317
Mhlaba, L. "Press Freedom in Zambia, or the Right of the Political Opposition to be Heard: Arthur Wina and Others v. the Attorney General 1990/HP/1878." *Zimbabwe Law Review* , no. 7/8 (1990): 174-180.

318
Mkhondo, Rich. *Reporting South Africa*. London: James Currey, 1993. 194pp.
  Personal account of the final days of apartheid by a South African journalist.

319
Modisane, Bloke. *Blame Me on History*. London: Thames and Hudson, 1963. 311pp.
  Autobiography of a Black South African journalist in the township of Sophiatown during the late 1950s.

320
Moffett, Martha Roadstrum. *Government Restrictions on the Press in South Africa: The State of Emergency and International Law*. Washington: The International Human Rights Group, 1987. 47pp.

321
Moghalu, Kingsley Chiedu. "Nigeria's Embattled Press." *Africa News* 33, no. 1 (19 January 1990): 7-8.
  Comments on the status of press freedom in Nigeria, summing up with a quote from the *Newswatch*: "...journalism in Nigeria is like walking blindfold through a minefield.".

322
Mohamed, Ali N. "South African Press Coverage of a Frontline African State." *Gazette* 42, no. 3 (1988): 177-191.
  A content analysis of the *Rand Daily Mail* to determine coverage of Mozambique in the year following the signing of the Nkomati Peace Treaty between South Africa and Mozambique, in March 1984.

323
Mollard, Pierre Jose. *Le Régime Juridique de la Presse au Maroc*. Rabat: Éditions La Porte, 1963. Collection de la Faculté des Sciences Juridiques, Économiques et Sociales, *Série de Langue Française*, no. 17. 183pp.
  A history of the press in Morocco in the 20th century, with emphasis on regulation by government. Appendices include text of relevant laws. 1 page bibliography.

The Press

324
How They Hate Us: South Africa, and in Particular the Afrikaners, Their Church, Culture and Leaders, under Fire in the World Press, compiled by H. M. Moolmam. Pretoria: Voortrekkerpers, 1965. 35pp.
> A collection of critical assessments of South Africa in the world press, concluding that this ill will is misguided.

325
Moore, Robert C. *The Political Reality of Freedom of the Press in Zambia.* Lanham, Maryland: University Press of America, 1992. 144pp.
> A study of freedom of the press in Zambia, including a discussion of Zambian Humanism, related issues in other media, and a proposal for democratizing the media. 10 page bibliography includes 6 pages of citations of newspaper articles and an index (unfortunately, page numbers in the index do not correspond to page numbers in the text.).

326
Moroney, Sean. "The Media in Africa." *Africa*, 1123-1131. Edited by Sean Moroney. New York: Facts on File, 1989.
> An overview of newspaper and magazine publishing in Africa, with some notes on journals and newsletters published elsewhere but focusing on African activities.

327
Morris, Roger. "Reporting the Race War in Rhodesia." *Columbia Journalism Review* (March 1979): 32-34.
> This critical examination of U.S. coverage of Zimbabwe's war of independence finds that most reports emphasized the 'savagery' of Black rebels and downplayed the brutality of the White Rhodesians.

328
Moseki, Mojalefa. "Black Journalists Under Apartheid." *Index on Censorship* 17, no. 7 (August 1988): 22-24.
> A description by a Black South African journalist of his own experiences and conditions for his colleagues.

329
Moundolock, Ignace Bertrand. *La Presse Écrite et la Liberté au Cameroun du Mandat à la Tutelle.* Yaoundé: Faculté de Droit et des Sciences Economiques, Université de Yaoundé, 1975. 51pp.
> History of the press and press freedom in Cameroon.

330
Muddathir, Ahmed. *Die Arabische Presse in den Maghreb-Staaten.* Hamburg: Deutsches Institut fur Afrika Forschung, 1966. *Hamburger Beitrage zur Afrika-Kunda*, Band 31. 48pp.
> An overview of the Arabic press in North Africa, including Morocco, Algeria, Tunisia and Libya. Appendices list newspapers for each country. 5 page bibliography.

331

Mugerwa, P. J. Nkambo. "The Attorney General of Uganda on the Press." *Transition* 8, no. 39 (1971): 29-31.
  A commentary on repression of the press in Uganda during the Amin regime, and the responsibility of journalists to report the truth regardless of that repression.

332

Mukenge, Mauadi. "Sensationalism at Work: Creating the Myth of Mau Mau." *Ufahamu* 21, no. 1/2 (March 1993): 14-26.
  A analysis and critique of coverage of Mau Mau and Kenya's State of Emergency by the Kenyan, British and U.S. press, concluding that articles in all three countries were biased, although in different ways, for different reasons.

333

Mukupo, Titus, Emmanuel Adagogo Jaja, Clyde Sanger, and William A. Payne. "A Symposium on the Press." *Africa Report* 11, no. 1 (January 1966): 39-48.
  Journalists from Zambia, Nigeria, England, and the U.S. discuss the press in Africa from several perspectives: the problems facing African journalists, the problems facing foreign correspondents in Africa, and the coverage of Africa in the U.S.

334

Muller, Johan. "Press Houses at War: A Brief History of Nasionale Pers and Perskor." *Narrating the Crisis: Hegemony and the South African Press*, 118-140. Edited by Ruth Tomaselli, Keyan G. Tomaselli, and Johan Muller. Johannesburg: Richard Lyon & Co., 1987.
  A study of two Afrikaner publishers and the newspapers they published, *Beeld* and *Die Transvaler*, with emphasis on their interaction with the National Party.

335

Muoria, Henry. *I, the Gikuyu and the White Fury*. Nairobi, Kenya: East African Educational Publishers, 1994. 186pp.
  Personal recollections of the Mau Mau "Emergency" by a Kenyan journalist, founder of the Kikuyu language paper *Mumenyereri*.

336

Murphy, Sharon M., and James F. Scotton. "Dependency and Journalism Education in Africa: Are There Alternative Models?" *Africa Media Review* 1, no. 3 (1987): 11-35.
  An historical and critical review of journalism training in Africa.

337

Mwaffisi, Samwilu. "Development Journalism: How Prepared are Tanzanian Journalists?" *Africa Media Review* 5, no. 2 (1991): 85-94.
  An analysis of a survey of 136 practicing Tanzanian journalists to determine their competence in handling development issues, with recommendations that media

institutions seek staff with better academic qualifications, then give them professional journalism training.

338

Mwase, Ngila R. L. "The Media and the Namibian Liberation Struggle." *Media, Culture and Society* 10, no. 2 (1988): 225-237.
   A study of the ways in which the colonial and the nationalist press in Namibia (formerly South West Africa) affected the outcome of the liberation struggle.

339

Nakasa, Nathaniel. *The World of Nat Nakasa.* Johannesburg: Ravan Press, 1985. 206pp.
   A collection of articles by the South African journalist, together with several tributes from colleagues.

340

Nasser, Munir K. *Press, Politics and Power: Egypt's Heikal and Al-Ahram.* Ames, Iowa: Iowa State University Press, 1979. 175pp.
   An account of the activities of Mohamed Hassanein Heikal, editor of Egypt's *Al-Ahram* newspaper during the years from Nasser through Sadat, with emphasis on freedom of the press and government reaction to dissent in the press. 4 page bibliography. Index.

341

Natsoulas, Theodore. "Harold G. Robertson: An Editor's Reversal from Settler Critic to Ally in Kenya, 1922-1923." *International Journal of African Historical Studies* 5, no. 4 (1972): 610-628.
   Commentary on the change in political stance of an editor in Kenya and his use of his newspaper in conveying his ideas.

342

Ndovi, Victor. "Censorship in Malawi." *Index on Censorship* 8, no. 1 (January 1979): 22-25.
   Interview with a Malawian journalist imprisoned in 1973 in a purge of the press reported by Peter Edwards (Item #127). Living in England at the time of the interview, Ndovi describes his arrest and press conditions in Malawi.

343

Nduru, Moyiga. "Reporting the Sudan." *Index on Censorship* 18, no. 1 (January 1989): 11-14.
   A Sudanese journalist reports on government use of visa restrictions to limit foreign journalists' access to Sudan, where they are accused of exaggerating religious conflict.

344

Negash, Ghirmai. "A Press in the Making." *Index on Censorship* 22, no. 4 (April 1993): 30-31.

A report on the establishment and development of the press in the newly independent nation of Eritrea.

345

Neier, Aryeh. "Selling Apartheid." *Nation* 229, no. 4 (11 August 1979): 104-106.
> A critique of South African claims that the creation of Bantu Homelands should be considered the reform of apartheid, pointing out continued government control of the South African press and manipulation of international media.

346

Nelson, Daniel. "Newspapers in Uganda." *Transition* 7, no. 35 (February 1968): 29-33.
> A brief overview of indigenous nationalist papers which appeared in Uganda after the Second World War but did not continue long after Independence. Includes commentary on press freedom and censorship in Uganda during the 1960s.

347

The News Agency of Nigeria: The First Decade. Lagos: News Agency of Nigeria, 1988. 136pp.
> An historical overview of the Nigerian News Agency since its establishment. Numerous photographs and facsimiles of newspaper articles.

348

Nga Ndongo, Valentin. *Les Médias au Cameroun: Mythes et Délires d'une Société en Crise.* Paris: L'Harmattan, 1993. 228pp.
> A discussion of the activities of Cameroonian newspapers in the context of strict government control.

349

Ng'weno, Hilary B. "All Freedom is at Stake." *The Third World and Press Freedom*, 127-134. Edited by Philip C. Horton. New York: Praeger, 1978.
> The editor of Kenya's *Weekly Review* discusses the forces putting restraints on the press in Third World countries and the effects of importing programming and news while neglecting local reporting and programming.

350

---. "The Nature of the Threat to Press Freedom in East Africa." *Africa Today* 16, no. 3 (June 1969): 1-4.
> An overview of the press in East Africa, assessing such problems as censorship, restraints on journalists, foreign ownership, and inadequate financing.

351

Nienaber, G. S. *Louis Henri Meurant: 'Nvoree Afrikaanse Joenalis'.* Bloomfontein: Nasionale Boekhandel, 1968. 188pp.
> Biography of a South African journalist.

352

Njawé, Pius. "La Censure au Cameroun." *Peuples Noirs, Peuples Africains*, no. 79 (January 1991): 4-15.
: An impassioned statement by the editor of the Cameroonian newspaper *Le Messager* describing state censorship of the press in his country.

353

Nkrumah, Kwame. *The African Journalist*. Dar es Salaam: Tanzania Publishers, 1965. 40pp.
: The text of an address to the Second Conference of Pan African Journalists held in Accra in 1963, in which the Ghanaian statesman exhorts the gathering to use the profession to inspire and educate the masses to withstand neo-colonialism.

354

Nolot, P. "La Presse Écrite Camerounaise de *Mulee Ngea* à *Cameroon Tribune*." *L'Afrique Littéraire et Artistique*, no. 42 (1976): 71-75.
: A history of the press in Cameroon from the first newspaper, *Mulee Ngea (The Guide)*, published during the German colonial period, through to the post independence period.

355

Nwabughuogu, Anthony I. "The Role of Propaganda in the Development of Indirect Rule in Nigeria, 1890-1929." *International Journal of African Historical Studies* 14, no. 1 (1981): 65-92.
: The author argues that initiation of the policy of indirect rule in Nigeria was the result of manipulation of British public opinion by pressure groups rather than a response to practical considerations. Newspaper articles and letters to the editor are cited as one means by which opinion was shaped on this matter.

356

Nwankwo, Clement et al. *Crisis of Press Freedom in Nigeria*. Lagos: Constitutional Rights Project, 1993. 137pp.

357

Nwankwo, Robert L. Nwafo. "Utopia and Reality in the African Mass Media: A Case Study." *Gazette* 19, no. 3 (1973): 171-182.
: Using Nigeria's *West African Pilot* as a case study, the author explores the effects of modernity, tradition, and changing socio-political situations on the content and coverage of the paper.

358

Nwankwo, Robert L. Nwafo, and William M. F. Shija. "The Communication Environment of the Food Crisis in Africa: Some Dependency Issues in the Political Economy of Development Communications." *Journal of Black Studies* 20, no. 3 267-286.
: Analysis of the coverage of food crises in Africa by the *Washington Post* and the *New York Times* for three months in 1984.

359
Nwokeafor, Cosmas, and Robert L. Nwafo Nwankwo. "Development Information Content in the African Mass Media: A Study of Two Nigerian Dailies." *Africa Media Review* 7, no. 3 (1993): 75-90.
>A comparison of the content of the *Daily Times* and the *Nigerian Tribune* in terms of development information over a 15 year period.

360
Nwosu, Ikechukwu E. "Foreign Media Coverage of African Liberation Struggles: A Content Analytical Case Study of the Angolan Crisis." *Africa Media Review* 2, no. 1 (1987): 76-103.
>Content analysis of three U.S. and three British newspapers' coverage of Angola from 1974 to 1976, concluding that coverage was biased and was among the factors causing the war.

361
---. "Mass Media Discipline and Control in Contemporary Nigeria: A Contextual Critical Analysis." *Gazette* 39, no. 1 (1987): 17-29.
>An exploration of self discipline and imposed control of media in Nigeria through professional training, codes of ethics, the Press Council, ombudsmen, and legal infrastructure.

362
---. "The Newspaper in the Development of Developing Nations." *Communicating for Development: a New Pan-Disciplinary Perspective*, 101-123. Edited by Andrew A. Moemeka. Albany, NY: State University of New York Press, 1994.
>A broad view of newspapers in development worldwide, with mostly African examples. 5 page bibliography.

363
Nwuneli, Onuora E., and Effiong Udoh. "International News Coverage in Nigerian Newspapers." *Gazette* 29, no. 1/2 (1982): 31-40.
>Report of a content analysis of five Nigerian daily newspapers to determine coverage of world events. Includes a survey of the literature on similar studies in other parts of the world. 1 page bibliography.

364
Nyamnjoh, Francis B. "How to 'Kill' an Underdeveloped Press: Lessons from Cameroon." *Gazette* 46, no. 1 (1990): 57-75.
>A brief history of the development of the press in Cameroon with a discussion of the problems journalists and editors face.

365
Nyika, Tambayi et al. "Unchaining Africa's Press." *West Africa*, no. 3821 (November 1990): 2854-2857.

Brief reports from Zimbabwe, Ghana, Nigeria, Cameroon and Mali on press freedom and censorship.

366

Obadina, Tunde. "How Free is Our Press?" *Index on Censorship* 17, no. 9 (October 1988): 31-34.
   A Nigerian journalist looks at his country's press, known as one of the liveliest in Africa, and points out the restrictions that hamper its effectiveness.

367

Obaze, Abraham I. "His Master's Voice: the Nigerian Press." *West Africa*, no. 3310 (5 January 1981): 17-18.
   A critical appraisal of the press in Nigeria and its relationship with the government, noting that journalists are failing in their responsibility to the Nigerian public.

368

O'Brien, Sue. "Eye on Soweto: a Study of Factors in News Photo Use." *Journal of Mass Media Ethics* 8, no. 2 (1993): 69-87.
   A discussion of the moral obligation of photojournalists taking and publishing photographs of violence. Based on controversy over photographs by Pulitzer-prize winning photographer Gregory Marinovich showing the burning of a man in Soweto. 3 page bibliography.

369

Ochieng, Philip. *I Accuse the Press: An Insider's View of the Media and Politics in Africa*. Nairobi: Initiatives Publishers, 1992. 210pp.
   A discussion of press freedom and press responsibility in Africa, using events in Kenya to illustrate the complexity of the relationship of the two factors. Chronology of events. Index.

370

Ochs, Martin. *The African Press*. Cairo: American University in Cairo Press, 1986. 138pp.
   An overview of the press in Africa, covering the entire continent. Opening chapters discuss general topics, followed by case studies from English, French and Arabic speaking countries. 3 page bibliography. Index.

371

Odhiambo, L. "Development Journalism in Africa: Capitulation of the Fourth Estate." *Africa Media Review* 5, no. 2 (1991): 17-29.

372

Ogan, Christine L., and Jo Ellen Fair. ""A Little Good News": the Treatment of Development News in Selected Third World Newspapers." *Gazette* 33, no. 3 (1984): 173-191.
   A content analysis of Nigeria's *Daily Times* and *New Nigerian*, Côte D'Ivoire's *Fraternité Matin*, Zimbabwe's *Herald*, and South Africa's *Rand Daily Mail*, along

with several Middle Eastern and Latin American newspapers to determine the topics and sources of news stories.

373
Ogbondah, Chris W. "British Colonial Authoritarianism, African Military Dictatorship and the Nigerian Press." *Africa Media Review* 6, no. 3 (1992): 1-18.
    An historical overview of the press in Nigeria, focusing on the British colonial era, 1895-1960, and the several indigenous military governments after independence in 1960, comparing and contrasting press laws and their effects.

374
---. "Can the Devil Speak the Truth? *The New York Times* Coverage of Mandela's U. S. Visit." *Africa Media Review* 8, no. 2 (1994): 89-109.
    Analysis of the coverage of Mandela's 1990 visit to the U. S. The favorable image presented is hypothesized to be the result of a change of U. S. foreign policy and public attitude toward South Africa.

375
---. *Military Regimes and the Press in Nigeria, 1966-1993: Human Rights and National Development.* Lanham, MD: University Press of America, 1994. 191pp.
    A summary of the decrees and laws governing freedom of the press in Nigeria during the regimes of Ironsi, Gowon, Mohammed, Obasanjo, Buhari and Babangida. Extensive bibliographic endnotes follow each chapter.

376
---. "Nigerian Journalism: A Bibliographical Essay." *Gazette* 36, no. 3 (1985): 175-192.
    This review of the literature provides an overview of the press in Nigeria.

377
---. "The Pen is Mightier than the "Koboko": A Critical Analysis of the Amakiri Case in Nigeria." *Political Communication and Persuasion* 8, no. 2 (April 1991): 109-124.
    An analysis of public reactions to the Amakiri incident of 1973 in which a Nigerian journalist was detained and beaten by military authorities, apparently for publishing a story concerning the military governor of the Rivers State, although no charges were brought.

378
---. "Press Freedom and Political Development in Africa." *Africa Media Review* 8, no. 3 (1994): 1-39.
    An overview of censorship of the press in Africa and an argument that a free press aids overall development. 8 page bibliography.

379
---. "Press Freedom in West Africa: an Analysis of One Ramification of Human Rights." *Issue* 22, no. 1/2 (1994): 21-26.
>A review of constitutional guarantees of press freedom and human rights violations which have an impact on press freedom. Covers West Africa, with emphasis on Nigeria. 8 page bibliography.

380
---. *The Press in Nigeria: an Annotated Bibliography*. New York: Greenwood Press, 1990. 127pp.
>A 501 item bibliography on the press and journalism in Nigeria. Alphabetical arrangement, with a subject index.

381
---. "The Sword Versus the Pen: A Study of Military-Press Relations in Chile, Greece and Nigeria." *Gazette* 44, no. 1 (1989): 1-26.
>Comparison of the relationship between military governments and the press, concluding that such regimes impose stiff controls with harsh penalties for infractions.

382
Ogbondah, Chris W., and Emmanuel U. Onyedike. "Origins and Interpretation of Nigerian Press Laws." *Africa Media Review* 5, no. 2 (1991): 59-70.
>Historical overview of Nigeria's press laws, illustrating the colonial legacies of current legislation.

383
Okeowo, Kunle. *Inside the Power House: The Press Secretary*. Ilorin: Atoto Press, 1991. 112pp.
>Personal account of the author's experiences as press secretary to the Military Governor of Ilorin State, Nigeria, with commentary on the press-government relationship. Numerous photographs.

384
Okere, Linus C. "The Press and Foreign Policy in Nigeria." *The Round Table*, no. 321 (January 1992): 61-71.
>An assessment of the role of the press in Nigeria as interpreter of Nigeria's foreign policy and shaper of public opinion about it.

385
Okigbo, Charles. "Gatekeeping in the Nigerian Press." *Africa Media Review* 4, no. 2 (1990): 1-10.
>Report of a survey of 21 senior reporters and editors in four Nigerian newspapers to determine the policies and philosophies that influenced their selection of news to publish.

386
---. "News Flow Imbalance: Quantifications of Nigerian Press Content." *Gazette* 36, no. 2 (1985): 95-108.
   A content analysis of five Nigerian newspapers during one continuous week and randomly selected days totaling one week between January and December 1983 to determine coverage of local versus foreign news.

387
---. "The Newsflow Controversy: Professional Journalists' Evaluation of News Imbalance." *Africa Media Review* 2, no. 1 (1987): 104-116.
   A survey of 400 Nigerian journalists on their opinion of NWICO.

388
Okonkwor, R. Chude. "The Press and the Formation of Pre-Independence Political Parties in Nigeria." *Nigeria Magazine*, no. 137 (1981): 66-73.
   A study of the relationship between early Nigerian newspapers and political parties within the independence and nationalist movements, with descriptions of individual newspapers and their editors.

389
Olasope, Biola. "The Nonaligned News Agencies Pool and the Free Flow of Meaningful News: An African Viewpoint." *The Third World and Press Freedom*, 162-172. Edited by Philip C. Horton. New York: Praeger, 1978.
   The director of news for the Nigerian Broadcasting Corporation outlines the ways in which Third World countries can get news, and measures underway for improvements in news flow.

390
Olayiwola, Rahman Olalekan. "Political Communications: Press and Politics in Nigeria's Second Republic." *Africa Media Review* 5, no. 2 (1991): 31-46.
   An examination of the relationship between ownership of the mass media and bias in political communications.

391
Omari, I. M. "The Kiswahili Press and Nationalism in Tanganyika 1954-1958." *Taamuli: A Political Science Forum* 2, no. 2 (July 1972): 34-46.
   An examination of newspapers publishing in Swahili during the pre-Independence nationalist movement in Tanzania, and the influence those papers had on formation and success of political parties.

392
Omu, Fred I. A. "The Dilemma of Press Freedom in Colonial Africa: the West African Example." *Journal of African History* 9, no. 2 (1968): 279-298.
   An historical overview of the press in British West Africa, pointing out that educated Africans, often trained in England, assumed that they were entitled to the same press freedom that the English enjoyed, but that when the African press was critical of the colonial regime, attempts were made to control it.

The Press

393

---. "The 'New Era' and the Abortive Press Law of 1857." *Sierra Leone Studies*, no. n.s. 23 (July 1968): 2-14.
    Account of the unsuccessful attempt by the Sierra Leone government to control the critical voice of the press during a period of public dissatisfaction with government.

394

---. *Press and Politics in Nigeria, 1880-1937*. Atlantic Highlands, NJ: Humanities Press, 1978. 290 pp.
    An overview of the development of the Nigerian press and its relationship to politics in the colonial period. Appendices include a list of newspapers, their dates of publication, editors, publishers and circulation. 10 page bibliography. Index.

395

Onagoruwa, G. Olu. *Press Freedom in Crisis: A Study of the Amakiri Case*. Ibadan: Sketch Publishing Co., 163pp.
    A discussion of freedom of the press in the context of the trial and punishment of a reporter who displeased Nigeria's military government with his coverage of a teacher's strike.

396

Onu, P. Eze. "The Dilemma of Presenting an African Image Abroad: The Kind of African News Contained in Canadian Newspapers." *African Studies Review* 22, no. 2 (September 1979): 95-110.
    Content analysis of three Canadian daily newspapers plus the *New York Times* to determine extent of coverage of African news, the kinds of stories reported, and the sources.

397

---. "The Use and Misuse of Scarce Newsprint: Mortuary Advertisements Compete for Space in African Daily Newspapers." *Gazette* 27, no. 2 (1981): 105-121.
    A survey of the appearance in Nigeria's *Daily Times* and Ghana's *Ghanaian Times* of paid announcements of deaths or memorials to previously deceased persons, comparing this kind of notice to coverage of news events and to other types of paid announcement and advertising.

398

Onyedike, Emmanuel U. "Coverage of Africa by the African-American Press: Perceptions of African-American Newspaper Editors." *Africa Media Review* 8, no. 2 (1994): 15-26.
    A survey, conducted by questionnaire, to determine how African-American editors select African news for their papers.

399

---. "Government-Press Relations in Nigeria: Effects of the Press Laws." *Gazette* 34, no. 1 (1984): 91-102.

An historical overview of press laws in Nigeria through four administrations: colonial (1891-1960), first civilian (1960-1966), military (1966-1979), and second civilian (1979 to the date of writing).

400
Oppenheimer, Harry. "The Press and South African Society." *Communications in Africa* 4, no. 1 (December 1972): 1-5.
    A discussion by the chairman of the Anglo-American Corporation of press freedom in South Africa.

401
Oreh, Onuma O. "'Developmental Journalism' and Press Freedom: An African Point of View." *Gazette* 26, no. 1 (1978): 36-40.
    A short assessment of press freedom in Western and African contexts.

402
Orlik, Peter B. "Under Damocles' Sword -- The South African Press." *Journalism Quarterly* (June 1969): 343-348.
    An examination of the press in South Africa, noting that while at the time of writing the National Party seemed more tolerant of press freedom, there were no legal safeguards.

403
Oso, Lai. "The Commercialization of the Nigerian Press: Development and Implications." *Africa Media Review* 5, no. 3 (1991): 42-52.
    An historical overview of press ownership in Nigeria, focusing on the interaction between commercial and political orientations.

404
Oton, Esuakema U. "Development of Journalism in Nigeria." *Journalism Quarterly* 35, no. 1 (1958): 72-79.
    A survey of the growth of Nigerian journalism since 1880, with descriptions of leading newspapers at the time of the article's publication.

405
---. "The Press in Liberia: A Case Study." *Journalism Quarterly* 38, no. 2 (March 1961): 208-312.
    Discussion of the legal framework of press freedom in Liberia, noting the existence of corruption in the press corps and lack of training for journalists.

406
Oudes, Bruce. "The Other Nigerian War: The Foreign Press Takes on the Federal Military Government in a Storm of Misunderstanding, Distrust and Confusion." *Africa Report* 15, no. 2 (February 1970): 15-17.
    A biting critique of U.S. coverage of the Nigerian Civil War, the Biafran propaganda campaign and the Nigerian federal government's policies restraining journalists.

407
Ozoh, Hilary. "Communication Research and Journalism Practice in Nigeria." *Communication Research in Africa: Issues and Perspectives*, 11-18. Edited by S. T. Kwame Boafo, and Nancy A. George. Nairobi: African Council on Communication Education, 1992.
   A brief discussion of ways to put communication research to practical use in Niger

408
---. "Newspaper Response to National Mobilization Efforts: An Examination of the Impact of a New Public Policy on Media Coverage." *Africa Media Review* 4, no. 2 (1990): 37-47.
   Content analysis of Nigerian newspapers before and after the establishment of the Directorate of Food, Roads and Rural Infrastructure to determine if coverage of rural areas changed in quantity and quality between the two periods.

409
Pachai, B. "Gandhi and his South African Journal *Indian Opinion*." *Africa Quarterly* 9, no. 2 (July 1969): 76-82.
   An account of Gandhi's activities and influence in South Africa in the early 1900s, emphasizing the role of his newspaper, *Indian Opinion*, in publicizing his advocacy of passive resistance to political oppression.

410
Page, Melvin E. "'With Jannie in the Jungle': European Humor in an East African Campaign, 1914-1918." *International Journal of African Historical Studies* 14, no. 3 (1981): 466-481.
   A look at the use of cartoons to boost moral in the British army in East Africa during the First World War, including commentary on negative images of Africans. Four reproductions of cartoons.

411
Pasquier, Roger. "Les Débuts de la Press au Sénégal." *Cahiers d'Études Africaines* 2, no. 3 (1962): 477-490.
   An historical overview of the press in Senegal during the 19th century. An appendix lists newspapers held at the Bibliothèque Nationale in Paris.

412
Pate, Umaru A. "Reporting African Countries in the Nigerian Press: Perspectives in International News." *Africa Media Review* 6, no. 1 (1992): 59-70.
   An examination of news of African countries in selected Nigerian newspapers, finding that coverage reflected Nigerian foreign policy.

413
Paterson, Adolphus A. "Why Africa Needs a Free Press." *Africa Report* 16, no. 4 (January 1971): 22-24.

Commentary by a Ghanaian freelance journalist on government control of the press and intervention in the activities of journalists.

414
Pather, Dennis. "In Memoriam: Percy Qoboza, Nieman Fellow '76." *Nieman Reports* 42, no. 1 (March 1988): 17-20.
The editor of *Post Natal* pays final tribute to a leading Black South African journalist and editor.

415
PEN American Center. Freedom to Write Committee. *Censorship and Apartheid in South Africa*. New York: PEN American Center, 1981. 78pp.
A discussion of writing and censorship in South Africa, covering the press, education, and publishing. Includes a list of detained, banned and imprisoned writers and a compilation of the major laws affecting the South African press.

416
Pennell, Richard. "News from Equatorial Guinea." *Index on Censorship* 11, no. 2 (April 1982): 35-36.
A brief note on the repression by Franco of any news about Equatorial Guinea in the Spanish press. This allowed the tyrannical cruelties of the dictator Francisco Macias Ngema to go unreported.

417
"The Percy Qoboza Case." *Nieman Reports* 31/32, no. 4/1 (March 1978): 34-37.
A list of citations to articles and copies of letters in support of Qoboza, editor of the Black South African newspapers *The World* and *The Weekend World*, and Nieman Fellow, who was imprisoned in a crackdown on dissenters.

418
Perkins, Kenneth J. "North African Propaganda and the United States 1946-1956." *African Studies Review* 19, no. 3 (December 1976): 65-77.
Discussion of the efforts of North African liberation movements to gain American public support and undermine French colonial administration through the dissemination of their own publications and the use of letters and contributed opinion pieces to prestigious U.S. newspapers.

419
Petley, Dexter. "*Munnansi*." *Index on Censorship* 14, no. 2 (April 1985): 44-45.
Report on the suppression of *Munnansi*, a small Ugandan weekly with a reputation for accuracy. Includes a list of journalists detained in Uganda and a facsimile of the paper's front page.

420
Pogrund, Benjamin. "Prisons and the Public Gaze: A Testimonial." *Nieman Reports* 35, no. 1 (March 1981): 25-28.

The Press

A transcript of evidence given to the Steyn Commission of Inquiry into the mass media by the author, an editor of the *Rand Daily Mail*, concerning restrictions on the press and the need for journalists to publicize conditions in South African prisons.

421

---. "The South African Press." *Index on Censorship* (August 1976): 11-16.

422

Pollak, Richard. *Up Against Apartheid: the Role and the Plight of the Press in South Africa*. Carbondale, IL: Southern Illinois University Press, 1981. 157pp.
　　An overview of the problems of the press in apartheid South Africa, including a precis of the Muldergate scandal and descriptions of harassment of South African and foreign journalists by South African security officials. Appendix includes documents relating to Muldergate. Index.

423

Pollock, Francis. "Junkets to Apartheid: America's Press on Safari." *Nation* 203, no. 15 (7 November 1966): 479-481.
　　A report on South Africa's efforts to influence what was written about that country and apartheid in the U. S. These included giving all-expenses-paid trips to selected American journalists and refusing visas for those who did not write favorable articles.

424

Potter, Elaine. *The Press as Opposition: the Political Role of South African Newspapers*. Totowa, NJ: Rowman and Littlefield, 1975. 228pp.
　　An overview of South African newspapers, their ownership, readership and circulation, and their respective experiences with censorship and restraint. 8 page bibliography. Index.

425

Pratt, Cornelius B. "Editorials in National Development: Perceptions of Nigerian Journalists." *Political Communication and Persuasion* 8, no. 4 (October 1991): 221-232.
　　Report of a survey of 348 Nigerian journalists asked for their perceptions of the role of newspaper editorials in national development.

426

---. "Ethics in Newspaper Editorials: Perceptions of Sub-Saharan African Journalists." *Gazette* 46, no. 1 (1990): 17-40.
　　Report of a survey of 348 journalists working on nine Nigerian newspapers who responded to questions concerning journalistic ethics as practiced by their papers.

427

---. "The Reportage and Images of Africa in Six U.S. News and Opinion Magazines: A Comparative Study." *Gazette* 26, no. 1 (1980): 17-45.

A content analysis of *Time, Newsweek, U.S. News and World Report, The Nation, The New Republic* and the *National Review* to determine the extent of coverage of Africa and the kinds of stories published.

428
---. "Responsibility and Ethical Reasoning in the Nigerian Press." *Africa Media Review* 2, no. 2 (1988): 46-64.
Content analysis of six Nigerian newspapers to determine their application of ethics to their reportage.

429
Pratt, Cornelius B., and Gerald W. McLaughlin. "Ethical Dimensions of Nigerian Journalists and Their Newspapers." *Journal of Mass Media Ethics* 5, no. 1 (1990): 30-44.
This survey of journalists at nine Nigerian newspapers explores attitudes on ethical issues. 2 page bibliography.

430
Press Freedom in Zimbabwe. Harare, Zimbabwe: Willie Muarurwa Memorial Trust, 1993. 99p.
A collection of papers presented at a seminar focusing on the role of freedom of the press in a democracy and the varieties of political constraints that can curtail it.

431
"The Press in a Democratic South Africa." *Africa Report* 37, no. 5 (September 1992): 61-64.
Report of a conference sponsored by the African-American Institute (publisher of *Africa Report*) and the Nieman Foundation and held in Johannesburg in July 1992, including statements by South African political figures.

432
The Press in Africa: Is It Dying? Kampala: Makerere University, 1966. 38pp.
Papers presented at a symposium held at Makerere University in October 1966 comprised of three newspaper editors, a Minister of Information, a reporter, a professor of political science, and the president of a journalists' union. The papers all focused on press freedom.

433
The Press Versus the Law in Africa. London: Article 19, 1993. *Censorship News* #23. 11pp.
A report on the "flowering of the independent press in Africa", and the concomitant repression, focusing on the legal framework.

434
Presse Francophone d'Afrique: vers la Pluralisme. Actes du Colloque Panos/UJAO, UNESCO-Paris, les 24 et 25 janvier 1991. Paris: Harmattan, 1991. 278pp.

Proceedings of an international conference on relations between the press and national governments, the development of the press as a business, training and career development of journalists, and international cooperation among journalists.

435

"Pretoria's New Press Controls." *Index on Censorship* 16, no. 2 (February 1987): 20-26.
Text of the press regulations passed in South Africa in December 1986, extending and expanding the state of emergency declared in June 1986.

436

Prince, Viv. *If Only My Mother Knew*. Cape Town: Don Nelson, 1977. 124pp.
Personal memoir of a woman reporter for the *Rand Daily Mail*. Contains photographs and some sample articles.

437

Prior, M. *Campaigns of a War Correspondent*. New York: Longmans, Green, 1912. 340pp.
Autobiography of a reporter-artist for the *Illustrated London News*, particularly his experiences in Africa.

438

Puri, Shamlal. "African Publishing: Crossroads in Britain." *East African Report on Trade and Industry* 20, no. 12 (January 1988): 22-23.
Brief report on the African publishing scene in London, focusing on magazines, and describing some of the problems faced by African publishers in London.

439

"Qoboza." *New Yorker* (18 November 1977): 41-42.

440

Qoboza, Percy. "Press Censorship in South Africa." *The Third World and Press Freedom*, 231-237. Edited by Philip C. Horton. New York: Praeger, 1978.
The former editor of *The World* (South Africa) discusses the laws governing the press in South Africa during apartheid.

441

Rees, Mervyn, and Chris Day. *Muldergate: the Story of the Info Scandal*. Johannesburg, South Africa: Macmillan South Africa, 1980. 222pp.
An account of the South African Department of Information scandal by two reporters whose probing brought the affair to light.

442

The Referendum in Malawi - Free Expression Denied. London: Article 19, 1993. *Censorship News* #22. 28pp.

An overview of freedom of the press and of expression in Malawi since 1964 and conditions during the 1993 referendum campaign.

443

Report of the Investigating Team Which Probed the Star Publishing Company and the Guinea Press Limited. Accra: Ministry of Information, 1969. 62pp.
    Report of a government investigation into possible misuse of public funds by the management of two Ghanaian publishing companies.

444

"Reward of Moderation: Suppression of the *World.*" *New Republic* (19 October 1977): 5-6.

445

Righter, Rosemary. *Whose News? Politics, the Press and the Third World.* New York: Times Books, 1978. 272pp.
    A discussion of the interrelationship of news coverage and politics and the challenges that the Third World press is raising to the traditional dominance of the Western press.

446

Roberts, John Storm. "Hilary Ng'weno, Publisher and Editor of the *Nairobi Times.*" *Africa Report* 23, no. 4 (July 1978): 22-24.
    Interview with Kenya's senior journalist, former editor of the *Daily Nation* and current editor of the *Weekly Review* and several other popular weeklies. Topics discussed include press freedom and training for journalists.

447

Ronan, Barry. *Forty South African Years: Journalistic, Political, Social, Theatrical and Pioneering.* London: Heath Cranton, 1923. 239pp.
    Personal memoir of a South African journalist.

448

Rosenthal, Eric. *Bantu Journalism in South Africa.* Johannesburg: Society of the Friends of Africa, 1950. 30pp.
    An overview of the Black South African press of the time, with useful facts despite occasional condescension.

449

---. *Today's News Today: the Story of the Argus Company.* Johannesburg: The Argus Printing and Publishing Co., 1956. 310pp.
    History of a South African company which published numerous newspapers, from its founding in 1857 through the end of World War II. Table of Events includes titles of all the newspapers, their proprietors and editors. Index.

The Press

450
Roser, Connie, and Lee Brown. "African Newspaper Editors and the New World Information Order." *Current Issues in International Communication*, 320-327. Edited by John L. Martin, and Ray Eldon Hiebert. New York: Longman, 1990.
> Report of a survey conducted on the editors of 171 newspapers from 45 African countries to determine their attitudes toward the United Nations proposed New World Information Order.

451
Rothmeyer, Karen. "The McGoff Grab." *Columbia Journalism Review* (November 1979): 33-39.
> A report on the attempt by Michigan publisher John P. McGoff to purchase *The Washington Star*, revealing that financing for the purchase, as well as for personal luxuries, had come from the South African Department of Information as part of their bid to control overseas reporting on South Africa.

452
---. "US Press: Telling It Like It Isn't." *Southern Africa* 11, no. 9 (December 1978): 5-6, 26.
> Critique of U.S. coverage of Africa, including events in Angola, Zaire, Rhodesia and South Africa. Illustrated by a Jules Feiffer cartoon.

453
Reporting Africa: A Manual for Reporters in Africa, edited by Don Rowlands and Hugh Lewin. London and Harare: The Thomson Foundation and the Friedrich Naumann Foundation, 1985. 181pp.
> A textbook aimed at young journalists in Africa, comprised of essays by journalists, editors and publishers. Reading lists follow each paper.

454
Rubin, Barry. "The Uncertain Future of South Africa's Press." *Washington Journalism Review* 2, no. 9 (November 1980): 41-45.
> A report on the difficulties the South African press has balancing between government restrictions and professional responsibility.

455
Rukuni, Charles. "Independent Press in Peril." *Index on Censorship* 20, no. 9 (October 1991): 17-19.
> A report on the press in Zimbabwe, where one form of repression is strict control of access to foreign currency, thereby limiting operations.

456
St. Leger, Fred. "The *World* Newspaper 1968-1976." *Critical Arts* 2, no. 3 (1981): 27-37.
> A content analysis of the *World* and its supplement, *Weekend World*, to determine how the newspaper's performance changed over the last two decades of its existence, comparing it to the *Rand Daily Mail*.

457
Sam, Albert. "Gloomy Future for Journalists?" *Index on Censorship* 16, no. 9 (October 1987): 23-24.
   A grim commentary on the efforts of newsmagazines on Africa published in Europe to report events in Africa accurately and the tactics used by some interests in Africa to suppress them.

458
Sampson, Anthony. *Drum: the Newspaper that Won the Heart of Africa.* Boston: Houghton Mifflin, 1957. 256pp.
   Personal recollections of *Drum* magazine by an editor.

459
Sauldie, Madan M. "Africa in the Indian Press." *Africa Quarterly* 8, no. 3 (October 1968): 257-262.
   Content analysis of four political and two economic daily newspapers in India for the month of October 1968 to assess coverage of African news.

460
Schmidt, Nancy J. "*Atlas* Looks at sub-Saharan Africa." *Africana Library Journal* 2, no. 4 (December 1971): 4-8.
   An index of citations from *Atlas*'s column, "Best of the World's Press", which provides excerpts of articles from African newspapers. Approximately 155 articles are listed, preceded by a short commentary and an analysis of geographic and subject coverage.

461
Schneider, William. *An Empire for the Masses: the French Popular Image of Africa, 1870-1900.* Westport, CT: Greenwood Press, 1982. 222pp.
   A study of the coverage of Africa in the French popular press during the late 19th century. Numerous reproductions from the illustrated press. Index. 5 page bibliographic essay.

462
Scott, Christina. *Notes on Intimidation and Violence Against Journalists in Natal.* Durban: University of Natal, Centre for Cultural and Media Studies, 1991. 10pp.
   A report on incidents of violence directed at journalists in Natal, refuting the claims of the editor of the Inkatha paper *Ilanga*, that there was an ANC conspiracy against him and his paper. The author contends that violence and intimidation against journalists was endemic in South Africa in the 1980s.

463
Scotton, James F. "The First African Press in East Africa: Protest and Nationalism in Uganda in the 1920s." *International Journal of African Historical Studies* 6, no. 2 (1973): 211-228.
   A description of the early newspapers in East Africa, with an assessment of their roles in independence movements.

464
---. "Kenya's Maligned Press: Time for Reassessment." *Journalism Quarterly* 52 (March 1975): 30-36.

465
---. "The Press in Kenya a Decade After Independence: Patterns of Readership and Ownership." *Gazette* 21, no. 1 (1975): 19-33.
> A survey of readership, content and news coverage of newspapers in Kenya following independence.

466
---. "Tanganyika's African Press, 1937-1960: A Nearly Forgotten Pre-Independence Forum." *African Studies Review* 21, no. 1 (April 1978): 1-18.
> A discussion of the African press in Tanzania under British colonial rule, focusing on its role in the move toward independence.

467
The Press: Papers Delivered During the First Seminar for Journalists Organised by the Uganda Authors Association in Association with the Press Club, edited by Aga Sekalala. Kampala: Milton Obote Foundation, 1969. 27pp.
> A collection of papers on topics relevant to the press in Uganda, including the responsibility of editors, the role of the press in adult education, and journalistic ethics.

468
Serfontein, J. H. P. *Die Verkrampte Aanslag*. Cape Town: Human and Rousseau, 1970. 269pp.

469
Shaloff, Stanley. "Press Controls and Sedition Proceedings in the Gold Coast 1933-1939." *African Affairs* 71, no. 284 (July 1972): 241-263.
> A study of the interrelationship of economic and social factors in the issue of press freedom and the attempts of government to control citizens by controlling the press.

470
Shaw, Gerald. *Some Beginnings: the Cape Times (1876-1910)*. London: Oxford University Press, 1975. 198pp.
> An account of the early days of the *Cape Times* of South Africa. Contains a list of directors of the *Cape Times* and Associated Newspapers Ltd. and transcripts of interviews with Paul Kruger and Cecil Rhodes. 3 page bibliography. Index.

471
---. *South Africa Telegraph versus Cape Times: an Examination of the Attempt by the South African Telegraph, financed by J. B. Robinson, to Challenge the Dominance of the Pro-Rhodes Press at the Cape, August,*

1895 to September 1896. Cape Town: University of Cape Town, Centre for African Studies, 1980. 85pp.
  An account of the exertion of political influence through newspapers. 2 page bibliography.

472
Sheehan, Edward R. F. "The Second Most Important Man in Egypt -- and Possibly the World's Most Powerful Journalist." *New York Times Magazine* (22 August 1971): 12-.

473
Sicherman, Carol. "Kenya. Creativity and Political Repression: The Confusion of Fact and Fiction." *Race and Class* 37, no. 4 (April 1996): 61-71.
  A discussion of the government harassment of journalists and writers in Kenya.

474
Sikakane, Joyce. *A Window on Soweto*. London: International Defense and Aid Fund, 1977. 80pp.
  A personal account by a Black South African journalist during the Soweto uprisings.

475
Silver, Louise. *Restrictions on Freedom of Publication in South Africa 1948 to 1968: A Select and Annotated Bibliography*. Johannesburg: The University of the Witwatersrand, Department of Librarianship, Bibliography and Typography, 1972. 54pp.
  A bibliography of government documents, laws and legal treatises on press freedom in South Africa.

476
Sing, Michael, and Gary T. Hunt. "The Press and Politics in Nigeria: A Case Study of Developmental Journalism." *Boston College Third World Law Journal* 6, no. 2 (1986): 85-110.

477
Skurnik, W. A. E. "Foreign News Coverage in Six African Newspapers: the Potency of National Interests." *Gazette* 28, no. 2 (1981): 117-130.
  Content analysis of four Francophone West African newspapers and two Anglophone East African papers to determine coverage of events and what influence national interests may have on that coverage.

478
---. "Foreign News Coverage in the Ivory Coast: A Statistical Profile of *Fraternité-Matin*." *Gazette* 24, no. 4 (1978): 271-282.
  Content analysis of *Fraternité-Matin* from April 1975 to March 1976 to determine the ratio of local to foreign news coverage.

The Press

479
---. "A New Look at Foreign News Coverage: External Dependence or National Interests?" *African Studies Review* 24, no. 1 (March 1981): 99-112.
> A study of the coverage of foreign news in African newspapers using a content analysis of *Fraternité Matin* (Côte D'Ivoire) and *Daily Nation* (Kenya) to compare them to the *New York Times*. The tables compare worldwide geographic coverage, geographic coverage within Africa, and the ratio of sensational or violent news to stories of peace and cooperation.

480
---. "Press Freedom in Africa: From Pessimism to Optimism." *Democracy and Pluralism in Africa*, 145-164. Edited by Dov Ronen. Boulder, CO: Lynne Rienner, 1986.
> An overview of press conditions in Africa, noting problems of government control and a credibility gap between journalists and readers, but sounding an optimistic note.

481
Sly, Liz. "The Anguish of Covering Africa." *Nieman Reports* 50, no. 1 (March 1996): 57-59.
> A personal account by a British journalist describing some of the difficulties facing foreign journalists in Africa, but ending on a hopeful note.

482
Smart, M. Neff. "How the Press Can Help Teach the Masses and Curb Starvation." *New African*, no. 166 (July 1981): 46.
> A brief note on the success of a community weekly newspaper in rural Ghana.

483
---. "School/Community Newspapers: An Experiment in Rural Ghana." *Rural Africana* 27 (March 1975): 53-58.
> A brief report on the *Densu Times*, a newspaper aimed at increasing literacy and interest in reading in Ghanaian rural schools.

484
Smith, H. Lindsay. *Behind the Press in South Africa*. Cape Town: Stewart, 1947. 172pp.
> An assessment of the press in South Africa after World War II, including a chapter on the Bureau of Information, which, in the decades to follow, assumed a central role in South African government-press relations.

485
Smith, Jasper K. "The Press and Elite Values in Ghana 1962-1970." *Journalism Quarterly* 49 (December 1972): 30-36.

486
Smith, Richard L. "Using French Newspapers as a Source for African History During the Period of Imperialism." *Africana Journal* 10, no. 1 (1979): 7-13.
    A bibliographic essay describing the kinds of information that a researcher can find in French newspapers. The author notes that while they present Africa from the French point of view, their reports can be extremely useful.

487
Smith de Sherif, Teresa K. "Wall Newspapers in the Desert: A Sahrawi Initiative for Problem Solving in Exile." *The Media as a Forum for Community Building: Cases from Africa, Asia, Latin America, Eastern Europe and the United States*, 3-7. Edited by Hamid Mowlana, and Margaret Hardt Frondorf. Washington: SAIS, 1992.
    An account of the mechanism developed by Western Sahara refugees to cope with the problem of disseminating information and giving voice to the needs of the people: newspapers produced on whatever materials were available and posted on designated walls in villages.

488
Sobowale, Idowu. "Image of the World Through the Eyes of Five Nigerian Newspapers." *Africa Media Review* 2, no. 1 (1987): 52-65.
    Content analysis of five Nigerian newspapers, concluding that they distort news coverage of the Third World in the same ways that Western papers do.

489
Sommerlad, Lloyd E. "Problems in Developing a Free Enterprise Press in Africa." *Gazette* 14, no. 2 (1968): 74-78.
    An assessment of the major difficulties encountered in establishing a private sector newspaper in East Africa, namely, money and government restrictions.

490
Souriau-Hoebrechts, Christiane. *La Presse Maghrebine: Libye-Tunisie-Maroc-Algérie. Évolution Historique - Situation en 1965 - Organisation et Problèmes Actuels*. Paris: Éditions du Centre National de la Recherche Scientifique, 1969. 369pp.
    An historical overview of the press in North Africa from the colonial period through 1965. Current (1965) papers are reviewed. 6 page bibliography. Index.

491
South Africa. Commission of Inquiry into the Press. *Summary of the Second Portion of the Report*. Pretoria: Govt. Printer, 1964. 223pp.
    Report of a detailed study of the reporting of foreign newspapers and news agencies in South Africa.

492

"South Africa and News Censorship." *Nieman Reports* 41, no. 3 (1987): 24-30, 55.
> Report of a conference sponsored by the Nieman Foundation and the African-American Institute.

493

"South Africa and the News: Conference Report." *Nieman Reports* 40, no. 3 (1986): 25-28.
> Report on a conference sponsored by the Nieman Foundation and the African-American Institute on news gathering in South Africa.

494

South Africa and Zimbabwe: The Freest Press in Africa? New York: Committee to Protect Journalists, 1983. 98pp.

495

Soyinka, Wole. "Electoral Fraud and the Western Press." *Index on Censorship* 12, no. 6 (December 1983): 11-14.
> The Nigerian Nobel Laureate chastises the Western press for failing to report accurately and thoroughly on the discrepancy in vote tabulations in the 1983 Nigerian national election, which returned presidential incumbent Shehu Shagari to office.

496

---. "The Last Despot and the End of Nigerian History?" *Index on Censorship* 23, no. 6 (November 1994): 67-75.
> The Nigerian Nobel Laureate speaks out on the occasion of the arrest of Ken Saro-Wiwa, a writer and environmental activist, and castigates the Nigerian media for failing to report Nigerian events accurately.

497

Sparks, Allister. "The Closing of the *Rand Daily Mail*." *Nieman Reports* 39, no. 2 (June 1985): 17-19.
> A former editor of the *Rand Daily Mail* discusses the economic and other pressures leading to the closure of that South African newspaper.

498

---. "South Africa. For the Media, the Opportunities of "Pretoriastoika"." *Media Studies Journal* 7, no. 4 (September 1993): 103-109.
> The former editor of the *Rand Daily Mail* discusses the parallels between Gorbachev's reforms of the Soviet Union and de Klerk's actions in South Africa in the context of the opportunities and challenges facing the press in the new political climate.

499
Ssali, Ndugu Mike. "The Uganda Press: A Commentary." *Ufahamu* 15, no. 3 (December 1986): 167-175.
A discussion of the state of the press in Uganda, with a brief historical overview.

500
Startt, James D. "H. W. Massingham, Radical Journalism, and the South African Racial Imperative, 1906-1910." *American Journalism* 8, no. 2/3 (March 1991): 142-159.
A discussion of the aftermath of the Boer War and how British policy in this period contributed to the development of apartheid in South Africa. Focuses on the attitudes and influence of the British radical press.

501
Stein, M. L. "UNESCO Debate Muted in Nairobi." *Quill* 70, no. 1 (January 1982): 10-11.
A brief commentary on Kenyan reaction to debates in Unesco over Third World news reporting.

502
Stevenson, Robert. "Western News Agencies and the Third World." *West Africa* , no. 3325 (April 1980): 865,867-869.
An assessment of the coverage and accuracy of Western news agencies reporting on the Third World.

503
Stewart, Desmond. "The Rise and Fall of Muhammad Heikal." *Encounter* 42, no. 6 (June 1974): 87-93.
A biographical sketch and assessment of the accomplishments of the political activist and editor of Egypt's *Al Ahram* newspaper, written following his removal from the editorship by Sadat in February 1974.

504
Stewart, Gavin. "Perfecting the Free Flow of Information." *Index on Censorship* 16, no. 1 (January 1987): 29-38.
A chronology of events pertaining to censorship during the South African state of emergency from 12 June to 18 November, 1986.

505
Storm, Roeland. "La Répartition des Nouvelles Régionales dans le Quotidien *Le Soleil* (Sénégal)." *Kroniek van Afrika* , no. 3 (1993): 277-282.
A brief survey of coverage of regional Senegalese news in *Le Soleil*.

506
Stuart, Kelsey William. *Newspaperman's Guide to the Law*. Durban: Butterworths, 1977. 303pp.

The Press

The second edition of a compendium of laws and court cases pertaining to the press in South Africa. Designed for journalists and editors, it provides a framework for maintaining a working relationship between the press and the state in the confusing and often dangerous political climate of the apartheid years. This work appeared in many editions, the latest of which is still in print. The 2nd edition is cited here because it was in print during the Muldergate scandal. 1 page bibliography. Index.

507

The Sudan and the Press: Headlines of Articles on Sudanese Problems and on the Southern Sudan Question in Particular Published in Newspapers and Magazines in English from 1960 to 1972. 117pp.
   A mimeographed list of articles, arranged by year and by newspaper. No publication information. Available at Boston University Library.

508

Sudan: Torture as Censorship. London: Article 19, 1992. *Censorship News* #13. 10pp.
   Report of the testimony of an exiled Sudanese journalist on his and others' detention and torture.

509

Sussman, Leonard R. *Mass News Media and the Third World Challenge*. Beverly Hills: Sage, 1977. The Washington Papers Volume 5, no. 46 . 80pp.
   An analysis of the problems of journalism in Third World countries, with numerous African examples. Topics include press freedom as well as the apparent neglect of news from the Third World by western journalists and editors. 3 page bibliography.

510

---. *Power, the Press and the Technology of Freedom: the Coming Age of ISDN*. New York: Freedom House, 1989. 496pp.
   An international overview and discussion of press freedom and the effect of the development of new information technologies. Contains numerous African examples. Index.

511

Switzer, Les. "The Ambiguities of Protest in South Africa: Rural Politics and the Press during the 1920s." *International Journal of African Historical Studies* 23, no. 1 (1990): 87-109.
   An historical analysis of the dynamics of Black protest in South Africa, with a content analysis of the Black newspaper *Imvo Zabantsundu* (Native Opinion), to determine coverage of protest.

512

---. *Media and Dependency in South Africa: a Case Study of the Press and the Ciskei "Homeland"*. Athens, Ohio: Ohio University Center for International Studies, 1985. *Monographs in International Studies, Africa Series* No. 47. 80pp.

A study based on content analysis of *Daily Dispatch*, and *Indaba (The News)* from Ciskei, and the weekly *Imvo Zabantsundu (Black Opinion)* from the Eastern Cape. 8 page bibliography.

513

Switzer, Les, and Elizabeth Ceirog Jones. "Other Voices: the Ambiguities of Resistance in South Africa's Resistance Press." *South African Historical Journal* 32 (May 1995): 66-113.

An examination of six newspapers published between 1919 and 1952 (four African nationalist and two socialist) with a content analysis to determine the discourse of resistance.

514

Switzer, Les, and Donna Switzer. *The Black Press in South Africa and Lesotho: a Descriptive Bibliographic Guide to African, Coloured, and Indian Newspapers, Newsletters, and Magazines, 1836-1976.* Boston: G. K. Hall, 1979. 307pp.

This list of 712 newspapers and magazines provides their dates of publication, frequency of appearance, language, and description of their contents as well as the libraries which hold them. The introduction gives an historical overview and defines the criteria for the inclusion of publications in this work.

515

Tanjong, Enoh, and Gary D. Gaddy. "The Agenda-setting Function of the International Mass Media: the Case of *Newsweek* in Nigeria." *Africa Media Review* 8, no. 2 (1994): 1-14.

A study based on two surveys: a content analysis of *Newsweek* and a questionnaire given to 1,213 Nigerian citizens to determine if awareness of international events is linked to reading of the magazine.

516

Tanner, Henry. "Congo: Reporter's Nightmare." *Nieman Reports* 15, no. 4 (October 1961): 5-7.

A reporter in the Congo (now Zaire) during the unrest following independence describes the difficulty of reporting events because of potential danger in the field and because potential readers might not understand the background of the country.

517

Tanzania. Ministry of Information and Tourism. Tanzania School of Journalism. *New Trends in Journalism Education and Practice in Tanzania (Official Report of the Joint Seminar of Journalism Teaching Staff of Tanzania School of Journalism and Nyegezi Social Training Centre and Representatives of Mass Media Institutions in Tanzania, held in Arusha between December 10-15, 1979).* Dar es Salaam: The Ministry, 1980. 124pp.

Collection of papers on training for journalists in Tanzania.

518

Tegambwage, Ndimara. *Who Tells the Truth in Tanzania?* Dar es Salaam: Tausi Publishers, 1990. 37pp.
> An exploration of the role of "gatekeeper" in Tanzanian journalism, using four incidents as examples: the Kilombero Sugar Company massacre, the fire that destroyed the Central Bank in Dar es Salaam, mining deaths at Nyarugusu and the International Monetary Fund. A second chapter looks at the impact of rumors in Tanzanian society.

519

Terrell, R. L. "Problematic Aspects of U.S. Press Coverage of Africa." *Gazette* 43, no. 2 (1989): 131-153.
> Overview of coverage of Africa by the U.S. press with commentary on the factors contributing to its unsatisfactory level and content.

520

Thompson, J. S. T. *Fractured Jail Sentence*. Enugu: Fourth Dimension, 1988. 174pp.
> A personal account of the interaction of Nigeria's several military regimes and the press by a correspondent of *The Guardian*. Includes his experience in prison as well as a philosophical analysis.

521

Thompson, James C. "African Nemesis?" *Nieman Reports* 31, no. 2/3 (June 1977): 2,31.
> A short, impassioned editorial decrying the crackdown on the press in South Africa. Rebutted by Louis Louw, editor of *Die Burger*, in the Autumn 1978 issue of *Nieman Reports*.

522

Timothy, Bankole. "The Press and National Development." *Africa: An International Business, Economic and Political Monthly*, no. 14 (October 1972): 60-65.
> A discussion of press freedom, with proposals for constitutional reforms and for greater responsibility to be taken by journalists.

523

Todd, Judith. "'Not in Rhodesia's Interest'." *Index on Censorship* 1, no. 3/4 (December 1972): 85-96.
> Report by a Rhodesian journalist on Ian Smith's suppression of the press, based on her personal experience of detention, described in a government document as "designed to prevent the detainee from engaging in any future subversive actions".

524

Tomaselli, Keyan G. "La Presse Communautaire et la Résistance en Afrique du Sud." *Politique Africaine* 15 (September 1984): 115-119.
> A brief overview of newspapers in the "homelands" of South Africa and their role in the struggle against apartheid.

525
---. "Race, Class and the Progressive Press." *International Journal of Intercultural Relations* 10 (1986): 53-74.

526
Tomaselli, Keyan G. et al. "Community and the Progressive Press: A Case Study in Finding Our Way." *Journal of Communication Inquiry* 12, no. 1 (1988): 26-44.

527
Tomaselli, Keyan G., and P. Eric Louw. "Alternative Press and Political Science: The South African Struggle." *Communication For and Against Democracy*, 203-220. Edited by Peter A. Bruck, and Marc Raboy. Montreal: Black Rose Books, 1989.
   An analysis of the press in South Africa, dividing it into nine broad categories according to ownership, affiliation and general philosophy, with discussion of the role of each category's publications in the apartheid struggle.

528
The Alternative Press in South Africa, edited by Keyan G. Tomaselli, and P. Eric Louw. Bellville, South Africa: Anthropos Publishers, 1991. 236pp.
   Collection of essays on the alternative press in South Africa, including an historical overview, examinations of particular time periods and specific newspapers. Contains notes on authors. 5 page bibliography. Index.

529
Tomaselli, Keyan G., Ruth Tomaselli, and Johan Muller. "The Construction of News in the South African Media." *Narrating the Crisis: Hegemony and the South African Press*, 22-38. edited by Ruth Tomaselli, Keyan G. Tomaselli, and Johan Muller. Johannesburg: Richard Lyon & Co., 1987.
   Strategies and philosophy of journalists in reporting news.

530
Narrating the Crisis: Hegemony and the South African Press, edited by Keyan G. Tomaselli, Ruth Tomaselli, and Johan Muller. Johannesburg: R. Lyon, 1987. 258pp.
   A collection of essays dealing with the media, predominantly the press, in South Africa. 14 page bibliography. Published in England and the U.S. as *The Press in South Africa*, by James Currey, and Lake View Press, respectively.

531
Tomaselli, Ruth, and Keyan G. Tomaselli. "The Political Economy of the South African Press." *Narrating the Crisis: Hegemony and the South African Press*, 39-117. Edited by Ruth Tomaselli, Keyan G. Tomaselli, and Johan Muller. Johannesburg: Richard Lyon & Co., 1987.
   A discussion of the forces at work in the dynamics of the press in South Africa.

The Press

532
Torchia, Andrew. "Assignment Africa." *Columbia Journalism Review* (May 1981): 41.
   A short statement on the difficulties encountered in covering Africa for the U.S. press, and the need for journalists to cover the continent responsibly.

533
Truth from Below: the Emergent Press in Africa. London: Article 19, 1991. 91pp.
   A report on the role of the free press in Africa's movement towards greater democracy. Preliminary chapters cover the major themes of the legal framework and the various forms that censorship can take; Part II provides sketches of the independent press in nine Africa countries. Appendices include transcripts of international documents dealing with press freedom.

534
Tudesq, André Jean. *Feuilles d'Afrique: Étude de la Presse de l'Afrique Sub-Saharienne*. Talence: Éditions de la Maison des Sciences de l'Homme d'Aquitaine, 1995. 335pp.
   An overview of the African press. 12 page bibliography. Index.

535
Turki, Mohamed. *Abdelaziz Laroui: Témoin de son Temps*. Tunis: Éditions Turki, 1988. 353pp.
   The biography of a Tunisian journalist, with selections from his writing. Includes a lexicon of Arabic terms in the text.

536
Twumasi, Yaw. "The Newspaper Press and Political Leadership in Developing Nations: the Case of Ghana 1964 to 1978." *Gazette* 26, no. 1 (1980): 1-16.
   The author summarizes political and communication theory in respect to development and compares the theory to his observations in Ghana.

537
Conflict and the Press: Proceedings of the Star's Centennial Conference on the Role of the Press in a Divided Society, edited by Harvey Tyson. Johannesburg: Argus, 1987. 317pp.
   Papers and remarks by journalists from South Africa and abroad and by South African government officials on a range of topics dealing with press freedom and responsibility.

538
Tyson, Harvey. *Editors Under Fire*. Sandton: Random House, 1993. 428pp.
   A collection of essays describing the experiences of editors and journalists as they attempted to publish accurate news in apartheid South Africa. Numerous reproductions of cartoons and pages of newspapers. Index.

539
African Journalism in Perspective, edited by Callix Udofia. Abak, Nigeria: Itiaba Publishers, 1991. 257pp.
    A collection of essays intended as a *vade mecum* for practicing African journalists. All media are covered, with the emphasis on reporting and writing. Bibliographic notes. List of centers for media research. List of notes on contributors to the book.

540
Ugboajah, Frank, and Idowu Sobowale. "The Press in West Africa: A Comparative Analysis of Mass Media Trends." *Studies in Third World Societies* 10 (December 1979): 133-151.
    A discussion of the press, with some commentary on other media, in West Africa, focusing on issues of censorship, ownership and professional training.

541
Ume-Nwagbo, Elebe N. "Foreign News Flow in Africa: A Content Analytical Study on a Regional Basis." *Gazette* 29, no. 1/2 (1082): 42-56.
    A content analysis of 15 newspapers from all regions of Africa to determine coverage of foreign news. North Africa was the most highly represented, with eight papers, West Africa the least, with one.

542
United Nations. Economic Commission for Africa. *Report: Study Visit of Women Journalists*. Addis Ababa: UNECA, 1978. 35pp.
    Report of a program for women journalists held at the African Training and Research Centre for Women in Addis Ababa, focusing on training and career development. List of participants.

543
Utomi, Patrick. "Historical-Philosophical Foundations of Government Ownership of Newspapers in Nigeria." *Gazette* 27, no. 1 (1981): 69-72.
    A brief note on the relationship between traditional government in Nigeria's three main regions and patterns of press ownership.

544
Uwazurike, Chudi. "Communication and Culture in Contemporary Nigeria: The Social Context of the 1980s Print Media Flowering." *Studies in Third World Societies* 46 (December 1991): 93-113.
    An examination of the tremendous expansion of the mass media, particularly the print media, in Nigeria during the 1980s, looking both for reasons and for potential future effects.

545
Uys, Stanley. "A Silenced Voice." *Index on Censorship* 14, no. 4 (August 1985): 7-8.
    Report on the closure of South Africa's *Rand Daily Mail*, described by President Botha as evidence of "a new spirit of national unity", but by its editor as the stilling of "a vigorous voice of dissent.".

546
Van Amelsvoort, Vincent. *Medical Anthropology in African Newspapers: An Annotated Facsimile Edition from the Third World*. Oosterhout: Anthropological Publications, 1976. 108pp.
> Facsimiles of articles from fifteen newspapers published in Ghana, Kenya, Nigeria and Tanzania which reflect attitudes and conceptions relating to culture as a concept; changing patterns of culture, particularly pertaining to dress and sexual behavior; witchcraft; traditional medicine; modern medicine and doctors. Introduction and commentary link the articles to the central themes.

547
Van Bol, Jean-Marie. *La Presse Quotiddienne au Congo Belge*. Brussels: La Pensée Catholique, 1959. 112pp.
> History of the press in the Belgian Congo (Zaire). Contains descriptions of nine daily newspapers.

548
van den Wijngaard, Rian. "Women as Journalists: Incompatibility of Roles?" *Africa Media Review* 6, no. 2 (1992): 47-56.
> An overview of the situation of women journalists in Senegal, focusing on attitudes toward women's role in society.

549
van Deventer, Hennie. "An Afrikaner Editor's View of the Afrikaans Press." *Nieman Reports* 44, no. 3 (1990): 14-15.
> A brief article by the editor of *Die Volksblad* attesting to the positive role Afrikaans journalists are playing in South Africa and the harassment they suffer for it.

550
Venkatasamy, Coll. *Coll Venkatasamy: Articles Choisis*. Mauritius: Editions Sigma, 1990. 85pp.
> Collection of articles by a Mauritian journalist.

551
Verbaan, Mark. "A Paper with a Conscience." *Index on Censorship* 18, no. 4 (April 1989): 10-11.
> Report of attacks on the Namibian newspaper *The Namibian* when it refused to exercise the self-censorship imposed by South Africa.

552
Versi, Anver. "PANA Goes on Sale." *African Business*, no. 19 (January 1995): 42.
> A report on the efforts to sell the Pan African News Agency to private investors.

553
Visser, Rud P. *Die Vaderland: Gedenboek*. Johannesburg: Afrikaanse Pers Boekhandel, 1957. 169pp.

History of the Afrikaans newspaper *Die Vaderland*.

554

Wason, Eugene. *Banned: the Story of the African Daily News, Southern Rhodesia, 1964*. London: Hamish Hamilton, 1976. 161pp.
   Personal account by an editor of a Rhodesian newspaper during the period of the Unilateral Declaration of Independence.

555

Watling, Cyril. *Ink in My Blood*. Cape Town: Purnell & Sons, 1966. 148pp.
   Personal memoir of a South African publisher.

556

Wauthier, Claude. "La Presse en Afrique du Sud." *Revue Française d'Etudes Politiques Africaines* , no. 88 (April 1973): 64-73.
   Survey of the various divisions of the press in South Africa: the papers of the ANC; the Black press; the opposition English language press; the Afrikaans press.

557

Weiss, Ruth. "Zimbabwe: Black Editors In." *Index on Censorship* 10, no. 3 (June 1981): 27-31.
   An assessment of the transition from White minority to Black majority government in Zimbabwe following independence, as reflected in the policies and news coverage in the major newspapers.

558

Weissman, Steve. "American Publisher Peddles South Africa." *Southern Africa* 11, no. 1 (January 1978): 2-4.
   A description of South Africa's efforts to ensure favorable international press coverage during the apartheid years.

559

White, Luise. "Firemen Do Not Buy People: Media, Villains and Vampires in Kampala in the 1950s." *Passages: A Chronicle of the Humanities* , no. 8 (1994): 11,16-17. Supplement to *Program of African Studies News and Events* (Northwestern University) Fall 1994, Vol. 5, no. 1.
   A discussion of sensational stories in Ugandan newspapers in the 1950s and their sociological ramifications.

560

Willan, Brian. *Sol Plaatje, South African Nationalist, 1876-1932*. Berkeley: University of California Press, 1984. 436pp.
   Biography of a political leader, author, and editor of the Tswana language newspaper *Koranta ea Becoana*.

The Press

561

Windrich, Elaine. "Rhodesian Censorship: the Role of the Media in the Making of a One-Party State." *African Affairs* 78, no. 313 (October 1979): 523-534.
> An examination of press censorship in Rhodesia following its Unilateral Declaration of Independence.

562

Woods, Donald. *Asking for Trouble: Autobiography of a Banned Journalist.* New York: Atheneum, 1981. 373pp.
> Autobiography of a South African journalist, author of *Biko*. Index.

563

---. *Biko.* New York: H. Holt, 1987. 418pp.
> An account of the imprisonment and death in detention of Steve Biko, leader of the Black Consciousness movement in South Africa by investigative journalist Woods. Includes texts of interviews with Biko, and analysis of press coverage of the events.

564

---. *South African Dispatches: Letters to My Countrymen.* New York: Henry Holt, 1987. 190pp.
> A collection of columns written by the editor of the *Daily Dispatch* between 1975 and 1977. While these columns complied with South African publication laws, the author was nevertheless banned in 1977.

565

Woodson, Dorothy C. *Decade of Discontent: An Index to "Fighting Talk", 1954-1963.* Madison, WI: African Studies Program, University of Wisconsin, 1992. 86pp.
> A chronological index to *Fighting Talk*, which had begun as a South African soldiers' magazine published by the Springbok Legion, a liberal veterans' organization, during World War II. Edited by Ruth First during its civilian phase, it continued as a liberation journal.

566

---. *"Drum": an Index to 'Africa's Leading Magazine', 1951-1965.* Madison, WI: African Studies Program, University of Wisconsin, 1988. *Bibliographies in African Studies*, 2. 207pp.
> A subject index to articles appearing in *Drum* arranged by broad subject category and further indexed by author, photographer and genre (i.e. short stories, poetry, reviews) and additional subject terms.

567

---. "'Pathos, Mirth, Murder, and Sweet Abandon': The Early Life and Times of *Drum*." *Africana Resources and Collections: Three Decades of Development and Achievement. A Festschrift in Honor of Hans Panofsky,*

229-246. Edited by Julian W. Witherell. Metuchen, NJ: Scarecrow Press, 1989.
>A history and celebration of *Drum*, the enormously popular South African magazine which the author describes as "an educing mirror of urban Black South African culture".

568

Yankah, Kojo. "Covering the Environment in the Ghanaian Media." *Africa Media Review* 8, no. 1 (1994): 47-56.
>A survey of the coverage of environmental issues in two Ghanaian daily x

569

--. *Dialogue with the North: an African Journalist Looks at Holland.* Accra: Uhuru Publications, 1990. 61pp.
>Account of "North-South Dialogue" aimed at clarifying stereotypical images of Africans in Europe and vice versa.

570

Yao, Faustin K., and Hugues Koné. *The African Drought Reported by Six West African Newspapers.* Boston: Boston University African Studies Center, 1986. African-American Issues Center Discussion Paper no. 14. 41pp.
>Content analysis of the *Cameroon Tribune*, *Daily Times* (Nigeria), *Fraternité Matin* (Côte d'Ivoire), *Ghanaian Times*, *Le Soleil* (Senegal), and the *New Nigerian* to determine coverage of the droughts in Africa in 1983.

571

Yata, Ali. *La Presse Démocratique au Maroc: Bilan et Difficultés.* Casablanca: Éditions Al Bayane, 1982. 100pp.
>A study of the problems of the democratic press in Morocco, including not only political pressures, but such practical considerations as shortages of paper and problems in distribution.

572

Zamparoni, Valdemir D. "A Imprensa Negra em Moçambique: a Trajetoria de "O Africano" - 1908-1920." *Africa (São Paulo)* 11, no. 1 (1988): 73-86.
>A study of the black press in Mozambique, following the fortunes of one newspaper, *O Africano*, to illustrate the influence of the press on the political conscience of the colonized.

573

Zaremba, Alan. "International Communication: Ghanaian Press Perspectives on the 1973 Middle East War." *Journal of Black Studies* 12, no. 4 (June 1982): 369-382.
>A content analysis of Ghana's *Daily Graphic* for a sixty day period following the outbreak of the 1973 war in the Middle East to determine the paper's representation of the merits of each side in the conflict.

The Press

574
Zaring, D. T. "Journalist Responses to Ethnic Tensions: A Study of the Press in Kenya." *Africa Media Review* 8, no. 1 (1994): 57-68.
> A content analysis of the Kenyan newspapers *Daily Nation* and *Kenya Times* to determine coverage of ethnic conflicts in Kenya.

575
Zeff, Eleanor E. "The Ghanaian Press as a Translator of Public Policy." *Journal of African Studies* 10, no. 2 (June 1983): 50-65.
> A more detailed analysis of the study described in item # , detailing the methodology and computer program used.

576
---. "New Directions in Understanding Military and Civilian Regimes in Ghana." *African Studies Review* 24, no. 1 (March 1981): 49-72.
> An analysis of editorials appearing in the Ghanaian *Daily Graphic* which attempt to determine the characteristics of four separate Ghanaian governments: the Nkrumah regime, the first military regime, the Second Republic, and the second military regime.

577
Zerbst, Jeff. "Getting into Bed with Democracy." *Index on Censorship* 24, no. 3 (May 1995): 134-137.
> Report on the growth of pornography in South Africa following the lifting of National Party censorship.

578
Zimbabwe: Attacks on Freedom of Expression. London: Article 19, 1992. *Censorship News* #17. 14pp.
> A report of government repression of the press in Zimbabwe.

579
Zindela, Theo. *Ndazana: the Early Years of Nat Nakasa.* Cape Town: Skotaville, 1990. 30pp.
> A personal appreciation of the South African journalist Nat Nakasa.

Broadcasting

580
Abu-Lughod, Lila. "Finding a Place for Islam: Egyptian Television Serials and the National Interest." Public Culture 5, no. 3 (1993): 493-513.
> An examination of the role of television programming in Egyptian national culture and Islamic identity.

581
Afrani, Mike, Barrack Otieno, and Herald Tagama. "Rise of the African Soap Opera." *New African*, no. 338 (February 1996): 8-12.
> Three short pieces describing television programming in Ghana, Kenya and Tanzania featuring serialized dramas in local languages. In Ghana and Kenya some of these shows have been running, with great success, since 1972.

582
African Conference on Radio Education. Harare, Zimbabwe 22-26 January, 1990. *Report on Conference Proceedings*. Harare, Zimbabwe: Ministry of Primary and Secondary Education, 1990. 176pp.
> Papers from the conference, covering all aspects of educational broadcasting throughout Africa.

583
Africa's Slanted Image." *New African*, no. 137 (January 1979): 88-90.
> A report on the coverage of Africa on foreign news services such as the BBC, Voice of America and Deutsche Welle, which broadcast into African nations and influence public opinion there.

584
Ajia, Olalekan. "Democratization and Economic Viability of Community Television: A Proposal for Nigeria." *Africa Media Review* 3, no. 3 (1989): 39-58.

585
Akam, Noble. "Télé-Niger: la Télévision Hors de Cause." *Afrique Contemporaine*, no. 172 (October 1994): 134-141.
> An examination of an educational television project in Niger, looking in particular at why educational broadcasting is no longer considered as effective as it was in the 1960s.

586
Akiwowo, Akinsola A. *A Statistical Report of the Radio Audience Survey in the Lagos and Western States of Nigeria: 1967*. Ibadan: Nigerian Institute of Social and Economic Research, 1967. 124pp.
> Report, mostly in statistical tables and graphs, of a listener survey conducted in Nigeria to determine programming preferences.

587
Amapula, Johannes Ndeshihala. *Developmental Radio Broadcasting in Namibia and Tanzania: A Comparative Study*. Tampere, Finland:

University of Tampere, Dept. of Journalism and Mass Communication, 1979. 119pp.
> Using Namibia's South-West Africa Broadcasting Corporation and Radio Tanzania Dar es Salaam as case studies to illustrate his theoretical approach to media policies, the author comments on the content of programming in the two countries. 5 page bibliography.

588

Amienyi, Osabuohien P. "Obstacles to Broadcasting for National Integration in Nigeria." *Gazette* 43, no. 1 (1989): 1-15.
> Overview of Nigeria's ethnic-cultural, linguistic and religious diversity and the problems this poses for national unity, with commentary on factors in the use of broadcasting to promote that unity.

589

Amosu, Akwe. *New Routes for Radio: A Paper*. Mowbray: IDASA, 1992. 25pp.
> An overview of broadcasting in South Africa with a critical analysis of changes in the South African Broadcasting Corporation following the end of apartheid and recommendations for the future.

590

Andrzejewski, B. W. "The Role of Broadcasting in the Adaptation of the Somali Language to Modern Needs." *Language Use and Social Change: Problems of Multilingualism with Special Reference to Eastern Africa*, 262-273. Edited by W. H. Whiteley. London: Oxford University Press, for the International African Institute, 1971.
> Discussion of the effects of broadcasting on the Somali language, including the development of a vocabulary for dealing with modern life and the growing dominance of one dialect type, "Common Somali", as the acceptable standard throughout the country.

591

Ansah, Paul A. V. *Golden Jubilee Lectures: Broadcasting and National Development*. Accra: Ghana Broadcasting Corp., 1985. 80pp.
> Transcripts of four lectures broadcast in Ghana to mark the Golden Jubilee of the Ghana Broadcasting Corporation in July 1985. The lectures trace the history of the GBC, its change from a colonial to a national medium, radio's influence on national development, and the future of broadcasting in Ghana.

592

---. "Problems of Localising Radio in Ghana." *Gazette* 25, no. 1 (1979): 1-16.
> An exploration of the dilemma of the need to broadcast to diverse language and ethnic groups, while at the same time fostering national integration, with an analysis of the experience of GBC-1, Ghana's service broadcasting in Ghanaian languages.

593

Ansu-Kyeremeh, Kwasi. "Cultural Aspects of Constraints on Village Education by Radio." *Media, Culture and Society* 14, no. 1 (1992): 111-128.

> A study of the use of radio in rural education in Ghana, concluding that radio, as one-way communication, is not effective as an educational medium. 2 page bibliography.

594

Armour, Charles. "The BBC and the Development of Broadcasting in British Colonial Africa 1946-1956." *African Affairs* 83, no. 332 (July 1984): 359-402.

> Exploration of the role of the BBC in the establishment of broadcasting services in British African colonies, with emphasis on financial and administrative structure.

595

---. "Broadcasting, Politics and the Story of African Independence." *Library Notes*, no. 301 (January 1991): 1-12.

> Transcript of a talk given at the Royal Commonwealth Society by a retired BBC executive who had been assigned to establish broadcasting in Nigeria in the 1950s. An overview of the early days of broadcasting throughout Africa in the pre-Independence era, with descriptions of the archival sources for research information on the topic.

596

Balon, R. E. "The Impact of *Roots* on a Racially Heterogeneous Southern Community: An Exploratory Study." *Journal of Broadcasting* 22, no. 3 (June 1978): 299-307.

> Report of a telephone survey conducted on 536 residents of Austin, Texas, to determine reactions to the television series *Roots* and how those reactions correlate to race of respondent.

597

Bebey, Francis. *La Radiodiffusion en Afrique Noire*. Issy-les-Moulineauc, France: Éditions Saint-Paul, 1963. 191pp.

> A survey of radio services in Sub-Saharan Africa with a brief history contrasting development of radio in Anglophone and Francophone African countries. 3 page bibliography.

598

Birck, Danielle. "La Télévision et le Rwanda ou le Génocide Déprogrammé." *Les Temps Modernes*, no. 583 (July 1995): 181-197.

> The author raises important and troubling questions about the role of television and reporting in the Rwandan tragedy.

599

Boisserie, Philippe, and Danielle Birck. "Rétour sur Images." *Les Temps Modernes*, no. 583 (July 1995): 198-216.

> The role of televised images in reporting on Rwanda.

Broadcasting

600

Bosompra, Kwadwo. "Television, Sexual Behavior and Attitudes Towards AIDS: A Study in Cultivation Analysis." *Africa Media Review* 7, no. 3 (1993): 35-62.
> An examination of the relationship of television to the number of sexual partners of persons in several demographic groups in Nigeria. 3 page bibliography.

601

Bourgault, Louise M. "The Liberian Rural Communications Network: A Study of the Contradictions of Development Communication." *Journal of Development Communication* 5, no. 2 (1994): 57-71.
> A study of the Liberian Rural Communications Network which, prior to the country's eruption in civil war and chaos, effected a revolution in development communication. Its grass-roots character and participation of local people in design and content of programming held great promise for progress, promise which was not given a chance to come to fruition.

602

Boyd, Douglas A. *Broadcasting in the Arab World: A Survey of the Electronic Media in the Middle East.* Ames, IA: Iowa State University Press, 1993. 386pp.
> Overview of technical and organizational aspects of radio and television broadcasting in the Middle East. Includes studies of North African countries. 26 page bibliography. Index.

603

---. *Egyptian Radio: Tool of Political and National Development.* Lexington, KY: Association for Education in Journalism, 1977. 33pp.
> A study of the development of radio broadcasting in Egypt during the regime of Gamal Abdel Nasser, who recognized radio's power to bring his message to the masses. The author notes that *Time* once referred to Nasser as "virtually a creature of radio.".

604

---. "International Broadcasting in Arabic to the Middle East and North Africa." *Gazette* 22, no. 3 (1976): 183-196.
> A survey of Western European, Eastern European, Asian, African, North and South American, and transnational religious broadcasting in Arabic, with discussion of motives and effects.

605

Bredin, Andrew. "His Master's Voice: Radio and TV in Africa." *Index on Censorship* 11, no. 5 (October 1982): 3-6.
> An overview of radio and television throughout Africa, with emphasis on government control and censorship, observing that, despite some notable exceptions, the overall picture is grim.

606
Broadcasting in Ghana. Accra: Ghana Broadcasting Corporation, 1978. 35pp.
   A report on the status of broadcasting in Ghana, with historical notes from the first radio broadcast in 1935.

607
Browne, Donald R. "Something New Out of Africa? South African International Radio's Presentation of Africa to Listeners in North America." *Journal of African Studies* 14, no. 1 (March 1987): 17-24.
   A discussion of Radio RSA, with a content analysis of its broadcasts monitored randomly during 1982 and 1983 to determine geographic coverage and selection of news stories.

608
Cancel, Robert. "Broadcasting Oral Traditions: The 'Logic' of Narrative Variants -- the Problem of 'Message'." *African Studies Review* 29, no. 1 (March 1986): 60-70.
   A discussion of the problems involved in radio broadcast of African oral traditions, when the medium loses the elements and nuances of the live performance with audience interaction.

609
Cassirer, Henry. *Mass Media in an African Context: an Evaluation of Senegal's Pilot Project.* Paris: Unesco, 1974. Reports and Papers on Mass Communication, no. 69. 53pp.
   Report of a Unesco project to develop educational television and radio in West Africa.

610
Celarie, André. "Une Entreprise en Expansion: la Radio-Télévision Gabonaise." *L'Afrique Littéraire et Artistique* , no. 1 (1968): 66-68.
   A brief description of the development of radio and television service in Gabon.

611
---. *Les Moyens d'Information au Cameroun: Recherche Préable a l'Établissement d'une Campagne Éducative par la Radiodiffusion.* Paris: Office de Cooperation Radiophonique, 1965. Tome 1, 114pp, Tome 2, 153pp.
   Detailed report on the planning and implementation of an educational radio project in Cameroon.

612
---. *Le Radiodiffusion Harmonisée au Service du Développement.* Paris: Créations de Presse, 1962. Les Cahiers Africains no. 61. 179pp.
   An overview of the use of radio and wire rediffusion to disseminate development information in Africa.

613

Social Conflict and Television News, edited by Akiba A. Cohen, Hanna Adoni, and Charles R. Lantz. Newbury Park, CA: Sage Publications, 1990. 258pp.
> An overview of social conflict as represented on television news programs. South Africa is surveyed, along with four non-African countries.

614

Coleman, William, Andrew A. Opoku, and Helen C. Abell. *An African Experiment in Radio Forums for Rural Development: Ghana, 1964/1965.* Paris: Unesco, 1968. 71pp.
> A report and assessment of an experiment using interactive radio discussion groups to disseminate information about Ghana's agricultural policy to rural farmers.

615

Collins, Richard. "Broadcasting Policy for a Post Apartheid South Africa: Some Preliminary Proposals." *Critical Arts* 6, no. 1 (1992): 26-51.
> Discussion of a wide range of issues dealing with broadcasting in South Africa, concentrating on television.

616

Collins, Richard, and P. Eric Louw. "Broadcasting Reforms: Fine Tuning Apartheid." *Indicator SA* 9, no. 1 (1991): 19-22.
> A critique of the report of the Viljoen Task Group on Broadcasting, which was charged with making recommendations for bringing broadcasting in South Africa into the post-apartheid era.

617

Cook, David. *In Black and White: Writings from East Africa with Broadcast Discussions and Commentary.* Nairobi, Kenya: East African Literature Bureau, 1976. 169pp.
> Transcripts of Radio Uganda's program *In Black and White*, in which samples of the work African writers were read aloud and discussed.

618

Cordeaux, Shirley. "The BBC African Service's Involvement in African Theatre." *Research in African Literatures* 1, no. 2 (September 1970): 147-155.
> A description of the BBC radio program "African Theatre" which debuted in 1962 with an adaptation of a medieval British drama but soon became an important showcase for African playwrights. Contains list of plays broadcast.

619

Corrigan, Edward C. "South Africa Enters the Electronic Age: The Decision to Introduce Television." *Africa Today* 21, no. 2 (March 1974): 15-28.

A report on South Africa's 1971 decision to reverse its long-standing policy of keeping television out of the country, and its plans to introduce it by 1976 with government controls on its programming.

620
Cripwell, Kenneth K. R. *Teaching Adults by Television: A Report of an Experiment in the Teaching of Elementary English and Arithmetic to Adult Africans on the Copperbelt, Zambia, 1963-1965*. Salisbury: University College of Rhodesia, 1966. 129pp.
: A report on an educational television project in Zambia. A brief narrative is followed by extensive statistical data.

621
Crowley, David, Alan Etherington, and Ross Kidd. *Mass Media Manual: How to Run a Radio Learning Group Campaign*. Bonn: Friedrich-Ebert-Stiftung, 1978. 197pp.
: A practical handbook for planning and implementing educational radio programming. Illustrated with sample task lists and timetables. 2 page bibliography.

622
Cruise O'Brien, Rita. *Professionalism in Broadcasting: Case Studies of Algeria and Senegal*. Brighton, England: Institute of Development Studies, University of Sussex, 1976. 50pp.
: A comparison of the political and social conditions in the two countries and how these factors influence the organization and content of broadcasting.

623
Cutter, Charles Hickman. *Nation-Building in Mali: Art, Radio and Leadership in a Pre-Literate Society*. Ann Arbor, Michigan: University Microfilms, 1980. Thesis: University of California, Los Angeles, 1971. 371pp.

624
Daoud, Zayka. "Le Paysage Audiovisuel Maghrebin: La Bataille des Images." *Afrique et l'Asie Modernes* , no. 162 (September 1989): 41-51.
: An overview of radio and television in North Africa, noting that much of the programming is imported from Europe and the U.S. and that this foreign programming is having a social and cultural effect.

625
de Fossard, Esta. *Writing the Instructional Radioscript*. Washington: Academy for Educational Development, 1982. 18pp.
: A USAID contracted instruction manual for a radio-based English language program series in Kenya. Includes sample scripts.

Broadcasting

626

de Koning, T. L. "Broadcasting in the Republic of South Africa." *Broadcasting Around the World*, 9-24. edited by William E. McCavitt. Blue Ridge Summit, PA: TAB Books, Inc., 1981.
> A brief overview of radio and television broadcasting in South Africa, with data on programming in various languages.

627

Decker, Thomas. "'This is Freetown Calling': The Story of Direct Broadcast in Sierra Leone." *Sierra Leone Studies*, no. n.s. 7 (December 1956): 166-168.
> A brief note on the inauguration of broadcasting in Sierra Leone in October 1955.

628

Defever, Armand. "Integrated Development Support Communication in Dahomey." *Communications Policy for National Development: A Comparative Perspective*, 205-224. Edited by Majid Teheranian, Farhad Hakimzadeh, and Marcello L. Vidale. London: Routledge & Kegan Paul, 1977.
> Description of an FAO project to bring agricultural information and training to rural areas via radio.

629

Deutsche Afrika-Gesellschaft. *Commercial Radio in Africa*. Bonn: German Africa Society, 1970. 307pp.
> A country-by-country compendium of information on broadcasting in Africa, including detailed technical information on radio stations.

630

Dexter, Gerry L. "Africa's Shadow Voices." *Africa Report* 31, no. 5 (September 986): 84-86.
> A brief overview of clandestine radio operations in Africa.

631

Diawara, Mamadou. "Production and Reproduction: The Mande Oral Popular Culture Revisited by the Electronic Media." *Passages: A Chronicle of the Humanities*, no. 8 (1994): 13,18,21-22. Supplement to *Program of African Studies News and Events* (Northwestern University) Fall 1995, Vol. 5, no. 1.
> An examination of Mande oral tradition and its adaptation to radio and other electronic media.

632

Discussion and Critique of the Democratic Party's Draft Principles on Telecommunications and Broadcasting. Durban, South Africa: Broadcasting and Telecommunications Working Group, Centre for Cultural

and Media Studies, University of Natal, 1991. *Draft Resource Document #3*. 13pp.
> Transcript of discussion of proposals to establish an independent body to control broadcasting, to separate commercial from public broadcasting, and to emphasize radio as the best means of reaching most people.

633
Domatob, Jerry Komia. "Radio Cameroun and Rural Exodus: Policies and Problems." *Gazette* 36, no. 2 (1985): 121-137.
> Description of the problem of migration from rural to urban areas and the Cameroon government's use of radio broadcasts to stop the trend.

634
Donkor, Clifford. "The Rural-Radio Forum." *Rural Radio: Programme Formats*, 37-48. Kiranmani A. Dikshit et al. Paris: UNESCO, 1979.
> A report on Ghana's educational radio programming for dissemination of agricultural information to rural villages, assessing the support needed to improve effectiveness.

635
Dosse Placca, Jean-Baptiste. "Is Togo Television Yours or Mine?" *Index on Censorship* 13, no. 4 (August 1984): 21-23.
> Report of a confrontation between Togo Television and President Eyadema, who posed the question in the article's title to a news reporter who failed to follow Eyadema's instructions on what story to highlight in the evening news broadcast.

636
Downer, Monica. "Clandestine Radio in Africa: A Study of the Eritrean Struggle for Self-Determination." *Journal of Communication Inquiry* 17, no. 2 (June 1993): 93-104.
> A study of the use of clandestine broadcasting by the Eritrean People's Liberation Front in the struggle for independence from Ethiopia.

637
Ebeogu, Afam. "Media Comedy for Nigerian Folk: The Adventures of the 'Masquerade' Drama Group." *Nigeria Magazine* 55, no. 2 (1987): 1-12.
> An analysis of a popular Nigerian weekly television show which satirizes all aspects of Nigerian political and social life, including the show's own characters.

638
Egbon, Mike. "Federal Television Service and the Issue of National Development and Unity in Nigeria." *Gazette* 29, no. 3 (1982): 179-188.
> A discussion of the centralization of television service by the military government in Nigeria despite the opposition of the Nigerian states, which wanted to set up their own local television stations.

639

Ekaney, Nkwelle. "Radio and National Development in Cameroon: A Descriptive Analysis." *Gazette* 22, no. 2 (1976): 115-128.
   An overview of the hours and kinds of programming on radio in Cameroon with suggestions for increasing the effectiveness of radio in distributing information for development.

640

Elaturoti, D. F. *Fifteen Years of Educational Broadcasting in Nigeria: A Bibliography*. Lagos, Nigeria: Nigerian Broadcasting Corp., 1979. 63pp.
   A bibliography of about 3,248 tapes produced by the Nigerian Broadcasting Corporation Schools' Unit from 1961 to 1976. Arranged by broad topic, indexed by subject.

641

Eone, Tjade. *Radio, Publics et Pouvoirs au Cameroun: Utilisation Officielles et Besoins Sociaux*. Paris: Harmattan, 1986. 287pp.
   Discussion of radio in Cameroon, including descriptions of national and foreign broadcasting services and the government-media relationship.

642

Everett, Anna. "'Operation Restore Hope': Recolonizing Africa for the 21st Century." *Ufahamu* 21, no. 1/2 (March 1993): 3-13.
   An analysis of the Fox TV documentary *Somalia Behind the Scenes,*. Seeing parallels with Conrad's *Heart of Darkness* and Kipling's *White Man's Burden*, the author contends that the show's underlying message is that Africa is still a dark and primitive place, in need of civilization through recolonization.

643

Eyoh, Hansel Ndumbe. "Theatre, Television and Development: A Case for the Third World." *Africa Media Review* 1, no. 3 (1987): 49-55.
   A discussion promoting the broadcast of locally developed theatre productions rather than importing television programs.

644

Fahim, Fawzia. "The Effect of Television on Children." *ASBU Review: The Quarterly Publication of the Arab States Broadcasting Union* (April 1979): 45-52.
   A discussion of foreign studies of the impact of television violence and criminal acts on child viewers and the implication of those studies for Egyptian broadcasting.

645

Fairchild, Halford H., Russell Stockard, and Philip Bowman. "Impact of *Roots*: Evidence from the National Survey of Black Americans." *Journal of Black Studies* 16, no. 3 (March 1986): 307-318.
   An analysis of the data (collected in the National Survey of Black Americans) on the telecast of *Roots*. From the large scale, broad spectrum survey conducted at the

University of Michigan in 1981, the authors of this article looked at two questions: whether the respondents had watched any of the *Roots* broadcasts and, if so, what they liked most about the programs.

646

Farounbi, Yemi. *In Defense of Nigerian Broadcasting*. Ibadan, Nigeria: The Cheeley Management Service, 1977. 66pp.

647

---. *Television and Society: Speeches by Yemi Farounbi, General Manager, Nigerian Television, Ibadan*. Ibadan, Nigeria: Nigerian Television,, 1979. 69pp.
   A collection of speeches and interviews on the challenges and progress of Nigerian television. 8 pages of photographs.

648

---. *Whither Nigerian Broadcasting: External or Self-Control*. Ibadan, Nigeria: Cheeley Management Service, 1977. 22pp.
   A review of regulations governing broadcasting in the U.S., Canada, and Britain, with commentary on what form regulation of broadcasting in Nigeria should take.

649

Fifty Years of Broadcasting in Ghana: Golden Jubilee July 1935-1985. Accra: Ghana Broadcasting Corporation, 1985. 61pp.
   Collection of essays and short articles celebrating the anniversary of the beginning of broadcasting in Ghana. Numerous photographs.

650

Fougeyrollas, Pierre. *Television and the Social Education of Women*. Paris: Unesco, 1966. 40pp.
   Report of a project using Wolof language television programs in Senegal to reach rural women with information on health and nutrition.

651

Fraenkel, Pierre. *Wayaleshi*. London: Weidenfeld and Nicolson, 1959. 225pp.
   Personal recollections of the operation of a radio service in colonial Rhodesia and Nyasaland (now Zambia, Zimbabwe and Malawi).

652

Gambia. Advisory Committee on Education Broadcasting. *Proposals for the Establishment of a Rural Broadcasting Service in the Gambia*. Banjul: Advisory Committee on Education Broadcasting, 1979. 6pp.
   Document preparatory to establishing the Rural Broadcasting Service in the Gambia.

Broadcasting

653

Gartley, John. "Electronic Media in Ethiopia: A Preliminary Inquiry." *Northeast African Studies* 2, no. 3 (1981): 163-170.
> An examination of the transformation of mass communication in Ethiopia from traditional to electronic media, with discussion of how the form and content of communication has changed in the process.

654

Gaudio, A., and P. Trichet. "Radio Hope." *Africans on Africa Series* #1, supplement to *IDOC Internazionale* 26, no. 1 (January 1995): 39-40.

655

George, Nancy A. "Using Radio for Community Mobilization: Experiences in Zimbabwe and Kenya." *Africa Media Review* 7, no. 2 (1993): 52-67.
> Report of an experiment to determine if radio could be used in Kenya to promote community oriented development among women as it was used successfully in Zimbabwe. 2 page bibliography.

656

Gibbs, James. "'Yapping' and 'Pushing': Notes on Wole Soyinka's *Broke Time Bar* Radio Series of the Early Sixties." *Africa Today* 33, no. 1 (1986): 19-26.
> A study of the Nigerian Nobel laureate's early radio scripts for a comedy serial which the playwright called "pun-demented dramas" but which were clearly precursors of his later work.

657

Giffard, C. Anthony, and Lisa Cohen. "The Impact of Censorship on U.S. Television News Coverage of South Africa." *Current Issues in International Communication*, 122-133. Edited by L. John Martin and Ray Eldon Hiebert. New York: Longman, 1990.
> A study of U.S. coverage of South African events from 1982 to 1987, using the *Television News Index and Abstracts* to determine the effects of curbs placed on the foreign press by the South African government. The authors found that coverage did not diminish in quantity but did change in quality.

658

---. "South African TV and Censorship: Does it Reduce Negative Coverage?" *Journalism Quarterly* 66, no. 1 (March 1989): 3-10.
> A study of the content of U.S. television coverage of events in South Africa between 1982 and 1987 to determine the effects of South African censorship on reports of violence in that country.

659

Gorelick, Nahum J. "The Challenges of Democratic Television." *Voices From Africa*, no. 4 (June 1992): 79-88.
> An overview of television broadcasting in Namibia, focusing on the development of policy and the problem of imported programming.

660

Grant, Stephen. "Educational TV Comes to the Ivory Coast." *Africa Report* 16, no. 2 (February 1971): 31-33.
> An evaluation of projects introducing television as a means of dealing with problems such as lack of teachers and rural-urban imbalance in the Ivoirien educational system.

661

Grenholm, Lennart H. *Radio Study Group Campaigns in the United Republic of Tanzania*. Paris: Unesco, 1975. 51pp.
> Report on use of radio for adult education in Tanzania.

662

Guidelines for Election Broadcasting in Transitional Democracies. London: Article 19, 1994. 109pp.
> Although not devoted to Africa, this work uses numerous African examples in its examination of issues relating to broadcast media's role in elections. Problems such as censorship, news coverage, voter education and the legal framework are explored.

663

Guyot, Michel, and René Wisselmann. *Une Expérience de Télévision Scolaire au Sénégal: Zuiguinchor, Diembereng, Boulome: Mars, 1974.* Dakar: Centre de Linguistique Appliquée de Dakar, 1974. 81pp.
> A report of an educational television scheme in Senegal devised to teach French to rural villagers.

664

Hachten, William A. "Policies and Performance of South African Television." *Journal of Communication* 29, no. 3 (June 1979): 62-72.
> An assessment of television in South Africa three years after broadcasting began in 1976. It operated with a clear policy of supporting the government's goals and to provide entertainment and educational programming in line with Afrikaner values.

665

Hall, Budd L. *Mta Ni Afya: Tanzania's Health Campaign*. Washington: Clearinghouse on Development Communication, 1978. 74pp.
> A report of an educational radio project designed to disseminate disease prevention information in Tanzania through radio broadcasts combined with discussion groups organized in villages throughout the country. Follow-up evaluation included surveys of villages to determine if specified health practices improved following the broadcasts and group discussions.

666

---. *Wakati Wa Furaha: An Evaluation of a Radio Study Group Campaign*. Uppsala: Scandinavian Institute of African Studies, 1973. 47pp.

Broadcasting

A report on an educational radio project designed to celebrate the tenth anniversary of Tanzania's independence (Wakati Wa Furaha is Swahili for "Time for Rejoicing") by highlighting achievements since independence and by fostering national unity.

667

Hall, Budd L., and Tony Dodds. *Voices for Development: the Tanzanian National Radio Study Campaigns*. Cambridge, England: International Extension College, 1974. *IEC Broadsheets on Distance Learning*, no. 6. 53pp.

A discussion of educational radio projects in Tanzania focusing on three major campaigns: *Uchaguzi Ni Wako* (The Choice is Yours), designed to educate voters prior to the 1970 national election; *Wakati Wa Furaha* (A Time for Rejoicing), aired in 1971 to celebrate Tanzania's tenth anniversary of independence by highlighting the achievements of the government to date; *Mtu Ni Afya* (Man Is Health), undertaken in 1973 to disseminate information on disease prevention.

668

Harrison, Randall, and Paul Ekman. "TV's Last Frontier: South Africa." *Journal of Communication* 26, no. 1 (December 1976): 102-109.

A brief commentary on the potential changes that the introduction of television to South Africa might bring.

669

---. "TV's Last Frontier: South Africa." *Mass Media Policies in Changing Cultures*, 189-196. Edited by George Gerbner. New York: John Wiley & Sons, 1977.

An analysis of the potential political and social effects of television in South Africa from its beginnings in 1976. Reprint of #.

670

Hayman, Graham, and Ruth Tomaselli. "Ideology and Technology in the Growth of South African Broadcasting, 1924-1971." *Currents of Power: State Broadcasting in South Africa*, 23-83. Edited by Ruth Tomaselli, Keyan G. Tomaselli, and Johan Muller. Bellville, South Africa: Anthropos, 1989.

An account of the early history of broadcasting in South Africa and the interplay of ideology and technology.

671

Head, Sydney W. "British Broadcasting Policies: The Case of the Gold Coast." *African Studies Review* 22, no. 2 (September 1979): 39-47.

A discussion of the role of broadcasting in pre-independence Ghana and how Britain used local broadcasting to explain the Second World War to Ghanaians and to justify and promote their participation in it.

672

Broadcasting in Africa, edited by Sydney W. Head. Philadelphia: Temple University Press, 1974. 453pp.

A collection of country overviews and essays on issues affecting broadcasting throughout Africa. 25 page bibliography. Index.

673
Head, Sydney W., and John Kugblenu. "GBC-1: A Survival of Wired Radio in Tropical Africa." *Gazette* 224, no. 2 (1978): 121-129.
A description of the content and technology of GBC-1, which broadcasts in Ghanaian languages by means of wire distribution to villages and rural locations.

674
Heath, Carla W. "Private Sector Participation in Public Service Broadcasting: the Case of Kenya." *Journal of Communication* 38, no. 3 (June 1988): 96-107.
An overview of broadcasting in Kenya pointing out the often conflicting goals of public and private sector broadcasting.

675
---. "Private Sector Participation in Public Service Broadcasting: the Case of Kenya." *Current Issues in International Communication*, 74-80. Edited by L. John Martin, and Ray Eldon Hiebert. White Plains, NY: Longman, 1990.
A discussion of continuing government control of broadcasting in Kenya, despite the advent of advertising and religious programming, which supply needed revenue but do not influence programming as much as the state.

676
---. "Structural Changes in Kenya's Broadcasting System: A Manifestation of Presidential Authoritarianism." *Gazette* 50, no. 1 (1992): 37-51.
A study of the motivation and effects of the transfer of Kenya's broadcasting system from the Ministry of Information to the semi-autonomous Kenya Broadcasting Corporation.

677
Communicating Across Cultural Barriers: a Dynamic Equivalent Approach to the Use of Radio and Other Media in Biblical Evangelism, edited by Charles T. Hein. Nairobi: Afrolit Society, 1977. 139pp.
Papers from the seminar "Communication of the Biblical Message by Radio and Associated Media", held at RVOG [Radio Voice of the Gospel, Addis Ababa] October 1-15, 1976.

678
Herbert, Boh, and Ofege Ntemfac. *Prison Graduate: the Story of "Cameroon Calling", a True Story*. Calabar, Nigeria: United News Service, 1991. 124pp.
Personal memoir of the Deputy Editor-in-Chief of Cameroon Radio Television Corporation (CRTC) Radio News, who developed a controversial radio program titled *Cameroon Calling*. He was jailed for his broadcasts, which were critical of the government. Includes transcripts of actual broadcasts.

Broadcasting

679

Howard, J., G. Rothbart, and L. Sloan. "The Response to *Roots*: A National Survey." *Journal of Broadcasting* 22 (1978): 279-287.
    Report of a survey of 971 adults who had watched two or more episodes of the television series *Roots*, tabulating responses according to race and sex.

680

Hur, K. Kyoon. "Impact of *Roots* on Black and White Teenagers." *Journal of Broadcasting* 22, no. 3 (June 1978): 289-298.
    Results of a survey conducted at 15 schools in the metropolitan Cleveland area to determine differences in perceptions of the television series *Roots* between Black and White adolescents.

681

Hur, K. Kyoon, and J. P. Robinson. "The Social Impact of *Roots*." *Journalism Quarterly* 55 (1978): 19-21, 83.

682

Ibelema, Minabere, and Ebere Onwudiwe. "*Today* in Africa." *Issue* 22, no. 1 (March 1994): 12-14.
    An analysis of the program series focusing on Africa, shot on location in Zimbabwe, and broadcast on NBC's *Today* show from November 13 through 20, 1993.

683

Ibrahim, Mohammed. *The Radio as a Campaign Instrument*. Maiduguri, Nigeria: University of Maiduguri Press, 1991. 47pp.
    A convocation address to the University of Maiduguri by the Director-General of the Nigerian Television Authority on radio's role in both election campaigns and programs of mass mobilization such as Nigeria's MAMSER.

684

Ihaddaden, Zahir. "The Postcolonial Policy of Algerian Broadcasting in Kabyle." *Ethnic Minority Media: An International Perspective*, 243-255. Edited by S. H. Riggins. Newbury Park: Sage, 1992.
    A discussion of Algerian broadcasting wherein one national corporation has three channels, one broadcasting in Arabic, one in Kabyle, a minority language, and the third in French and other European languages. Includes a detailed description of Kabyle broadcasts.

685

Twentieth Anniversary History of WNTV, First in Africa, edited by Obaro Ikime. Compiled by Staff of NTV. Ibadan: Heinemann, 1978. 114pp.
    An historical overview of the services and programming of WNTV, a television station in Ibadan, Nigeria. Numerous photographs, sample program schedules, organization charts and financial records.

686
Imhoof, Maurice. *Practical Decisions in Instructional Radio Innovation.* Washington: Academy for Educational Development, 1982. 11pp.
The report of the planning phase of the Radio Language Arts Project in Kenya.

687
Imhoof, Maurice, Philip R. Christensen, and Kurt Hein. *English By Radio: Implications for Non-Formal Language Education.* East Lansing, MI: Non-Formal Education Center, Michigan State University, 1984. *Occasional Paper* #12. 42pp.
A report on the Radio Language Arts Project in Kenya which broadcasts a series of English language lessons, *English In Action*, to primary schools. The adaptation of the project to non-formal education situations is discussed in the conclusion.

688
International Workshop on the Radio Learning Group Approach to Mass Education (1982: Cooperative Development Center, Ezulwini Swaziland). *Report.* Mbabane, Swaziland: Ministry of Health, 1982. 191pp.
Papers and reports from a conference on the use of radio in education in Eastern and Southern Africa.

689
Jabulani! Freedom of the Airwaves: Towards Democratic Broadcasting in South Africa. Amsterdam: African-European Institute OMREAP Voor Radio Freedom, 1991. 83pp.
Papers from a conference held in Doorn, The Netherlands in August 1991, covering cultural diversity, training, media ownership and the Viljoen Task Group's work.

690
Jackson, Gordon. "TV2 -- The Introduction of Television for Blacks in South Africa." *Gazette* 29, no. 3 (1982): 155-171.
An assessment of the potential effects of the new service for Black South Africans.

691
Jere, Annette. *Facts About Reception.* Gaborone: University College of Botswana, Institute of Adult Education, 1979. 23pp.

692
Landmarks: An Exploration of the South African Mosaic, edited by Barry Jones, and Joy Cameron-Dow. Sloane Park, South Africa: Premier Book Publishers, 1991. 246pp.
A collection of scripts from the "Landmarks" series on Radio South Africa.

Broadcasting

693
Kalter, Joanmarie. "The Untold Stories of Africa: Why TV is Missing Some Big Ones." *TV Guide* (24 May 1986).

694
Independent Broadcasting in Ghana: Implications and Challenges, edited by Kwame Karikari. Accra: Ghana Universities Press, 1994. 129pp.
> A collection of essays on technical and administrative aspects of developing private sector broadcasting in Ghana.

695
Karikari, Kwame. "My Brief for Ghana Radio." *Index on Censorship* 13, no. 1 (February 1984): 29-31.
> The acting Head of the Ghana Broadcasting Corporation responds to charges that the government of Jerry Rawlings has tried to muzzle the press.

696
---. "Radio Pluralism and Manpower Needs." *Africa Media Review* 7, no. 3 (1993): 105-110.
> A short analysis of the staffing needs of radio broadcasting in the context of democracy movements and increased non-government broadcasting.

697
Katz, Elihu, and George Wedell. *Broadcasting in the Third World: Promise and Performance*. Cambridge, MA: Harvard University Press, 1977. 305pp.
> An overview of broadcasting facilities and services worldwide, with significant African coverage. Appendices include statistical tables, the methodology, and an outline of the level of development of the countries surveyed. 12 pages of bibliographic notes. Index.

698
Keane, Fergal. *Season of Blood: A Rwandan Journey*. New York: Viking, 1996. 198pp.
> A British television correspondent's personal account of travels in Rwanda during the unrest of mid 1994.

699
Keekeh, Florida. "Radio for Rural Development in Liberia." *Intermedia* 15, no. 2 (March 1987): 27-29.
> A brief report on the activities of the Liberian Rural Communications Network.

700
Keene-Young, Bronwyn. "SABC and the Massacre." *African Communist*, no. 130 (1903): 28-32.
> Extracts from the Campaign for Open Media report on coverage by the South African Broadcasting Corporation of the massacre at Bisho, Ciskei, in which

Ciskei forces, trained by the South African Defense Force, opened fire on an ANC rally killing 33 people and injuring over 300. The report concluded that SABC had misrepresented the ANC and failed to fulfill its responsibility to provide unbiased information to the public.

701

Kiwanuka-Tondo, James. "Educational Broadcasting in Africa: The Case of Uganda." *Africa Media Review* 4, no. 2 (1990): 48-63.
> A discussion of how broadcast media have been used for formal and non-formal education in Uganda.

702

Klee, Hans Dieter. "The Video Invasion of Africa." *Intermedia* 19, no. 2 (March 1990): 27-29.
> A report on the proliferation of videos in African countries, outlining the problems that this causes for development of local television and film, as well as the distortion these foreign videos cause in traditional ways of life. Followed by short sketches of video use in Zimbabwe, Kenya and Tanzania.

703

Koffi, Atta. "Télévision et Colonisation Culturelle en Afrique Noire." *Présence Africaine*, no. 88 (1973): 98-112. Special Issue: *Mass Media and Black Civilization*.
> A commentary on television and radio, noting that in the West they are entertainment media, while in Africa they have become instruments of governmental control.

704

Kojima, Hiroshi. "Effects of Mass Media on Contraception and Fertility in African Countries." *Fertility in the Developing Countries: A comparative Study of the Demographic and Health Surveys*, 133-151. edited by Shigemi Kono and Yasuko Hayase. *IDE Statistical Data Series*, 66. Tokyo: Institute of Developing Economies, 1994.
> A study of radio ownership and exposure to broadcasts concerning family planning as factors in fertility and contraception. 2 page bibliography.

705

Koné, Hugues. *Les Radios et les Télévisions Africaines à l'Aube du 21e Siècle. La Planification et la Gestion des Systèmes de Radiodiffusion dans les Pays Non-Anglophones de la Région de l'Afrique Australe et de l'Afrique Centrale*. Brazzaville: Friedrich Ebert Stiftung, 1989.

706

Kotane, Solomon. "Restructuring and Privatization in South African Broadcasting." *Sechaba* 24, no. 12 (December 1990): 6-9.
> A critical assessment of Task Force appointed to investigate broadcasting in South Africa and consider options of restructuring and privatization, with a list of ANC demands and proposals for change.

Broadcasting

707
Kozol, Wendy. "Representations of Race in Network News Coverage of South Africa." *Television Studies: Textual Analysis*, 165-182. Edited by Gary Burns and Robert J. Thompson. New York: Praeger, 1989.
> A discussion of the format and content of news coverage of South Africa, including use of unusual camera angles to accentuate violent scenes, cutting and editing to juxtapose footage of Blacks at rallies following statements about security measures and other techniques that reinforce racial stereotypes.

708
Kulakow, Allan. *Rural Radio in the Sahel*. Bamako: Prepared for the Institut du Sahel, 1979. 2 vol. (*Sahel Documents and Dissertations*, AS277. Ann Arbor: UMI, 1980.)

709
Kushner, James M. "African Liberation Broadcasting." *Journal of Broadcasting* 18, no. 3 (June 1974): 299-309.
> An exploration of the ways that liberation groups in Africa use radio to further their aims and carry their message to their own people and the rest of the world.

710
Ladele, Olu, V. Olufemi Adefela, and Olu Lasekan. *History of the Nigerian Broadcasting Corporation*. Ibadan: Ibadan University Press, 1979. 251pp.
> History of radio and television broadcasting in Nigeria since the establishment of the Nigerian Broadcasting Service in the early 1950s, with a description of the organization and administration of today's Nigerian Broadcasting Corporation. Appendices include copies of relevant legislation. Index.

711
Land, Mitchell. "Ivoirien Television, Willing Vector of Cultural Imperialism." *Howard Journal of Communications* 4, no. 1/2 (June 1992): 10-
> Report of television in Côte d'Ivoire in 1987-1988 focusing on its role in politics and national unity, and its cultural influences, particularly in the tension between traditional identity and the inroads of foreign cultural influences.

712
Lasode, Obafemi. *Television Broadcasting: the Nigerian Experience 1959-1992*. Ibadan: Caltop Publications, 1993. 297pp.
> An historical overview of television in Nigeria through several political regimes, with notes on future developments. Appendices include copies of relevant documents.

713
Lems-Dworkin, Carol. *Videos of African and African-Related Performance: An Annotated Bibliography*. Evanston, IL: Carol Lems-Dworkin Publishers, 1996. 300pp.

714

Liberia Broadcasting System. *Plan of Action for the Interim Period.* [Monrovia]: Liberia Broadcasting System, 1991. 58 leaves.
>A proposal and justification for rebuilding the Liberian Broadcasting System.

715

Liberté Pour les Radios Africaines. Paris: L'Harmattan, 1994. 220pp.
>Proceedings of the Bamako symposium "Le Pluralisme Radiophonique en Afrique de l'Ouest".

716

Louw, P. Eric. "Obstacles to Digging out the Dirt: Frustrations in Researching Broadcast Policy in the New South Africa." *Critical Arts* 6, no. 2 (1993): 68-77.
>An analysis of current research and recommendations on broadcasting policy in South Africa, with a discussion of the difficulties encountered in compiling the information.

717

Luc, Jean-Claude. "Que Sera l'Avenir de Télé-Niger?" *L'Afrique Littéraire et Artistique* , no. 14 (1970): 23-32.
>Assessment of the achievements of an educational television project, inaugurated in Niger in 1967, designed to combine instruction in the French language with practical training.

718

Lyons, Andrew P. "The Television and the Shrine: Towards a Theoretical Model for the Study of Mass Communications in Nigeria." *Visual Anthropology* 3, no. 4 (1990): 429-456.
>A study of the context of Nigerian television, viewing habits of audiences and the socio-cultural background.

719

MacKay, Ian K. *Broadcasting in Nigeria*. Ibadan: Ibadan University Press, 1964. 159pp.
>A history of radio in Nigeria, with some notes on television, from the first BBC broadcast through the establishment of the Nigerian Broadcasting Corporation on into the early 1960s. The author was the last expatriate director of the NBC. Appendices include copies of government documents relevant to the NBC. 3 page bibliography.

720

Malden, Sue. "Images of Africa: Television's Eye." *African Research and Documentation* , no. 68 (1995): 69-74.
>A description of the film library of the BBC, emphasizing its holdings on Africa. A paper given at the annual meeting of the Standing Conference on Library Materials on Africa, London, 9-10 June, 1994.

721

Maren, Michael. "A Video Version of Constructive Engagement." *Africa Report* 30, no. 3 (May 1985): 78-80.

> A report on the broadcasting of Ted Koppel's *Nightline* on location in South Africa for five nights, during which time the show brought together supporters and opponents of apartheid. Despite the production's attempts to appear unbiased, South African president P. W. Botha called the broadcast "negative and one-sided.".

722

Matabane, Paula W. "Through the Prism of Race and Controversy: Did Viewers Learn Anything from *The Africans*?" *Journal of Black Studies* 19, no. 1 (September 1988): 3-16.

> A report of a telephone survey of 120 viewers of public television in the Washington D.C.. area to determine how much knowledge of Africa had been retained six weeks after the airing the Ali Mazrui's *The Africans*.

723

Matheson, H. "Broadcasting in Africa." *Journal of the Royal African Society* 34, no. 137 (October 1935): 387-390.

> A brief appeal for development of broadcasting in Africa both for educational and news purposes.

724

Mazrui, Ali A. "Roots: The End of America's Amnesia?" *Africa Report* 22, no. 3 (May 1977): 6-11.

> A review of Alex Haley's *Roots*, and discussion of the effects of the television movie on American audiences.

725

McAnany, Emile. "African Rural Development and Communication: Five Radio-Based Projects." *Rural Africana* 27 (1975): 52-72.

> A discussion of radio projects disseminating development information in Niger, Senegal, Dahomey (now Benin), Tanzania, and Botswana.

726

McLean, Polly E. "Radio and Rural Development in Swaziland." *Africa Media Review* 6, no. 3 (1992): 51-64.

> An historical overview of the use of radio for development in Swaziland, with recommendations for more staff with specialized training in the topics covered in broadcasts.

727

McLellan, Iain. *Television for Development: the African Experience.* Ottawa: IDRC, 1986.

> A report of a field survey of television and its uses in development programs in Africa, including educational and entertainment programs.

728

Mersham, Gary M. "Mass Media Discourse and the Semiotics of Zulu Nationalism." *Critical Arts* 7, no. 1/2 (1993): 78-119.
> An analysis of the South African TV series, *Shaka Zulu*, and how the series relates to ethnic politics in modern South Africa.

729

Misser, François. "New African TV Network." *African Business*, no. 208 (March 1996): 12-13.
> A brief note on a new Pan-African satellite television network, Africasat TV, planned by Afric & Co., a Paris based company headed by the former Director of Burundian radio, Athanase Karayenga. Although the project has only completed a feasibility study, it has received substantial advertising revenues.

730

Miyouna, Ludovic-Robert. "Télévision et Développement? L'Exemple du Congo." *Mondes en Développement* 19, no. 73 (1991): 57-61.
> A study of the programming of Télé-Congo focusing on the disparity between the plans for projects and their eventual reality.

731

Moemeka, Andrew A. *Local Radio: Community Education for Development*. Zaria, Nigeria: Ahmadu Bello University Press, 1980. 118pp.
> A discussion of the uses of radio and television for education and development in Nigeria, with recommendations for appropriate strategies.

732

---. "Radio Strategies for Community Development: a Critical Analysis." *Communicating for Development: a New Pan-Disciplinary Perspective*, 124-140. Edited by Andrew A. Moemeka. Albany, NY: State University of New York Press, 1994.
> An overview of the use of radio for education, with African examples. 2 page bibliography.

733

Mohammed, Jubril Bala. "Democratization and the Challenge of Private Broadcasting in Nigeria." *Africa Media Review* 8, no. 1 (1994): 81-95.
> A discussion of the potential consequences of privatization of Nigerian radio and television. 1 page bibliography.

734

Moshiro, G. "The Role of Radio Tanzania Dar es Salaam in Mobilising the Masses." *Africa Media Review* 4, no. 3 (1990): 18-35.
> A discussion of the use of radio to build self reliance and economic output, concluding that the major radio station in Tanzania will have to get closer to the grassroots, or introduce smaller community-based stations.

Broadcasting

735

Mosia, Lebona, Charles Riddle, and James J. Zaffiro. "From Revolutionary to Regime Radio: Three Decades of Nationalist Broadcasting in Southern Africa." *Africa Media Review* 8, no. 1 (1994): 1-24.
> The history of the last four anti-Apartheid radio stations in Africa: Radio Freedom (ANC); Voice of Namibia (SWAPO); Voice of Zimbabwe (ZANU); Voice of the Revolution (ZAPU).

736

Mostefaoui, Belkacem. "La Télévision au Maghreb." *Médiaspouvoirs* (July 1991): 27-37.
> A discussion of the way that television in North Africa is changing as broadcasting becomes more regional, and more European programs are imported.

737

Mthombothi, Barney. "South African Broadcasting: Desegregation at the Top." *Nieman Reports* 50, no. 1 (March 1996): 60-62.
> A report on the changes and new appointments in the South African Broadcasting Corporation and on the establishment of the Independent Broadcasting Authority to determine and enforce guidelines in the industry.

738

Mueller, Claus. *Third World Television Access to U. S. Media: Distributing Television Programs from Developing Countries in U. S. Television, New Electronic and Nontheatrical Markets.* New York: Friedrich Naumann Foundation, 1989. 119pp.
> A report of the status of and opportunities for importation of programs produced in the Third World for broadcast to U.S. audiences. Although the report is not focused on Africa, tables of survey statistics indicate that African material is attractive to U.S. viewers.

739

Munger, Edwin S. "Africa in 240 Minutes: A Review of ABC-TV's *Africa*." *Africa Report* 12, no. 7 (October 1967): 67-70.
> An assessment of a prime time four hour special documentary on the whole of Africa. It was generally perceived to have been of high quality and was well received by audiences, who preferred it to *Lassie*, which was aired at the same time.

740

Mwaffisi, M. Samwilu. "Direct Broadcast Satellites and National Sovereignty: Can Developing Nations Control Their Airwaves?" *Africa Media Review* 5, no. 1 (1991): 87-96.
> Examination of the inroads on national broadcasting in Africa by Direct Broadcasting Satellites from other countries, calling for better laws and regulations to control international propaganda.

741
---. "Zambia Broadcasting Corporation: A Content Analysis." *Africa Media Review* 3, no. 3 (1989): 70-85.

742
National Symposium on Broadcasting in Nigeria (1st: 1978: University of Ife). *Proceedings*. Ife, Nigeria: Nigerian Association of Planetary and Radio Sciences, 1978. 255pp.
: Collection of papers and reports from the Symposium, focusing on technical aspects, with some policy issues.

743
Nazareth, Peter. *Two Radio Plays*. Nairobi: East African Literature Bureau, 1976. 36pp.
: Scripts of two plays, *The Hospital* and *X*, with an introduction describing their production for radio, and an appendix with copies of correspondence between the producer and playwright.

744
Ngomba, Mbella M., and Robert L. Nwafo Nwankwo. "The Context of Television Broadcasting in Cameroon: a Policy Delphi Study." *Journal of Black Studies* 20, no. 3 (1990): 335-341.
: An overview of television in Cameroon, using the analytic device "Policy Delphi" and summarizing interviews with experts in the field.

745
Niambele, Abdramne. *Médias et Enfance (Essai d'Étude Sociologique de l'Information pour Enfants au Mali de 1960 à 1993. Cas des Journaux de la Radio et de la Télévision à Bamako District)*. Bamako, Mali: Bibliothèque Nationale-Bamako, 1993. 14pp.
: A study of the ways that the media fill the information needs of children in Bamako. Tables show hours of television watched, and whether programs were local or imported.

746
Nichols, Lee. "The Voice of America Series, *Conversations with African Writers*: An Adventure in International Communication." *Research in African Literatures* 8, no. 3 (December 1977): 293-303.
: A personal account of the launching of the VOA program in which African writers were interviewed on the air. Contains list of the writers interviewed.

747
Nixon, Rob. "South Africa: Cultural Protectionism and the Censorship of Television." *Intermedia* 20, no. 3 (May 1992): 24-25.
: A brief discussion of the changes in control of television in South Africa after the end of apartheid.

748

Nyamnjoh, Francis B. "Broadcasting in Francophone Africa: Crusading for French Culture?" *Gazette* 42, no. 2 (1988): 81-92.
   An assessment of the motivation and effects of French broadcasting in Africa.

749

---. "The Last Laugh: Television in Cameroon." *Intermedia* 16, no. 1 (January 1988): 36-39.
   A report of the introduction of television to Cameroon in 1985, with discussion of the problems involved.

750

Nyirenda, J. E. "Development Broadcasting in Zambia: Challenges for the 1990s." *Zambia in the 1990s*, 101-114. Edited by F. K. M. Sumaili and G. Lungwangwa. Lusaka: Professors World Peace Academy of Zambia, 1991.

751

Oduko, Segun. "From Indigenous Communication to Modern Television: A Reflection of Political Development in Nigeria." *Africa Media Review* 1, no. 3 (1987): 1-10.
   A discussion of mass media in Nigeria and its role in developing national unity.

752

Ogunbi, Adebayo. *Select Bibliography on Mass Communication in Africa (with Emphasis on Broadcasting)*. East Lansing, MI: Michigan State University, Dept. of Television and Radio, 1973. 49pp.
   A bibliography of books, reports and articles in journals and newspapers dealing with broadcasting in Africa.

753

Ogundimu, Folu. "Images of Africa on US Television: Do You Have Problems With That?" *Issue* 22, no. 1 (March 1994): 7-11.
   A report of a study in which 14 high school teachers of African history and social studies were shown three videotapes of U.S. television segments on Africa and asked to discuss the images of Africa presented in them.

754

Okigbo, Charles. "Nigerian Radio News and the New Information Order." *Gazette* 41, no. 3 (1988): 141-150.
   A content analysis of two Nigerian radio stations during two weeks in the late 1980s comparing coverage of national, regional, and global events.

755

Okonkwo, Jerome Ikechukwu. *The History and Some Problems of Television Service in Anambra State of Nigeria: A Review of Television*

Technology in the Context of a Developing Country. Frankfurt: Peter Lang, 1986. 443pp.
> The author's dissertation at the University of Munich. A broad description and analysis of television in Nigeria, including a brief discussion of traditional means of communication, the development of television broadcasting, relevant Western theories of communications and the legal framework in which broadcasting operates in Nigeria. 16 page bibliography.

756
Okoye, Innocent. "Video in the Lives of Nigerian Children: Some Socio-Cultural Implications." *Africa Media Review* 7, no. 3 (1993): 63-74.
> An analysis of the video viewing habits of children under the age of 16 in Lagos. 2 page bibliography.

757
Okunna, Chinyere Stella. "Development Communication Action Research: Rural Women in Nigeria." *Journal of Development Communication* 4, no. 1 (June 1993): 24-32.
> A report on a study of a pottery-making project sponsored by Nigeria's Better Life for Rural Women Programme, using interviews to determine the effectiveness of broadcast media in disseminating development information.

758
Onah, J. O., and A. V. Anyanwu. "Viewer Preference for Television Stations and Programming: A Pilot Study Report of Two Nigerian Television Stations." *Africa Media Review* 2, no. 3 (1988): 1-18.
> Report of a survey of 500 viewer to determine preferences between two Nigerian television stations.

759
Orivel, François. *La Télévision Scolaire du Sénégal: Évaluation Économique et Perspectives.* Washington: World Bank, 1981. *Discussion Paper no.* 81-50. 26pp.

760
Orlik, Peter B. "South Africa: How Long Without TV?" *Journal of Broadcasting* 14, no. 2 (March 1970): 245-258.
> A discussion of South Africa's ban on the introduction of television in the country, outlining the rationale of the policy and assessing the possibilities for its change.

761
Oso, Lai. "Agriculture on Nigerian Television: A Critique of Current Practice." *Africa Media Review* 7, no. 2 (1993): 30-43.
> An analysis of the kinds of agricultural information available on Nigerian television and their effectiveness. 1 page bibliography.

Broadcasting

762
Ossman, Susan. *Picturing Casablanca: Portraits as Power in a Modern City*. Berkeley, CA: University of California Press, 1994. 246pp.
> A study of the effect of mass images, i.e. television, photographs, etc. on social interaction in Casablanca. 11 page bibliography. Index.

763
Ozoh, Hilary C. "Some Critical Factors in the Perception of the Credibility of Television Endorsements." *Africa Media Review* 5, no. 1 (1991): 49-60.
> A survey of students in the Department of Mass Communication at the Anambra State University of Technology (Nigeria) to measure the effect on their attitudes toward Lux soap of a sophisticated endorser of that soap in a commercial.

764
Pate, Umaru A. "Status of Women in Nigerian Broadcasting Media: A Case for Representation and Upward Mobility." *Journal of Development Communication* 5, no. 1 (June 1994): 75-85.
> A report of a study using questionnaires to survey female staff of eight Nigerian broadcasting stations to determine their job satisfaction and opportunities for advancement.

765
Paterson, Christopher. "Who Owns TV Images from Africa?" *Issue* 22, no. 1 (March 1994): 15-18.
> A discussion of the motives of the major news services which "own" news stories, their role as "gatekeepers" controlling the flow of news to international audiences, and how coverage of African events is thus affected.

766
Pawlouschek, Andreas. "Arabvision: A New Player in the World of News Exchange." *Intermedia* 19, no. 2 (March 1992): 34-36.
> A report on a cooperative arrangement among North African and Middle Eastern nations to pool their news reports for broadcast via satellite.

767
Petty, Sheila. "*Miseria*: The Evolution of a Unique Melodramatic Form." *Passages: A Chronicle of the Humanities* , no. 8 (1994): 19-20. Supplement to *Program of African Studies News and Events* (Northwestern University) Fall 1994, Vol.. 5, no. 1.
> Discussion of a Cameroonian television serial melodrama in terms of its popular appeal and depiction of women.

768
Pige, François. *Radiodiffusion et Télévision au Maghreb*. Paris: Fondation Nationale des Sciences Politiques, 1966. 183pp.

A report on radio and television in Algeria, Morocco, and Tunisia, covering technical and administrative issues.

769

Platzbecker, Toni. *Étude Financière de la Radiodiffusion de la République Rwandaise*. Kigali: Office Rwandais d'Information, 1981. 38pp.
A report on the budget and expenditures of Radio Rwanda with tables providing detailed information on operations.

770

Le Pluralisme Radiophonique en Afrique de l'Ouest. Enquête Réalisée par l'Institut Panos Paris et l'Union des Journalistes d'Afrique de l'Ouest. Paris: Institute Panos; l'Harmattan, 1993. Vol. I, 163pp; Vol. II, 149pp.
A country-by-country review of political pluralism and its relationship to radio broadcasting in the countries of West Africa. The survey covers private radio facilities, including clandestine stations with political agendas, government broadcast services, and programming for development, education and entertainment.

771

Prince, Bill. *Laughing at Life*. Cape Town: Timmins, 1975. 188pp.
Personal memoir of a South African broadcast announcer.

772

Quarmyne, Wilna W. "Managing Radio Organizations for Participation: Research Issues." *Communication Research in Africa: Issues and Perspectives*, 69-88. Edited by S. T. Kwame Boafo, and Nancy A. George. Nairobi: African Council on Communication Education, 1992.
A report on the undertaking by the African Media Women (Zimbabwe) to write a training manual on the management of the media for development.

773

Quaye, Paa Keow. *The Challenge of Media in Africa Today*. Nairobi: Foccam, 1991. 168pp.
A country by country review of Christian religious broadcasting facilities and capabilities in Africa.

774

Rattley, Sandra. "The Impact of *Roots*: Real or Imagined?" *Africa Report* 22, no. 3 (May 1977): 12-16.
A discussion of the ways in which Alex Haley's book and the television version of it have affected readers and viewers, particularly in regard to images of Africa.

775

Raya, Gamal Abu. "Preparing Children's Programmes and How to Deal with Them." *ASBU Review: the Quarterly Publication of the Arab States Broadcasting Union* (July 1979): 33-60.

A review of psychological and educational factors involved in developing programs for children, along with the legal infrastructure and a framework of national and cultural goals in Egypt.

776

Reda, Adly Sayed Mohamed. "The Flow of Programmes From Abroad on Egypt Television: The Content Analysis of Some Foreign Material in Egypt Television." *ASBU Review: The Quarterly Publication of the Arab States Broadcasting Union* (July 1979): 25-31.
> A summary of the author's master's thesis at Cairo University, reviewing the foreign content of Egyptian television, the kinds of programs imported, and recommendations for increasing local production both in Egypt and in the broader Arab world.

777

Report on Task Group into the Future of Broadcasting. Durban: Centre for Cultural and Media Studies, University of Natal, 1991. 7pp.
> Report of discussions on reforming broadcasting in South Africa.

778

Revill, Stuart. "The SABC Takes the Path to the High Veldt." *Intermedia* 22, no. 3 (June 1994): 4-6.
> A report on the changes in the South African Broadcast Corporation following the end of apartheid.

779

Ricard, Alain. "The ORTF and African Literature." *Research in African Literatures* 4, no. 2 (September 1973): 189-191.
> A brief note on the role of the French Office de Radio-diffusion Television in promoting African literature through its broadcasts. Contains list of works broadcast.

780

Riddle, Charles. "South African Attempts to Dominate Political Communication in Namibia Through Control of Radio, 1966-1989." *Gazette* 52, no. 1 (1993): 25-41.
> A study of South Africa's authoritarian control of radio and the use of disinformation in broadcasts to maintain its hold on Namibia and its people.

781

Ridore, Charles. *La Signification de l'Éducation dans le Développement: Télévision et Éducation au Niger.* Fribourg: Éditions Universitaires, 1979. Documents Économiques v. 10. 60pp.
> Discussion of the use of educational television in Niger, focusing on language use and staffing issues.

Broadcasting

782
Robert, Guy. *Les Radio-Clubs du Niger*. Paris: Ocora, 1967. 79pp.
   A description of an educational radio project in Niger involving instructional broadcasts which were followed up by volunteers who taped interviews with listeners, then sent the tapes to the broadcaster to be incorporated into future programs.

783
Rogerson, C. M. "Corporate Strategy, State Power and Compromise: Television Manufacture in Southern Africa." *South African Geographical Journal* 60, no. 2 (1978): 89-102.
   A study of corporate strategies and their political implications in planning of the manufacturing television sets in South Africa.

784
Rosenthal, E. *You Have Been Listening: A History of the Early Days of Radio in South Africa*. Cape Town: Purnell, 1974. 165pp.
   The study covers the period from the first radio broadcast on July 1, 1924, through the establishment of the South African Broadcasting Corporation in 1936. Numerous photographs. Index.

785
Rural Primary Schools Extension Project: Radio Language Arts. Implementation Plan. Washington: Academy for Education Development, 1981. 38pp.
   A report on a USAID project using radio for teaching English language in Kenya. Appendices include job descriptions, resumes of staff and lesson plans.

786
Salama, Girgis. *Nigerian Television Authority. Television in a Developing Country*. Jos, Nigeria: Nigerian Television Authority, 1978. 360pp.

787
Sambe, John A. "Network Coverage of the Civil War in Nigeria." *Journal of Broadcasting* 24 (1980): 61-67.
   Content analysis of news programs on ABC, CBS and NBC from August 1968 to the end of the Nigerian Civil War to determine if there was bias in favor of Biafra.

788
Seeking the Barefoot Technologist: A Report of a Workshop on Distance Teaching and Rural Development Held by the International Extension College at Dartington Hall, Devon, England, 3-9 September, 1977. Cambridge, UK: International Extension College, 1978. 53pp.
   A discussion of the technical problems in setting up radio-based educational projects, focusing on the need for skilled maintenance personnel.

789
Senekal, J. E. *Effect of Television on the Religious Activities of English-Speaking Secondary School Pupils*. Pretoria: Human Sciences Research Council, 1985. 61pp.

790
Sherrington, R. W. "The Organization of a Schools Television Service: Its Use in Language Teaching." *Language Education in Eastern Africa*, 195-206. Edited by T. P. Gorman. Nairobi: Oxford University Press, 1970.
>A position paper outlining the elements necessary for successful use of television in teaching English in East Africa.

791
Silla, Mactar. *Le Paria du Village Planètaire ou l'Afrique à l'Heure de la Télévision Mondiale*. Dakar: Les Nouvelles Éditions Africaines du Sénégal, 1994. 159pp.
>A study of television in Francophone Africa.

792
Silverman, Theresa. *Télé-Niger: Adapting an Electronic Medium to a Rural African Context*. Washington, DC: Clearinghouse on Development Communications, 1976. Information Bulletin no. 8. 45pp.
>Report on an early project to use television for elementary school education in Niger during the 1960s. Besides an overview of the structure of the project, the report includes an updated evaluation twelve years after the project.

793
Smith, Howard. "Apartheid, Sharpeville and "Impartiality": The Reporting of south Africa 1948 - 1961." *Historical Journal of Film, Radio and TV* 13, no. 3 (1993): 251-298.
>A detailed survey and analysis of BBC's news coverage and documentary programs on South Africa during the buildup of apartheid, ending with particular focus on the incident at Sharpeville. 7 pages of bibliographic notes.

794
Sock, Boubacar. "L'Utilisation de la Radiodiffusion pour l'Animation et l'Éducation des Communautés de Base (L'Expèrience Sénégalaise)." *Présence Africaine*, no. 107 (1978): 93-110.
>A discussion of the use of radio in disseminating information for development, focusing on the language of transmission and the need to express modern ideas in the context of traditional values in ways that will be appealing to listeners.

795
South Africa. Commission of Inquiry into Matters Relating to Television. *Report*. Pretoria: Government Printer, 1971. 57pp.
>Report of a commission charged with determining if television should be introduced in South Africa, concluding that it should be, with "suitable" controls.

796
South Africa. Task Group on Broadcasting in South and Southern Africa. *Report of the Task Group on Broadcasting in South And Southern Africa.* Pretoria: Govt. Printer, 1991. Christo Viljoen, Chairman. 141pp.

797
Sow, Mamadou Aliou. "School Radio in Guinea." *Educational Media International* 27, no. 2 (June 1990): 135-136.
   Brief overview of Radio Scolaire de Guiné, an educational broadcasting project for elementary schools in Guinea.

798
Spitulnik, Debra. "Radio Cycles and Recyclings in Zambia: Public Words, Popular Critiques, and National Communities." *Passages: A Chronicle of the Humanities* , no. 8 (1994): 10,12,14,16. Supplement to *Program of African Studies News and Events* (Northwestern University) Fall 1994, Vol. 5, no. 1.
   A discussion of the use of political slogans in Zambian radio programming and its effect on listeners.

799
Sreberny-Mohammadi, Annabelle, and Helio Belik. "The U.N. as International Communicator: Portuguese Broadcasting to Lusophone Africa." *Gazette* 45, no. 2 (1990): 117-133.
   Discussion of a U.N. project to broadcast in Portuguese to Lusophone countries of Africa as part of a broader effort to develop broadcasting capabilities locally.

800
Stanley, Joyce, and Alisa Lundeen. *Audio Cassette Listening Forums: a Participatory Women's Development Project.* Washington: USAID Office of Women in Development, 1978. 92pp.
   A report of a USAID project using audio cassettes to augment radio campaigns to bring health and nutrition information to rural women in Tanzania. 3 page bibliography. Appendix contains sample questionnaires.

801
Surlin, S. H. "Race and Authoritarianism: Effect on the Perception of *Roots.*" *Journal of Black Studies* 12, no. 1 (1981): 71-82.
   A survey of Black residents of Athens, Georgia, who had viewed the television series *Roots* to test several hypotheses about the relationship of authoritarianism to reaction to the series.

802
---. "*Roots* Research: A Summary of the Findings." *Journal of Broadcasting* 22, no. 3 (June 1978): 309-320.
   A summary and evaluation of survey research done on audience reactions to the television series *Roots*.

Broadcasting

803
Teaching English by Radio. Washington, DC: Academy for Educational Development, 1986. 333pp.

804
Teboho, Moja. "Teacher Education from Classroom Broadcasts in the New South Africa." *Educational Media International* 29, no. 3 (September 1992): 171.

805
Teer-Tomaselli, Ruth. "Moving Towards Democracy: the South African Broadcasting Corporation and the 1994 Election." *Media, Culture and Society* 17, no. 4 (October 1995): 577-601.
   A discussion of the change of the SABC from the propaganda arm of the National Party to an effective means of conveying information for the 1994 election to potential voters via radio and television.

806
Theroux, Paul. *Education by Radio: an Experiment in Rural Group Listening for Adults in Uganda*. Kampala: MASC, 1966. 22pp.
   A report of a Makerere University history course on the comparative experiences of immigration and national development in the United States and in East Africa which was broadcast to adult learners throughout Uganda. Discussion groups were arranged as part of the course, and a follow-up survey accompanies the report.

807
Tomaselli, Keyan G. et al. "Square Vision in Colour: How TV 2/3 Negotiates Consent." *Currents of Power: State Broadcasting in South Africa*, 153-176. Edited by Ruth Tomaselli, Keyan G. Tomaselli, and Johan Muller. Bellville, South Africa: Anthropos, 1989.
   A description of the programming and administration of television for the Black African populations of South Africa.

808
Tomaselli, Keyan G., and B. Boster. "Mandela, MTV, Television and Apartheid." *Popular Music and Society* 17, no. 2 1-20.
   An assessment of the incorporation of Mandela and anti-apartheid messages into popular videos, television and music in the 1970s and 1980s, and this popularization's possible effect on events in South Africa.

809
Tomaselli, Keyan G., and Ruth Tomaselli. "Between Policy and Practice in the SABC, 1970-1981." *Currents of Power: State Broadcasting in South Africa*, 84-152. Edited by Ruth Tomaselli, Keyan G. Tomaselli, and Johan Muller. Bellville, South Africa: Anthropos, 1989.

An overview of the philosophical basis of broadcasting policy and programming decisions.

810

---. "Change and Continuity at the SABC." *Indicator SA* 3, no. 3 (June 1986): 18-20.
A report and analysis of change in the South African Broadcasting Corporation under the control of the South African Department of Foreign Affairs.

811

Tomaselli, Ruth. *The Covering of Current Affairs in Broadcasting*. Durban: Centre for Cultural and Media Studies, University of Natal, 1991. 5pp.
Report of a seminar hosted by the Human Sciences Research Council of South Africa, noting that the wide range of opinions voiced was something of a breakthrough for South African media.

812

---. "Restoring the Dignity of the Local Community: A Case-Study of Impartiality, SABC-Style." *Reality* 20, no. 6 (November 1988): 7-11.
An analysis of television coverage of violence in Pietermaritzburg demonstrating bias and stereotyping.

813

Currents of Power: State Broadcasting in South Africa, edited by Ruth Tomaselli, Keyan G. Tomaselli, and Johan Muller. Bellville, South Africa: Anthropos, 1989. 227pp.
A collection of essays on broadcasting in South Africa covering both the technological and the theoretical and philosophical aspects. 7 page bibliography.

814

Tudesq, André-Jean. *L'Afrique Noire et ses Télévisions*. Paris: Anthropos, 1992. 340pp.
A detailed overview of television in Africa, including a history of its development, the organization and staffing of television services, programming and studies of the effect of television on its audiences. 8 page bibliography. Index.

815

---. *La Radio en Afrique Noire*. Paris: Pedone, 1983. 312pp.
A study of radio and radiodiffusion in Africa including an historical overview, discussion of radio's role in several African coups d'etat and other crises, technical and programming information, and a profile of Africa's radio audience. Appendices include transcripts of laws, reports of projects, and samples of broadcast programs from several countries. 12 page bibliography. Index.

816

---. "Radios et Télévisions Scolaires." *Afrique Contemporaine*, no. 172 (October 1994): 126-133.

Broadcasting

In this historical overview of educational radio and television in Africa, the author notes that such broadcasting, considered indispensable for educating large numbers of rural people in the years following independence, now has gone out of vogue.

817

Tusa, John. *Fourth Estate or Fifth Column: Media, the Government and the State*. Nigerian Institute of International Affairs, 1992. *Lecture Series* no. 75. 18pp.
An address by the Managing Director of the BBC World Service on the responsibility of broadcast journalists to get the news, and how their role has changed over time.

818

"TV Schedules: Africa." *Intermedia* 18, no. 2 (March 1990): 40-45.
A listing of regularly scheduled evening television programs for African countries.

819

Uche, Luke Uka. "The Politics of Nigeria's Broadcast Industry: 1932-1983." *Gazette* 35, no. 1 (1985): 19-29.
An historical overview of the development of broadcasting in Nigeria, with commentary on radio's importance during coups and similar periods of unrest.

820

Uganda. *Broadcasting in Uganda: Memorandum by the Protectorate Government on Chapter VI of the Report of the Committee of Enquiry into the Organization, Policy and Operation of the Government's Information Service*. Kampala: Government Printer, 1960. 8pp.
A government document establishing a broadcasting service in Uganda.

821

Ugboajah, Frank Okwu. "Media Habits of Rural and Semi-Rural (Slum) Kenya." *Gazette* 36, no. 3 (1985): 155-174.
A report of a survey in six neighborhoods on the outskirts of Nairobi to determine radio listening patterns as correlated with socio-economic factors.

822

---. "Mind Management: An Analysis of South African Broadcasts Into Neighbouring African States." *Current Research on Peace and Violence* 4, no. 4 (1981): 287-309.
Content analysis of Radio SA broadcasts to neighboring countries in March 1981 to determine events covered and treatment of the news items.

823

---. "Some Issues in Nigerian Broadcasting." *Mass Media Policies in Changing Cultures*, 185-188. Edited by George Gerbner. New York: John Wiley & Sons, 1977.

A brief discussion of programming and listener participation in Nigerian broadcasting.

824
Ugochukwu, F. "La Guerre de Biafra à la Radio: Situation Militaire et Livraisons d'Armes en 1968-1969." *Peuples Noirs, Peuples Africains* 14, no. 80 (1991): 60-76.
A discussion of the role of foreign radio journalists in the Nigerian Civil War following the secession of Biafra.

825
Ume-Nwagbo, Ebele N. E. ""Cock Crow at Dawn": A Nigerian Experiment with Television Drama in Development-Communication." *Gazette* 37, no. 3 (1986): 155-167.
A report of a "television success story" in Nigeria: the promotion of mechanized agriculture through a serial drama which achieved great popularity.

826
Umeh, Charles C. "The Advent and Growth of Television Broadcasting in Nigeria: Its Political and Educational Overtones." *Africa Media Review* 3, no. 2 (1989): 54-66.

827
United Nations. Economic Commission for Africa. *Study of Broadcasting Techniques for Promoting the Extension of Coverage and Improvement of Mass Communications*. Addis Ababa, Ethiopia: UNECA, 1981. 56pp.
Report of field missions to eleven African countries to determine the feasibility of introducing alternative technologies for increasing radio service to rural areas.

828
Van Tonder, J. W. "South Africa: Apartheid of the Airwaves Still Rules." *Intermedia* 20, no. 6 (November 1992): 28-29.
A report noting that independent broadcasters are still excluded from South African radio, and that some clandestine radio stations still are operating.

829
Van Zyl, J. A. F. *Media and Myth: The Construction of Television News*. Mowbray: IDASA, 1991. 5pp.
An analysis of South African Television's news coverage during the two months prior to the 1989 general election to illustrate the ways television can be used to shape public opinion to a particular political agenda.

830
van Zyl, Mikki, and Leandra Elion. "Trauma by Installment: Springbok Radio Soap Operas." *Currents of Power: State Broadcasting in South*

Africa, 177-219. Edited by Ruth Tomaselli, Keyan G. Tomaselli, and Johan Muller. Bellville, South Africa: Anthropos, 1989.
>A review of the content and planning process of a popular South African radio series.

831
Vergeldt, Vicki. *Non-Formal Education and Radio: A Selected, Annotated Bibliography*. East Lansing, MI: Michigan State University, Non-Formal Education Center, 1983. 48pp.

832
Versi, Anver. "Noah Samara: Africa's Radio Renaissance Man." *African Business*, no. 208 (March 1996): 8-12.
>An interview with Noah Samara, an African entrepreneur headquartered in the U.S., who founded WorldSpace, a satellite broadcast service for Africa. The service is expected to be operational in 1998.

833
Vittin, Theophile. "L'Écoute des Radios Étrangères en Afrique Noire." *Mondes en Développement* 19, no. 73 (1991): 45-56.
>An assessment of the popularity of foreign radio programs in Africa and the role which they can play in the politics of the countries where they are heard.

834
Wander, Philip. "On the Meaning of *Roots*." *Journal of Communication* 27, no. 4 (1977): 64-69.
>A commentary on the audience reaction to the broadcast of *Roots*, which had extremely high ratings.

835
Wasburn, Philo C. "Counterpropaganda of Radio RSA: the Voice of South Africa." *Journal of Broadcasting and Electronic Media* 33, no. 2 (March 1989): 117-138.
>A content analysis of the broadcasts of Radio RSA to North America, outlining their major themes and discussing their propaganda value.

836
---. "*Voice of America* and *Radio Moscow* Newscasts to the Third World." *Journal of Broadcasting and Electronic Media* 32, no. 2 (March 1988): 197-218.
>A content analysis of U.S. and Soviet broadcasting to the Third World with tables showing statistics for each area, including Africa.

837
Waterman, Christopher A. "Celebrity and the Public in Yoruba Popular Music Video." *Passages: A Chronicle of the Humanities*, no. 8 (1994): 3-

4,7-8,10. Supplement to *Program of African Studies News and Events* (Northwestern University) Fall 1994, Vol.. 5, no. 1.
> Discussion of the content and form of traditional and modern Yoruba music and the effect of their video formats on audiences.

838

Making Broadcast Useful: The African Experience. The Development of Radio and Television in Africa in the 1980s, edited by George Wedell. Manchester, UK: Manchester University Press, 1986. 306pp.
> An overview of issues and problems affecting the development of radio and television in Africa. Includes studies describing the state of broadcasting in each of nine African nations. 2 page bibliography. Index.

839

Welsh, B. W. W. "Educational Broadcasting in Tanzania." *Gazette* 14, no. 2 (1968): 111-128.
> The history, current policies and content of educational broadcasting for all levels in Tanzania.

840

Wendland, Wend. "Tightroping Freedom of Expression and Broadcasting Regulation: the New Bill of Rights and the Independent Broadcasting Authority Act, 1993." *South African Journal on Human Rights* 10, no. 2 (1994): 280-286.
> A commentary on the legislation creating the Independent Broadcasting Authority, which removes control of the media from the government and assures freedom of speech under the new Bill of Rights.

841

Who Rules the Airwaves? Broadcasting in Africa. London: Article 19, 1995. 155pp.
> A collection of articles on broad themes of broadcasting and the legal framework of freedom to broadcast in Africa, followed by case studies of nine eastern and southern African nations and recommendations for protection and promotion of broadcasting freedom. Appendices include relevant provisions of international instruments and Article 19 guidelines for election broadcasting.

842

Wilkinson, J. F. "The BBC and Africa." *African Affairs* 71, no. 283 (April 1972): 176-185.
> An historical overview of BBC activities in Africa since the beginning of broadcasting in the British African colonies in Kenya in 1928.

843

Wilson, Des. "Organizing a Television Service for Rural Areas." *Africa Media Review* 1, no. 3 (1987): 36-48.
> A discussion of television in Nigeria and an assessment of its service to rural areas.

Broadcasting

844

Zaffiro, James J. *From Police Network to Station of the Nation: a Political History of Broadcasting in Botswana, 1927-1991.* Gaborone: The Botswana Society, 1991. 109pp.
> A history of broadcasting in Botswana prior to Independence and its development since Independence in 1966. 7 pages of bibliographic endnotes.

845

---. "Political Legitimacy and Broadcasting: the Case of Zimbabwe." *Gazette* 37, no. 3 (1986): 127-138.
> A report of a survey using interviews with Zimbabwean media theorists and practitioners to determine linkages between state, party, and media institutions during five years of majority rule.

846

--. "Political Change, Regime Legitimation and Zimbabwe Broadcasting: Lessons for a Post-Apartheid South Africa?" *Critical Arts* 6, no. 1 (1992): 61-75.
> A comparative analysis of the first decade of the Zimbabwe Broadcasting Corporation under the Zimbabwe African National Union (ZANU) and the possibilities for change in the South African Broadcasting Corporation under majority rule government.

847

Zemoniaco, Patrice. "La Radiodiffusion, une Université Populaire." *Présence Africaine*, no. 88 (1973): 29-49. Special Issue: *Mass Media and Black Civilization.*
> A call for radio to be used to improve the life of all citizens of African nations, emphasizing the need to tailor programming to potential audiences and to take those audiences' needs and preferences into consideration.

848

Ziegler, Dhyana, and Bette J. Dickerson. "Breaking the Barriers: Using Video as a Tool for Intercultural Communication." *Journal of Black Studies* 24, no. 2 (December 1993): 159-177.
> A discussion of images of Africa in Western media and the mixed messages these images give to African Americans, with a report on a video letter exchange project between two groups of women, one in Knoxville, Tennessee, the other in Ngodiba, Senegal. The videos, depicting ordinary day-to-day life in the two locations, enhanced understanding of both cultures.

Film

849

Adelman, Larry. *Using Films on South Africa: an Activation Kit on Investments.* New York: Africa Fund, 1980. 45pp.
> A planning guide for developing effective educational sessions on divestment as a means of causing the end of apartheid. Contains synopses of five films and background materials to foster discussion.

850

Africa on Film and Videotape, 1960-1981: A Compendium of Reviews. East Lansing, MI: Michigan State University, 1983. 551pp.
> A filmography of 7495 films, most with a short synopsis and assessment of potential classroom use, and some with critiques. Appendices list without commentary additional films: those no longer distributed, with no known distributor, or available only from foreign sources. 6 page bibliography of filmographies. Index.

851

Africa on Film and Videotape: A Guide to Audio-Visual Resources Available in Canada. Montreal: CIDIHCA, 1990. 139pp.
> An annotated filmography of 396 films and videos made in Africa or dealing with Africa. Indexed by subject, geographic area, and director with a list of distributors' addresses.

852

Afrique Noire: Quel Cinéma? Actes du Colloque, Université de Paris X Nanterre, Décembre 1981. Nanterre: Association du Ciné-Club de l'Université de Paris X, 1983. 97pp.
> Transcripts of a conference focusing on three debates: the relationship of France and Africa; the structure of African cinema; the future form of African cinema.

853

Ahmed, Osman Hassan. *Bibliography of Documentary and Educational Films on Sudan.* Washington: Embassy of Sudan, 1982. *Sudan Publications Series* no. 7. 114pp.
> A 116 item list, with synopses and descriptive information, of films on the Sudan. Appendices list additional films, including UN, commercial news service and USIA films plus a miscellany of transcripts and reviews, and a list of distributors. Photographs. 2 page bibliography.

854

Aig-Imoukhuede, Frank. "A National Film Industry: Assessment of Problems and Suggested Solutions." *The Development and Growth of the Film Industry in Nigeria: Proceedings of a Seminar on the Film Industry and Cultural Identity in Nigeria,* 61-72. Edited by Alfred E. Opubor and Onuora E. Nwuneli. New York: Third Press International, 1979.
> A Nigerian writer assesses the problems of the images of Africa and Africans presented by some foreign films and suggests ways in which Nigerian films can overcome them.

855
Anderson, P. "The Tiakeni Report: The Maker and the Problem of Method in Documentary Video Production." *Critical Arts* 4, no. 1 (1985): 1-79.
> A long report and analysis of the making of a documentary film on a textile-printing cooperative in South Africa by a group of student filmmakers from the University of the Witwatersrand. The author outlines the philosophical and theoretical framework of documentary production, and describes the practical and cinematic problems encountered and overcome in the production of this documentary.

856
Andrade-Watkins, Claire. "Francophone African Cinema: French Financial and Technical Assistance, 1961-1977." Ph.D. diss., Boston University, 1989. 307pp.

857
---. "A Mirage in the Desert? African Women Directors at FESPACO." *Cinemas of the Black Diaspora: Diversity, Dependence and Oppositionality*, 145-152. Edited by Michael T. Martin. Detroit: Wayne State University Press, 1995.
> Report of a workshop on Women, Cinema, TV and Video in Africa held at the Festival Panafricain du *Cinéma* du Ouagadougou (FESPACO) in 1991, which erupted in controversy when non-African women were unexpectedly asked to leave. Nevertheless it may have served as a catalyst for development of women filmmakers in Africa and for better dialog between African and non-African filmmakers.

858
---. "Portuguese African Cinema: Historical and Contemporary Perspectives - 1969 to 1993." *Research in African Literatures* 26, no. 3 (September 1995): 134-150.
> An historical overview of filmmaking in Lusophone Africa, tracing its development from liberation films through the post-independence transition from government-sponsored production to free market, private sector filmmaking.

859
Armes, Roy. "Black African Cinema in the Eighties." *Screen* 26, no. 3/4 (May 1985): 60-73.
> A survey of feature films made in Africa during the first half of the 1980s, with a discussion of the problems the film industry has encountered there.

860
---. *Third World Film Making and the West*. Berkeley, CA: University of California Press, 1987. 381pp.
> Overview of Third World cinema and its relationship to national identity, western influences and capitalism. One full chapter on Ousmane Sembene. 34 page bibliography. Index.

861
Arulogun, Adegboyega. "The Role of Film in Cultural Identity." *The Development and Growth of the Film Industry in Nigeria: Proceedings of a Seminar on the Film Industry and Cultural Identity in Nigeria*, 23-38. Edited by Alfred E. Opubor, and Onuora E. Nwuneli. New York: Third Press International, 1979.
   An analysis of the use of film as propaganda and to promote stereotypes, and the ways in which Nigerian film can counteract these tendencies.

862
Asch, Timothy, and Patsy Asch. "Images that Represent Ideas: The Use of Film on the !Kung to Teach Anthropology." *The Past and Future of !Kung Ethnography: Critical Reflections and Symbolic Perspectives. Essays in Honour of Lorna Marshall*, 327-358. Edited by Megan Biesele, Robert Gordon, and Richard Lee. Hamburg: Helmut Buske Verlag, 1986.
   A discussion of the variety of documentary films and their use in teaching anthropology, focusing on twelve films portraying the !Kung which the authors found useful.

863
Association des Trois Mondes. *Dictionnaire du Cinéma Africain*. Paris: Karthala, 1991. 398pp.
   A country by country list of filmmakers and their films. Some film entries are annotated with a synopsis. Indexed by filmmaker and film title.

864
Attenborough, Richard. *Richard Attenborough's "Cry Freedom"*. New York: Alfred A. Knopf, 1987. unpaged.
   A collection of photographs from the film, with captions synopsizing the film's story. A ten page introduction by Attenborough describes his personal approach to the film.

865
Auge, Marc, and Jean-Paul Colleyn. *Nkpiti: La Rancune et le Prophète*. Paris: Éditions de l'École des Hautes Études en Sciences Sociales, 1990. 85pp.
   Anthropological study of a traditional healer in Côte d'Ivoire, with a description and the script of a film made of his practice. Numerous photographs.

866
Awed, Ibrahim M., Hussein M. Adam, and Lionel Ngakane. *Pan-African Cinema ...Which Way Ahead? Proceedings of the First Mogadishu Pan-African Film Symposium*. Mogadishu, Somalia: Mogpafis Management Committee, 1983. 126pp.
   The papers and country reports from the Symposium.

Film

867

Ayu, Iyorchia D. "Film as a Weapon: the Cultural Question in African Liberation." *Ufahamu* 17, no. 3 (September 1989): 5-16.
A discussion of the role of films in culture generally, the depiction of Africa in U.S. films, and the ways that some African films have contributed to liberation struggles.

868

Bachy, Victor. *Le Cinéma au Gabon*. Brussels: OCIC, 1986. 156pp.
Cinema in Gabon has been strongly supported by the government, due to the personal interest of President Omar Bongo. This overview traces the history, and includes 16 pages of photographs, biographical notes on filmmakers, a filmography, and a 13 page bibliography.

869

---. *Le Cinéma au Mali*. Brussels: OCIC/L'Harmattan, 1983. 84pp.
An overview of film in Mali. Photographs. 6 page bibliography.

870

---. *Le Cinéma de Tunisie 1956-1977*. Tunis, Tunisia: Societé Tunisienne de Diffusion, 1978. 510pp.
An overview of film in Tunisia, looking at the influences of Islam and language, and the role of government and private organizations. Appendices include biographical information on filmmakers. 52 page bibliography.

871

---. *Le Cinéma en Côte d'Ivoire*. Brussels: OCIC/L'Harmattan, 1983. 82pp.
Overview of cinema and filmmaking in Côte d'Ivoire. Numerous photographs. 10 page bibliography.

872

---. *La Haute Volta et le Cinéma*. Brussels: OCIC/L'Harmattan, 1983. 86pp.
Overview of film and filmmaking in Burkina Faso (formerly Upper Volta). Several pages of photographs. 8 page bibliography.

873

---. *To Have a History of African Cinema*. Brussels: OCIC, 1987. 65pp.
A short commentary on the history of film in Africa, with the problem of definition, namely, what is an African film? 16 pages of photographs.

874

Badday, Moncef S. "Naissance Ajournée pour le Cinéma Tunisien?" *L'Afrique Littéraire et Artistique*, no. 2 (1968): 71-77.
A discussion of the problems confronting Tunisian filmmakers: disagreement on what themes and kinds of films are most appropriate and lack of government support for the industry.

875
Baker, Raymond William. "Egypt in Shadows: Films and the Political Order." *American Behavioral Scientist* 17, no. 3 (February 1974): 393-423.
>A discussion of political themes in Egyptian films and the influence those films have on political events.

876
Balogun, Françoise. *Le Cinéma au Nigéria*. Paris: OCIC/L'Harmattan, 1984. 137pp.
>Original French version of item no. 877.

877
---. *The Cinema in Nigeria*. Enugu, Nigeria: Delta Publications, 1987. 144pp.
>A study of the film industry in Nigeria, including both government documentaries and commercial films. Profiles of leading film personalities, with 8 pages of photographs, are included, as are texts of articles and reviews. 13 page filmography. 8 page bibliography.

878
Balogun, Olu. "Africa." *The Education of the Film-maker: an International View*, 33-41. Paris: Unesco, 1975.
>A brief overview of some issues relating to filmmaking in Africa, and suggestions for training new filmmakers.

879
Barbash, Ilisa, and Lucien Taylor. "Reframing Ethnographic Film: A "Conversation" with David Macdougall and Judith MacDougall." *American Anthropologist* 98, no. 2 (June 1996): 371-387.
>Two major ethnographic filmmakers, whose work includes many films on Africa, discuss their philosophies and techniques.

880
Barkas, N. *Thirty Thousand Miles for the Cinema: The Story of the Filming of "Soldiers Three" and "Rhodes of Africa"*. London: Blackie and Son, 1937. 197pp.
>Personal account of the filming of "Rhodes of Africa" on location in Rhodesia (now Zimbabwe) and South Africa. Numerous photographs.

881
Barnes, John. *Filming the Boer War*. London: Bishopsgate Press, 1992. 340pp.
>A documentary history of the fledgling film industry at the end of the 19th century, when the Boer War provided impetus to its growth by demand for both news footage from the front and dramatic productions depicting war scenes.

Film

882

Barrett, Lindsay. "Liberation War is Brought to the Screen." *West Africa*, no. 3325 (20 April 1981): 858-861.
    A review of *Cry Freedom*, a feature film of Nigerian filmmaker Olu Balogun, based on the novel *Carcase for Hounds* by Kenyan writer Meja Mwangi. Although the novel was set in Kenya during the Mau Mau era, Balogun has generalized the location in his adaptation.

883

Bassori, Timité. "Will the African Cinema be Still-Born?" *Présence Africaine*, no. 49 (1964): 108-112.
    The Ivoirien filmmaker discusses the problems facing the African film industry both from the practical and artistic viewpoints.

884

Bellman, Beryl L., and Bennetta Jules-Rosette. *A Paradigm for Looking: Cross-Cultural Research with Visual Media*. Norwood, NJ: Able Publishing Corporation, 1977. 210pp.
    An account of ethnographic research in a rural Liberian village and a shanty compound on the outskirts of Lusaka. In both locations local people as well as the anthropologists used cameras to record events, providing both insiders' and outsiders' views. Appendices provide detailed descriptions of the films. 3 page bibliography. Index.

885

ben Ammar, Abdellatif. "Putting Forward a Clear View on Life." *Film and Politics in the Third World*, 109-117. Edited by John D. H. Downing. New York: Praeger, 1987.
    Interview with Tunisian filmmaker Abdellatif ben Ammar covering the themes and language used in his films.

886

ben Barka, Souhail. "A Cinema Founded on the Image." *Film and Politics in the Third World*, 89-99. Edited by John D. H. Downing. New York: Praeger, 1987.
    A conversation between Guy Hennebelle and Moroccan filmmaker Souhail ben Barka, focusing on cinematic techniques.

887

Bensusan, David. "*My Country, My Hat*: ne pas Interesser Seulement les Convainçus de Méfaits de l'Apartheid." *Le Cinéma Sud-Africain Est-il Tombé sur la Tête?*, 48-51. Edited by Keyan G. Tomaselli. Paris: Cerf, 1986.
    South African filmmaker David Bensusan discusses the theme and structure of his film.

888
Bentsi-Enchill, Nii K. "Money, Power and Cinema." *West Africa* , no. 3393 (16 August 1982): 2093-2094.
> A review of Nigerian filmmaker Olu Balogun's feature film, *Money Power*, which depicts corruption in Nigerian life and has struck a powerful chord with its audiences.

889
Biella, Peter. "Against Reductionism and Idealist Self-Reflexivity: the Ilparakuyo Maasai Film Project." *Anthropological Filmmaking: Anthropological Perspectives on the Production Film and Video for General Public Audiences*, 47-72. Edited by Jack R. Rollwagen. Chur, Switzerland: Harwood Academic Publishers, 1988.
> The author uses his experience studying and filming the Maasai to illustrate his contention that erroneous theoretical structures lead to ethnographic film techniques that inhibit rather than enhance understanding of the peoples filmed. 3 page bibliography.

890
Binet, Jacques. "L'Argent dans les Films Africains." *L'Afrique Littéraire et Artistique* , no. 43 (1977): 90-93.
> An exploration of money, either as a symbol of prestige or an agent of corruption, as a theme in African films, based on analysis of 46 films. Money was found to be the primary theme in nine, and a secondary theme in seven.

891
---. *Cinéma Noirs d'Afrique*. Paris: L'Harmattan, 1983. Also issued as *Cinémaction* no. 26, 1982. 206pp.
> A collection of essays on African film, with such themes as language, images of women and audience.

892
---. "La Nature dans le Cinéma Africain." *L'Afrique Littéraire et Artistique*, no. 39 (1976): 52-59.
> A discussion of the use of nature in African films, as setting and symbol.

893
---. "Violence et Cinéma Africain." *L'Afrique Littéraire et Artistique*, no. 44 (1977): 73-80.
> A comparison of African film with American, European, and Japanese film in terms of the amount and kind of violence portrayed. The author finds that while violence is not absent in Africa films, it plays a limited, secondary role to other plot elements.

Film

894

Movies - Moguls - Mavericks: Current South African Film, 1979-1991, edited by Johan Blignault, and Martin Botha. Cape Town: Showdata, 1992. 486pp plus separately paged filmographies.
> A collection of essays focusing on identity, individual directors, the end of racism and Afrikaans film and television productions. Lengthy separately paged filmographies.

895

Bosseno, Christian. *Youssef Chahine l'Alexandrin*. Paris: Editions du Cerf, 1985. 158pp. Also *Cinémaction* 33.
> Biography and critical review of the Egyptian filmmaker, Youssef Chahine. Includes interviews and an annotated filmography with texts of reviews. Numerous photographs.

896

Boudjedra, Rachid. *Naissance du Cinéma Algérien*. Paris: Maspero, 1971. 101pp.
> This history of film in Algeria moves from French impressions of the country through the emergence of local filmmakers, with emphasis on the war of independence. 4 page filmography. 2 page bibliography.

897

Boughedir, Ferid. *African Cinema from A to Z*. Brussels: OCIC, 1992. 185pp.
> A short historical overview precedes a detailed country-by-country list of African filmmakers. 13 pages of photographs.

898

---. "A Cinema Fighting for its Liberation." *Cinemas of the Black Diaspora: Diversity, Dependence and Oppositionality*, 111-117. Edited by Michael T. Martin. Detroit: Wayne State University Press, 1995.
> An outline of important events in the history of African filmmaking and its relationship with the film industry overseas.

899

Boulanger, Pierre. *Le Cinéma Colonial: de "l'Atlantide " à "Lawrence d'Arabie."* Paris: Seghers, 1975. 291pp.
> Focusing on North Africa, this history examines film and the effects of its images of the North African peoples in Europe and elsewhere, with emphasis on colonial attitudes. 32 pages of photographs. 2 page bibliography. Index.

900

Bouteba, P. M. "Cultural Heritage in African Film." *Ufahamu* 17, no. 3 (September 1989): 17-43.
> An examination of the need for African cultural heritage in films and strategies of African filmmakers for incorporating that heritage in their films, using the films *Yeelen, The Swamp Dwellers* and *Wend Kuuni* as examples.

901
L'Algérie Vue par Son Cinéma, edited by Jean-Pierre Brossard. Locarno: International Film Festival, 1981. 184pp.
    Essays reviewing contemporary Algerian film and its role in projecting an Algerian image.

902
Burton, Julianne. "Marginal Cinemas and Mainstream Critical Theory." *Screen* 26, no. 3/4 (May 1985): 2-21.
    An examination of the relationship between Third World cinema and 'First World' criticism. Rebutted by Teshome H. Gabriel (Item # 1150).

903
Camera Nigra: Le Discours du Film Africain. Brussels: OCIC/L'Harmattan, 1984. 227pp.
    Collection of essays on African film, including use of language, historical and technical aspects.

904
Cameron, Kenneth M. *Africa on Film: Beyond Black and White*. New York: Continuum, 1994. 240p.
    A study of the way that Africa and Africans are depicted in American and British films, examining not only racism but issues of class and gender. 18 page filmography. 5 page bibliography. Index.

905
---. "Paul Robeson, Eddie Murphy and Film Text of "Africa"." *Text and Performance Quarterly* 10, no. 4 (October 1990): 282-293.
    A discussion of the image of Africa in Western films, comparing roles played by Paul Robeson and Eddie Murphy to illustrate the ways that image has changed over time. The author makes the point that the pain and humiliation that Robeson endured provided a necessary foundation for Murphy's self-confident comedy.

906
Cancel, Robert. "Nadine Gordimer Meets Ngugi wa Thiong'o: Text into Film in "Oral History"." *Research in African Literatures* 26, no. 3 (September 1995): 36-48.
    An analysis of the transformation of Nadine Gordimer's short story "Oral History" into a film made for television.

907
Carchidi, Victoria. "Representing South Africa: Apartheid from Print to Film." *Film and History* , no. 1 (February 1991): 20-27.
    An analysis of three recent major films on South Africa: *Cry Freedom*, *A World Apart*, and *A Dry White Season*, noting that in each the focus is on the effects of apartheid and the events of the film on a White character, although each depicts the arrest, torture and death of a Black South African. The author feels that this reflects the difficulty of portraying apartheid to audiences outside South Africa.

Film

908

Cham, Mbye Baboucar. "African Women and Cinema: A Conversation with Anne Mungai." *Research in African Literatures* 25, no. 3 (September 1994): 93-104.
>Transcript of an interview with the Kenyan filmmaker Anne Mungai done at the Second Milan Festival of African Cinema, focusing on her film *Saikiti*.

909

---. "Art and Ideology in the Work of Sembene Ousmane and Haile Gerima." *Présence Africaine* , no. 1 (1984): 79-91.
>A study of two major African filmmakers, who, while very different in background, have both contributed to defining what the author calls "the quintessential African film".

910

---. "Film Production in West Africa: 1979-1981." *Présence Africaine* , no. 4 (1982): 168-187.
>An overview of filmmaking in West Africa, noting activities in Nigeria and Ghana, where new filmmakers were emerging, and in Francophone Africa, which already had an established reputation in the film industry.

911

---. "Film Production in West Africa, 1979-1981." *Film and Politics in the Third World*, 13-29. Edited by John D. H. Downing. New York: Praeger, 1987.
A survey of film making in Ghana, Nigeria, Senegal, Ivory Coast and Cameroon. Bibliographic footnotes. Reprint of #910.

912

---. "Ousmane Sembene and the Aesthetics of African Oral Traditions." *Africana Journal* 13, no. 1/4 (1982): 24-40.
>A discussion of the use of oral tradition in Sembene's films, noting especially the recurring themes of hero and trickster and the use of stylistic language to convey the filmmaker's ideas.

913

Blackframes: Critical Perspectives on Black Independent Cinema, edited by Mbye Baboucar Cham, and Claire Andrade-Watkins. Cambridge: MIT Press, 1988. 85pp.
>Collection of essays on Black filmmakers in Africa and the U.S.

914

Cheriaa, Tahar. *Écrans d'Abondance...ou Cinémas de Liberation en Afrique*. Tunis, Tunisia: Societé Tunisienne de Diffusion, 1979. 312pp.
>An examination of the distribution infrastructure and policies of African countries in regard to film. Nearly half the book is devoted to an appendix containing texts of

national legislation and international conventions concerning film production and distribution.

915

Chirol, Marie-Magdeleine. "The Missing Narrative in *Wend Kuuni* (Time and Space)." *Research in African Literatures* 26, no. 3 (September 1995): 49-56.
> An analysis of the symbolism in the film *Wend Kuuni* by Burkina Faso filmmaker Gaston Kabore.

916

"Cinéastes d'Afrique Noire." *L'Afrique Littéraire et Artistique*, no. 49 (1978): 1-192.
> A special issue devoted to Sub-Saharan African film, with profiles of fifty African filmmakers, essays discussing themes, economics, and ethics of African films, and a country-by-country chronology of the development of filmmaking.

917

"Le Cinéma et l'Afrique." *La Vie Africaine*, no. 15 (June 1961): 3-49. Special Issue.
> A collection of short articles on all phases of African film.

918

"The Cinema of Jean Rouch." *Visual Anthropology* 2, no. 3/4 (1989): Special Issue.
> A special issue containing articles on the French filmmaker, highlighting his African films. 34 page filmography.

919

Cinémas du Maghreb. Paris: L'Afrique Littéraire, 1981. Special issue of *Afrique Littéraire* No. 59-60, 1981. 248pp.
> An overview of cinema in Algeria, Tunisia and Morocco, with articles covering the main trends and influences in each country, interviews with filmmakers and filmographies. Numerous photographs.

920

Colleyn, Jean-Paul. "Manières et Matières du *Cinéma* Anthropologique." *Cahiers d'Études Africaines* 33, no. 1 (1990): 101-116.
> A review of anthropological films and literature about them noting changes in approach, subject matter and technique. 2 page filmography.

921

Collinge, J. "Under Fire." *American Film* 11, no. 2 (1985): 30-38, 78.
> A South African journalist discusses the problems of independent South African filmmakers under apartheid. Inserts in the article comment on the cultural boycott and actions of U.S. filmmakers and entertainers.

Film

922

Convents, Guido. *Préhistoire du Cinéma en Afrique 1897-1918: à la Recherche des Images Oubliées*. Brussels: OCIC, 1986. 235pp.
 A study of film in Africa during the early colonial period, with emphasis on the uses of film for propaganda purposes by the colonial powers, both in their dealings with their African colonies and their interaction with the rest of the world. Numerous photographs and reproductions of posters and flyers of the period. 13 page bibliography. Index.

923

Cotlow, Lewis. *Zanzabuku (Dangerous Safari)*. New York: Rinehart, 1956.
 An account by British filmmaker Cotlow of his travels in Africa during the making of *Zanzabuku* and *Savage Splendor*. The twenty pages of photographs, along with the titles of the films, illustrate the negative image of Africa projected by his work. Index.

924

Crowdus, Gary, and Udayan Gupta. "A Luta Continua: An Interview With Robert Van Lierop." *Cinéaste* 9, no. 1 (September 1978): 26-31.
 An interview with a Black American political activist who became a filmmaker in his frustration in trying to find an established filmmaker who would undertake a film on the liberation struggle in Portuguese Africa. His films are *A Luta Continua* and *O Povo Organizado*.

925

Cyr, Helen W. *A Filmography of the Third World*. Metuchen, N. J.: Scarecrow, 1976. 319pp.
 African section contains 38 pages of films, mostly documentaries, with brief annotations as well as a short section, "The Third World in Europe", which lists several African films dealing with the experience of Africans in Europe or the European view of Africa. List of distributors. Index.

926

---. *A Filmography of the Third World (1976-1983). An Annotated List of 16mm Films*. Metuchen, N. J.: Scarecrow, 1985. 275pp.
 A filmography of documentary films. 31 pages of entries on Africa.

927

---. *The Third World in Film and Video, 1984-1990*. Metuchen, NJ: Scarecrow Press, 1991. 246pp.
 A filmography of film and videos concerning the Third World. 32 pages of citations for African films, mostly documentaries.

928

Dadci, Younes. *Dialogues Algérie-Cinéma: Première Histoire du Cinéma Algérien*. Paris: Editions Dadci, 1970. 150pp.
 A collection of articles tracing the history of Algerian film and its role in Algerian history.

929

Davis, Peter. "*Les Dieux Sont Tombés sur la Tête*, de Jamie Uys: Délices et Ambiguités de la Position du Missionaire!" *Le Cinéma Sud-Africain Est-il Tombé sur la Tête?*, 52-58. Edited by Keyan G. Tomaselli. Paris: Cerf, 1986.
>A discussion of the conflicting views and interpretations of Jamie Uys' film *The Gods Must Be Crazy*. The French translation of the film title is the source of the title of the volume.

930

Davis, Peter, and Daniel Riesenfeld. *A Viewer's Guide for "In Darkest Hollywood: Cinema and Apartheid", Two One-Hour Video Programs on Hollywood and South African Filmmaking During the Apartheid Years*. Bloomington, IN: Indiana University African Studies Program, 1995. 56pp.
>Outline of the videos, with an introduction focusing on filmmaking and relations between Blacks and Whites in South Africa, suggested before- and after-viewing questions to guide group discussion, and a list of suggested further reading. Numerous photographs. Foreword by Lewis Nkosi.

931

DeBona, Guerric. "Into Africa: Orson Welles and *Heart of Darkness*." *Cinema Journal* 33, no. 3 (March 1994): 16-34.
>An analysis of Welles' planned, but never produced, film version of Conrad's *Heart of Darkness*, a novel that many African and other scholars feel expresses racism and contributes to a negative image of Africa.

932

Debrix, Jean-René. "Le Cinéma Africain." *Afrique Contemporaine* , no. 38/39 (July 1968): 7-12.
>An overview of African film and filmmaking, noting the image of Africa as savage and exotic in early films by Western filmmakers, and the progress of African filmmakers in dispelling those negative images.

933

---. "Le Cinéma Africain." *Afrique Contemporaine* , no. 49 (November 1968): 2-6.
>Continuing an examination of the African film industry begun in an earlier issue of *Afrique Contemporaine*, the author explores the economic side of the industry.

934

DeLuca, Laura, and Shadrack Kamenya. "Representation of Female Circumcision in *Finzan, a Dance for the Heroes*." *Research in African Literatures* 26, no. 3 (September 1995): 83-87.
>Discussion of the issues of female circumcision as portrayed in the Malian film *Finzan* by filmmaker Cheik Oumar Sissoko.

Film

935
Description et Analyse Filmique: "Touki Bouki" de Djibril Diop Mambety.
Abidjan: Université Nationale de Côte D'Ivoire, 1982. 159pp.
    An analytic presentation of the script of Mambety's *Touki Bouki*, with notes on filming techniques and sound effects, accompanied by critical essays.

936
Diakite, Madubuko. "Film and Cultural Signification: Reconsidering Minority and Third World Films." *Journal of the University Film Association* 30, no. 3 (June 1978): 19-23.
    A discussion of Black and Third World filmmaking arguing that these films are largely ignored or misunderstood in global film history.

937
---. *Film, Culture, and the Black Filmmaker: A Study of Functional Relationships and Parallel Developments.* New York: Arno Press, 1980. 184pp.
    A reprint of the author's dissertation at the University of Stockholm, this work focuses mostly on Black American filmmakers but includes an overview of Black African filmmakers and an analysis of the films of Ousmane Sembene.

938
Diawara, Manthia. "African Cinema: The Background and the Economic Context of Production." Ph.D. diss., Indiana University, 1985. 209pp.

939
---. "African Cinema: FESPACO, an Evaluation." *Third World Affairs* (1986): 404-411.
    An historical overview and assessment of the Festival Panafricain du *Cinéma* de Ouagadougou (FESPACO) from its beginning in 1969 to the writing of the article.

940
---. *African Cinema: Politics and Culture.* Bloomington, IN: Indiana University Press, 1992. 192pp.
    With chapters focusing on individual regions, this study examines the technical and social history of filmmaking in Africa. 7 page bibliography. Index.

941
---. "The Artist as the Leader of the Revolution: The History of the Federation Panafricaine des Cinéastes." *Cinema of the Black Diaspora: Diversity, Dependence, and Oppositionality*, 95-110. Edited by Michael T. Martin. Detroit: Wayne State University Press, 1995.
    A history of the Federation Panafricaine des Cinéastes (FEPACI) with a discussion of the problems facing African filmmakers.

942
---. "Film in Anglophone Africa: A Brief Survey." *Blackframes: Critical Perspectives on Black Independent Cinema*, 37-49. Edited by Mbye Baboucar Cham, and Claire Andrade-Watkins. Cambridge, MA: MIT Press, 1988.
   A brief overview of feature film production in English speaking Africa. Photographs.

943
---. "Oral Literature and African Film: Narratology in *Wend Kuuni*." *Présence Africaine*, no. 142 (1987): 36-49.
   A discussion of the theory advanced by Ethiopian filmmaker Haile Gerima that African filmmakers should turn to oral rather than written literature, using as an example *Wend Kuuni*, a film by Gaston Kabore of Burkina Faso.

944
---. "Oral Literature and African Film: Narratology in *Wend Kuuni*." *Questions of Third Cinema*, 199-211. edited by Jim Pines, and Paul Willemen. London: British Film Institute, 1989.
   A discussion of the relationship of oral literature and film, using the film *Wend Kuuni* as an example.

945
---. "Popular Culture and Oral Traditions in African Film." *Film Quarterly* 41, no. 3 (1988): 6-14.
   A discussion of the frames of reference used in criticism of African film. Most Western critics ignore or misinterpret the use of oral tradition in African films, and do not understand how those oral traditions shape cinematic technique.

946
Diawara, Manthia, and Elizabeth Robinson. "New Perspectives in African Cinema: An Interview with Cheick Oumar Sissoko." *Film Quarterly* 41, no. 2 (1988): 43-48.
   The Malian filmmaker discusses his latest film, *Nyamanton* (The Garbage Boys), and the problems of producing films in Africa.

947
Dickson, W. K-L. *The Biograph in Battle: Its Story in the South African War Related with Personal Experiences.* Madison, NJ: Fairleigh Dickinson University Press, 1995. 296pp. Facsimile reprint of work originally published by T. Fisher Unwin, London, in 1901.
   Personal account, in diary format, of the inventor of an early movie camera (the biograph) who filmed the Boer War.

948
Dine, Philip. *Images of the Algerian War: French Fiction and Film, 1954-1992.* Oxford: Clarendon Press, 1994. 267pp.

Film

A study of propaganda and image manipulation in France concerning the war in Algeria. Filmography. 19 page bibliography. Index.

949

Ditmars, Hadani. "The Economics of African Cinema." *African Business*, no. 195 (January 1995): 38-39.
A report focusing on the Carthage Film Festival in Tunisia which analyses the financial status of the African film industry in general.

950

Dosumu, Sanya. "The Shortcomings of Producing Films in Nigeria." *The Development and Growth of the Film Industry in Nigeria: Proceedings of a Seminar on the Film Industry and Cultural Identity in Nigeria*, 61-72. Edited by Alfred E. Opubor, and Onuora E. Nwuneli. New York: Third Press International, 1979.
A frank discussion of the problems of film production in Nigeria: money, infrastructure, dishonest practices.

951

Film and Politics in the Third World, edited by John D. H. Downing. New York: Praeger, 1987.
A collection of essays, more than half dealing with Africa.

952

Dunn, Kevin. "Lights...Camera...Africa: Images of Africa and Africans in Western Popular Films of the 1930s." *African Studies Review* 39, no. 1 (April 1996): 149-175.
An analysis of the categories of images of Africa and Africans in selected films and the influence they had on American and British audiences during the Depression and years prior to World War II.

953

Anthropology - Reality - Cinema: The Films of Jean Rouch, edited by Mick Eaton. Colchester: Spottiswoode Ballantyne, 1979. 77pp.

954

Educational Media Resources on Egypt. Washington: U. S. Dept. of Health, Education and Welfare, 1977. 57pp.
Annotated filmography of films, videos and filmstrips suitable for use in most classroom situations. Index.

955

Egbe, Edison. "The Language of Film: Its Application to the Nigerian Cultural Environment." *The Development and Growth of the Film Industry in Nigeria: Proceedings of a Seminar on the Film Industry and Cultural*

Identity in Nigeria, 89-96. Edited by Alfred E. Opubor, and Onuora E. Nwuneli. New York: Third Press International, 1979.
    A theoretical approach to the way in which film expresses the ideas of the filmmaker.

956

Der Afrikanisch-Arabische Film: Eine Dokumentation: Retrospektive zur XXVII Internationalen Filmwoche Mannheim, edited by Ambros Eichenberger et al. Mannheim: Direktorium der Internationalen Filmwoche Mannheim, 1978. 270pp.
    Papers from a film festival and conference held in Mannheim, Germany, in 1969.

957

Ekwuazi, Hyginus. *Film in Nigeria*. Ibadan: Moonlight Publishers, 1987. 142pp.
    An assessment of approaches to the study the role of film in Nigerian culture as well as the development of filmmaking in Nigeria.

958

---. "Toward the Decolonization of the African Film." *Africa Media Review* 5, no. 2 (1991): 95-.
    A discussion of what makes a truly African film, with arguments that the popularity of U.S. and Indian films shapes both films made in Africa and the film industry there.

959

---. "Towards a Development Scheme for the Nigerian Film Culture." *Nigeria Magazine* 54, no. 2 (April 1986): 56-67.
    An historical overview of the Nigerian film industry, both pre-Independence and post-Independence, with suggestions for further development.

960

---. "Towards a Theory of Film Acting: The Nigerian Experience." *Africa Media Review* 4, no. 3 (1990): 96-.
    A discussion of theory and technique for film acting in Nigeria, and how it is similar and differs from acting on the stage in traditional dramas.

961

No...Not Hollywood: Essays and Speeches of Brendan Shehu, edited by Hyginus Ekwuazi, and Yakubu Nasidi. Jos, Nigeria: Nigerian Film Corporation, 1992. 189pp.
    A collection of speeches and writing by the General Manager of the Nigerian Film Corporation. Index.

Film

962
Operative Principles of the Film Industry: Towards a Film Policy for Nigeria, edited by Hyginus Ekwuazi, and Yakubu Nasidi. Jos, Nigeria: Nigerian Film Corporation, 1992. 347pp.
   A collection of essays on policies for the film industry in Nigeria, including issues of copyright, censorship, cultural content and development.

963
Ekwuene, Laz. "The Music Composer, Film and Nigerian Cultural Identity." *The Development and Growth of the Film Industry in Nigeria: Proceedings of a Seminar on the Film Industry and Cultural Identity in Nigeria*, 105-112. Edited by Alfred E. Opubor, and Onuora E. Nwuneli. New York: Third Press International, 1979.
   An overview of music in Nigerian film.

964
Enahoro, Augustine-Ufua. "Film Makers and Film Making in Nigeria: Problems and Prospects." *Africa Media Review* 3, no. 3 (1989): 98-109.

965
---. "Towards a Philosophy of African Cinema." *Africa Media Review* 3, no. 1 (1988): 134-148.
   A review of the filmmaker's responsibility to express a true African culture and to combat the inroads of Euro-American media, which is eroding that culture.

966
Enckell, Monique, and Smail Benassir. "*Noua*, un Chef-d'Oeuvre du "Cinéma *Djidid*" Algérien." *L'Afrique Littéraire et Artistique*, no. 28 (April 1973): 88-93.
   A discussion of the work of Algerian filmmaker Abdelaziz Tolbi, analyzing both Tolbi's message and the artistic techniques used to portray it.

967
Essoe, Gabe. *Tarzan of the Movies: A Pictorial History of More than Fifty Years of Edgar Rice Burroughs' Legendary Hero*. Secaucus, NJ: Citadel Press, 1973. 208pp.
   With numerous photographs, this work describes the productions and casts of hundreds of versions of the adventures of Tarzan and discusses the personality of the man who created the now controversial fictional character.

968
Faris, James C. "*Southeast Nuba*: A Biographical Statement." *Anthropological Filmmaking: Anthropological Perspectives on the Production of Film and Video for General Public Audiences*, 111-121. Edited by Jack R. Rollwagen. Chur, Switzerland: Harwood Academic Publishers, 1988.

A personal account of the making of the BBC documentary *Southeast Nuba* describing the ethical and political issues and their implications for other anthropological filmmaking.

969

Films on Africa: an Educators Guide to 16mm films. Madison, WI: African Studies Program, University of Wisconsin, 1979. 71pp.

Annotated filmography of 16mm films on Africa suitable for use in most classrooms.

970

Gadjigo, Samba et al. *Ousmane Sembene: Dialogues with Critics and Writers.* Amherst, MA: University of Massachusetts Press, 1993. 122pp.

Proceedings of a conference culminating a visit of the filmmaker to the Five Colleges African Studies Council. Contains critical perspectives on Sembene's work, and remarks on language and the writer by Toni Cade Bambara, Earl Lovelace, Ngugi wa Thiong'o, John Wideman and Ousmane Sembene. Includes a transcription of their discussion and Sembene's remarks following a showing of *Camp de Thiaroye*. 3 page bibliography of critical works on Sembene.

971

Gardies, André. *Cinéma d'Afrique Noire Francophone: l'Espace-Miroir.* Paris: L'Harmattan, 1989. 191pp.

An exploration of the themes of Francophone African film using the metaphor of space as its theoretical framework.

972

Gardies, André, and Pierre Haffner. *Régards Sur le Cinéma Négro-Africain.* Brussels: OCIC, 1987. 234pp.

A discussion of several aspects of African film: aesthetics, symbolism, and expression of identity, together with analysis of specific films and notes on the 10th FESPACO in 1987. 16 pages of photographs.

973

Gavshon, Harriet. "Levels of Intervention in Films Made for African Audiences in South Africa." *Critical Arts* 2, no. 4 (1983): 13-21.

An overview of controls on films made for Black South Africans, focusing on the changes - and lack thereof - since the Muldergate scandal.

974

Gerogakas, Dan, and Lenny Rubenstein. *The Cinéaste Interviews on the Art and Politics of the Cinema.* Chicago: Lake View Press, 1983. 396pp.

Contains an interview with Ousmane Sembene.

975

Ghali, Noureddine. "An Interview with Sembene Ousmane." *Film and Politics in the Third World*, 41-54. edited by John D. H. Downing. New York: Praeger, 1987.

Film

The interview focuses on *Emitai* and *Xala*.

976

Gray, John. *Blacks in Film and Television: A Pan-African Bibliography of Films, Filmmakers and Performers.* New York: Greenwood Press, 1990. 496pp.

977

Grella, George. "The Colonial Movie and *The Man Who Would be King.*" *Texas Studies in Literature and Language* 22, no. 2 (June 1980): 246-262.
   Although the discussion centers on a film set in India, this commentary on colonial attitudes, as expressed in modern films, includes African examples.

978

Guback, Thomas. "American Films and the African Market." *Critical Arts* 3, no. 3 (1984): 1-14.
   An analysis of films as a commodity and what effect the importation of American films has on the economies and social agendas of African countries.

979

Gutsche, Thelma. *The History and Social Significance of Motion Pictures in South Africa, 1895-1940.* Cape Town: Howard Timmins, 1972. 404pp.
   An in-depth history of film production and the cinema in South Africa, including commentary on censorship. Index.

980

Haffner, Pierre. "Entretien avec le Père Alexandre Van den Heuvel, Pionnier d'un "Cinéma Missionaire" au Congo." *L'Afrique Littéraire et Artistique* , no. 48 (1978): 86-95.
   An interview with a Roman Catholic missionary who was instrumental in developing films for African audiences which furthered missionary efforts.

981

---. *Essai sur les Fondements du Cinéma Africain.* Abidjan: Nouvelles Éditions Africaines, 1978. 274pp.
   A study of cinema in Africa focusing on the role of imported films in African society and reactions of African audiences to them. Includes an appraisal of the aesthetics of African film. Appendices include texts of interviews and other documents used in the analysis.

982

---. *Palabres sur le Cinématographe: Initiation au Cinéma.* Kinshasa, Zaire: Les Presses Africaines, 1978. 270pp.
   A study which places African film in the context of films made worldwide. Theoretical discussion with synopses of films. Photographs. 6 page bibliography.

Film

983
Haile Gerima. "Triangular Cinema, Breaking Toys and Dinknesh vs Lucy." *Questions of Third Cinema*, 65-89. Edited by Jim Pines, and Paul Willemen. London: British Film Institute, 1989.
    The Ethiopian filmmaker explores the concepts of cinema as a medium both for storytelling and activism, and encourages Third World cinema to remain true to its origins.

984
Hall, Susan. "African Women on Film." *Africa Report* 22, no. 1 (January 1977): 15-17.
    A brief commentary on women in African films, based on a review of eight documentary and feature films in which women play a central role.

985
Hallis, Ron. "Movie Magic in Mozambique." *Cinéma Canada*, no. 62 (February 1980): 18-24.
    A personal account of the experiences of a Canadian *Cooperante* recruited by the Mozambique Ministry of Information to teach motion picture laboratory technique who used the opportunity to make documentary films of village life.

986
Hanna, Judith Lynne. "Frame by Frame: Revelation of Sex Roles Through Distinctive Feature Analysis and Comments on Field Research, Film and Notation." *Journal of Black Studies* 19, no. 4 (June 1989): 422-441.
    Discussion of the uses of film in research on African dance.

987
Harrow, Kenneth. "Sembene Ousmane's *Xala*: the Use of Film and Novel as Revolutionary Weapon." *Studies in Twentieth Century Literature* 4, no. 2 (1980): 177-188.
    An analysis of Sembene's *Xala* comparing the effectiveness of film and novel respectively in conveying the message of social and political protest.

988
Haynes, Jonathan. "Nigerian Cinema: Structural Adjustments." *Research in African Literatures* 26, no. 3 (September 1995): 97-119.
    History and critical overview of filmmaking and its development in Nigeria.

989
Hennebelle, Guy. "ben Ammar: Dans *Une Si Simple Histoire* Je Me Demande: Que Faire des Intellectuels Tunisiens?" *L'Afrique Littéraire et Artistique*, no. 12 (1970): 83-87.
    Interview with Tunisian filmmaker Abdellatif ben Ammar.

Film

990
---. "Le Cinéma Africain à Cannes." *L'Afrique Littéraire et Artistique*, no. 11 (1970): 60-69.
Interviews with Mauritanian filmmaker Med Hondo on his first feature length film *Soleil O* and French filmmaker on his film *Ramparts d'Argile*, a Franco-Algerian production.

991
---. "Cinéma et Émigration." *L'Afrique Littéraire et Artistique*, no. 9 (1970): 56-78.
A discussion of African filmmakers working in France with reviews of three films and interviews with their directors.

992
---. "Les Cinémas Africains en 1972." *L'Afrique Littéraire et Artistique*, no. 20 (1972): 371pp.
A special issue of *L'Afrique Littéraire et Artistique* devoted to African film. Chapters include overviews of the films of Egypt, the Maghreb, and Francophone Sub-Saharan Africa, along with discussion of their themes, filmographies and biographical notes on filmmakers.

993
---. "Ecare: *A Nous Deux, France* est l'Analyse Clinique d'un Processus d'Acculturation." *L'Afrique Littéraire et Artistique*, no. 12 (1970): 76-82.
Interview with the Ivoirien filmmaker Desiré Ecare following a special award for his film *A Nous Deux, France!* at the Festival of Young Film at Hyeres.

994
---. "Entretien avec Jean-René Debrix." *L'Afrique Littéraire et Artistique*, no. 43 (1977): 77-89.
Interview with the French Minister for Cooperation, who had made an important contribution to the development of African film, discussing his views on the possibility of a Pan-African film industry encompassing North Africa as well as sub-Saharan Africa, and the potential for nationalism in African film.

995
---. "Jean Rouch, Regarde-t-il les Africains "Comme des Insectes"?" *L'Afrique Littéraire et Artistique*, no. 10 (1970): 66-80.
Report of an interview and debate with French filmmaker Jean Rouch, Senegalese filmmaker Mahama Traore and Ivoirien filmmaker Bassori Timite, in which individual film techniques and artistic visions are discussed, along with Sembene's assessment that Jean Rouch 'regards Africans as insects'.

996
---. "Michael Raeburn Parle de son Film Tanzanien: "Par delà les Plaines où l'Homme Est Né"." *L'Afrique Littéraire et Artistique*, no. 45 (1977): 82-87.
Interview with the maker of *Beyond the Plains Where Man Was Born*, who discusses the making of that film and his own conception of himself as an African filmmaker, despite his nationality.

997

---. "Où Va le Cinéma Algérien, que Devient le "Cinéma *Djidid*"?" *L'Afrique Littéraire et Artistique* , no. 40 (1976): 83-105.
    A round table discussion with four Algerian filmmakers on the idea of *Cinéma Djidid* (New Cinema) and their individual approaches to their craft.

998

---. "Ousmane Sembene: "Pour Moi, le Cinéma est un Moyen d'Action Politique, Mais....."." *L'Afrique Littéraire et Artistique* , no. 7 (1969): 73-82.
    Interview with the Senegalese filmmaker discussing his political and social philosophies as they affect his filmmaking.

999

---. "*Les Passagers* Un Reportage d'Annie Tresgot sur l'Émigration Algérienne en France." *L'Afrique Littéraire et Artistique* , no. 17 (June 1971): 75-83.
    Interview with French filmmaker Annie Tresgot on her film depicting the life of Algerian immigrants in France.

1000

---. "*Poulou le Magnifique*." *L'Afrique Littéraire et Artistique* , no. 18 (August 1971): 72-77.
    Interview with Algerian filmmaker Derri Berkani discussing his techniques.

1001

---. "Pour le Declenchement de l'Insurrection Noire en Rhodesie Blanche le Compte à Rebours est Commencé." *L'Afrique Littéraire et Artistique* , no. 6 (1969): 45-51.
    Interview with filmmaker Michael Raeburn on the making of his film *Rhodesia Count Down*, which depicts the buildup to the Zimbabwe war of independence, touching on the censorship he encountered and his strategies for getting around it.

1002

---. "Une Révélation dans le Cinéma Egyptien: *La Momie* de Chadi Abdel Salam." *L'Afrique Littéraire et Artistique* , no. 14 (1970): 62-70.
    Interview with Egyptian filmmaker Chadi Abdel Salam about his film *La Momie* which depicted the illegal trade in Egyptian antiquities.

1003

---. "Table Ronde: Pour ou Contre un Cinéma Africain Engagé?" *L'Afrique Littéraire et Artistique* , no. 19 (October 1971): 87-93.
    A roundtable discussion among filmmakers Sarah Maldoror (Guadaloupe), Ousmane Sembene (Senegal), Youssef Chahine (Egypt), Timité Bassori (Côte d'Ivoire), and Samir Nasri (Lebanon) at the Carthage film festival in October 1970, about the concept and practice of 'engagement' in African film.

Film

1004

---. *"Traces*. Hamid Bennani: 'J'ai Voulu Denoncer la Sclèrose de la Societé Marocaine et Musulmane." *Afrique Littéraire et Artistique* , no. 16 (April 1971): 71-78.
>Interview with the Moroccan filmmaker Hamid Bennani on his film *Traces* and the filmmakers who influenced on his work.

1005

---. "Le IIIe Festival de Carthage." *L'Afrique Littéraire et Artistique* , no. 15 (1971): 66-84.
>A report on the 3rd Carthage Film Festival, and an interview with Egyptian filmmaker Youssef Chahine on his film *Al Ikhtyar* (*Le Choix*).

1006

---. "Le Troisième Festival Panafricain du Cinéma de Ouagadougou." *L'Afrique Littéraire et Artistique* , no. 22 (March 1972): 88-100.
>Report on the Third Pan African Film Festival held in Ouagadougou in 1972 discussing themes of the films and noting the success of Nigerien films both in terms of prize and audience response.

1007

---. "*Yan-Diga*: l'Exode Rural au Niger vu par Serge Moati." *L'Afrique Littéraire et Artistique* , no. 13 (1970): 58-67.
>Interview with Nigerien filmmaker Serge Moati on his career, techniques and artistic vision.

1008

Hennebelle, Monique. "Cinéma et Émigration." *L'Afrique Littéraire et Artistique* , no. 32 (August 1974): 20-34.
>An exploration of the lives of African immigrants in France as portrayed in films. Summaries of films are arranged in three main thematic categories: reasons for immigration, conditions of immigrant life, and labor organization.

1009

---. "Coup de Tonnerre dans le Cinéma Algérien: le "Cinéma *Djidid*" Fait Irruption." *L'Afrique Littéraire et Artistique* , no. 29 (June 1973): 53-92.
>An exploration of Algeria's "new cinema" and its political and aesthetic manifestations, with interviews with seven Algerian filmmakers.

1010

---. "Entretien avec Tewfik Salah: "Mes Six Films Sont Fables sur le Destin des Peuples Arabes"." *L'Afrique Littéraire et Artistique* , no. 26 (December 1972): 89-105.
>Interview with Egyptian filmmaker Tewfik Salah on the themes of his films, his experiences in making them, and the filmmakers who have influenced his craft.

1011
---. "La Nouvelle Vague du Cinéma Tunisien." *L'Afrique Littéraire et Artistique*, no. 25 (October 1972): 67-81.
   Interviews with three Tunisian filmmakers discussing their techniques, philosophies, and political messages.

1012
---. "*Sambizanga*: un Film de Sarah Maldoror sur les Débuts de la Guerre de Liberation en Angola." *L'Afrique Littéraire et Artistique*, no. 28 (April 1973): 78-87.
   An interview with Guadaloupe filmmaker Sarah Maldoror, wife of Angolan Mario de Andrade, discussing her work and her realistic style of film.

1013
Hepburn, Katherine. *The Making of The African Queen or How I Went to Africa with Bogart, Bacall and Huston and Almost Lost my Mind*. New York: Knopf, 1987. 129pp.
   The actress's recollection of the filming of *The African Queen* on location,.

1014
Hondo, Abid Med. "The Cinema of Exile." *Film and Politics in the Third World*, 69-76. Edited by John D. H. Downing. New York: Praeger, 1987.
   The author is a filmmaker born in Mauritania and uses his own experience of exile as a basis for his films' themes.

1015
Horatio-Jones, Edward B. "Historical Review of the Cinema in West Africa and the Black World and its Implication for a Film Industry in Nigeria." *The Development and Growth of the Film Industry in Nigeria: Proceedings of a Seminar on the Film Industry and Cultural Identity in Nigeria*, 73-88. Edited by Alfred E. Opubor and Onuora E. Nwuneli. New York: Third Press International, 1979.
   A brief historical overview and firm statement of the bitterness of Nigerian filmmakers that the country imports more films than it supports locally.

1016
Ilbo, Ousmane. *Le Cinéma au Niger*. Brussels: OCIC, 1993. 140pp.
   History and overview of film in Niger, including biographical and critical notes on Nigerien filmmakers. 31 page bibliography.

1017
Iyam, David Uru. "The Silent Revolutionaries: Ousmane Sembene's *Emitai*, *Xala* and *Ceddo*." *African Studies Review* 29, no. 4 (December 1986): 79-87.
   A discussion of common themes and character types in Sembene's films, where strength is expressed by silence.

Film

1018

Jaidi, Moulay Driss. *Le Cinéma au Maroc.* Rabat: Assabah, 1991. 174pp.
> A study of film in Morocco, covering government involvement, distribution infrastructure, themes of films, and problems of production. 8 page bibliography. Filmography of feature length films.

1019

Jell-Bahlsen, Sabine. "On the Making *Eze Nwata - The Small King.*" *Anthropological Filmmaking: Anthropological Perspectives on the Production of Film and Video for General Public Audiences*, 197-221. Edited by Jack R. Rollwagen. Chur, Switzerland: Harwood Academic Publishers, 1988.
> A personal account of the author's fieldwork among the Igbo in eastern Nigeria and the subsequent making of an ethnographic film of religious ceremonies. Technical and theoretical issues are discussed.

1020

Jutras, Dominque. *Images d'Ailleurs: Films Canadiens sur l'Afrique et le Monde Créole 1947 à 1988.* Montréal: Les Éditions du Cidihca, 1991. 474pp.
> An analysis of images of "the other", peoples of the Third World in Canadian film. Features interviews with 14 filmmakers. 228 page filmography. Index.

1021

Kamphausen, Hannes. "Cinema in Africa, A Survey." *Cinéaste* 5, no. 2 (March 1972): 28-41.
> An overview of films and filmmaking throughout Africa, with statistical tables showing figures for cinema facilities as well as data on radio, television, and newspaper development.

1022

Kasongo Ibanda Ngozulu. *Le "Cinéma Pour Africains", Acte d'Influence à Visée Persuasive.* Louvain-la-Neuve: Université Catholique de Louvain, 1989. 193pp.
> Analysis of the ways that film can affect opinion, and a discussion of theoretical issues. 14 page bibliography.

1023

Kerr, David. "The Best of Both Worlds? Colonial Film Policy and Practice in Northern Rhodesia and Nyasaland." *Critical Arts* 7, no. 2 (1993): 11-42.
> An historical overview of Colonial filmmaking and distribution, focusing on policy, the educational and propaganda objectives and the audiences of the films made.

1024

Khan, M. *An Introduction to the Egyptian Cinema.* London: Informatics, 1969. 93pp.
> An historical overview of film in Egypt with biographical sketches and filmographies of major filmmakers and actors. Numerous photographs.

1025
Khlifi, Omar. *L'Histoire du Cinéma en Tunisie*. Tunis, Tunisia: Societé Tunisienne de Diffusion, 1970. 239pp.
> History of film production in Tunisia, including capsule descriptions of films. Photographs.

1026
Kindem, Gorham H., and Martha Steele. "Women in Sembene's Films." *Jump Cut*, no. 36 (1991): 52-60.
> A discussion of the realistic and symbolic role of women in Sembene's work.

1027
Klotman, Phyllis Rauch. *Frame by Frame: A Black Filmography*. Bloomington: Indiana University Press, 1979. 700pp.
> A large and inclusive listing of films which involve Blacks in any capacity. Includes African produced films and films about Africa, filmed outside Africa.

1028
Landy, Marcia. "Political Allegory and Engaged Cinema: Sembene's *Xala*." *Cinema Journal* 23, no. 3 (March 1984): 31-46.
> A discussion of Sembene's themes and techniques, specifically the use of allegory, montage and satire.

1029
---. "Politics and Style in *Black Girl*." *Jump Cut*, no. 27 (July 1982): 23-25.
> The author relates Sembene's film *La Noire de...* (*Black Girl*) to the political philosophies of Amilcar Cabral and Frantz Fanon.

1030
Larson, Charles R. "The Film Version of Achebe's *Things Fall Apart*." *Africana Journal* 13, no. 1/2 (1982): 104-110.
> A commentary on the film of Achebe's novel, which was not distributed commercially in the U.S. and only shown on PBS ten years after its filming. The reviewer finds the film, which combines both *Things Fall Apart* and the later novel *No Longer At Ease*, stunning, but takes note of some of the problems in making a film appealing to both Nigerian and American audiences.

1031
Le Roy, Marie Claire. "Africa's Film Festival." *Africa Report* 15, no. 4 (April 1970): 27-28.
> Report from Ouagadougou's second African Film Festival, with an interview with filmmaker Ousmane Sembene.

1032
Leahy, James. "Taking Apart *A World Apart*." *Monthly Film Bulletin* 57, no. 672 (January 1990): 6-7.
> Report of a seminar on the cinema of apartheid held in London.

Film

1033
Lee, R. B. "The Gods Must Be Crazy - But the Producers Know Exactly What They Are Doing." *Southern Africa Report* (June 1985): 19-20.

1034
Lee, Raymond, and Vernell Coriell. *A Pictorial History of the Tarzan Movies*. Los Angeles: Golden State News, 1966. 80pp.
> An enthusiastic celebration of the popular and controversial films, illustrating many of the points made by more critical analysts. Numerous photographs.

1035
Leprohon, Pierre. *L'Exotisme et le Cinéma*. Paris: J. Susse, 1945. 302pp.
> A discussion of the "exotic" in films, with numerous African examples. Themes include films of explorations, big game hunting, and representations of the colonies. Numerous photographs.

1036
Lester, Julius. "*Mandabi*: Confronting Africa." *Evergreen Review* 14, no. 78 (May 1970): 55-58; 85-89.

1037
Loizos, Peter. *Innovation in Ethnographic Film: From Innocence to Self-Consciousness, 1955-85*. Chicago: University of Chicago Press, 1993. 224pp.
> An examination of ethnographic film practices and techniques with numerous African examples. 10 page bibliography. 5 pages of film references. Index.

1038
Lorber, Howard Z., and Margo Cornelius. "*Bottle Babies* Grave Markers." *Jump Cut*, no. 27 (1982): 33-34.
> Review and discussion of Peter Krieg's documentary *Bottle Babies*, which exposes the infant mortality in Africa caused by use of commercial baby formula rather than breast feeding. The filmmaker blames the firms promoting these products; the reviewers call the practice "social murder".

1039
Lydall, Jean. "Confronting Hamar With Their Films: Questions About Death." *Eyes Across the Water II: Essays on Visual Anthropology and Sociology*, 11-18. Edited by Robert M. Boonzajer Flaes, and Douglas Harper. Amsterdam: Het Spinhaus, 1993.
> A discussion of the making of *The Women Who Smile*, a BBC documentary shot in Ethiopia, including transcripts of conversations with the subjects after they had viewed the film.

1040
---. "Filming *The Women Who Smile*." *Ethnographic Film Aesthetics and Narrative Traditions*, 141-158. Peter Ian Crawford, and Jan Ketil Simonsen. Aarhus, Denmark: Intervention Press, 1992.

A reflection on the making of a documentary film on the Hamar of southern Ethiopia, which used an all-women film crew to capture the true day-to-day lives of women. 2 page bibliography.

1041

MacRae, Suzanne H. "Yeelen: A Political Fable of the *Komo* Blacksmith/Sorcerers." *Research in African Literatures* 26, no. 3 (September 1995): 57-66.
A political and anthropological analysis of Malian filmmaker Souleymane Cisse's film *Yeelen*.

1042

Maillot, Dominique. *Le Régime Administratif du Cinéma au Maroc: Etude Théorique et Pratique*. Rabat: Éditions la Porte, 1961. Collection de la Faculté des Sciences Juridiques, Économiques et Sociales, *Série de Langue Française*, no. 13. 186pp.
History of state-controlled film in Morocco. Appendices include statistical tables, relevant laws, reproductions of forms and permits. 3 page bibliography.

1043

Majerzi, Lotfi. *Le Cinéma Algérien: Institutions-Imaginaire-Idéologie*. Algiers, Algeria: SNED, 1980. 414pp.
Social and cultural history of film in Algeria, focusing on both colonial and post-independence films. 7 page filmography. 7 page bibliography.

1044

Makedonsky, Erik. "Route Étroite pour le Jeune Cinéma Sénégalais." *L'Afrique Littéraire et Artistique*, no. 1 (1968): 54-62.
An exploration of the Senegalese film industry in its early days noting the problems both in presenting African films to European audiences and developing African audiences for those films.

1045

Malkmus, Lizbeth, and Roy Armes. *Arab and African Film Making*. London: Zed Press, 1991. 264pp.
A thorough study of the sociological context, technique and aesthetics of Arab and African cinema, with many of the Arab examples from North Africa. Dictionary of filmmakers. 11 page bibliography. Index.

1046

Mantoux, Thierry. "A Madagascar: Silence, on Tourne!" *L'Afrique Littéraire et Artistique*, no. 27 (April 1973): 71-75.
A vignette of filmmaking in Madagascar, featuring the film *L'Accident* by filmmaker Benoît Ramampy.

1047

Marshall, John. "At the Other End of the Camera." *Visual Anthropology* 5, no. 2 (1992): 167-173.
> Further discussion of Paul Myburgh's *People of the Great Sandface*. (See Items 1188 and 1233)

1048

African Films: the Context of Production, edited by Angela Martin. London: British Film Institute, 1982. *Dossier* no. 6. 126pp.
> A collection of short pieces on film and Africa. Several sections give general background for the understanding of Africa; the sections on film vary from a list of films showing at movie houses in Ghana and Burkina Faso to interviews with African filmmakers. 5 page bibliography.

1049

Cinemas of the Black Diaspora: Diversity, Dependence and Oppositionality, edited by Michael T. Martin. Detroit: Wayne State University Press, 1995. 522pp.
> A collection of essays on Black cinema including a substantial section on film in continental Africa, as well as the Caribbean and South America, Western Europe, and the United States, with some discussion of general theoretical issues. Appendices include reports of conferences. 4 page bibliography. Index.

1050

Masilela, Ntongela. "*Come Back Africa* and South African Film History." *Jump Cut*, no. 36 (1991): 61-65.
> Examines a banned film made by an American in the context of Apartheid censorship, raising questions about the role of South African filmmakers.

1051

Mativo, Kyalo. "Resolving the Cultural Dilemma of the African Film." *Ufahamu* 13, no. 1 (September 1983): 61-65.
> The author gives a precis of the films shown at the second Festival of African Films at UCLA and discusses the themes of cultural deprivation and loss of tradition. This follows up his remarks on the first festival, twelve years earlier. See # 1052.

1052

Mativo, Wilson. "Cultural Dilemma of the African Film." *Ufahamu* 1, no. 3 (December 1970): 64-68.
> Using synopses of several African films as examples, the author explores the themes of cultural deprivation and the loss of traditional ways of life. See # 1051.

1053

Maynard, Richard A. *Africa on Film: Myth and Reality*. Rochelle Park, NJ.: Hayden Books, 1974. 84pp.
> A collection of excerpts from film scripts, reviews and articles illustrating ways in which Africa is misrepresented in film, along with the author's commentary.

Questions for discussion aid its use as a textbook. 3 page filmography and list of film rental sources.

1054
McCaffrey, Kathleen. "African Women on the Screen." *Africa Report* 26, no. 2 (March 1981): 56-58.
   An analysis of the portrayal of women in selected films by African filmmakers, including one by the Guadaloupean woman filmmaker, Sarah Maldoror, who works in Angola.

1055
Megherbi, Abdelghani. *Les Algériens au Miroir du Cinéma Colonial.* Algiers: SNED, 1982. 280pp.
   Examines the image of Algerians as portrayed in French films prior to independence, looking in detail at a large number of films. 2 page bibliography. 5 page filmography.

1056
Mellen, Joan. *Filmguide to the Battle of Algiers.* Bloomington, IN: Indiana University Press, 1973. 82pp.
   Analysis, critique and general information about the film *Battle of Algiers*. 10 page bibliography. Filmography of Gillo Pontecorvo's works.

1057
Mercer, Kobena. "Third Cinema at Edinburgh: Reflections on a Pioneering Event." *Screen* 27, no. 6 (November 1986): 95-102.
   A report of the conference, *Third Cinema: Theories and Practices,* held at the 40th Edinburgh International Film Festival, August 11-13, 1986, which explored the philosophy and technique of African and other Third World filmmakers.

1058
Mermin, Elizabeth. "A Window on Whose Reality? The Emerging Industry of Senegalese Cinema." *Research in African Literatures* 26, no. 3 (September 1995): 120-133.
   A discussion of Senegalese filmmaking as it becomes a full-fledged industry, with emphasis on the financial aspects of filmmaking as well as the content and themes of the films.

1059
Merzak, Allouache. "The Necessity of a Cinema which Interrogates Everyday Life." *Film and Politics in the Third World*, 93-99. Edited by John D. H. Downing. New York: Praeger, 1987.
   An interview with Algerian filmmaker Allouache Merzak on the themes of his films.

1060
Minot, Gilbert. "Toward the African Cinema." *Ufahamu* 12, no. 2 (1983): 37-43.

Film

A brief overview of the status of filmmaking in Africa, its problems, and some proposed solutions.

1061

Morgenthau, Henry. "On Films and Filmmakers." *Africa Report* 14, no. 5/6 (May 1969): 71-75.
   Notes and commentary on the African Film Festival held at Brandeis University in May 1969.

1062

Mortimer, Robert A. "Engaged Film-Making for a New Society." *Africa Report* 15, no. 8 (November 1970): 28-30.
   A discussion of the political commitment of Senegalese filmmakers, and the market for their films in their own country.

1063

Morton-Williams, P. *Cinema in Rural Nigeria: A Field Study of the Impact of Fundamental-Education Films on Rural Audiences in Nigeria.* Ibadan, Nigeria: West African Institute of Social and Economic Research, 1950[?]. 195pp.
   Evaluation of films made for rural education by the Colonial Film Unit.

1064

Mpoyi-Buatu, Th. "Sembene Ousmane's *Ceddo* and Med Hondo's *West Indies*." *Film and Politics in the Third World*, 55-67. Edited by John D. H. Downing. New York: Praeger, 1987.
   A discussion of the two films in terms of political and social implications.

1065

Ngakane, Lionel. "The Cinema in South Africa." *Présence Africaine* 80, no. 4 (1971): 131-133.
   A discussion of films imported to South Africa which are cut, distorted or banned by the Board of Censors, and of films made in South Africa which are not allowed artistic freedom or documentary accuracy, with an appeal to keep struggling against this situation.

1066

Ngansop, Guy Jeremie. *Le Cinéma Camerounais en Crise.* Paris: L'Harmattan, 1987. 143pp.
   Overview of filmmaking and the cinema in Cameroon. Appendices include filmmakers and their films; a filmography; synopses, excerpts from reviews and other information on nine films; reproductions of laws and other documents; descriptions and capacities of movie houses. 6 pages of photographs. 1 page bibliography.

1067
Niang, Sada, and Samba Gadjigo. "Interview With Ousmane Sembene." *Research in African Literatures* 26, no. 3 (September 1995): 174-178.
    The interview focuses on the film *Guelwaar*.

1068
Nixon, Rob. *Homelands, Harlem and Hollywood: South African Culture and the World Beyond*. New York: Routledge, 1994. 305pp.
    A collection of essays looking at South Africa's cultural contacts with the rest of the world, touching on images of South Africa in world media, the influence of Harlem on South African Black artistic expression, and the cultural boycott, among many other topics. Bibliographic notes. Index.

1069
Notcutt, L. A., and G. C. Latham. *The African and the Cinema: an Account of the Work of the Bantu Educational Cinema Experiment During the Period March 1935 to May 1937*. London: Edinburgh House Press, 1937. 256pp.
    Descriptions of the films made and the conditions for production, distribution and screening. Index.

1070
Novicki, Margaret A. "Burkina Faso: A Revolutionary Culture." *Africa Report* 32, no. 4 (July 1987): 57-60.
    A discussion of the place of the Pan African Film Festival (FESPACO) in the life and politics of its base, Burkina Faso.

1071
---. "Interview with King Ampaw." *Africa Report* 32, no. 4 (July 1987): 53-56.
    The Ghanaian filmmaker discusses his own films and the future of African cinema.

1072
Ohrn, Steven G., and Rebecca Riley. *Africa From Reel to Real: An African Filmography*. Waltham, MA: African Studies Association, 1976. 144pp.
    An annotated filmography of 1,300 16mm films on Africa distributed in the United States and Canada. 6 page bibliography.

1073
Okomba Wetshisambi. *Histoire du Cinéma au Zaire Pendant l'Époque Coloniale*. Kinshasa: Institut de Recherches Économiques et Sociales, Université de Kinshasa, 1986. *Lettre de l'I.R.E.S.* no. 11-12. 28pp.
    Historical overview of film in Zaire, focusing on the purposes of the films, their distribution, and the laws governing filmmaking.

Film

1074
Okome, Onookome. "From London to Lagos: the Evolution of Film in Nigeria." *AfterImage* 20, no. 9 (April 1993): 6-7.
    A brief history of filmmaking in Nigeria and a discussion of present-day problems.

1075
The Development and Growth of the Film Industry in Nigeria: Proceedings of a Seminar on the Film Industry and Cultural Identity in Nigeria, edited by Alfred E. Opubor, and Onuora E. Nwuneli. New York: Third Press International, 1979. Published for the National Council for Arts and Culture, Lagos, Nigeria. 119pp.
    A collection of papers by filmmakers, writers and scholars on filmmaking in Nigeria.

1076
Opubor, Alfred E., Onuora E. Nwuneli, and O. Oreh. "The Status, Role and Future of the Film Industry in Nigeria." *The Development and Growth of the Film Industry in Nigeria: Proceedings of a Seminar on the Film Industry and Cultural Identity in Nigeria*, 1-22. Edited by Alfred E. Opubor, and Onuora E. Nwuneli. New York: Third Press International, 1979.
    An overview of the film industry in Nigeria, with recommendations for training of personnel and government support.

1077
Opubor, Alfred E., and Adeyayo Ogunbi. "Ooga Booga: The African Image in American Films." *Other Voices, Other Views: An International Collection of Essays from the Bicentennial*, 343-375. Edited by Robin W. Winks. Westport, CT: Greenwood Press, 1978.
    A discussion of Africa and Africans as portrayed in American films and how the images have changed over time. 17 page filmography.

1078
Otten, Rik. *Le Cinéma dans les Pays des Grands Lacs: Zaire, Rwanda, Burundi*. Brussels: OCIC/L'Harmattan, 1984. 122pp.
    Historical overview of film and filmmaking in the three countries. 12 page list of Zairian filmmakers and their films. 12 pages of photographs. 6 page bibliography.

1079
Overballe, Henrik. "Narrative Traditions Among the Mandinka of West Africa." *Ethnographic Film Aesthetics and Narrative Traditions*, 176-201. Edited by Peter Ian Crawford, and Jan Ketil Simonsen. Aarhus, Denmark: Intervention Press, 1992.
    A study of the role of griots and traditional tales in Mandinka society, concluding with a discussion of Diawara's essay "Oral Literature and African Film: Narratology in *Wend Kuuni*". arguing that Diawara's premise that griots advocate a return to traditionalism and filmmakers want to break out of its straight-jacket is a misrepresentation.

1080

L'Afrique et le Centenaire du Cinéma/Africa and the Centenary of Cinema, Edited by PanAfrican Federation of Filmmakers/FEPACI. Dakar: *Présence Africaine*, 1995. 412pp.
> The papers from the 14th FESPACO conference in Ouagadougou, focusing language, Africa in foreign films and prospects for African filmmaking.

1081

Patterson, James. "Africa on Film." *African Research and Documentation*, no. 68 (1995): 75-79.
> A description of the holdings on Africa of the British National Film and Television Archive. Paper presented at the annual meeting of the Standing Conference on Library Materials on Africa, London, 9-10 June, 1994.

1082

Peters, Jonathan. "Aesthetics and Ideology in African Film: Ousmane Sembene's "Emitai"." *African Literature in Its Social and Political Dimensions*, 69-75. Edited by Eileen Julien, Mildred Mortimer, and Curtis Schade. Washington: Three Continents Press, 1986.
> A discussion of the work of Ousmane Sembene, focusing on his film *Emitai*, and its balance of art and political ideas.

1083

Petty, Sheila. "Cities, Subject, Sites: Sub-Saharan Cinema and the Reorganization of Knowledge." *AfterImage* 19, no. 1 (June 1991): 10-11, 18.
> A discussion of themes of identity in several African films, remarking on a shift from ethnic or national identity to a universal African identity.

1084

Pfaff, Françoise. *The Cinema of Ousmane Sembene: a Pioneer of African Film*. Westport, CT: Greenwood Press, 1984. 207pp.
> An assessment of Sembene's filmmaking career with commentary and analysis of several of his films. Appendices include a biographical sketch, casting and credits for his films, and a collection of quotes from reviews. 14 pages of photographs. 5 page bibliography. Index.

1085

---. "Conversation with Ghanaian Filmmaker Kwaw Ansah." *Research in African Literatures* 26, no. 3 (September 1995): 186-193.
> The filmmaker discusses some of the practical aspects of producing films in Ghana.

1086

---. "Sembene, A Griot of Modern Times." *Cinemas of the Black Diaspora: Diversity, Dependence and Oppositionality*, 118-128. Edited by Michael T. Martin. Detroit: Wayne State University, 1995.
> An assessment of the Senegalese filmmaker as storyteller.

Film

1087

---. "Three Faces of Africa: Women in *Xala*." *Jump Cut*, no. 27 (1982): 27-31.
> An interpretation of the complex symbolism of the female characters in Sembene's *Xala*.

1088

---. *Twenty-five Black African Filmmakers: A Critical Study with Filmography and Bio-Bibliography*. Westport, CT: Greenwood Press, 1988. 332pp.
> Biographies and critical assessment of African filmmakers, with filmographies and bibliographies of criticism, and interviews for each. 14 page general bibliography. Index.

1089

Pike, Charles Ben. "Colonial Africa and Exile Cinema." *AfterImage* 13, no. 5 (December 1985): 14-16.
> A discussion of the early films of the British Colonial Film Unit contrasting its influence on later Anglophone African filmmakers with that of the French colonial government on Francophone African filmmakers.

1090

---. "Film Image and the Oral Tradition." *Ba Shiru*, no. 5 (1973): 1-9.
> An analysis of an Mbundu tale from Angola and Cocteau's film *Beauty and the Beast*, illustrating the parallels in imagery between film and oral tradition.

1091

---. "Tales of Empire: The Colonial Film Unit in Africa, 1939-1950." *AfterImage* 17, no. 1 (June 1989): 8-9.
> A brief discussion of the work of the Colonial Film Unit, the technical problems it encountered, and its influence on subsequent independent filmmaking.

1092

Questions of Third Cinema, edited by Jim Pines and Paul Willemen. London: British Film Institute, 1989. 246pp.
> A collection of essays dealing with "Third Cinema", a phrase coined by Teshome H. Gabriel which denotes both cinema of the Third World and cinema with an ideology opposed to imperialism and class oppression.

1093

Poirier, Leon. *24 Images à la Seconde: Du Studio au Désert, Journal d'un Cinéaste Pendant Quarante-Cinq Années de Voyages à Travers les Pays, les Evénements, les Idées. 1907-1952*. Tours: Éd. Mame, 1953. 266pp.
> Personal account by a French filmmaker of his experiences making documentaries and other films in Africa. 16 pages of photographs.

1094
Pommier, Pierre. *Cinéma et Développement en Afrique Noire Francophone.* Paris: Pedone, 1974. 184pp.
Historical overview of the film industry in Africa.

1095
Poussaint, Renée. "African Film: The High Price of Division." *Ufahamu* 1, no. 3 (December 1970): 51-63.
In a discussion of the problems facing African filmmakers, the author notes several areas of artificial division which inhibit or distort growth and development: arbitrary geographic classification, particularly separating North African film from Sub-Saharan Africa; excessive influence of the former colonial rulers; disagreements between filmmakers and their own national governments.

1096
Predal, René. *Jean Rouch, un Griot Gaulois: Dossier Réuni par René Predal.* Paris: L'Afrique Littéraire, 1981. Special Issue of *L'Afrique Littéraire* #61-62. 191pp.
A special issue devoted to the French filmmaker known for his many films on Africa. Articles include discussion of his ethnographic films, the psychological and social themes of his films, and his cinematic technique. Included are interviews and discussions with African filmmakers.

1097
Pretorius, William. "La Télévision, la Comédie et le Film Afrikaans." *Le Cinéma Sud-Africain Est-il Tombé sur la Tête?*, 59-65. Edited by Keyan G. Tomaselli. Paris: Cerf, 1986.
An overview of the tastes and preferences of Afrikaner filmgoers and television viewers.

1098
Raeburn, Michael. "Absent de Ouagadougou: Le Cinéma Ghanéen Va-t-il Décoller?" *L'Afrique Littéraire et Artistique*, no. 23 (June 1972): 88-98.
Ghanaian films, indeed films from most of Anglophone Africa, were absent or very poorly represented at the Pan African Film Festival in Ouagadougou in March 1972. The author interviews one South African and three Ghanaian filmmakers who discuss their craft and their themes.

1099
Rayfield, F. R. "The Use of Films in Teaching About Africa." *Film Library Quarterly* 17, no. 2/3/4 (1984): 34-52.
The author, an anthropologist, sets a framework for selecting and using films from and about Africa in classrooms, and discusses the merits and faults of a wide range of films.

1100
Rayfield, J. R. "*Hyenas*: The Message and the Messenger." *Research in African Literatures* 26, no. 3 (September 1995): 78-82.

Film

    Analysis of the film *Hyenas* made by Senegalese filmmaker Djibril Diop-Mambety and based on Durrenmatt's play *The Visit*.

1101
Reid, Mark A. "Dialogic Modes of Representing Africa(s): Womanist Film." *Black American Literary Forum* 5, no. 2 (June 1991): 375-388.
    A theoretical discussion of women's issues as portrayed in African films and films made in the African diaspora.

1102
---. "Interview with Andrée Daventure: Producing African Cinema in Paris." *Jump Cut*, no. 36 (1991): 47-51.
    The interviewee is the founder of the French film company Atria, and has edited and produced a number of African films.

1103
Roberts, Andrew. "Africa on Film to 1940." *History in Africa* 14 (1987): 189-227.
    This survey of documentaries and newsreels on Africa explores film as a resource for historical research. 13 pages of bibliographical notes.

1104
Robinson, Cedric. "Domination and Imitation: *Xala* and the Emergence of the Black Bourgeoisie." *Race and Class* 22, no. 2 (1980): 147-158.
    A sociological and political analysis of the films of Ousmane Sembene.

1105
Anthropological Filmmaking: Anthropological Perspectives on the Production of Film and Video for General Public Audiences, edited by Jack R. Rollwagen. London: Harwood Academic Publishers, 1988.
    A collection of essays on anthropological filmmaking, including African examples.

1106
Rouch, Jean. "The Awakening African Cinema." *UNESCO Courier* 15, no. 3 (March 1962): 10-15.
    A brief overview of the progress of African film in several steps: films made outside of Africa which highlight the "exotic", ethnographic films, films depicting Africa in the course of modernization, the beginnings of true African cinema; films made by and for Africans.

1107
Rouch, Jean, and Oumarou Ganda. *Moi, un Noir. Cabascabo*. Paris: L'Avant-Scène du Cinéma, 1981. 50pp.
    Still photographs and excerpts from the scripts of the films *Moi, Un Noir*, directed by Jean Rouch and set in Treichville, Côte d'Ivoire, and *Cabascabo*, directed by Nigerien filmmaker Oumarou Ganda.

1108
Cinema of John Marshall, edited by Jay Ruby. Philadelphia: Harwood Academic Pub., 1993. 282pp.
   A collection of essays on the anthropologist and documentary filmmaker known best for his films of the San people of Namibia. 38 page filmography.

1109
Salmane, Hala, Simon Hartog, and David Wilson. *Algerian Cinema*. London: British Film Institute, 1976. 58pp.
   Essays on the history and cultural context of film in Algeria.

1110
Sauer, Matthew E. "Nigeria and India: The Use of Film for Development - Whispers In a Crowd." *Africa Media Review* 6, no. 1 (1992): 25-34.
   A comparison of Nigerian and Indian experiences using film for development, finding similar problems: lack of government support and lack of popular interest in the films produced.

1111
Schmidt, Nancy J. "African Literature on Film." *Research in African Literatures* 13, no. 4 (December 1982): 518-531.
   A discussion of the use in film of African literature, both oral and published.

1112
Schmidt, Nancy J. "Culture and Nationalism in sub-Saharan African Filmmaking." *Visual Anthropology* 2, no. 1 (1989): 85-91.
   A discussion of the theoretical issues relating to African filmmaking.

1113
---. "Films by Sub-Saharan African Women Filmmakers (A Preliminary Filmography)." *ALA Bulletin* 18, no. 4 (1992): 12-14.
   A list of African women filmmakers and the films they have made. Dr. Schmidt does a continuing listing of films by African filmmakers in this journal.

1114
---. "Nigerian Filmmaking into the 1990s: A Review Article." *Research in African Literatures* 168-173.
   In a review of four books and two new journals all published in Nigeria and all dealing with filmmaking, the author gives an overview of the film industry in that country.

1115
---. "Publications on African Film: Focus on Burkina Faso and Nigeria." *African Book Publishing Record* 16, no. 3 (1990): 153-156.
   A commentary on books and articles dealing with African films in Burkina Faso and Nigeria, with some general observations on FESPACO and its publications.

Film

1116
---. "Review Essay: African Filmmakers and Their Films." *African Studies Review* 37, no. 1 (April 1994): 175-181.
   A discussion of filmographies and recent books on African film.

1117
---. *Sub-Saharan African Films and Filmmakers: an Annotated Bibliography/Films et Cinéastes Africains de la Région Subsaharienne: Une Bibliographie Commentée.* London: Hans Zell, 1988. 401pp.
   A 3993 entry bibliography of books, monographs, theses, articles, reviews and pamphlets with indexes of actors and actresses, film festivals, film titles, filmmakers, countries, and general subjects.

1118
---. *Sub-Saharan African Films and Filmmakers, 1987-1992.* London: Hans Zell, 1994. 468pp.
   A 3198 entry bibliography updating the author's 1988 publication, indexed by author and co-authors, actors and actresses, film festivals, film titles, filmmakers, other film personnel, countries, and general subjects.

1119
---. "Visualizing Africa: The Bibliography of Films by Sub-Saharan African Filmmakers." *Africana Resources and Collections: Three Decades of Development and Achievement. A Festschrift in Honor of Hans Panofsky,* 151-177. Edited by Julian W. Witherell. Metuchen, NJ: Scarecrow Press, 1989.
   A discussion of the author's experience in compiling bibliographies on film and filmmaking in Sub-Saharan Africa and an evaluation of the literature.

1120
Scott, Chuck. *Lesotho Herders Video Project: Explorations in Visual Anthropology.* Durban: Centre for Cultural and Media Studies, University of Natal, 1991. 123pp.
   An honours essay in visual anthropology at the University of Natal, this report describes the making of a documentary film of herders in Lesotho, wherein the subjects of the film also did some of the filming.

1121
"Seminar on the Role of the African Filmmaker in Rousing an Awareness of Black Civilization, Ouagadougou, 8-13 April 1974." *Présence Africaine* 90, no. 2 (1974): 3-204.
   The papers and transcribe discussion from a conference held by the Society of African Culture focusing on the political and cultural responsibilities of African filmmakers.

1122
Senghor, Blaise. "Prerequisites for a Truly African Cinema." *Présence Africaine*, no. 49 (1964): 101-107.
: A discussion of the practical needs of the incipient African film industry.

1123
Serceau, Daniel. "Sembene Ousmane: Dossier Réuni par Daniel Serceau." *L'Afrique Littéraire*, no. 76 (1985): 96pp.
: A special issue devoted to Ousmane Sembene with articles discussing his biography and development as a novelist and filmmaker; a filmography plus reviews and commentary on his films; an exploration of his style; an interview with French filmmaker Jean Rouch.

1124
Shaka, Femi Okiremuete. "Vichy Dakar and the Other Story of French Colonial Stewardship in Africa: A Critical Reading of Ousmane Sembene and Thierno Faty Sow's *Camp de Thiaroye*." *Research in African Literatures* 26, no. 3 (September 1995): 67-77.
: Discussion of the historical and political significance of the events portrayed in the film *Camp de Thiaroye*, specifically the massacre by Vichy French soldiers of a group of repatriated *tirailleurs* awaiting their discharge in Senegal.

1125
Directory of African Film-Makers and Films, compiled and edited by Keith Shiri. Westport, CT: Greenwood, 1992. 194pp.
: An alphabetical list of filmmakers from 29 African countries, covering sixty years of film production in Africa, with biographical and career information and a filmography for each. Indexed by country and film title. Supplemented by a general index which includes names of organizations and film personalities other than those listed as main entries, titles of books and plays. 3 page bibliography.

1126
Shohat, Ella. "Egypt: Cinema and Revolution." *Critical Arts* 2, no. 4 (1982): 22-32. (The author's name appears in the journal as both Ella Schochat and Ella Schohat. Her later work is established as Ella Shohat.)
: An historical overview of the film industry in Egypt, with an examination of the consequences of the 1952 revolution in Egypt, when Nasser seized power of that industry.

1127
Smihi, Moumen. "Moroccan Society as Mythology." *Film and Politics in the Third World*, 77-87. Edited by John D. H. Downing. New York: Praeger, 1987.
: A conversation between Guy Hennebelle and Moroccan filmmaker Moumen Smihi on the origins and meanings of his films.

Film

1128

Smyth, Rosaleen. "The British Colonial Film Unit and Sub-Saharan Africa, 1939-1945." *Historical Journal of Film, Radio and Television* 8, no. 3 (1988): 285-298.
>A discussion of the activities and goals of the British Colonial Film Unit in Africa during the Second World War, focusing on its propaganda efforts.

1129

---. "The Central African Film Unit's Images of Empire 1948-1963." *Historical Journal of Film, Radio and Television* 3, no. 2 (1983): 132-147.
>A study of the instructional films produced by the Central African Film Unit for use in the territories of Northern Rhodesia, Southern Rhodesia and Nyasaland (now Zambia, Zimbabwe and Malawi) focusing on the images projected: Africans as inferior and dependent; English as wise, powerful and benevolent.

1130

---. "The Development of British Colonial Film Policy 1927-1939, With Special Reference to East and Central Africa." *Journal of African History* 20, no. 3 (1979): 437-450.
>An historical overview of the change in British film policy from the use of film as a propaganda tool to its use as a means of educating African populations.

1131

---. "The Feature Film in Tanzania." *African Affairs* 88, no. 352 (July 1989):
>An historical overview of filmmaking in Tanzania, from the International Missionary Council's Bantu Educational Kinema Experiment in the 1930s to the post Independence era when government policy is to limit imports of foreign film in order to encourage local production.

1132

---. "Movies and Mandarins: the Official Film and British Colonial Africa." *British Cinema History*, 129-143. Edited by James Curran, and Vincent Porter. Totowa, N. J.: Barnes and Noble Books, 1983.
>An exploration of the use of film in Africa by the British Colonial Office, including educational films and propaganda films aimed at strengthening the position of colonial governments.

1133

---. "Post-War Career of the Colonial Film Unit in Africa, 1946-1955." *Historical Journal of Film, Radio and TV* 12, no. 2 (1992): 163-177.
>A study of the Colonial Film Unit following World War II, when the emphasis shifted from war-related themes to mass education and community development, until its end in 1955, when the Unit was deemed to be ineffective and not worth its high cost.

1134
Solanas, Fernando E., and Octavio Gettino. "Towards a Third Cinema." *Movies and Methods*, 44-64. Edited by Bill Nichols. Berkeley. CA: University of California Press, 1976.
>Two filmmakers discuss the philosophical and practical aspects of "Third Cinema", a concept developed by Teshome H. Gabriel.

1135
Gillo Pontecorvo's The Battle of Algiers: a Film Written by Franco Solinas, edited by PierNico Solinas. New York: Scribners, 1973. 206pp.
>The screenplay of the movie, with numerous photographs and interviews with both Gillo Pontecorvo and Franco Solinas. 4 page bibliography.

1136
Soyinka, Wole. "The Theatre and the Emergence of the Nigerian Film Industry." *The Development and Growth of the Film Industry in Nigeria: Proceedings of a Seminar on the Film Industry and Cultural Identity in Nigeria*, 97-103. Edited by Alfred E. Opubor, and Onuora E. Nwuneli. New York: Third Press International, 1979.
>The Nigerian playwright and Nobel laureate on the interaction between theater and film, and the need for the integrity of the creative vision.

1137
Spass, Lieve. "Female Domestic Labour and Third World Politics in *La Noire de....*" *Jump Cut* , no. 27 (July 1982): 26-27.
>A discussion of the oppression of women as illustrated in Sembene's film *La Noire de....*

1138
Spence, Louise et al. "Racism in the Cinema: Proposal for a Methodological Evaluation." *Critical Arts* 2, no. 4 (1983): 6-12.
>A methodological model for analysis of racism in the film industry, focusing on employment opportunities, economics of production, marketing and distribution.

1139
Ssali, Ndugu Mike. "Apartheid and Cinema." *Ufahamu* 13, no. 1 (1983): 105-133.
>A discussion of film in South Africa, with emphasis on the portrayal of Blacks in both South African and imported films and the use of film in social control.

1140
Stam, Robert, and Louise Spence. "Colonialism, Racism and Representation." *Screen* 24, no. 2 (March 1983): 2-20.
>This general discussion of racist messages in film uses two African examples: *The Wild Geese*, a story of glorifying White mercenaries in Africa, and *Battle of Algiers*, which drew audience sympathies to the Algerians.

Film

1141
Steenveld, Lynette. "Les Documentaires de Propagande." *Le Cinéma Sud-Africain Est-il Tombé sur la Tête?*, 68-72. Edited by Keyan G. Tomaselli. Paris: Cerf, 1986.
> An analysis of documentaries produced both to convince South African Blacks to accept the idea of Homelands, and to favorably present the practice of apartheid to outsiders.

1142
Stoller, Paul. *The Cinematic Griot: the Ethnography of Jean Rouch.* Chicago: University of Chicago Press, 1992. 247pp.
> A biography and appreciation of French ethnographic filmmaker Jean Rouch, whose major works were filmed in Africa. Appendices include a bibliography and filmography of Jean Rouch. 8 page bibliography. Index.

1143
Strebel, Elizabeth Grottle. "Imperialist Iconography of Anglo-Boer War Film Footage." *Film Before Griffith*, 264-271. Edited by John L. Fell. Berkeley: University of California Press, 1983.
> A discussion of film as record and propaganda in the Anglo-Boer War of 1899-1901, one of the first wars recorded in moving pictures.

1144
---. "Primitive Propaganda: the Boer War Films." *Sight and Sound* 46, no. 1 (December 1976): 45-47.
> An exploration of the use of film, then a novelty, as propaganda to build public support in England for the Boer War.

1145
---. "*The Voortrekkers*: A Cinematic Reflection of Afrikaner Nationalism." *Film and History* 9, no. 2 (1972): 25-32.
> A discussion of the film *The Voortrekkers*, made in South Africa in 1916, comparing it in scope and message to the US film *Birth of A Nation*.

1146
Strong, John A. "Images of a Liberation Struggle: the Film as Document." *Africa Today* 20, no. 1 (December 1973): 85-92.
> A discussion of five documentaries on the civil war in Angola, focusing on the selection and juxtaposition of images to convey differing messages.

1147
Sumo, Honoré de. "Genèse et Avenir du Cinéma Camerounais." *L'Afrique Littéraire et Artistique*, no. 39 (1976): 59-62.
> A brief note on the development of filmmaking in Cameroon.

1148
Tamzali, Wassyla. *En Attendant Omar Gatlato: Regards Sur le Cinéma Algérien Suivi de Introduction Fragmentaire au Cinéma Tunisien.* Algiers, Algeria: Édition EN. P. P., 1979. 228pp.
   A study of films and filmmakers in Algeria and Tunisia.

1149
Taylor, Elyseo J. "Film and Social Change in Africa South of the Sahara." *American Behavioral Scientist* 17, no. 3 (1974): 424-438.
   A discussion of support for African filmmaking in Africa, films made elsewhere about Africa, and films imported for African audiences.

1150
Teshome H. Gabriel. "Colonialism and 'Law and Order' Criticism." *Screen* 27, no. 3/4 (May 1986): 140-147.
   The author responds to criticism of his theoretical framework for understanding Third World cinema as "Third Cinema", "anti-imperialist, militant and confrontational". (See Item #902)

1151
---. "Teaching Third World Cinema." *Screen* 24, no. 2 (March 1982): 60-64.
   Using examples from African films, the author outlines three themes of his course in Third World film: its cinematic grammar, the production milieu and the need for a framework for criticism.

1152
---. "Third Cinema as Guardian of Popular Memory: Towards a Third Aesthetics." *Questions of Third Cinema,* 53-64. Edited by Jim Pines, and Paul Willemen. London: British Film Institute, 1989.
   Explores the relationship between folklore and cinema in the Third World.

1153
---. *Third Cinema in the Third World: the Aesthetics of Liberation.* Ann Arbor, MI: UMI Research Press, 1982. 146pp.
   An elaboration of the author's thesis that the themes and techniques of many Third World films merge into a "Third Cinema" which rejects the "concepts and propositions of traditional cinema as represented by Hollywood." 7 page bibliography. Index.

1154
---. "Towards a Critical Theory of Third World Films." *Questions of Third Cinema,* 30-52. Edited by Jim Pines, and Paul Willemen. London: British Film Institute, 1989. Also in *Third World Affairs* 1985.
   A discussion of similarities and differences among films made throughout the Third World, including both philosophies and the technical aspects.

Film

1155

---. "*Xala*: A Cinema of Wax and Gold." *Présence Africaine*, no. 116 (1980): 202-214.
> A discussion of Sembene's technique in terms of a traditional Ethiopian poetic form, *sem-enna-worq*, literally "wax and gold", referring to the lost-wax process of metal casting. The "gold", or true meaning of the poem, is embedded in the "wax", or superficial meaning.

1156

---. "*Xala*: A Cinema of Wax and Gold." *Jump Cut*, no. 27 (1982): 31-33.
> A reprint of the article which appeared in *Présence Africaine* in 1980.

1157

Thoraval, Yves. *Regards sur le Cinéma Egyptien*. Beirut: Dar el-Mashreq, 1975. 140pp.
> History of film and filmmaking in Egypt from the first films shown in the country in the early 1900s through the 1970s. 16 pages of photographs. 7 page bibliography.

1158

Tomaselli, Keyan G. "'African' Cinema - Theoretical Perspectives on Some Unresolved Questions." *Critical Arts* 7, no. 1/2 (1993): 1-10.
> The author notes that South Africa is often excluded from discussion and study of African film, and poses a set of questions as the basis for further analysis of film in all of Africa.

1159

---. "Capitalism and Culture in South African Cinema: Jingoism, Nationalism and the Historical Epic." *Wide Angle* 8, no. 2 (1986): 33-43.
> An historical overview of South African film with commentary on the political and social messages conveyed by early films.

1160

---. "Le Censure: de la Rigueur à la Subtilité." *Le Cinéma Sud-Africain Est-il Tombé sur la Téte?*, 73-78. Edited by Keyan G. Tomaselli. Paris: Cerf, 1986.
> History and analysis of various kinds of film censorship as practiced in South Africa.

1161

---. "Le Cinéma Anti-Apartheid à l'Extérieur." *Le Cinéma Sud-Africain Est-il Tombé sur la Tête?*, 90-98. Edited by Keyan G. Tomaselli. Paris: Cerf, 1986.
> A discussion of anti-apartheid films made outside South Africa by South African filmmakers and others.

1162

---. "Le Cinéma et la Video d'Opposition." *Le Cinéma Sud-Africain Est-il Tombé sur la Tête?*, 79-83. Edited by Keyan G. Tomaselli. Paris: Cerf, 1986.
   Video has added a new dimension and opportunity to those making films countering apartheid.

1163

Tomaselli, Keyan G. *The Cinema of Apartheid: Race and Class in South African Film.* New York: Smyrna/Lake View Press, 1988. 300pp.
   A study of the complexities of filmmaking during apartheid, including government attempts to control information and ideas through censorship and attempts to mold thought by itself producing films with "acceptable" themes. 17 page filmography, including feature films and documentaries. 17 page annotated bibliography. Index.

1164

Le Cinéma Sud-Africain Est-il Tombé sur la Tête?, edited by Keyan G. Tomaselli. Paris: Cerf, 1986. *Cinémaction* 39. Also published as a special issue of *L'Afrique Littéraire*, #78, 1986. 128pp.
   A special issue of *Cinémaction* providing a collection of essays on film in and about South Africa. Appendices include an interview with filmmaker Lionel Ngakane, an annotated list of thirty South African filmmakers, synopses of typical South African films, a 13 page filmography, and an annotated list of anti-apartheid films made in Paris. (The title of this collection is based on the French translation of Jamie Uys's film *The Gods Must Be Crazy, Les Dieux Sont Tombé Sur la Tête*.).

1165

Tomaselli, Keyan G.. "Les Cinémas "Noirs" de l'Afrique du Sud Blanche." *Le Cinéma Sud-Africain Est-il Tombé sur la Tête?*, 36-47. Edited by Keyan G. Tomaselli. Paris: Cerf, 1986.
   An overview of films made by White filmmakers for Black audiences in South Africa. A "No politics, no Whites" policy was observed and only themes deemed "suitable" were allowed.

1166

---. "Class and Ideology: Reflections in South African Cinema." *Critical Arts* 1, no. 1 (1980): 1-13.
   An examination of South African film in social and historical terms rather than an aesthetic and literary perspective. Major themes of race, class and ethnic identity are explored.

1167

---. "'Colouring It In': Films in 'Black' or 'White' - Reassessing Authorship." *Critical Arts* 7, no. 1/2 (1993): 61-77.
   Beginning with Spike Lee's reaction to a White director filming *The Autobiography of Malcolm X*, the author explores racial attitudes and theories in filmmaking, pointing out contradictions and inconsistencies in much writing on this topic.

Film

1168

---. "'Culture' as Theatre-Going, 'Arts' as Buildings: A Critique of 'Difference' in a South African Propaganda Film." *South African Theatre Journal* 1, no. 2 (1987): 63-75.

    An analysis of an early South African Department of Information documentary film, "South Africa's Performing Arts", which he finds to be ethnocentric propaganda.

1169

---. "L'Evolution du Cinéma Sud-Africain." *Le Cinéma Sud-Africain Est-il Tombé sur la Tête?*, 18-23. Edited by Keyan G. Tomaselli. Paris: Cerf, 1986.

    Historical overview of filmmaking in South Africa.

1170

---. "Film and Literature (South Africa)." *Encyclopedia of Post-Colonial Literatures in English*, 509-511. Edited by E. Benson, and L. W. Conolly. London: Routledge, 1994.

    A discussion of South African literary works which have been made into films.

1171

---. "Grierson in South Africa - Culture, State and Nationalist Ideology in the South African Film Industry: 1940-1981." *Cinéma Canada*, no. 122 (1985): 24-27.

    A discussion of the influence of John Grierson on government control of film in South Africa and the establishment of the National Film Board.

1172

---. "Ideology and Censorship in South African Film." *Critical Arts* 1, no. 2 (1980): 1-15.

    An examination of South Africa's censorship regulations as a reflection of the dominant ideology, and thus not amenable to reform.

1173

---. *Myth, Race and Power: South Africans Imaged on Film and TV.* Bellville, South Africa: Anthropos, 1986. 126pp.

    Examination of ethnographic and documentary films about South Africa made locally and overseas, combining a theoretical approach with concrete analysis of specific films.

1174

---. "Popular Memory and the Voortrekker Films." *Critical Arts* 3, no. 3 (1985): 15-24.

    A study of the themes of films dealing with the *Voortrek*, the mass movement of Boers or Afrikaners from the Cape to Natal in 1837, and the Boer War at the end of the 19th century, placing the symbolism in a modern political context.

1175
---. "The Post Apartheid Era: The San as a Bridge Between Past and Future." *Eyes Across the Water II: Essays on Visual Anthropology and Sociology*, 81-90. edited by Robert M. Boonzajer Flaes, and Douglas Harper. Amsterdam: Het Spinhaus, 1993.
> A discussion of changing attitudes toward the San people of the Kalahari as reflected in documentaries and anthropological writing.

1176
---. "Racism in South African Cinema." *Cinéaste* 6, no. 1 (1983): 32-35.

1177
---. "Revisualizing the San in the Nineteen Eighties." *Visual Anthropology* 6, no. 1 (1993): 97-104.
> A review essay discussion films and writings on the San.

1178
---. "Le Rôle de la Jamie Uys Film Company dans la Culture Afrikaner." *Le Cinéma Sud-Africain Est-il Tombé sur la Tête?*, 24-33. Edited by Keyan G. Tomaselli. Paris: Cerf, 1986.
> An analysis of the work of the filmmaker Jamie Uys and his effect of Afrikaner ideas. Contains filmography of Jamie Uys's work.

1179
---. "[South Africa] Independent Cinema." *Cinema of the Black Diaspora: Diversity, Dependence and Oppositionality*, 129-144. Edited by Michael T. Martin. Detroit: Wayne State University Press, 1995.
> An overview of independent filmmaking in South Africa focusing on practical considerations such as funding and production facilities, but also discussing philosophical and theoretical issues.

1180
---. "The South African and Australian Film Industries: A Comparison." *Breaker Morant*, 31-50. Edited by Keyan G. Tomaselli, and John van Zyl. Johannesburg: University of the Witwatersrand, 1984. Critical Arts Monograph No. 1.
> Comparison of filmmaking in South Africa and Australia in terms of types of films, their themes, and industry infrastructure.

1181
---. *The South African Film Industry*. Johannesburg: African Studies Institute, University of the Witwatersrand, 1980. 152pp.
> A broad overview of film in South Africa, covering theoretical and practical topics.

Film

1182
---. "Strategies for an Independent Radical Cinema in South Africa." *Marang* 4 (1983): 51-85.

1183
---. "Theoretical Perspectives in African Cinema: Culture, Identity and Diaspora." *Visual Anthropology* 7, no. 4 (1995): 297-330.

1184
Tomaselli, Keyan G., and Maureen Eke. "Perspectives on Orality in African Cinema." *Oral Tradition* 10, no. 1 (March 1995): 111-128.
> A theoretical discussion of orality in cinema, with particular reference to Cameroonian filmmaker Jean-Marie Teno's *Afrique, Je Te Plumerai*, and the South African film, *The Two Rivers*, a history of the Venda people.

1185
Tomaselli, Keyan G., and Richard J. Haines. "Toward a Political Economy of the South African Film Industry in the 1980s." *Multinational Culture: Social Impacts of a Global Economy*, 155-166. Edited by C. Lehman, and R. M. Moore. Westport, CT: Greenwood Press, 1992.
> A discussion of the financial backing of the South African film industry by hotel and vice industries and the effects of this backing on the films made.

1186
Tomaselli, Keyan G., Arnold Shepperson, and Maureen Eke. "Towards a Theory of Orality in African Cinema." *Research in African Literatures* 26, no. 3 (September 1995): 18-35.
> Analysis of African film using two theoretical approaches: orality (Walter Ong) and semiotics (Arnold Shepperson and Keyan G. Tomaselli).

1187
Tomaselli, Keyan G., and Edgard Sienaert. "Ethnographic Film/Video Production and Oral Documentation: The Case of Piet Draghoender in *Kat River: The End of Hope*." *Research in African Literatures* 20, no. 2 (June 1989): 242-264.
> A discussion of a documentary telling the history of a coloured peasant farming settlement in South Africa from its founding in 1829 through the early 20th century, with a transcript and translation of a remarkable speech by one of the farmers interviewed.

1188
Tomaselli, Keyan G., Teshome H. Gabriel, Ntongela Masilela, and Amie Williams. "People of the Great Sandface: A Different Kind of Dialogue." *Visual Anthropology* 5, no. 1 (1992): 153-166.
> Transcript of a discussion of the documentary film *People of the Great Sandface*, which has raised considerable controversy. (See items #1047 and #1223)

1189
Turecamo, David. "A Celebration of Cinema." *Africa Report* 38, no. 3 (May 1993): 68-69.
   A report from the 1993 Pan African Film Festival (FESPACO), notes that its 200 films from 60 countries around the world are evidence of the festival's growth over the 23 years of its existence.

1190
Turner, Patricia A. *Ceramic Uncles and Celluloid Mammies: Black Images and their Influence on Culture*. New York: Anchor Books, 1994. 238pp.
   An analysis of images of Blacks in popular culture. Chapter 11, "Of Primates, Porters and Potables: Images of Africa on the Screen", examines the ways Africa is portrayed in films.

1191
Turvey, Gerry. "*Xala* and the Curse of Neocolonialism." *Screen* 26, no. 3/4 (1985): 75-87.
   Using a technique the author describes as "narrative as parable", Sembene projects a profound political message while telling the story of a middle-aged African civil servant.

1192
---. "African Cinematic Reality: the Documentary Tradition as an Emerging Trend." *Research in African Literatures* 26, no. 3 (September 1995): 88-96.
   Examining the films *Allah Tantou*, filmed in Guinea by David Achkar. and *Afrique, Je Te Plumerai*, filmed in Cameroon by Jean-Marie Teno, the author addresses the portrayal of Africa in African films.

1193
Ukadike, N. Frank. "African Films: A Retrospective and a Vision for the Future." *Critical Arts* 7, no. 1/2 (1993): 43-60.
   An historical overview of film in Africa, with a strongly optimistic assessment of the future.

1194
---. *Black African Cinema*. Berkeley, CA: University of California Press, 1994. 371pp.
   An extensive, in-depth history of film in Africa. 12 page bibliography. Index.

1195
---. "Depictions of Africa in Documentary Film." *Black Film Review* 4, no. 1 (December 1987): 13-15.

1196
---. "Framing FESPACO: Pan-African Cinema in Context." *AfterImage* 19, no. 4 (November 1991): 6-9.

Film

A report of the 1991 Pan African Film Festival in Ouagadougou, noting some of the themes of discussions, primarily problems of distribution in Africa and abroad, questions of the language(s) in which films should be made and the hope that films will lead to a validation of culture.

1197

---. "In Guinea Bissau, Cinema Trickles Down: An Interview with Flora Gomes." *Research in African Literatures* 26, no. 3 (September 1995): 179-185.
Conducted in New York after the screening of *The Blue Eyes of Yonta* in 1993, the interview introduces filmmaker Gomes, who was relatively unknown in the U.S.

1198

---. "Representing Native Kenya on Film: *Lorang's Way* and the Turkana People." *Ufahamu* 17, no. 1 (1988): 3-14.
A biting discussion of documentary films, using David and Judith MacDougall's *Lorang's Way* as an example. The author finds the film disrespectful and exploitative of the people filmed.

1199

---. "Toward an African Cinema." *Cinemas of the Black Diaspora: Diversity, Dependence and Oppositionality*, 167-180. Edited by Michael T. Martin. Detroit: Wayne State University Press, 1995.
Text of an interview with Nigerian filmmaker Eddie Ugbomah covering his own films, the relationship of traditional Yoruba theater to Nigerian films, and the need to redefine the image of Africa in the eyes of the world.

1200

---. "Western Film Images of Africa: Genealogy of an Ideological Formulation." *Black Scholar* 21, no. 2 (March 1990): 30-48.
A commentary on the depiction of Africa in Western films since the beginning of the 20th century, with discussion of the themes and underlying motivations.

1201

Van Bever, L. *Le Cinéma pour Africains*. Brussels: G. Van Campenhout, 1952. 62pp.
An overview of the production and distribution of films made specifically for viewing by Africans in the colonial context.

1202

Van Den Heuvel, Alex. "Le Cinéma Missionaire au Congo." *Grands Lacs* , no. 181 (1955): 27-32.
Discussion of films with religious themes made for African audiences in the Congo (now Zaire) during the 1930s and 1940s, focusing on animated films using folk tales to convey their messages.

1203
Van Wert, William. "Ideology in the Third World Cinema: A Study of Sembene Ousmane and Glauber Rocha." *Quarterly Review of Film Studies* 4, no. 2 (March 1979): 207-226.
   An examination of political ideology in the works of Senegalese Sembene and Brazilian Rocha focusing on the symbolism and cinematic techniques used to express their ideas.

1204
van Zyl, Hannes. "*De Voortrekkers* (1916): Some Stereotypes and Narrative Conventions." *Critical Arts* 1, no. 1 (March 1980): 24-31.
   An analysis of the themes and techniques of early South African epic films.

1205
Van Zyl, John. "Une Expérience: le Centre du Cinéma Direct." *Le Cinéma Sud-Africain Est-il Tombé sur la Tête?*, 84-89. Edited by Keyan G. Tomaselli. Paris: Cerf, 1986.
   The author's experience with a workshop dedicated to the training and nurturing of Black filmmakers in South Africa. Includes list of films made.

1206
Vaughn, J. Koyinde. "Africa and the Cinema." *An African Treasury*, 85-94. Edited by Langston Hughes. New York: Crown, 1960.
   A discussion several aspects of Africa in film: the stereotypes of Africa and Africans in American and British films; the messages of British colonial educational films; portrayal of African societies in anthropological films.

1207
Vieyra, Paulin Soumanou. "African Cinema: Solidarity and Difference." *Questions of Third Cinema*, 195-198. edited by Jim Pines, and Paul Willemen. London: British Film Industry, 1989.
   A brief note on the status of African filmmaking and the spirit of cooperation evident among African filmmakers, despite their differences.

1208
---. *Le Cinéma Africain des Origines à 1973*. Paris: Présence Africaine, 1975. 444pp.
   Tome I is a country-by-country historical overview of filmmaking in Africa. Tome II is a philosophical and theoretical discussion. Photographs. Filmography. Lists of filmmaking personnel. Statistical tables. 15 page bibliography.

1209
---. *Le Cinéma au Sénégal*. Paris: Editions OCIC/L'Harmattan, 1983. 170pp.
   Overview of filmmaking in Senegal, covering production, distribution, and critiques of major filmmakers. Numerous photographs. 13 page bibliography.

Film

1210
---. *Le Cinéma et L'Afrique*. Paris: Présence Africaine, 1969. 218pp.
Collection of essays on film in Africa.

1211
---. "Le Cinquième FESPACO." *Présence Africaine* , no. 98 (1976): 187-192.
A summary of events at the fifth Pan-African Film Festival, with a list of the winners.

1212
---. "Five Major Films of Sembene Ousmane." *Film and Politics in the Third World*, 31-39. Edited by John D. H. Downing. New York: Praeger, 1987.
Synopses of the stories of *Black Girl*, *Mandabi*, *Emitai*, *Xala*, and *Ceddo*, with additional comments on cinematic technique and the place of these films in Senegalese society.

1213
---. *Ousmane Sembene, Cinéaste*. Paris: Présence Africaine, 1972. 244pp.
A critical biography of the noted Senegalese filmmaker and author, including personal information on his life, analysis of seven of his films and his writings, and transcripts of critical reviews and articles. Numerous photographs.

1214
---. "Responsabilité du Cinéma dans la Formation d'une Conscience Nationale Africaine." *Présence Africaine* , no. 27 (1960): 303-315.
Discussion of the role of film developing a sense of national identity in African nations.

1215
Walling, William. "Algerian Cinema: To Give Them New Faces." *Africa Report* 16, no. 6 (June 1971): 29-31.
Comments on the changes in the themes and content of Algerian cinema since independence.

1216
Weaver, Harold D. Jr. "Interview with Ousmane Sembene." *Issue* 2, no. 4 (December 1972): 58-64.
The Senegalese filmmaker discusses his film *Emitai* and his opinions of films by or about African Americans.

1217
---. "Politics of African Cinema." *Black Cinema Aesthetics*, 83-92. Edited by Gladstone L. Yearwood. Athens, Ohio: Ohio University Center for Afro-American Studies, 1982.
A commentary on the contexts, themes and styles of films made in Africa.

1218

Weinberger, Eliot. "The Camera People." *Transition*, no. 55 (1992): 24-54.
   A discussion of ethnographic filmmakers, with numerous African examples. The author criticizes the filmmakers' attitudes towards their subjects and their daily lives.

1219

Wellington, Nicholas. "*Cry Freedom, Lethal Weapon 2, A Dry White Season*: Hollywood's Apartheid." *Jump Cut*, no. 36 (1991): 66-72.
   A critical discussion of three films depicting apartheid.

1220

Werman, Marco. "African Cinema: A Market in the U.S.?" *Africa Report* 34, no. 3 (May 1989): 68-70.
   A report on the 1989 Pan African Film Festival (FESPACO) in Ouagadougou, focusing on discussions of the problems encountered in distributing African films in the U.S.

1221

Willemen, Paul. "The Making of an African Cinema." *Transition*, no. 58 (1992): 138-150.
   In a lengthy review of Diawara's *African Cinema: Politics and Culture*, the author comments on Diawara's ideas and adds examples from his own experience.

1222

Williams, Amie. "Dancing with Absences: The Impossible Presence of Third World Women in Films." *Ufahamu* 17, no. 3 (September 1989): 44-56.
   A discussion of the representation of women in African and other Third World films, making the point that often women are mis-represented.

1223

Wilmsen, Edwin M. "Comment on *People of the Great Sandface*." *Visual Anthropology* 5, no. 1 (1992): 174-181.
   Additional discussion of Myburgh's film. (See Items #1047 and #1188)

1224

Woods, Donald. *Filming with Attenborough: the Making of Cry Freedom.* New York: H. Holt, 1987. 163pp.
   Account of the production of a film based on the author's books *Asking for Trouble* and *Biko*. Numerous photographs.

1225

Woolford, Pamela. "Filming Slavery: a Conversation with Haile Gerima." *Transition* 65 90-104.
   Interview with the Ethiopian filmmaker on his film *Sankofa*.

Film

1226
Wright, Rob. "Africa's Film Capital." *Africa Report* 40, no. 1 (January 1995): 61-63.
   A short introduction to the Ouagadougou Pan-African Film Festival (FESPACO).

1227
Yakir, Dan. "*Ciné-Transe*: The Vision of Jean Rouch. An Interview." *Film Quarterly* 31, no. 2 (December 1977): 2-11.
   French filmmaker Jean Rouch, known for his African films, discusses his life and art.

1228
Zacks, Stephen A. "The Theoretical Construction of African Cinema." *Research in African Literatures* 26, no. 3 (September 1995): 6-17.
   A discussion of African film as the expression of a range of philosophical theories.

1229
Zimmermann, Patricia R. "Our Trip to Africa: Home Movies as the Eyes of the Empire." *AfterImage* 17, no. 8 (March 1990): 4-7.
   The author uses two items from the Smithsonian Institution's Human Studies Film Archives, amateur footage shot by an American woman touring Africa and her diary, to illustrate a discussion of the intrusiveness of ethnographic filming, amateur and professional alike.

General

1230
Abdel Rahman, Awatef. "Communication Technology in Africa: Dependency or Self-Reliance?" *Africa Media Review* 5, no. 3 (1991): 11-.
> An analysis of the role of technology in communication and the impact of multinational corporations in news coverage, with recommendations for technology policy in Africa.

1231
Aborampah, Osei-Mensah, and Kwadwo Anokwa. "Communication and Agricultural Development: Some Theoretical and Conceptual Considerations." *Gazette* 34, no. 1 (1984): 103-115.
> A discussion of the theoretical basis for communication strategies in development, with examples from Ghana.

1232
Abu-Lughod, Ibrahim. "The Mass Media and Egyptian Village Life." *Social Forces* 42, no. 1 (October 1963): 97-104.
> Report of a 1961 survey of 300 heads of household in six Egyptian villages using reaction to one news event, the death of King Mohammed V of Morocco, to determine exposure to mass media.

1233
Achile, Yves. "Extraversion et Développement Autocentre: L'Exemple de l'Industrie Audio-Visuelle en Afrique." *Mondes en Développement* 19, no. 73 (1991): 63-76.
> A critique of the role of foreign media in Africa. The author contends that "dumping" of Western programs inhibits the development of local programs and endangers national sovereignty.

1234
Adagala, Esther K., and Wambui Kiai. *Situation of Women and the Media in Africa*. Nairobi: Women in Communication Trust, 1993. 59pp.
> Discussion of employment patterns for women journalists and coverage of women in African media.

1235
Adi, Isabella E. *Judicial Attitudes to Freedom of Speech and the Press*. Lagos: Nigerian Institute of Advanced Legal Studies, 1983. 23pp.

1236
"Africa and the World: Competing for Attention." *Nieman Reports* 44, no. 4 (December 1990): 9-23.
> Report of a media conference sponsored by the Nieman Foundation and the African-American Institute.

1237
"The African Media." *Nieman Reports* 50, no. 1 (March 1996): 47-76.
> A special section containing articles and brief notes by Nieman Fellows on the media in Africa.

General

1238

"The African Media in a Changing Africa." *Nieman Reports* 47, no. 3 (September 1993): 30-62.
> Report of a conference sponsored by the Nieman Foundation and the African American Institute, with the International Women's Media Foundation, held in Harare, Zimbabwe.

1239

Ahcene-Djaballah, Belkacem. *Aspects du Nouvel Ordre International de l'Information: Étude et Documents*. Algiers: Office des Publications Universitaires, 1980. 217pp.
> A discussion of the New World Information Order with commentary on information media in Algeria since independence. Appendices contain documents of the United Nations and the Non-Aligned Nations concerning the New World Information Order.

1240

Aig-Imoukhuede, Frank. "The Film and Television in Nigeria." *Présence Africaine*, no. 58 (1966): 89-93.
> A brief report on the work of Nigeria's Federal Film Unit and the television stations in Western Nigeria (WNTV) and Eastern Nigeria (ENTV).

1241

Ajibola, William A. *Foreign Policy and Public Opinion: A Case Study of British Foreign Policy Over the Nigerian Civil War*. Ibadan: Ibadan University Press, 1978. 213pp.
> A description of British Policy toward Nigeria during the Nigerian civil war, emphasizing the role of the media. 4 page bibliography. Index.

1242

Akene, Emman. *Democratization of Mass Communication in Nigeria*. Jos, Nigeria: Industrial Training Fund Printing Press, 1992. 60pp.
> A textbook for journalists by a Nigerian broadcast journalist. Includes theoretical discussion and transcripts of the author's broadcasts.

1243

Akigbo, Charles. "Media Education in Anglophone Africa: Perspectives and Problems." *Africans on Africa Series* #1, Supplement to *IDOC Internazionale* 26, no. 1 (January 1995): 20-26.

1244

Contemporary Issues in Mass Media For Development and National Security, edited by Ralph A. Akinfeleye. Lagos: Unimedia Publications, 1988. 235pp.
> A collection of essays on a broad range of issues relating to the media in Nigeria.

General

1245
Media Nigeria: Dialectic Issues in Nigerian Journalism, edited by Ralph A. Akinfeleye. Lagos: Nelson Publishers, 1990. 117pp.
> A collection of essays on topics including journalistic professionalism and responsibility, media ownership and press freedom. Appendices include codes of conduct.

1246
Ali, Ibrahim Abukar. "Female Circumcision and its Coverage in the Mass Media." *Communicating Health In Africa: Research Papers of the Second Training Course of African Communicators*, 1-13. Edited by Osmo Apunen and Pirjo Huida. Tampere, Finland: University of Tampere, Unit of Peace Research and Development Studies, 1988.
> An introduction to the practice of female circumcision, with a brief overview of its coverage on Somali radio and press.

1247
The Visual Role of the 'Rubicons' as Part of P. W. Botha's 'Reform' Strategy, edited by Mark Allison-Broomhead et al. Durban: Centre for Cultural and Media Studies, University of Natal, 1986. 19pp.
> A study of the "Rubicon" speeches of President P. W. Botha of South Africa which attacked the press.

1248
Amatokwu, F. Nwaokedi. *Dynamic Concepts and Problems of Communication Development in Nigeria*. Ikeja, Nigeria: Taorgan Publications, 1992. 172 pp.
> Discussion of problems of communication in Nigeria, particularly in regard to promotion of democracy, protection of the environment, and economic development.

1249
Amienyi, Osabuohien P. "The Actual Contribution of Mass Media Use to Integrative Tendency in Nigeria." *Africa Media Review* 6, no. 2 (1992): 31-46.
> A study of the contribution of mass media to integration of three ethnic groups in Nigeria, concluding that Nigeria needs to streamline media policy.

1250
---. "Adult Attitude Towards Mass Media in Nigeria." *Africa Media Review* 7, no. 1 (1993): 19-32.
> Results of a survey of three ethnic groups in Nigeria's Plateau State on attitudes toward radio and newspapers. 1 page bibliography.

1251
---. *Journalism Profession in Nigeria*. Lagos: Citadel Resources for Taorgan, 1989. 182pp.

General

A discussion of the Nigerian Media Council Decree of 1988 and conditions for journalists in that country.

1252

Anani, Elma Lititia, Alkaly Miriama Keita, and Awatef Abdel Rahman. *Women and the Mass Media in Africa: Case Studies from Sierra Leone, the Niger and Egypt*. Addis Ababa: African Training and Research Centre for Women, 1981. 38pp.
   The study examines the image of women as portrayed in the media of the three countries, as well as the roles and opportunities for women as media professionals.

1253

Andrade, Mario de. "Communication for Cultural Decolonization in Africa." *Cultures* 8, no. 3 (1982): 15-25.
   Focusing on the PAIGC's official cultural policies for an independent Cape Verde and Guinea Bissau, the author looks at communication as a political as well as a cultural tool. Film and radio emphasized.

1254

Anokwa, Kwadwo, and Osei-Mensah Aborampah. "The Mass Media, Political Attitudes and Behavior in Ghana." *Gazette* 37, no. 3 (1986): 139-154.
   An historical overview of the relationship between the media, particularly newspapers, and successive political regimes in Ghana, with a survey of similar studies done elsewhere.

1255

Ansah, Paul A. V. "African Responses to the NWICO Debate." *Communication for All: New World Information and Communication Order*, 57-69. Edited by Philip Lee. Maryknoll, NY: Orbis Books, 1985.
   A discussion of the effects of the New World Information and Communication Order on African media, focusing on relations between state and press, the Pan-African News Agency, community media and training of journalists.

1256

---. "In Search of a Role for the African Media in the Democratic Process." *Africa Media Review* 2, no. 2 (1988): 1-16.
   A discussion of ways the media in Africa can promote democracy and development.

1257

Communicating Health Crisis in Africa. Report of the Follow-up Seminar Training Course in Primary Health Care for Eastern and Southern African Communicators, edited by Osmo Apunen. Tampere, Finland: University of Tampere, Unit of Peace Research and Development Studies, 1989. 103pp.
   Follow up reports and evaluation of a training course for East African journalists to increase their proficiency in reporting on health issues.

1258
Communicating Health in Africa: Research Papers of the Second Training Course of African Communicators, edited by Osmo Apunen, and Pirjo Huida. Tampere, Finalnd: University of Tampere, Unit of Peace Research and Development Studies, 1988. 305pp.
   A collection of essays on various aspects of health and health care in Africa, many focusing on the use of media in communicating health information.

1259
Armstrong, A. "'Hear No Evil, See No Evil, Speak No Evil': Media Restrictions and the State of Emergency." *South African Review* 4 (1987): 199-214.
   An overview of media restrictions in South Africa prior to the state of emergency declared on 12 June, 1986, the restrictions that were imposed at that time, and their effect on South African society.

1260
International Perspectives on News, edited by L. Erwin Atwood, Stuart J. Bullion, and Sharon Murphy. Carbondale: Southern Illinois University Press, 1982. 203pp.
   Papers from a symposium which brought together American journalists and mass communications scholars with journalists and scholars from other countries. Includes several papers on Nigeria and Egypt as well as relevant general analysis of the media in the Third World.

1261
Austin, Sydney Bryn. "AIDS and Africa: United States Media and Racist Fantasy." *Cultural Critique* , no. 14 (December 1989): 129-152.
   A discussion of the media coverage of the AIDS epidemic in Africa, making the case that racial stereotyping and misrepresentation could lead U.S. readers to assume that heterosexually transmitted AIDS is only an African or Black problem and, thus, ignore it.

1262
Awa, Njoku E. "Communication in Africa: Implications for Development and Planning." *Howard Journal of Communication* 1, no. 3 (September 1988): 131-143.
   A discussion of traditional forms of communication in Africa, concluding that most forms of mass media are aimed at and consumed by the urban elite. The exception is radio, which is an extension of oral tradition.

1263
---. "Mass Communication and Change in Africa: Implications for the Commonwealth Caribbean." *Journal of Black Studies* 13, no. 1 (September 1982): 7-22.
   An overview of traditional oral communication, radio, television and newspapers and their effects on development in Africa, with commentary on the implications of Africa's experience for the Caribbean.

General

1264
Ayish, Muhammad I. "International Communications in the 1990s: Implications for the Third World." *International Affairs* 68, no. 3 (July 1992):487-510.
> A general discussion of the New World Information and Communication Order (NWICO), raising issues important to Africa, although it does not focus directly on that continent.

1265
Ayodele, Lumuyiwa. "Objectivity, Sycophancy and the Media Reality in Nigeria." *Africa Media Review* 3, no. 1 (1988): 106-123.
> An argument that objectivity in the media is an attainable that the journalist must strive for, despite the obstacles placed in his way.

1266
Bagdley, Christine, and Motombo Mpanya. "Africa: Made in the USA." *AfterImage* 20, no. 1 (June 1992): 16-17.
> A brief discussion of bias and misrepresentation of Africa in U.S. media and advertising, and its effect on both American and African audiences.

1267
Balogun, Olu. "Traditional Arts and Cultural Development in Africa." *Cultures* 2, no. 3 (1975): 145-176.
> A noted Nigerian film-maker surveys the spectrum of traditional and modern art forms, including film, for the Intergovernmental Conference on Cultural Policies in Africa organized by Unesco in Accra, Ghana, 17 October to 6 November, 1975.

1268
Bamouni, Babou Paulin. "L'Afrique et l'Information dans le Monde." *Peuples Noirs-Peuples Africains*, no. 22 (January 1981): 85-99.
> A discussion of African news services and the influence on them of foreign media. The author recommends more use of Pan-African news agencies to supplement underfunded local news media.

1269
Barrett, Mike. *Rural Communications: Report on a Seminar for Managers/Planners/Policy-makers at Kericho Tea Hotel April 10-14, 1978 and a Workshop for Production/Research/Field Officers at Egerton College, Njoro, April 17-21, 1978.* Nairobi: Kenya. Ministry of Finance and Planning, 1978. 75pp.
> Examination of activities in press, film and television for rural areas in Africa.

1270
Becker, Jorg. *Africa on the Way to A New International Information Order.* Geneva: Institut Universitaire d'Études du Développement, 1980. *Notes et Travaux* no. 550pp.

A discussion of racism, both subtle and blatant, in much of the Western media's coverage of Africa and the misleading messages projected by Western-influenced media within Africa.

1271
Beltran, Luis. "Information and Social Communication in Zaire: an Annotated Bibliography." *Africana Journal* 11, no. 1/2 (1980): 5-30.
A bibliography of 188 citations to works on the press, broadcasting, and film in Zaire, indexed by time period and subject.

1272
Bensusan, A. D. *Silver Images: History of Photography in Africa*. Cape Town: Howard Timmins, 1966. 146pp.
Emphasis is on photography in South Africa, with chapters on cinematography and war correspondent photographers. Index.

1273
Bertelsen, Eve. "Selling Change: Advertisements for the 1994 Election." *African Affairs* 95, no. 379 (April 1996): 225-252.
A survey and analysis of political ads appearing in South African newspapers during the 1994 election campaign.

1274
Black List: The Concise Reference Guide to Publications and Broadcasting Media of Black America, Africa and the Caribbean. New York: Panther House, 1971. 289pp.
Lists newspapers, periodicals and broadcasting stations in Africa with figures for circulation and numbers of radios and television sets.

1275
Blake, Cecil A. "Communication Development in Africa and Its Impact on Cultural Synchronization of Africa and Its Peoples." *Africa Media Review* 2, no. 2 (1988): 17-28.
A discussion of theoretical issues and their potential relevance for African media.

1276
---. "Communication Research and African National Development." *Journal of Black Studies* 10, no. 2 (December 1979): 218-230.
The author suggests two areas for study: the curriculum for training in communication and the patterns and effects of ownership of the media in Africa.

1277
Blay-Amihere, Kabral. "Guinea: A Case for Optimism?" *Index on Censorship* 20, no. 1 (January 1991): 29-30.
A report on the improving conditions for the news media in Guinea.

General

1278

---."Sankara's Legacy." *Index on Censorship* 19, no. 2 (February 1990): 14-15.
  A report on the condition of the press and news media in Burkina Faso by a Ghanaian journalist.

1279

Bled, Cynthia A. "Review of Audience Research in Some Developing Countries of Africa." *Journal of Broadcasting* 13, no. 2 (March 1969): 167-180.
  A survey of studies done on audience response to media in Africa, with a summary of the major issues.

1280

Boadu, Samuel Osei. "Mass Media and Modernization: An Assessment of Theoretical Problems." *Journal of Black Studies* 12, no. 2 (December 1981): 193-200.
  A theoretical discussion of the relationship of media and development, with reference to Africa.

1281

Boafo, S. T. Kwame. *Bibliography of Teaching and Study Materials on African Media and Communication Systems.* Nairobi: African Council for Communication Education, 1991. 11pp.
  A bibliography of books on print and electronic media in Africa.

1282

Communication and Culture: African Perspectives, edited by S. T. Kwame Boafo. Nairobi: Africa Church Information Service, 1989. 56pp.
  A collection of essays on mass communication in Africa presented at the First World Association of Christian Communication Congress in Manila, October 1989. 4 page bibliography.

1283

Boafo, S. T. Kwame. "Communication Policy-Making in Sub-Saharan African Countries: Some Major Policy Issues." *Communication Policy-Making in Subsaharan African Countries and Latin America,* 3-20. S. T. Kwame Boafo, and Raquel Salinas. Budapest: Mass Communication Research Centre, 1988.
  An overview of communications policies in effect in African countries with discussion of the differing philosophies of policy-makers throughout that continent.

1284

---. "Democratizing Media Systems in African Societies: The Case of Ghana." *Africa Media Review* 2, no. 1 (1987): 24-37.
  A discussion of and proposals for ways that media systems in Ghana can be meaningfully democratized.

General

1285
---. "Democratizing Media Systems in African Societies: the Case of Ghana." *Gazette* 41, no. 1 (1988): 37-51.
> An overview of the media in Ghana, with commentary on the predominantly urban focus of writing and programming, with suggestions for improving the rural/urban balance.

1286
Media and Environment in Africa: Challenges for the Future, edited by S. T. Kwame Boafo. Nairobi: African Council on Communication Education, 1993. 111pp.
> A collection of essays on the role of the media in environmental problems in Africa, including issues of population, child health, drought, and media coverage of environmental problems.

1287
Boafo, S. T. Kwame. "Utilising Development Communication Strategies in African Societies." *Gazette* 35, no. 2 (1985): 83-92.
> Definition and discussion of the concept of "development communication" in the African context.

1288
Boafo, S. T. Kwame, and Rahab Gatura. *Communications Studies in Africa: A Bibliography*. Nairobi: African Council for Communication Education, 1994. 75pp.
> A bibliography of works on mass communications in Africa, arranged in sections by format: books, journal articles, documents, unpublished works and microfiche. Indexed by author and country or region.

1289
Communication Processes: Alternative Channels and Strategies for Development Support. Selected Papers Prepared for a Seminar Held in Nairobi, Kenya, November 14-16, 1990, edited by S. T. Kwame Boafo and Nancy A. George. Ottawa: IDRC, 1990. 97pp.
> A collection of papers discussing radio, television and newspapers as means of delivering information for development.

1290
Communication Research in Africa: Issues and Perspectives, edited by S. T. Kwame Boafo and Nancy A. George. Nairobi: African Council on Communication Education, 1992. 161pp.
> Collection of essays from a series of seminars on communications in Africa. 3 page bibliography. Index.

1291
Bojuwade, Dokun. *Mass Media on Trial*. s.n., 1981. 101pp.

General

A Nigerian journalist discusses the responsibility of the news media, examining news coverage between September 1978 and September 1979, the transition period from a military to a civilian regime, to determine how well this process was reported.

1292
---. *Press and Public Policy: A Guide to Information Managers.* Ibadan: Ibadan University Press, 1991. 53pp.
A description of the state of press policy in Nigeria, intended as a guide for media professionals. Includes the Nigeria Media Council Decree of 1988.

1293
Bosompra, Kwadwo. "Sources of Health Information Among Rural Dwellers in Africa: A Case Study of Two Ghanaian Villages." *Africa Media Review* 1, no. 2 (1987): 120-133.
Report of a survey to determine the efficacy of radio, newspapers and more traditional means of communication in disseminating health information in two villages in Ghana.

1294
Botombele Ekanga Bokonga. *Communication Policies in Zaire.* Paris: Unesco, 1980. 59pp.
A discussion of the press, radio, television and film in Zaire, with commentary on the effect of Zairian "authenticity" on the form and content of media presentation. Appendices include copies of relevant legislation.

1295
Bourgault, Louise M. *Mass Media in Sub-Saharan Africa.* Bloomington, IN: Indiana University Press, 1995. 294pp.
An historical overview of broadcasting and the press in Africa with theoretical commentary on traditional communication, modern discourse style, and sociological analysis. 17 page bibliography. Index.

1296
---. "Press Freedom in Africa: A Cultural Analysis." *Journal of Communication Inquiry* 17, no. 2 (June 1993): 69-92.
An examination of the relationship of traditional cultural patterns in African society and press freedom in Africa.

1297
---. "Training African Media Personnel: Some Psychocultural Considerations." *Africana Journal* 16 (1994): 51-65.
A discussion of the conflict between Western and traditional African approaches to communication, and the problems it raises in training African media staff.

1298
---. "Training Researchers for Development Communication in Africa." *World Communication* 18, no. 1 (1989): 73-92.

An examination of the problems in building a pool of professionals prepared to do meaningful research in development communication in Africa, based on the author's experience with development projects in several African countries.

1299

Bourges, Hervé. "Reflexion sur le Rôle de la Presse en Afrique." *Revue Française d'Études Politiques Africaines*, no. 84 (December 1972): 24-37.
A discussion of the problems facing the press and news broadcasting in Africa. They are, mainly, lack of funding for the industry's infrastructure, general poverty which reduces the potential readership and audience, and a growing sense of alienation.

1300

Boyd, Douglas A., and Jim Kushner. "Media Habits of Egyptian Gatekeepers." *Gazette* 25, no. 2 (1979): 106-113.
An exploration of "gatekeepers" of news, using interviews with 25 leading Egyptian radio, television, newspaper and magazine editors to determine the extent and pattern of their selection of news to disseminate.

1301

Braimoh, Dele. "Communication Strategies for Effective Literacy Campaign in Nigeria." *Nigeria Magazine*, no. 145 (1983): 16-27.
An assessment of the Mass Literacy Campaign in Nigeria in 1982 and its use of radio, television, film, and newspapers, with some comparison to literacy campaigns in Tanzania and Senegal.

1302

Brown, Trevor. "Why Has the U.S. Media Spotlight Turned Away From South Africa?" *Current Issues in International Communication*, 167-169. Edited by L. John Martin, and Ray Eldon Hiebert. New York: Longman, 1990.
A brief discussion of U.S. coverage of South Africa, concluding that it had diminished mainly because the American audience's attention had simply shifted elsewhere.

1303

Budlender, Debbie. "Resisting Seductive Technology in the New South Africa." *Social Dynamics* 21, no. 1 (1995): 79-82.
A response to P. Eric Louw's article "Rethinking Cultural Studies..." in the same journal, pointing out that South Africa's rural poor would benefit from more conventional development priorities than from the high level information technology Louw proposes. See # 1467.

1304

Buntman, Barbara. "Selling With the San: Representations of Bushman People and Artefacts in South African Print Advertisements." *Visual Anthropology* 8, no. 1 (1995): 33-54.
An examination of the uses of San images in South African advertising for such diverse products as airlines, hotels and telecommunications.

General

1305
Burgess, Julian et al. *The Great White Hoax: South Africa's International Propaganda Machine*. London: Africa Bureau, 1977. 119pp.
   A report on South Africa's propaganda efforts during the apartheid era, with sections on official and private sector activities, and descriptions of initiatives in the U.S., Britain, and the rest of Europe. Features reprints of ads and other propaganda materials. Index.

1306
Burton, Simon, and John Gultig. "Media in the "New" South Africa: "The More It Changes, the More It Stays the Same"." *Africa Quarterly* 32, no. 1-4 (1993): 115-125.
   A critique of media in South Africa following the end of apartheid.

1307
"Capturing the Continent: U.S. Media Coverage of Africa." *Africa News* 33, no. 10/11 (18 June 1990): 1-15.
   A special report, largely critical of the content and style of U.S. reporting on Africa.

1308
Carruthers, Susan L. *Winning Hearts and Minds: British Governments, the Mass Media and Colonial Counter-Insurgency, 1944-1960*. London: Mansell, 1995. 307pp.
   Essays on British propaganda during several liberation struggles of its colonies. Chapter 3, p. 128-193, looks at the Mau Mau insurgency, 1952-1960.

1309
Censorship in Kenya: Government Critics Face the Death Sentence. London: Article 19: International Centre Against Censorship, 1995. 33pp.
   Report on recent crackdowns by the Moi government on the press and other media in Kenya.

1310
Chakaodza, Bornwell. *Communication Policies in the African Context: Towards an Operational and Conceptual Framework*. Harare: Zimbabwe Institute of Development Studies, 1989. *Discussion Paper Series* No. 4. 9pp.
   An outline of factors to be considered in formulating national communication policies in Africa.

1311
Cheh, Mary M. "Systems and Slogans: The American Clear and Present Danger Doctrine and South African Publications Control." *South African Journal on Human Rights* 2, no. 1 (March 1986): 29-48.
   Comparison of U.S. and South African laws controlling the media when national security is at issue.

1312

Cheney-Coker, Syl. "African Artists and Mass Media." *Présence Africaine*, no. 88 (1973): 59-69. Special Issue: *Mass Media and Black Civilization*.
> An argument by a Sierra Leonean poet that racism and continued foreign domination, along with lack of encouragement for African artists, hamper creativity in African media.

1313

Chevaldonne, François. "Nationalization, Market Economy and Sociocultural Development: the Structures of Audiovisual Communication in Independent Algeria." *Media, Culture and Society* 10, no. 3 (1988): 269-284.
> A review of the private and public sectors in Algeria, with an analysis of the effect of economic status on access to the media.

1314

Chimutengwende, Chenhamo C. "The Media and the State in South African Politics." *Black Scholar* (September 1978): 44-57.
> An overview of all forms of media in South Africa and the restraints on them imposed by the legal infrastructure and police actions.

1315

---. "The Role of Communication Education in the Development and Democratization of African Society." *Africa Media Review* 2, no. 2 (1988): 29-45.
> A study of the interrelationship of the media and democracy in Africa.

1316

---. *South Africa: the Press and the Politics of Liberation*. London: Barbican Books, 1989. 208pp.
> The author defines "press" broadly to include all mass media. The work analyses the relationship of the media and socio-political events in South Africa. Appendices include documents dealing with mass media from anti-apartheid groups. 2 page reading list. Index.

1317

Clarke, L. J. "How Censorship Becomes Propaganda." *Index on Censorship* 16, no. 5 (May 1987): 2, 6.
> A former writer of propaganda for the South African Department of Information compares South African manipulation of the media to that of Nazi Germany.

1318

Club of Ten. *Ephemeral Materials*. London: Club of Ten.
> Reprint and letter from Gerald Sparrow, the putative chair of the Club of Ten, which was a cover for South Africa's Department of Information in its propaganda campaigns. Held in the Wilcox Collection of Contemporary Political Movements, University of Kansas Library.

General

1319

---. *The Phoenix*. London: Knightly Vernon. vol. 1-."Devoted mainly to the exposure of double standards in international affairs".
> A journal published by the Club of Ten, a cover group for the South Africa Department of Information for its propaganda campaign.

1320

Collinge, Jo-Anne et al. "What the Papers Don't Say." *Index on Censorship* 17, no. 3 (March 1988): 27-36.
> A survey of the restrictions on the press in force in South Africa through 1987, with some interpretation of the statutes in place. These number more than one hundred, most of which are deliberately vaguely worded.

1321

Coltart, James M. "The Influence of Newspaper and Television in Africa." *African Affairs* 62, no. 248 (July 1963): 202-210.
> A transcript of an address by a British newspaper publisher to the Royal African Society and the discussion following the address. The author notes the lack of media infrastructure throughout Africa and England's responsibility to help improve the situation.

1322

Communications and the Democratic Process in Africa: 6th Biennial Conference Report. Nairobi: African Council on Communication Education, 1989. 112pp.
> Summary of papers and workshops of the African Council on Communication Education conference held in Jos, Nigeria, in 1988, focusing on democratization and government-media relations.

1323

Condon, John C. "Some Guidelines for Mass Communications Research in East Africa." *Gazette* 14, no. 2 (1968): 141-151.
> Summary of suggested areas of scholarly investigation in the broad topic of mass communications in East Africa.

1324

Coombes, Annie E. *Reinventing Africa: Museums, Material Culture and Popular Imagination in Late Victorian and Edwardian England*. New Haven: Yale University Press, 1994. 280pp.
> While not dealing with images of Africa in the media, this work makes important observations concerning images of Africa portrayed in museums, including public events such as the Franco-British Exhibition in London in 1908. Bibliographic notes. 16 page bibliography. Index.

1325

Coulson, Anita. "The Party Line." *Index on Censorship* 19, no. 5 (May 1990): 22-24.

General

A report on the condition of the news media in Angola, where the ruling party exercises control but the new Press Law promises to reduce that control.

1326

---. "Press Freedoms Beckon... But the Door is Only Half Open." *Index on Censorship* 19, no. 5 (May 1990): 25-27.
> A report on the news media in Mozambique focusing on self censorship about controversial topics such as war, drought, famine, and the economic crisis, while noting that press freedoms are beginning to be implemented.

1327

"Creating a Vision." *Africa News* 28, no. 6 (30 November 1987): 9-11.
> Interview with Marty Rogol, head of United Support of Artists for Africa (USA for Africa), whose concerts and recording *We Are the World* raised $60 million in aid for Africa. He discusses new plans for the organization and the status of projects using the funds already raised.

1328

De Beer, Arnold S. "Censorship of Terror and the Struggle for Freedom: A South African Case Study." *Journal of Communication Inquiry* 17, no. 2 (June 1993): 36-51.
> A discussion of the means used by the South African government to control coverage of South African events, particularly incidents of violence and terrorism, by South African and foreign journalists. See Item #1683 for response.

1329

Mass Media for the Nineties: The South African Handbook of Mass Communication, edited by Arnold S. De Beer. Van Schaik, 1993. 426pp.
> A collection of essays discussing all forms of mass communications. General information is combined with material dealing with Africa as a whole and with South Africa in particular.

1330

DeBeer, Arnold S. "The Role of the Media in Building a Nation for a Unified South Africa." *Plural Societies* 22, no. 1/2 (1992): 214-237.
> A frank and blunt discussion of the media conditions in post-apartheid South Africa, where not all change is necessarily for the better.

1331

De Villiers, Les. *Secret Information*. Cape Town: Tafelberg, 1980. 182pp.
> An "insider's" account of Muldergate, the clandestine efforts of the South African Department of Information to build a favorable image of South Africa internationally.

1332

---. *South Africa: Skunk Among Nations*. London: Tandem, 1975. 186pp.
> Written by a principal participant in the Muldergate scandal, this discussion of South Africa's image in world media claims distortion and unfair treatment. Index.

General

1333
de Villiers, Trish, and Gaby Cheminais. "Investigating the Relationship between Women, Media and Violence: A CAP Media Project Course." *Critical Arts* 8, no. 1&2 (1994): 110-124.
> A description of a course taught in South Africa aimed at teaching women from a variety of community groups how to develop media campaigns to combat violence directed at women.

1334
Demafouth, Jean-Jacques. "Landlocked and Uninformed." *Index on Censorship* 14, no. 5 (October 1985): 22-23.
> Report on suppression of news in the Central African Republic by a CAR journalist now living in exile following charges of "revealing state secrets.".

1335
Dia, Saidou. "The Many Roles of Communications and Media in Africa." *Voices From Africa* , no. 4 (June 1992): 65-78.
> A discussion of the roles of media in development in Africa, concluding that radio is probably the best means currently available to spread necessary information and provide an opportunity for broad-based feedback.

1336
Dingamsangde, Ocsar Valentin. *Les Média d'Information en République du Tchad*. Ottawa: Institute for International Cooperation, University of Ottawa, 1974. 93pp.
> An overview of radio, press and other means of disseminating news in Chad. Appendices include statistical tables and a list of periodicals. 2 page bibliography.

1337
"Dirty Linen Gets Washed in Public." *Southern Africa* 12, no. 1 (January 1979): 13-17.
> Report of Muldergate, the scandal over the South African Ministry of Information's use of government funds to control information and disinformation. Sidebars illustrate parallels with the U.S. Watergate scandal.

1338
Distrust in Democracy: A Lawyers for Human Rights Commentary on the Report of the Steyn Commission of Inquiry into the Mass Media. Cape Town: Lawyers for Human Rights, 1982. 120pp.

1339
Dodson, Don, and William Hachten. *Communication and Development: African and Afro-American Parallels*. Lexington, Kentucky: Association for Education in Journalism, 1973. 37pp.
> A broad-ranging comparison, including use of language, media preference, and journalistic approaches.

1340
Domatob, Jerry Komia. "Communication Training for Self-Reliance in Black Africa: Challenges and Strategies." *Gazette* 40, no. 3 (1987): 167-182.
   A discussion of the need for self-reliance and the problems that hinder its realization in all phases of African life, including media production.

1341
---. "Communication Training for Self-Reliance in Black Africa: Challenges and Strategies." *Africa Media Review* 2, no. 1 (1987): 9-23.
   A critical evaluation of concepts of self-reliance in Africa, calling for a revamping of communication education to reach that ideal.

1342
---. "International Entertainment and the Fallacy of Free Information Flow." *The African Review* 13, no. 2 (1986): 1-11.
   A discussion of the concept of "free flow of information", and the controversy over it which is at the core of the debate about the New World Information and Communication Order (NWICO). The author contends that broadcasts of Western entertainment to African nations impede local development of the media.

1343
---. "Introducing Media Education into Sub-Saharan Africa." *Educational Media International* 28, no. 2 (June 1991): 91-99.
   Media education is here defined as teaching audiences how to understand and interpret the information they receive through the various media formats available to them. The author discusses the special problems involved in developing such programs in Africa.

1344
---. "Media and Adult Education in Sub-Saharan Africa: Role and Challenges." *Educational Media International* 27, no. 2 (June 1990): 108-114.
   An examination of the problems involved in the use of media in adult education in Africa, mainly lack of trained personnel and adequate funding, exacerbated by low levels of literacy and a multiplicity of local languages, with suggested strategies for overcoming them.

1345
---. "Propaganda Techniques in Black Africa." *Gazette* 36, no. 3 (1985): 193-212.
   An analysis of the ways in which the media are used in Africa to shape and influence opinions and actions.

1346
---. "Serious Problems Face Media Education in Sub-Saharan Africa." *Media Development* 38, no. 1 (1991): 31-34.

General

1347

---. "Sub-Saharan Africa's Media and Neocolonialism." *Africa Media Review* 3, no. 1 (1988): 149-174.
>A discussion of the role of the media in neo-colonial situations, contending that the media can work for or against this phenomenon.

1348

Domatob, Jerry Komia, and Stephen William Hall. "Development Journalism in Black Africa." *Gazette* 33, no. 1 (1983): 9-33.
>The authors define "development journalism" as the special situation of media in Third World societies, counteracting the dependency of colonialism and promoting the new nation state over the traditional societies. In this context they survey the achievements and frustrations of African media.

1349

Mass Media and the African Society, edited by Jerry Komia Domatob, A. Jika, and Ikechukwu E. Nwosu. Nairobi: African Council on Communication Education, 1987. 388pp.
>A collection of essays dealing with mass media in Africa, focusing on policy, media and development, global information flow, public relations and advertising, language in communication, and training of media professionals.

1350

Downing, John D. H. "US Media Discourse on South Africa." *Discourse and Society* 1, no. 1 (July 1990): 39.
>In a longitudinal study of the coverage of South Africa in *Time* and *Newsweek*, the author examines articles appearing in the two magazines in 1948, 1960 and 1976, focusing on the choice of terms and general tone and attitude.

1351

Dseagu, Njoroge. "A Matter of Words." *West Africa*, no. 3331 (1 June 1981): 1227-1228.
>A discussion of the inaccurate and biased terms used by foreign journalists reporting on events in Africa, compared to terms used to report similar events in Europe. Examples include: Ukrainians are "resisting Russian cultural domination", while "Ewes are fighting Ashanti tribalism"; a broadcast of ethnic music may include "Scottish bagpipe" and "African tribal drumming".

1352

Duyile, Dayo. *Media and Mass Communication in Nigeria*. Ibadan: Gong-Duyison Publishers, 1979. 384pp.
>An overview of press and broadcasting in Nigeria covering production and management, press freedom, public relations, and the relationship of the press and the military government.

1353
Dyck, Evellyne J., and Gary Coldevin. "Using Positive vs. Negative Photographs for Third-World Fund Raising." *Journalism Quarterly* 69, no. 3 (1992): 572-579.
>Report of a study done with the cooperation of World Vision Canada, a humanitarian relief and development organization. Fund raising appeals were sent to three groups: one receiving no photographs at all, one receiving positive photographs, the third receiving negative photographs. Contrary to conventional wisdom, the negative photographs were least effective in raising funds. While not dealing specifically with Africa, the study has great relevance to African concerns.

1354
Edeani, David O. "Priority Position of Communication in the African Development Process." *African Studies Review* 23, no. 2 (September 1980): 63-79.
>Description of a model of the relationship of communication to other factors in African development devised by using statistics concerning communication, urbanization, education, political participation, and press freedom garnered from several reliable standard reference works.

1355
---. "Role of *Africa Media Review* in the Sustainable Development of Communication Research." *Africa Media Review* 9, no. 1 (1995): 24-52.
>An examination of the nature of communication research published in *Africa Media Review*, concluding that more rigorous scholarship is needed.

1356
---. "Role of Development Journalism in Nigeria's Development." *Gazette* 52, no. 2 (1993): 123-143.
>An exploration of the benefits of both Nigeria's increased priority on rural communication infrastructure in the late 1980s and the efforts of a new breed of journalist committed to information service for development.

1357
---. "West African Communication Research At Major Turning Point." *Gazette* 41, no. 3 (1988): 151-183.
>An historical overview of communication research from colonial times to 1988. Analysis of problems caused by inappropriate theories and research tools along with stereotyped interpretations of results leads to recommendations for future research. 8 page bibliography.

1358
Egyptian Organization for Human Rights. *Freedom of Opinion and Expression in Egypt: A Report*. New York: Lawyers Committee for Human Rights, 1990. 33pp.

General

1359
Eilers, Franz-Josef, and Wilhelm Herzog. *Catholic Press Directory, Africa/Asia*. Munich: Paderborn, 1975. 318pp.
  A country-by-country list of Catholic periodical titles published in Africa with additional information on printing presses and broadcasting facilities.

1360
Nigerian Press Law, edited by T. O. Elias. Lagos: University of Lagos Press, 1969. 148pp.
  A collection of essays reviewing and discussing the principal statutes and case law relevant to the press, which the authors define broadly as including the broadcast and print media. Appendices include a tables of cases and statutes. Index.

1361
Emenyeonu, Bernard Nnamdi. "Communication and Adoption of Agricultural Innovations: Quantifications and Notes Toward a Conceptual Model." *Africa Media Review* 1, no. 2 (1987): 105-119.
  Report of a study of the correlation of rural Nigerian farmers' responsiveness to technical innovations and the media used to communicate the technology.

1362
---. "Motivations for Choice of Course and Career Preferences of Nigerian Female Students: Implications for the Status of Media Women in a Developing Nation." *Africa Media Review* 5, no. 2 (1991): 71-84.
  A survey of Nigerian female journalism students to determine their motivations for choosing that course of study and factors that affect their future career choices.

1363
Window on Africa: Democratization and Media Exposure, edited by Festus, Eribo, O. Oyediran, M. Wubneh, and L. Zonn. Greenville, NC: Center for International Programs, East Carolina University, 1993. 161pp.

1364
Eribo, Festus, and Stephen Vaughn. "Politics and Media in Russian-Sub-Saharan African Relations." *Journal of Communication Inquiry* 17, no. 2 (June 1993): 23-35.
  An overview of the coverage of Africa in Russian media and the relationship of that media coverage to politics and foreign policy.

1365
Issues and Problems in Mass Communications, edited by Nelson Etukudo. Calabar: Development Digest, 1986. 225pp.

1366
Ewane, F. Kange. "Les Légendes Ont la Vie Dure." *L'Afrique Littéraire* , no. 58 (1981): 10-24.

An overview of the image of Africans in European literature and journalism, pointing out how historical events have changed European perceptions to some extent, but also how stereotypes have persisted.

1367

Ewumbue-Munono, Churchill. "The Mass Media and Regional Integration in Africa." *Africa Media Review* 5, no. 1 (1991): 17-36.
An examination of media policies objectives, and the success of media in ensuring regional integration.

1368

Fair, Jo Ellen. "Black on Black: Race, Space and News of Africans and African Americans." *Issue* 22, no. 1 (March 1994): 35-40.
An analysis of the concept of "black on black" violence, beginning with the observation that crime or violence occurring between or among whites is not labeled "white on white". The author's point is that the phrase serves to distance and isolate both African-Americans and Africans from a white mainstream.

1369

---. "War, Famine and Poverty: Race in the Construction of Africa's Media." *Journal of Communication Inquiry* 17, no. 2 (June 1993): 5-22.
A discussion of U.S. coverage of African events and the images projected in that coverage, concentrating on the role of racial bias in choice of stories and terms.

1370

Fiofori, Ferdinand O. "Traditional Media, Modern Messages: A Nigerian Study." *Rural Africana* 27 (1975): 43-52.
A discussion of the use of tales and other traditional oral forms in modern media to disseminate development information.

1371

Frederikse, Julie. *None But Ourselves: Masses vs. Media in the Making of Zimbabwe*. Johannesburg: Ravan Press, 1982. 386pp.
Documentation of Zimbabwe's war of independence through interviews and analysis of print and non-print media. Extensive illustrations, including photographs, facsimiles of newspapers, advertisements, film clips and cartoons.

1372

Freeman, David K. "Mass Media: a Challenge." *Africans on Africa* # 1, Supplement to IDOC *Internazionale* 26, no. 1 (January 1995): 27-32.

1373

Friedenberg, Daniel M. "The Public Relations of Colonialism: Salazar's Mouthpiece in the U.S." *Africa Today* 9, no. 3 (April 1962): 4-6, 15-16.
Report describing the activities of a U.S. public relations firm with strong ties to domestic right wing conservative groups which conducted an extensive campaign of misinformation, playing on fears of Communism to promote support for Portugal's

General

colonial regime in Africa. Refers to a similar propaganda campaign for support of Katanga in its secession a few years earlier.

1374
Fuglesang, Minou. *Veils and Videos: Female Youth Culture on the Kenya Coast*. Stockholm: Dept. of Social Anthropology, Stockholm University, 1994. 322pp.
> An ethnography with chapters on the effect of video recording on ceremonial occasions and on the film and television preferences of women in Lamu and other Kenyan coastal communities with commentary on how the media is changing life there.

1375
Fussell, Paul. "The Smut Hounds of Pretoria." *New Republic* (23 February 1980): 20-23.

1376
Gambia: Democracy Overturned Violations of Freedom of Expression. London: Article 19, 1994.

1377
Mass Media Policies and Changing Cultures, edited by George Gerbner. New York: John Wiley & Sons, 1977. 291pp.
> Essays dealing with a broad spectrum of issues concerning the mass media in the Third World. Several essays dealing specifically with Africa, others on more general topics with relevance to Africa. Index.

1378
Getachew Tadesse Azmera. "Communicable Diseases and Media Coverage in Tigray." *Communicating Health in Africa: Research Papers of the Second Training Course of African Communicators*, 290-305. Edited by Osmo Apunen and Pirjo Huida. Tampere, Finland: University of Tampere, Unit of Peace Research and Development Studies, 1988.
> An overview of the major communicable diseases in Tigray, Ethiopia, and the messages disseminated on radio and in the press concerning them.

1379
Ghana Journalists Association. *State of the Media in Ghana*. University of Ghana Bookshop, 1994. 73pp.
> Proceedings of a workshop assessing the media in Ghana two years after the country's return to constitutional rule. Topics covered include the 1992 Constitution and its relation to journalistic practice, rural journalism, and journalistic ethics.

1380
Ghejam, Ali M. "Mass Communications in the Libyan Jamahiriya." *Journal of Black Studies* 20, no. 3 (1990): 324-334.

An overview of mass media in Libya and its role in achieving the goals of the revolution. A table accompanying the article compares Libyan mass media to those of the U.S. and the U.S.S.R.

1381
Giffard, C. Anthony. "The Impact of Television on South African Daily Newspapers." *Journalism Quarterly* (June 1980): 216-223.

1382
---. "Role of Media in a Changing South Africa." *Gazette* 46, no. 3 (1990): 143-153.
Discussion of possible future scenarios for the media in South Africa during the tumultuous change from the apartheid regime to democracy.

1383
---. "South African Attitudes Toward News Media." *Journalism Quarterly* (December 1976): 653-660.

1384
Gill, Peter. *A Year in the Death of Africa: Politics, Bureaucracy and the Famine*. London: Grafton Books, 1986. 191pp.
A British television journalist reports on the conduct of aid institutions engaged in famine relief in Ethiopia, with considerable commentary on media coverage of events.

1385
Gilwald, Alison. "Women, Democracy and Media in South Africa." *Africana on Africa Series* #1, Supplement to IDOC *Internazionale* 26, no. 1 (January 1995): 11-19.

1386
Green, Nick, and Reg Lascaris. *Communication in the Third World: Seizing Advertising Opportunities in the 1990s*. Cape Town: Tafelberg, 1990. 196pp.
A "how-to" book on advertising in the Third World, focusing on Africa. Includes numerous examples of ads.

1387
Green, Pippa. "Getting South Africa Back into the News." *Columbia Journalism Review* (January 1990): 46-47.
A short report on the efforts of journalists to overcome the restrictions imposed by South Africa's government and report anti-apartheid activities.

1388
Griffin, Michael. "The Case of Mike Kilongson." *Index on Censorship* 15, no. 10 (November 1986): 18, 50.

General

Description of the arrest and detention of a Sudanese radio journalist who reported on famine in the Sudan, against the government's order to suppress such news. (See Item # 1446).

1389

Gueye, Amadou Mactar. "Decolonising the Media on Africa." *West Africa*, no. 3709 (12 September): 1660-1662.

A report on the activities of the Pan-African News Agency in providing accurate and broad news coverage for Africa, thereby correcting the imbalance in the flow of information.

1390

Hachten, William A. *The Growth of Media in the Third World: African Failures, Asian Successes*. Ames, Iowa: Iowa State University Press, 1993. 128pp.

A comparison of media development in Africa and Asia concentrating on the press. 2 page bibliography. Index.

1391

Mass Communications in Africa: An Annotated Bibliography, compiled by William A. Hachten. Madison, WI: Center for International Communication Studies, 1971. 121pp.

This bibliography of 537 citations to works on mass communications in Africa covers newspapers, magazines, radio, television, and film, as well as broad topics such as press freedom, training of journalists, and technology.

1392

Hachten, William A. "Mass Media in Africa." *Mass Communication -- a World View*, 91-111. Edited by Alan Wells et al. New Orleans: Tulane University, 1974.

An historical overview of the development mass communication media in Africa, emphasizing the diversity of national and ethnic settings and noting the changes since most African nations achieved independence.

1393

---. "Moroccan News Media Reflect Divisive Forces While Unifying." *Journalism Quarterly* 48, no. 1 (March 1971): 100-110.

A survey of press, radio and television in Morocco noting how modern media are supplementing rather than supplanting traditional means of communication.

1394

---. *Muffled Drums: the News Media in Africa*. Ames, Iowa: Iowa State University Press, 1971. 314pp.

Overview of news media in Africa, with emphasis on the press, but including broadcast media. Case studies from Nigeria, Ghana, Côte d'Ivoire, Senegal, Kenya, Zambia and South Africa. Statistical tables. 9 page bibliography. Index.

1395

Hamdane, Mohamed. *Le Droit de l'Information en Tunisie*. Tunis: Centre National Universitaire de Documentation Scientifique et Technique, 1989. 413pp.
    Overview of Tunisian laws pertaining to the press, broadcasting, and organizations whose activities are related to information provision and distribution. Appendix provides a list of relevant legislation. 6 page bibliography.

1396

Hamelink, Cees J. *The Politics of World Communication: a Human Rights Perspective*. London: Sage, 1994. 337pp.
    Global overview of communications technologies and policies, with African examples. 8 page bibliography. Index.

1397

Hardy, Pauline. "The War of Words in Southern Africa." *Index on Censorship* 13, no. 1 (February 1984): 23-25.
    A report on the Kadoma Declaration, a set of resolutions signed by the Ministers of Information of the "Frontline" states of Southern Africa to counteract South Africa's campaign of destabilization through propaganda and disinformation.

1398

Harrison, Paul, and Robin Palmer. *News Out of Africa: Biafra to Band Aid*. London: H. Shipman, 1986. 147pp.
    Accounts of the forces which shape African news stories in the Western media, illustrating indifference alternating with sensationalism.

1399

Africa's Media Image, Edited by Beverly G. Hawk. New York: Praeger, 1992. 268pp.
    A collection of essays on coverage of African news in the U.S. press and other media, with specific examples of the Mau Mau, Algerian civil war, Nigerian civil war and South Africa. 2 page bibliography. Index.

1400

Haysom, Nicholas, and Gilbert Marcus. "'Undesirability' and Criminal Liability under the Publications Act 42 of 1974." *South African Journal on Human Rights* 1, no. 1 (May 1985): 37.
    A commentary on, and interpretation of, the Publications Act which was the basis of most of South Africa's censorship.

1401

Head, Sydney W. "African Mass Communication: Selected Information Sources." *Journal of Broadcasting* 20, no. 3 (June 1976): 381-415.
    A 460 item bibliography on the media of mass communication in Africa, grouped by type of publication and indexed by country.

General

1402
---. "Trends in Tropical African Societies." *Mass Media Policies in Changing Cultures*, 83-103. Edited by George Gerbner. New York: John Wiley & Sons, 1977.
> Discussion of the state of African broadcasting and the press with recommendations for the future.

1403
Hennebelle, Guy. "Slim: (Auteur de *Zid ya Bouzid*) La Bande Dessinée est un Moyen d'Expression Très Subtil." *L'Afrique Littéraire et Artistique*, no. 14 (1970): 2-6.
> Interview with Algerian cartoonist Slim (Menouar Merabtene) and discussion of the message of his comic strip *Zid ya Bouzid*.

1404
Herbstein, Denis. "Namibia: How South Africa Controls the News." *Index on Censorship* 14, no. 4 (August 1985): 8-10.
> A report on South Africa's manipulation and suppression of the news media in Namibia.

1405
Hoben, Susan J. *Language Use, Language Policy, and the Spread of Communications Systems in Africa*. Boston: Boston University African Studies Center, 1984. African American Issues Center Discussion Paper no. 7. 34pp.
> An exploration of issues of language and their implications for mass communications, including broadcasting and the press. 15 page bibliography.

1406
Hortop, Stella. "Media Representations: Towards Understanding the Selection and Construction of Media Messages; Learning in the Multicultural Classroom." *Critical Arts* 8, no. 1&2 (1994): 77-109.
> A study of the ways students in South Africa can be taught techniques of understanding the repercussions of images in media and of developing positive images.

1407
Hull, Galen. "South Africa's Propaganda War: A Bibliographic Essay." *African Studies Review* 22, no. 3 (December 1979): 79-98.
> An account of the activities of the South African Ministry of Information leading up to and during the Muldergate affair with numerous bibliographic references.

1408
Ibie, Nosa Owens. "The Commercialization of the Mass Media in Nigeria: the Challenge of Social Responsibility." *Journal of Development Communication* 4, no. 1 (June 1993): 60-68.

A discussion of privatization of the mass media in Nigeria in the context of structural adjustment, with emphasis on the debate over whether public or private media better serve the nation.

1409

---. "Media/Cultural Imperialism and Nigerian Women: Whose Culture, Which Imperialism." *Journal of Social Development in Africa* 7, no. 2 (1992): 39-52.
A discussion of the status of women in modern Nigeria, whose treatment is shaped both by traditional and the colonialist attitudes adopted by modern rulers. The author makes the point that the media could combat this problem but do not.

1410

---. "Public Opinion Research in Emergent African Democracies: the Case of Nigeria." *Communication Research in Africa: Issues and Perspectives*, 19-28. Edited by S. T. Kwame Boafo, and Nancy A. George. Nairobi: African Council on Communication Education, 1992.
An overview of methodologies for doing public opinion research in Nigeria.

1411

---. "Public Relations and the Structure of Reality: A Nigerian Perspective." *Studies in Third World Societies* ,52, no. 3 (December 1991): 207-255.
An assessment of the use of media in public relations in Nigeria, focusing on both government and private sector activities.

1412

Ibrahim, Salah M. *The Flow of International News Into Sudan, The Middle East and Africa: New Information Order*. Khartoum: Ministry of Culture and Information, 1981. 25pp.
An overview of the foreign and local news services providing news to Egypt and the Sudan, with a theoretical discussion of the best way for local news media to develop.

1413

Ijere, M. O. "The Nigerian Experience." *Présence Africaine* , no. 88 (1973): 10-28. Special issue: *Mass Media and Black Civilization*.
An historical overview of the development of mass media in Nigeria, arguing that modern mass media encourage adoption of foreign ideas and culture, with proposals for making the Nigerian media more Nigerian.

1414

Images de l'Afrique en Occident: La Presse, les Médias et la Littérature: Colloque Organisé par le Centre d'Études et de Recherches sur les Civilisations, Langues et Littérature d'Expression Française (CERCLEF). Paris: L'Afrique Littéraire, 1981. Special issue of *L'Afrique Littéraire*, #58. 147pp.

General

A special issue with papers from a colloquium organized by the Centre d'Etudes et de Recherches sur les Civilisations, Langues et Littérature d'Expression Française (CERCLEF), concentrating mainly on literature, with a few articles dealing with the press.

1415
In African Accents: A Report of a Conference on Communications in Development. Lusaka: Multimedia, 1971. 76pp.
Papers and reports from a meeting of the Association of the Episcopal Conferences in Eastern Africa focusing on Christian communication and use of media in church work and development.

1416
"Informaçao e Colonialismo." *Tempo*, no. 471 (21 October 1979): 29-43.
A report on the press and film in Africa.

1417
L'Information au Maghreb. Tunis: Ceres Éditions, 1992. 362pp.
A collection of essays dealing with the press and broadcast news in Algeria, Mauritania, Morocco and Tunisia. Topics include press freedom and the legal framework.

1418
"L'Information en Afrique." *Afrique Contemporaine* 16, no. 95 (January 1978): 1-16.
A collection of short pieces on the status of the press and other media in Africa.

1419
"Information Scandal Revelations Continue." *Southern Africa* 12, no. 4 (May 1979): 10-12.
Continuing coverage of Muldergate, the misuse of government funds by South Africa's Ministry of Information to control information and influence international opinion.

1420
Isaacs, Gayla Cook. "Media and the Ideal Women." *Africa Report* 28, no. 2 (March 1983): 48-51.
A discussion of the ways Africa women are portrayed in modern media, particularly advertising, contrasted to traditional portrayals of women.

1421
Jack, Abner. "The Steyn Commission: An Annotated Bibliography." *Critical Arts* 2, no. 3 (1982): 29-32.
A collection of citations to articles in South African publications reacting to the Steyn Commission report on mass media.

1422
James, Sybil L. "A Critical Appraisal of the Communication Gap and the Liberation Struggle." *Africa Media Review* 2, no. 1 (1987): 108.
> A critical analysis of politically loaded words used in Western coverage of African and other liberation struggles.

1423
---. "Development of Indigenous Journalism and Broadcast Formats: Curricular Implications for Communications Studies in Africa." *Africa Media Review* 4, no. 1 (1990): 1-14.

1424
Jefkins, Frank William, and Frank Okwu Ugboajah. *Communication in Industrialising Countries*. London: Macmillan, 1986. 220pp.
> Overview with emphasis on advertising and public relations containing numerous African examples. Index.

1425
Jimada, Usman. "Authoritarianism and Mass Media Participation in the Democratic Process in Africa: Problems and Prospects." *Western Journal of Black Studies* 15, no. 1 (March 1991): 60-65.
> The author argues that authoritarian regimes in many African countries stifle the media, which are an essential component of democracy.

1426
---. "Eurocentric Media Training in Nigeria: What Alternative?" *Journal of Black Studies* 22, no. 3 (March 1992): 366-379.
> A review of the training opportunities available to Nigerians for careers in the media, the problems with Western bias in most training, and proposals for alternative training methods.

1427
John-Kanem, Anthony V. "Mass Media and Black Civilization." *Présence Africaine*, no. 88 (1973): 80-97. Special Issue: *Mass Media and Black Civilization*.
> A commentary on the sense of inferiority that was the result of colonial attitudes towards African life and culture, with a call to action to use mass media in Africa to reassert pride in traditional culture.

1428
Johnson, Shaun. "Barometers of the Liberation Movement: A History of South Africa's Alternative Press." *Media Development* 32, no. 3 (June 1985): 18-21.

General

1429

Jules-Rosette, Bennetta. *Terminal Signs: Computers and Social Change in Africa*. Berlin: Mouton de Gruyter, 1990. 424pp.
   A thoughtful study of the ways computers and electronic information technology are affecting traditional African life and culture, focusing on Côte d'Ivoire and Kenya. 16 page bibliography. Index.

1430

Kahn, Ellison. "*When the Lion Feeds* -- and the Censor Pounces: A Disquisition on the Banning of Immoral Publications in South Africa." *South African Law Journal* 83 (1966): 278-336.
   An historical analysis of the South African laws pertaining to obscenity and immoral literature, illustrating the ways in which government control of reading matter has expanded.

1431

Kamara, Musa S. "Western Free Flow of Information Doctrine in a Borderless World Threatens Developing Nations' Cultures and National Identities." *The Journal of African Communications* 1, no. 1 (March 1996):
   A discussion of NWICO and its potential effect on national identity in Africa and the rest of the Third World, focusing on the global dominance of Western media.

1432

Kamuhanda, Sethi. "The Role of the Mass Media in the Implementation of Tanzania's Foreign Policy: Reality and Prospects." *Africa Media Review* 3, no. 3 (1989): 25-38.

1433

Kandaki, D. E. S. "The Role of Research in Development Communication at the Liberian Rural Communications Network." *Africa Media Review* 3, no. 1 (1988): 64-82.
   A study of the place of research in development communication, focusing on the Liberian Rural Communications Network, and making some general recommendations.

1434

Kaplan, David. *The Crossed Line: The South African Telecommunications Industry in Transition*. Johannesburg: Witwatersrand University Press, 1990. 227pp.

1435

---. "The Development of Telecommunications in South Africa: The Equipment Supply Industry." *Critical Arts* 6, no. 1 (1992): 96-109.
   A study of the technical aspects of telecommunications, particularly as they affect the expansion of media services to formerly disadvantaged groups.

1436

Karikari, Kwame. "Media Policy: A Factor in the Search for Democracy." *Africa Media Review* 4, no. 1 (1990): 27-41.

A discussion of national media policies in the context of military regimes in Ghana, which exercised tight control of the media.

1437

Kasoma, Francis P. *Communication Policies in Botswana, Lesotho and Swaziland*. Tampere, Finland: University of Tampere, 1992.

Overview of policies and regulations of the media of mass communication including radio, television, and the press in Botswana, Lesotho and Swaziland. Appendix provides the code of professional standards and operational procedures for broadcasting in Swaziland. 6 page bibliography.

1438

---. *Communication Policies in Zambia*. Tampere, Finland: University of Tampere, 1990. 104pp.

An overview of mass communications in Zambia including the infrastructure, newspapers, broadcasting, film publishing and advertising. Sections include summaries of communication laws and recommendations for policy.

1439

Katz, Elihu. "Can Authentic Cultures Survive New Media." *Journal of Communication* 27 (1977): 113-121.

A global overview of the problems of Western entertainment and news media imported to Third World countries, with some African examples.

1440

Kenya: Recent Threats to Freedom of Expression. London: Article 19, 1992. Censorship News #10. 8pp.

Report of repression of the press and other government critics.

1441

Kenya: Shooting the Messenger. London: Article 19, 1993. *Censorship News* #28. 11pp.

Report on efforts of the Moi government to suppress reportage of political violence in the Rift Valley area.

1442

Kern-Foxworth, Marilyn. "The Effect of Advertising Stimuli on American Perception of Africa: A Descriptive Analysis." *Journal of Black Studies* 16, no. 2 (December 1985): 155-168.

Report of a study using thirteen color slides of African scenes selected from travel brochures which were shown to 126 students at the University of Tennessee, recording how the slides fit the students' preconceived ideas of Africa, and whether seeing scenes of modern cities in Africa, for example, changed those preconceptions.

General

1443
Kerr, David. *African Popular Theatre From Pre-Colonial Times to the Present Day.* London: James Currey, 1995. 278pp.
    Chapter 9, "Popular Theatre and Macro-Media" discusses the interaction of media and other forms of popular theatre, particularly the development of locally produced film, radio and television. Endnotes for the chapter refer to a 14 page bibliography. Index.

1444
Khelil, Hedi. *Journalism, Cinéphilie et Télévision en Tunisie: Six Essais.* Sherbrooke, Quebec, Canada: Éditions Naaman, 1985. 66pp.
    A discussion of the use of the media in manifesting political power in Tunisia.

1445
Kifle Sede. "Health Information: Coverage on Ethiopian Mass Media." *Communicating Health in Africa: Research Papers of the Second Training Course of African Communicators,* 273-289. Edited by Osmo Apunen, and Pirjo Huida. Tampere: University of Tampere, Unit on Peace Research and Development Studies, 1988.
    An overview of the amount and kind of health coverage in all Ethiopian languages in Ethiopian radio broadcasts and newspapers.

1446
Kilongson, Mike. "Reports of Famine are Prohibited." *Index on Censorship* 15, no. 10 (November 1986): 17-18.
    A report by a Sudanese radio journalist on the suppression of news reports of famine in Sudan while the country's leaders assured the world that they had the situation under control. Kilongson was later arrested and exiled (See Item 1388).

1447
Kivikuru, Ullamaija. "Communication in Transition: the Case of Tanzanian Villages." *Gazette* 43, no. 2 (March 1989): 109-130.
    Commentary on the use of radio and newspapers to promote *Ujamaa*, Tanzania's comprehensive programme of social transformation, based on a survey of nine villages.

1448
---. "Participation or the Popular: Where to Find a Nest for the Restless Minds of Rural Transition?" *Africa Media Review* 8, no. 3 (1994): 40-77.
    A case study of the partial success of a rural communication project in nine Tanzanian villages. 3 page bibliography.

1449
---. *Tinned Novelties or Creative Cultures? A Study of the Role of Mass Communication in Peripheral Nations.* Helsinki: University of Helsinki, Department of Communication, 1990. 514pp.

A theoretical introduction is followed by a comparison of communications in Finland and Tanzania.

1450
Kizito, Robert N. *Communication and Human Rights in Africa: Implications for Development*. Nairobi: African Council on Communication Education, 1992. 162pp.
> A collection of essays exploring the relationship of communication and human rights in Africa.

1451
Klee, Hans Dieter. "In Africa, the Media Hold the Key to Democratic Reform." *Intermedia* 1992, no. 20 (November/December): 6.
> A discussion of the interdependence between the media and political reform in Africa.

1452
Konde, Hadji. *Press Freedom in Tanzania*. Arusha, Tanzania: Eastern Africa Publications, 1984. 242pp.
> Historical overview of censorship in Tanzania, focusing on the press, but touching on film and broadcasting.

1453
Koné, Hugues. "Circulation de l'Information et Pluralisme: Quels Défies Pour la Presse Africaine?" *Africa Media Review* 6, no. 2 (1992): 1-12.
> An assessment of the potential role for the press in Africa's democratization movements.

1454
---. "Démocratisation des Médias, Démocratie par les Médias: Une Imperieuse Necessité." *Africa Media Review* 2, no. 2 (1988): 100-114.
> A discussion of the role of the media in strengthening the democratic process.

1455
---. "Recherche en Communication en Matière de Population: Cas d'un Projet de Communication en Planification Familiale." *Africa Media Review* 7, no. 1 (1993): 51-71.
> A study of several means of communication, including radio, television, newspapers, word of mouth, and leaflets, in spreading understanding and acceptance of family planning measures in Côte d'Ivoire.

1456
Kramer, Jane. "In the Garrison." *New York Review of Books* (1 December 1982): 8-12.

General

1457
Kramer, Reed. "Africa News Online." *Nieman Reports* 50, no. 1 (March 1996): 74-76.
   A report on efforts to establish African news services on the Internet, with emphasis on the activities of the Africa News Service.

1458
Kumbula, Tendayi S. "[Review of *Africa's Media Image* by Beverly Hawk]." *Journal of Third World Studies* 11, no. 1 (March 1994): 460-466.
   A review of Hawk's book, with considerable commentary from the author's own experience with Africa's media image.

1459
Lardner, Tunji. "Africa: Rewriting the Tale of the "Dark Continent"." *Media Studies Journal* 7, no. 4 (September 1993): 95.
   An analysis of the rhetoric of U.S. coverage of Africa, noting racism, Eurocentrism and a Cold War frame of reference.

1460
Laurence, John. *The Seeds of a Disaster: A Guide to the Realities, Race Policies and World-Wide Propaganda Campaigns of the Republic of South Africa*. New York: Taplinger, 1968. 333pp.
   A discussion of South Africa's propaganda campaigns using the media of mass communications to influence opinion concerning South Africa and its apartheid policy both at home and overseas.

1461
Lederbogen, Utz. *Watchdog or Missionary? A Portrait of African News People and Their Work: A Case Study in Tanzania*. Frankfurt: P. Lang, 1992. 180pp.
   A study of print and broadcast journalism in Tanzania, including a detailed profile of journalists and the outlook for the future. Includes a press directory. 5 page bibliography. Index.

1462
Lepine, Richard M.. "Representations of the Printed Text and of Electronic Media Artforms in Swahili Popular Fiction." *Passages: A Chronicle of the Humanities*, no. 8 (1994): 5-6. Supplement to *Program of African Studies News and Events*, Northwestern University, Volume 5, No. 1, Fall 1994.
   Discussion of popular Swahili fiction in books, magazines, newspapers, television and film and the readers and audiences it attracts.

1463
Levi, Antonia. "How Heathens Treat Women: *Sati*, Footbinding and the American Campaign Against Genital Mutilation." *Africa in the Contemporary International Disorder: Crises and Possibilities*, 153-181.

Edited by Mulugeta Agonafer. Lanham, MD: University Press of America, 1996.
> Comparing Western reactions to female genital mutilation in Africa to similar reactions to the practice of *sati* in India and footbinding in China the author highlights use of media in shaping those reactions.

1464
Lodge, Tom. "Soviets and Surrogates: Black Nationalism and the Steyn Commission." *Critical Arts* 2, no. 3 (1982): 23-28.
> A commentary on the Steyn Commission's assertions that efforts of the ANC and other organizations to end apartheid were part of a Soviet Union attack on South Africa.

1465
Louw, P. Eric. *A Critical Analysis of the Durban Media Trainers' Group.* Durban: Centre for Cultural and Media Studies, University of Natal, 1991. 12pp.
> A report on a project to develop a pool of media activists skilled not only in the technical and business aspects of media production but also in its theoretical and philosophical bases.

1466
---. "Media, Media Education and the Development of South Africa." *Screen* 32, no. 4 (December 1991): 388-399.
> A leftist approach to planning for media and media education in the new South Africa.

1467
---. "Rethinking Cultural Studies to Meet the Challenge of the "Information Age" in South Africa." *Social Dynamics* 21, no. 1 (December 1995): 71-78.
> An optimistic discussion of electronic media as a powerful force with the potential of improving the lot of all South Africans. Rebutted by Debbie Budlander in # 1303.

1468
South African Media Policy: Debates of the 1990s, edited by P. Eric Louw. Chicago: Lake View Press, 1993. 380pp.
> A collection of essays on issues relating to development of South Africa's media policy in the post-apartheid era.

1469
Louw, P. Eric, and Keyan G. Tomaselli. "Considerations on the Role of Media and Information in Building a New South Africa." *Africa Media Review* 8, no. 1 (1994): 57-72.
> A leftist theoretical approach to the use of media, with practical recommendations for training media workers and educating the public to understand media. 2 page bibliography.

General

1470
Louw, Raymond et al. *Open Media: Media in a New South Africa.* Mowbray, South Africa: IDASA, 1990. 21pp.
> A collection of short papers on the future of media in Southern Africa, focusing on South Africa, with commentary on Namibia and Mozambique.

1471
---. "South Africa's Newspapers Press on from Pan-African Pay-TV to Cellular Telephones." *Intermedia* 21, no. 1 (January 1993): 3-5.
> An overview of pay-TV in South Africa from its beginning in 1986, when it was managed by a newspaper group supportive of the government which drained advertising revenues from opposition newspapers, to the present, when it cooperates with the print media and helps develop alternative publishing ventures.

1472
Maingard, Jacqueline. "Trends in South African Documentary Film and Video: Questions of Identity and Subjectivity." *Journal of Southern African Studies* 21, no. 4 (December 1995): 657-667.
> A study of South African anti-apartheid documentary film from the late 1970s to the early 1990s, focusing on the main themes and the companies organized to produce the films.

1473
Maissara, Neema Mussa. "The Role of the Media in Combating Malaria in Zanzibar." *Communicating Health in Africa: Research Papers of the Second Training Course of African Communicators*, 95-117. Edited by Osmo Apunen and Pirjo Huida. Tampere, Finland: Tampere University, Unit of Peace Research and Development Studies, 1988.
> A study of how a popular magazine, a newspaper, a health newsletter, radio, and television worked in a malaria eradication campaign in Zanzibar. 3 page bibliography, including citations of articles in Zanzibar newspapers.

1474
Maja-Pearce, Adewale. "Censorship in Sub-Saharan Africa." *Third World Affairs* (1988): 209-219.
> A report on censorship and government control of the press and broadcast media in Africa.

1475
Directory of African Media, edited by Adewale Maja-Pearce. Brussels: International Federation of Journalists, 1996. 384pp.

1476
Maja-Pearce, Adewale. *Who's Afraid of Wole Soyinka? Essays on Censorship.* Portsmouth, NH: Heinemann Educational Books, 1991. 109pp.
> Collection of the author's essays, which had originally appeared in *Index on Censorship*, commenting on censorship in the press and literature.

1477
Malawi: The Elections and the Need for Media Reform. London: Article 19, 1994.

1478
Malawi's Elections: Media Monitoring, Freedom of Expression and Intimidation. London: Article 19, 1994. *Censorship News* #34. 22pp.

1479
Malawi's Past: the Right to Truth. London: Article 19, 1993. *Censorship News* #29. 18pp.
   An appeal for a "truth commission" to bring out in the open the facts on deaths and disappearances of journalists and other activists in Malawi.

1480
Maqetuka, Sello. "The Media of the ANC and the New Situation." *Sechaba* 24, no. 6 (June 1990): 21-17.
   An assessment of the publications and broadcast media of the ANC following its unbanning in 1990 and how their functions and formats might change to meet the challenges of change.

1481
Marchand, Jacques. *La Propagande de l'Apartheid: Comment l'Afrique du Sud se Crée une Image de Marque.* Paris: Karthala, 1985. 284pp.
   An overview of the use of propaganda in mass media, with emphasis on the Muldergate scandal of the Ministry of Information and the activities of South African lobbyists in France.

1482
Marcus, Gilbert. "The Wider Reaches of Censorship." *South African Journal on Human Rights* 1, no. 1 (May 1985): 69-74.
   A survey of and commentary on legal cases of censorship in South Africa and their ramifications.

1483
Martin, Robert. "Building Independent Mass Media in Africa." *Journal of Modern African Studies* 30, no. 2 (1992): 331-340.
   A discussion of the role of Africa's media in finding solutions to Africa's economic and political problems, with some practical recommendations.

1484
Masmoudi, Mustapha. "Media and the State in Periods of Crisis." *Media, Crisis and Democracy: Mass Communication and the Disruption of Social Order*, 34-43. Edited by Marc Raboy, and Bernard Dagenais. London: Sage Publications, 1992.
   Using several examples from Tunisia and other Third World countries, the author builds a case for a proposed code of conduct for journalists covering crises.

General

1485

---. *Voie Libre Pour Monde Multiple*. Tunis: Dar el Amal, 1986. 294pp.
  A discussion of the effects of the New World Information Order on North Africa and the rest of the Arab world. 7 page bibliography.

1486

Mathews, Anthony S. *The Darker Reaches of Government: Access to Information about Public Administration in Three Societies*. Cape Town: Juta, 1978. 245pp.
  Comparison of laws relating to press freedom and access to information in the United States, United Kingdom, and South Africa. Index.

1487

Matovu, Jacob. "Mass Media as Agencies of Socialization in Uganda." *Journal of Black Studies* 20, no. 3 (1990): 342-361.
  This overview of print and broadcast media in Uganda since independence, concludes that, as presently organized, they are not effective as vehicles of national unity and development.

1488

Mau-Mauing the Media: New Censorship for the New South Africa. Johannesburg: South African Institute of Race Relations, 1991. 66pp.
  Papers delivered at a seminar on censorship by journalists, editors and entertainers.

1489

Mayer, Doe. "Problems of Teaching Film and Video Production in Developing Countries: Tales form the Field." *Visual Anthropology* 5, no. 3/4 (1993): 355-367.
  An account of the author's experiences in Kenya, Nigeria, and the Maldives, with commentary on cultural and other factors affecting training.

1490

Mazrui, Ali A. "Wole Soyinka as a Television Critic: A Parable of Deception." *Transition*, no. 54 (1991): 165-177.
  A rebuttal by the Kenyan scholar, widely known for his television series *The Africans*, of Nobel Laureate Soyinka's criticism of those programs. The article (and Soyinka's response) allude to disagreements while Mazrui was a Board member and Soyinka the editor of *Transition*, as well as basic ideological differences. See #1668.

1491

M'Bayo, Ritchard, and Robert N. Nwankwo. "The Political Culture of Mass Communication Research and the Role of African Communication Scholars." *Africa Media Review* 3, no. 2 (1989): 1-15.
  A discussion of research in mass communication in Africa and how it is affected by political events as well as internal dynamics in the field.

1492
M'Bayo, Ritchard, Cosmas Nwokeafor, and Chuka Onwumechili. "Press Freedom and the Imperatives of Democracy: Towards Sustainable Development." *Africa Media Review* 9, no. 3 (1995): 32-53.
    Drawing from research findings in Nigeria and Sierra Leone, the authors explore the relationship of press freedom and democracy in Africa.

1493
Mbejume, Onyero. "Constraints on Mass Media Policies in Nigeria." *Africa Media Review* 5, no. 2 (1991): 47-58.
    A discussion of the social and political forces shaping media policy in Nigeria.

1494
McCarthy, Jeffrey, and Michelle Friedmann. "Black Housing, Ideology and the Media in South Africa 1970-1979." *Critical Arts* 2, no. 2 (1981): 51-66.
    A survey and analysis of the coverage of issues of housing for Black South Africans in South African newspapers and broadcasting.

1495
McCarthy, Michael. *Dark Continent: Africa as Seen by Americans.* Westport, Connecticut: Greenwood Press, 1983. 192pp.
    An analysis of American impressions of Africa from the 19th through the 20th centuries, drawn from articles in popular magazines, books and other media sources.

1496
McIntyre, Joseph, and Hilke Meyer-Bahlburg. *Hausa in the Media: A Lexical Guide: Hausa-English-German, English-Hausa, German-Hausa.* Hamburg: H. Buske, 1991. 289pp.
    A dictionary aimed at helping users translate journalistic texts, containing some 6000 words and phrases. Examples such as "cold war" and "structural adjustment" illustrate its potential utility.

1497
McKay, Vernon. "The Propaganda Battle for Zambia." *Africa Today* 18, no. 2 (April 1971): 18-26.
    A report on the use of radio broadcasts aimed at Zambia by South African and Rhodesian stations and rumors and disinformation in Zambian newspapers to destabilize the Kaunda government.

1498
---. "South African Propaganda: Methods and Media." *Africa Report* 11, no. 2 (February 1966): 41-46.
    A discussion of South Africa's prodigious efforts to spread its message to all audiences in the U.S. and garner sympathy for its apartheid regime.

General

1499

---. "South African Propaganda on the International Court's Decision." *African Forum* 2, no. 2 (September 1966): 51-64.
> South Africa capitalized on the International Court's confirmation its mandate in South West Africa with a blitz of media propaganda conducted by its Department of Information, which would later be the center of the Muldergate scandal.

1500

McLean, Polly E. "Methodological Shortcomings of Communication Research in Southern Africa: a Critique Based on Swaziland Experience." *Communication Research in Africa: Issues and Perspectives*, 89-108. Edited by S. T. Kwame Boafo and Nancy A. George. Nairobi: African Council for Communication Education, 1992.
> Analysis and critique of methodologies and results of studies undertaken in southern Africa, with focus on Swaziland. 4 page bibliography.

1501

Media and Human Rights in Southern Africa. Report of the Proceedings of the Southern African Workshop on Human Rights and the Media. Harare, Zimbabwe, April 11-13, 1994. Harare, Zimbabwe: Inter Press Service, 1994. 59pp.
> Contains country briefs, discussion of issues, list of attendees.

1502

Media Institute of Southern Africa. *Round-Table on the Media in a Changing Southern Africa, Ezulwini Valley, Swaziland, November 21-22, 1994.* Windhoek: Media Institute of Southern Africa, 1995.

1503

---. *So this is Democracy? Report on Media Freedom in Southern Africa.* Windhoek: Media Institute of Southern Africa, 1995. 84pp.

1504

Menga, Guy. "The Congo Censorship Commission." *Index on Censorship* 15, no. 5 (May 1986): 31-34, 37.
> A report on censorship of press, broadcasting, and publishing in Congo.

1505

Merrett, Christopher. *A Culture of Censorship: Secrecy and Intellectual Repression in South Africa.* Cape Town: David Philip, 1994. 296pp.
> A history of censorship in South Africa during the 20th century up to the election in April 1994, with commentary on the legacy of censorship in the new democratic South Africa. Extensive bibliographic notes. Index.

1506
Meyer, William H. *Transnational Media and Third World Development: The Structure and Impact of Imperialism*. New York: Greenwood Press, 1988. 132pp.
> A theoretical and philosophical overview of media freedom within Third World countries and the flow of information into those countries, with significant coverage of Africa. 6 page bibliography. Index.

1507
Miller, Seumas. "Freedom of the Media: A Philosophical Analysis." *Quest Philosophical Discussions: An International African Journal of Philosophy* 9, no. 1 (June 1995): 66-83.
> A philosophical justification for the concept of freedom of the press, broadly based, but with references to South Africa.

1508
---. "Freedom of the Press." *Politikon: The South African Journal of Political Studies* 22, no. 1 (June 1995): 24-35.
> An assessment of the justification of freedom of the press and other media, particularly in the Third World where such freedom is rare. A general argument, with focus on South Africa.

1509
M'inoti, Kathurima, and Wachira Maina. "The Press Council of Kenya Bill and the Kenya Mass Media Commission Bill: A Critical and Comparative Review." *Nairobi Law Monthly*, no. 60 (January 1996): 15-48.
> The authors argue that the two proposed pieces of legislation, which severely limit press freedom and freedom of speech, should be prevented from becoming law. Copies of the two bills are provided.

1510
Mlama, Penina M. "Culture, Women and the Media." *Communication and Culture: African Perspectives*, 11-18. Edited by S. T. Kwame Boafo. Nairobi: African Church Information Service, 1989.
> An overview of women's roles in development and the media pointing out that women are too often ignored in both development and media planning.

1511
Mody, Bella. *Designing Messages for Development Communication: an Audience Participation-Based Approach*. New Delhi: Sage, 1991. 211pp.
> Methodology for writing media scripts for development, based on the author's experience in the Third World, including several African countries. 2 page bibliography with additional notes and references for each chapter. Index.

General

1512

Communicating for Development: a New Pan-Disciplinary Perspective, edited by Andrew A. Moemeka. Albany, NY: State University of New York Press, 1994. 280pp.
   A collection of essays examining the media in Third World development, several focusing on Africa. Index.

1513

Moemeka, Andrew A.. "Mass Media and Rational Domination: A Critical Review of a Dominant Paradigm." *Africa Media Review* 3, no. 1 (1988): 1-33.
   A theoretical discussion of the relationship between economic and socio-political structures and the utilization of mass media.

1514

---. "Perspectives on Development Communication." *Africa Media Review* 3, no. 3 (1989): 1-24.
   An overview of mass communication in Africa and its effectiveness in promoting development.

1515

Mohammed, Jubril Bala. "Development Communication Training in Nigeria: Notes and Observations." *Africa Media Review* 4, no. 1 (1990): 75-
   A discussion of strategies for communications training in Nigeria, with recommendations for changes in the current approaches.

1516

---. "The Mediation of Dependence: Development Communication Planning for Agricultural Development in Northern Nigeria." *Africa Media Review* 7, no. 2 (1993): 1-16.
   An examination of the role of communication planning in the context of Nigeria's effort to develop agriculture in Northern Nigeria. 2 page bibliography.

1517

Momoh, John. "Liberia's Dual Post-War Press Structure." *Index on Censorship* 20, no. 2 (February 1991): 28-29.
   A report on the effects of Liberia's civil war on the country's news media.

1518

Motlomelo, Samuel. *Survey of the Potential Media in Lesotho.* Maseru: Research and Evaluation, Lesotho Distance Teaching Centre, 1987. 81pp.
   A survey of radio and newspaper access and use in Lesotho, and their effectiveness in communicating health information.

General

1519
The Media as a Forum for Community Building: Cases from Africa, Asia, Latin America, Eastern Europe and the United States, edited by Hamid Mowlana and Margaret Hardt Frondorf. Washington: SAIS, 1992. 41pp.
   A collection of papers from a conference which focused on case studies of grass roots use of press, radio and video for community development. Two papers deal with Africa.

1520
Mozambique: Freedom of Expression and the Elections. London: Article 19, 1994. *Censorship News* #36 17pp.

1521
Mphahlele, Ezekiel. "Censorship in South Africa." *Voices in the Whirlwind and Other Essays*, 199-215. Edited by Ezekiel Mphahlele. New York: Hill and Wang, 1972.
   A commentary on the far-reaching censorship laws in South Africa and their detrimental effects on the press and creative writing, noting the different treatment and attitudes of English, Afrikaans and Black journalists and writers.

1522
Mukamba Longesha. *La Cible Manquée: Une Étude Pratique des Média dans une Ville Africaine, Lubumbashi*. Louvain-la-Neuve, Belgium: Cabay, 1983. 214pp.
   A study of access to and use of radio, television, the press, and film in Lubumbashi, Zaire. Statistical tables of surveys. 6 page bibliography.

1523
Mukasa, Stanford G., and Lee B. Becker. "Towards an Indigenized Philosophy of Communication: An Analysis of Africa Communication Educational Resources and Needs." *Africa Media Review* 6, no. 3 (1992): 31-50.
   The authors find too much foreign influence in educational communication in Africa, with the result that development messages are not being successfully disseminated.

1524
Mukela, John. "My 28 Days in Captivity." *Index on Censorship* 15, no. 8 (September 1986): 26-27.
   Description of news censorship in Lesotho by a Zambian journalist who was arrested, detained for four weeks, and deported following his report of a coup attempt.

1525
Mulu, John. "Rural Press and Control of Malaria in Kenya." *Communicating Health in Africa: Research Papers of the Second Training Course of African Communicators*, 191-206. Edited by Osmo Apunen and Pirjo Huida. Tampere,

General

Finland: Tampere University, Unit of Peace Research and Development Studies, 1988.
> A study of the role and effectiveness of Kenya radio and television, major newspapers and small rural newspapers in disseminating information on malaria control. Sketch map shows regions covered by nine rural newspapers.

1526

Munanga, Jonathan. "Information, Education and Communication (IEC) on AIDS in Uganda." *Communicating Health in Africa: Research Papers of the Second Training Course of African Communicators*, 170-190. Edited by Osmo Apunen and Pirjo Huida. Tampere, Finland: University of Tampere, Unit of Peace Research and Development Studies, 1988.
> An overview of various means of communicating information on AIDS, including radio, television and the press.

1527

Mutere, Absalom. "An Analysis of Communication Policies in Kenya." *Africa Media Review* 3, no. 1 (1988): 46-63.
> An overview of mass communication in Kenya, focusing on policies and making recommendations for improvements.

1528

Muzavazi, Christopher. "Media in West Africa." *Democratic Journalist* 37, no. 4 (April 1990): 5.
> A brief report of the seminar, "The Situation of the Media in West Africa", held in Dakar by the West Africa Journalists Association and the International Organization of Journalists in December 1990. The seminar examined the relationship of the media and national governments.

1529

Mwaura, Peter. *Communications Policies in Kenya*. Paris: Unesco, 1980. 94pp.
> An overview of the status and prospects of media development in Kenya.

1530

Mwendamseke, Nancy. "The Female Image in the Mass Media: The Reality and Possible Remedies." *Africa Media Review* 4, no. 2 (1990): 64-71.
> Drawing from examples in Tanzania, the author analyses of women's position in society and their image in the media and suggests major reforms.

1531

Mytton, Graham L. *Listening, Look ing and Learning: Report on a National Mass Media Audience Survey in Zambia (1970-1973)*. Lusaka: Institute for African Studies, University of Zambia, 1974. 133pp.
> Results and analysis of a survey covering language, distribution of mass media and news, attitudes to broadcasting, educational and foreign programming. Appendices

include a list of the research needs of the Zambia Broadcasting Service, the questionnaire used and statistical tables.

1532
---. *Mass Communication in Africa*. London: Edward Arnold, 1983. 159pp.
An overview of press and broadcasting in Africa, with case studies of Zambia, Tanzania and Nigeria. 8 pages of photographs. 3 page bibliography. Index.

1533
---. "Tanzania: the Problems of Mass Media Development." *Gazette* 14, no. 2 (1968): 89-100.
Discussion of newspapers and radio ownership, audience, content, and effectiveness in Tanzania.

1534
---. "A Third World News Deal? Tanzania -- A Case Study." *Index on Censorship* 6, no. 5 (September 1977): 35-46.
An assessment of the problems the Tanzanian news media faced in the 1970s; namely, whether to report on failures of development projects or to allow the government some leeway for trial and error. Includes an historical overview of news media in Tanzania.

1535
Nabwa, Ali. "Media Problems in the Comoros." *Index on Censorship* 9, no. 2 (April 1980): 33-37.
A report on the news media in the Comoros where the government is developing a broadcast infrastructure to carry its information to the people while opposition factions depend on mimeographed leaflets.

1536
Ndiaye, A. Raphael. *Communication à la Base: Enraciner et Épanouir*. Dakar, Sénégal: ENDA-Éditions, 1994. *Série Études et Recherches* no. 162-163-164. 302pp.
A survey of the issues and problems of communicating agricultural and other development information to all the populations of West Africa, including those who lack literacy and knowledge of European languages. Includes discussion of rural newspapers, radio and rediffusion.

1537
Ndifang, David. "Ending Colonialism in Communications." *West Africa*, no. 3291 (25 August 1980): 1599-1602.
A report on a Unesco sponsored conference on Communication Polices in Africa, AFRICOM 80, held in Yaoundé, Cameroon, in 1980. Includes the text of the Yaoundé Declaration on the free flow of information.

1538
Nederveen Pieterse, Jan. *White on Black: Images of Africa and Blacks in Western Popular Culture*. New Haven: Yale University Press, 1992. 259pp.

General

An exploration of the uses of negative images of Africa and Blacks in advertising, film and cartoons. 10 page bibliography. Index.

1539

Newman, Johanna. *Lights, Camera, War: Is Media Technology Driving International Politics?* New York: St. Martins Press, 1995. 327pp.

A discussion by the foreign editor of *USA Today* of the potential influence of the media on the events they are covering. Numerous examples from the U.S. invasion of Somalia and the genocide in Rwanda. 8 pages of photographs, including the Pulitzer Prize winning picture by Kevin Carter of a Sudanese child collapsed from hunger. Index.

1540

Newsinger, John. "Lord Greystoke and Darkest Africa: The Politics of the Tarzan Stories." *Race and Class* 28, no. 2 (1986): 59-71.

Although this study is based on the books of Edgar Rice Burroughs, rather than on the comic books and films derived from them, the analysis of colonialist themes and racism is relevant for study of those media products.

1541

N'Gosso, Gaston Same, and Catherine Ruelle. *Cinéma et Télévision en Afrique: de la Dépendance à l'Interdépendance*. Paris: UNESCO, 1983. 84pp.

Discussion of the organization of the film and television industries in Africa, the audiences and programming for both, an historical overview of them and proposals for development and cooperation among African nations.

1542

Ngure wa Mwachofi. "Unmasking President de Klerk's Obfuscating Rhetoric." *Journal of Communication Inquiry* 17, no. 2 (June 1993): 52-68.

An analysis of the rhetoric de Klerk uses in the media to shape public opinion about South Africa.

1543

Ngwainmbi, Emmanuel Komben. *Communication Efficiency and Rural Development in Africa: the Case of Cameroon*. Lanham, MD: University Press of America, 1995. 181pp.

A broad-based study covering communications policy, cultural values and theoretical approaches to analyzing data. 7 page bibliography. Index.

1544

Ng'wanakilala, Nkwabi. *Mass Communication and Development of Socialism in Tanzania*. Dar es Salaam: Tanzania Publishing House, 1981. 149pp.

An overview of the press, broadcasting, and film in Tanzania with an analysis of how the media interact with the social and political structures of socialism. 2 page bibliography.

1545

The Transport and Communications Sector in Southern Africa, edited by Sindiso Ngwenya. Harare: SAPES Trust, 1993. 136pp.

A sector study by the Southern Africa Political Economy Series (SAPES), in its Regional Cooperation Series, of the strategies and activities of the Southern Africa Development Coordination Conference (SADCC). The book focuses on transportation but telecommunications is included. Contains copies of documents. Bibliographic notes. Index.

1546

Nnaemeka, Tony Ike. "Cultural Influences, Modern Changes, and the Sociology of Modern African Political Communication." *Journal of Black Studies* 20, no. 3 (1990): 306-323.

A study of traditional and modern styles of communication with emphasis on mass media's role in African politics.

1547

Nordenstreng, Kaarle, and Nkwabi Ng'Wanakilala. *Tanzania and the New Information Order: A Case Study of Africa's Second Struggle*. Dar es Salaam: Printpak Tanzania, 1987. 54pp.

An analysis of Tanzania's mass media as a factor in the country's independence and development. Appendices include reports of four mass media seminars held in Tanzania from 1973 to 1983.

1548

National Sovereignty and International Communication, edited by Kaarle Nordenstreng, and Herbert I. Schiller. Norwood, NJ: Ablex Pub. Co., 1979. 286pp.

A collection of essays dealing with the relationship of national policies and the free flow of information. Numerous African examples. Index.

1549

Nowrojee, Binaifer. *Kenya: Multipartyism Betrayed in Kenya: Continuing Rural Violence and Restrictions on Freedom of Speech and Assembly*. New York: Human Rights Watch/Africa, 1994. 33pp.

1550

Nse, Alberto Elo. "Los *Mass Media* en una Sociedad de Cambio." *Africa 2000* 7, no. 18/19 (1993): 22-31.

A study of mass media in Equatorial Guinea.

1551

Nwankwo, Robert L. Nwafo, and Teresa K. Mphahlele. "Communication Rule Structure and the Communication Management of the South African Crisis." *Journal of Black Studies* 20, no. 3 287-305.

Analysis of coverage of news from South Africa by American television networks and the South African newspaper, the *Star*.

General

1552
Nwosu, Ikechukwu E. "Effective Reporting of Rural Africa: Towards Improved Strategies and Practices." *Africa Media Review* 2, no. 3 (1988): 35-55.
   Suggestions for improving news coverage of rural areas, with examples of successful projects.

1553
---. "Research and Training for Rural Development Communication: Adopting the Tri-Modular Training and Sequential Result Models." *Africa Media Review* 1, no. 2 (1987): 66-86.
   Examination of the utility of several Western training and research techniques for rural communications in Africa.

1554
Nwosu, Peter O., and Eronini Megwa. "Communication and Rural Development in Swaziland." *Africa Media Review* 7, no. 1 (1993): 1-17.
   An examination of media, particularly newspapers and radio, in disseminating information for agricultural development to farmers in Swaziland. 1 page bibliography.

1555
Mass Communication in Nigeria: a Book of Reading, edited by Onuora Nwuneli. Enugu: Fourth Dimension, 1985. 227pp.

1556
Nwuneli, Onuora et al. "Media Use, Knowledge of World Affairs and Image of Nations Among Nigerian Youth." *Africa Media Review* 7, no. 1 (1993): 33-49.
   A survey of 368 Nigerian undergraduate students to determine how effective the media (radio, television and newspapers) are in building knowledge of events in the rest of the world. 1 page bibliography.

1557
Nyamnjoh, Francis B. "Contrôle de l'Information au Cameroun: Implication Pour la Recherche en Communication." *Afrika Spektrum* 28, no. 1 (1993): 93-115.
   A critical assessment of decades of strict government control of press and broadcasting in Cameroon, pointing out that lack of access to information makes the people dependent on rumor and news from foreign broadcasts and inhibits the development of a well-informed and responsible public.

1558
Nyirenda, Kambona. "The Malawian Experience." *Présence Africaine*, no. 88 (1973): 50-58. Special Issue: *Mass Media and Black Civilization*.
   A brief overview of mass media in Malawi, noting that there was no television as of the early 1970s, radio was largely controlled by the government, and local writers

were and are frustrated by the lack of outlets in the press or publishing houses for their work.

1559
Nyong'o, Dorothy. "Generating Public Awareness in Africa." *Planned Parenthood Challenges*, no. 1 (1996): 2-4.
   A report of efforts of the International Planned Parenthood Foundation to use local media facilities to bring family planning information to the general public in Africa.

1560
Obeng-Quaidoo, Isaac. "Assessment of the Experience in the Production of Messages and Programmes for Rural Communication Systems: The Case of the Wonsuom Project in Ghana." *Gazette* 42, no. 1 (1988): 53-67.
   A report of a Unesco-sponsored project to promote rural newspapers and broadcasts in Ghana.

1561
---. "Culture and Communication Research Methodologies in Africa: A Proposal for Change." *Gazette* 36, no. 2 (1985): 109-120.
   A critique of Western theories and research methods, often learned by African media scholars in the course of higher education abroad, which do not have sufficient relevance and validity in African situations.

1562
---. "New Development-Oriented Models of Communication Research for Africa: The Case for Focus Group Research in Africa." *Africa Media Review* 1, no. 2 (1987): 52-65.
   Discussion of adaptation of the "focus group" approach in African situations.

1563
---. "Socio-Economic Factors Affecting Journalistic Expression in Africa." *Africa Media Review* 2, no. 2 (1988): 85-99.
   A report of focus group discussions among media personnel in Ghana to determine what elements affect their coverage of health issues.

1564
Ochieng, Mark. "Kenya (with CNN) Unmuffles its Press and TV." *Intermedia* 21, no. 4/5 (August 1993): 59-60.
   A discussion of press freedom and responsibility in Kenya where government repression of the news media has been harsh, but where the information infrastructure makes good news service possible.

1565
Ochilo, Polycarp J. Omolo. "Press Freedom and the Role of the Media in Kenya." *Africa Media Review* 7, no. 3 (1993): 19-33.
   An examination of the development of the media in Kenya, and how their history affects their role in the circumstances of government censorship today. 1 page bibliography.

General

1566
Ochola, Francis W. *Aspects of Mass Communication and Journalism Research on Africa.* Nairobi: Africa Book Services, 1983. 103pp.
> An overview of research on mass communication and journalism in Africa. 16 page bibliography. Index.

1567
---. *Mass Communications/Journalism Dissertations and Theses on Black Africa 1960-1980 Accepted by Universities in the U. S.* Nairobi: Africa Book Services, 1983. 69pp.
> A bibliography of doctoral dissertations and Master's theses dealing with mass communications and the press completed at U.S. universities. Indexed by author and title.

1568
Ogbondah, Chris W. "Colonial Laws: Model for Contemporary African Press Laws?" *International Third World Studies and Review* 1, no. 1 (1989): 191-192.
> To illustrate his point that contemporary African press laws are largely influenced by British and French colonial legal structures, the author examines in detail Nigeria's 1984 decree protecting public officers from false accusation. This decree is the basis of most of Nigeria's control of the press and broadcast media, and echoes laws passed during the British colonial regime.

1569
Ogundimu, Folu. "Communicating Knowledge of Immunization for Development: a Case Study from Nigeria." *Communicating for Development: a New Pan-Disciplinary Perspective*, 219-243. Edited by Andrew A. Moemeka. Albany, NY: State University of New York Press, 1994.
> A study of media's role in Nigeria's Extended Programme on Immunization to eliminate six major childhood diseases. 2 page bibliography.

1570
Ogundipe-Leslie, Molara. "The Image of Women and the Role of the Media in a New Political Culture in Nigeria." *Africa Media Review* 4, no. 1 (1990): 52-59.
> A discussion of the stereotypical images of women as they are portrayed in Nigerian media, with a call to women to change this situation.

1571
Okigbo, Charles. "American Communication Theories and African Communication Research: Need for a Philosophy of African Communication." *Africa Media Review* 1, no. 2 (1987): 18-31.
> Discussion of U.S. theory and the ways it can apply to African realities.

1572
---. "Communication Ethics and Social Change: A Nigerian Perspective." *Communication Ethics and Global Change*, 124-136. Edited by Thomas W. Cooper, Clifford G. Christians, Frances Forde Plude, and Robert A. White. White Plains, NY: Longman, 1989.
> A discussion of ethics in communications, including the press, advertising and public relations, focusing on interpretation of ethics codes in Nigeria.

1573
---. "National Images in the Age of the Information Superhighway: African Perspectives." *Africa Media Review* 9, no. 2 (1995): 105-121.
> The author contends that new information technologies, such as the Internet, are not improving the validity of Africa's image in the West.

1574
---. "Sources of Political Information in a Rural Nigerian Community." *Africa Media Review* 4, no. 3 (1990): 49-61.
> A discussion of political communication to voters during an election campaign in Nigeria, highlighting the need for the individual to sort the barrage of often conflicting information into comprehensible categories.

1575
Okoth-Owiro, A. "Law and the Mass Media in Kenya." *Africa Media Review* 4, no. 1 (1988): 15-26.
> Description and analysis of the law affecting the mass media in Kenya, focusing on government control.

1576
Okoye, Felix N. *The American Image of Africa: Myth and Reality*. Buffalo, NY: Black Academy Press, 1971. 157pp.
> A study of American images of Africa in literature and scholarly writing as well as in the popular press. 6 page bibliography.

1577
Okunna, Chinyere Stella. "Female Faculty in Journalism Education in Nigeria: Implications for the Status of Women in the Society." *Africa Media Review* 6, no. 2 (1992): 47-58.
> Addressing gender issues in the training of Nigerian journalists, the author suggests that more women journalism faculty could have a multiplier effect on attitudes toward and the status of women in the general society.

1578
---. "Small Participatory Media Technology as an Agent of Social Change in Nigeria: A Non-Existent Option?" *Media, Culture and Society* 17, no. 4 (October 1995): 615-627.
> A report of a survey of media technology available to and used by rural women in Nigeria for dissemination of development information.

General

1579

---. "Sources of Development Information Among Rural Women in Nigeria." *Africa Media Review* 6, no. 3 (1992): 65-78.
    Report of a study determining what communication media are used by rural women as sources of development information.

1580

Okwudishu, Chris. "Patterns of Ownership and Accessibility to Information and Media Facilities in Democratizing the Media in Nigeria." *Africa Media Review* 3, no. 1 (1988): 121-133.
    A discussion of two hypotheses: that democratization of the mass media in any society is a factor of accessibility of information, and also of the patterns of ownership of the media.

1581

Olkes, Cheryl. *Information Seeking with Mass Media in the Republic of Niger: an Exploratory Study of Town and Country*. Ann Arbor, Michigan: University Microfilms, 1980. Thesis: University of Texas at Austin, 1978.

1582

O'Meara, D. ""Muldergate" and the Politics of Afrikaner Nationalism." *Work in Progress*, no. 22 (supplement) (1982).

1583

O'Meara, Patrick. *South Africa's Watergate: The Muldergate Scandals*. Hanover, NH: American Universities Field Staff, 1979. *American Universities Field Staff Report* 1979/4. 39pp.
    An analysis of the multi-million dollar covert propaganda offensive to improve South Africa's image abroad undertaken by that country's Department of Information between 1972 and 1977.

1584

Onyango-Obbo, Charles. "East Africa Doors Unlocking -- Except in Kenya." *Nieman Reports* 50, no. 1 (March 1996): 69-73.
    An overview of improvements in press freedom in East Africa, counterbalanced by descriptions of restrictions on the press and oppression of journalists in Kenya.

1585

Opubor, Alfred E., and Mary Kay Hobbs. "Development Communication: A Selective Annotated Bibliography." *Rural Africana* 27 (1975): 127-156.
    A 151 item bibliography in the broad domain of development communication in Africa.

1586
Orewere, Ben. "Possible Implications of Modern Mass Media for Traditional Communication in a Nigerian Rural Setting." *Africa Media Review* 5, no. 3 (1991): 53-.
   An exploration of the interaction of modern means of communication with traditional means in Nigerian villages.

1587
Osakue, John. "Domestic Financing of Communication in Developing Countries: a Preliminary Investigation of the Nigerian Case." *Africa Media Review* 2, no. 3 (1988): 123-134.
   A study of public and private financing of mass communication in Nigeria from 1960-1980.

1588
Osinbajo, Yemi. *Nigerian Media Law*. Lagos: Gravitas Publishments, 1991. 385pp.

1589
Communication and Rural Development in Nigeria, edited by Lai Oso and Lanre Adebayo. Abeokuta, Nigeria: Millenium Investments, 1990. 170pp.

1590
Palmer, Robin. "Africa in the Media." *African Affairs* 86, no. 343 (April 1987): 241-247.
   Report of a symposium sponsored by the African Studies Association of the United Kingdom dealing with coverage of Africa by Western, particularly British, media.

1591
Payne, W. A. J. "Through a Glass Darkly: The Media and Africa." *Africa From Mystery to Maze*, 219-247. Edited by Helen Kitchen. Lexington, MA: Lexington Books, 1976.
   An assessment of African coverage in U.S. media and the status of the media in Africa, concluding that the former continues to present a mythical Africa, and the latter is too tightly controlled by national governments to serve its public.

1592
"Peace, War and Total Strategy." *South Africa Outlook* 110, no. 1308 (June 1980): 1-17.
   Most of this issue is devoted to short articles dealing with press censorship, Muldergate, and bias on television in South Africa.

1593
Perraton, Hilary D., Dean T. Jamison, and François Orivel. *Mass Media for Agricultural Extension in Malawi*. Washington: World Bank, 1981. 53pp.

General

Report of a World Bank study on the use of film and radio in teaching agricultural techniques to Malawian farmers.

1594

Phelan, John M. *Apartheid Media: Disinformation and Dissent in South Africa*. Westport, CT: Lawrence Hill, 1987. 220 pp.
    An assessment of the role the press and other media played in apartheid, both in its continuation and in its dissolution. Appendices list reactions to the Eloff Commission which examined the media activities of the South African Council of Churches. 6 page bibliography. Index.

1595

Pinnock, Don. "Culture as Communication: The Rise of the Left-Wing Press in South Africa." *Race and Class* 31, no. 2 (October 1989): 17-35.
    An exploration of the relationship between media and the anti-apartheid movements in South Africa, focusing on the left-wing media which evolved there in the early 1980s, when the mainstream media were less willing or less able to express freely the mood and actions of activists.

1596

Prakke, Heinrichus Johannes. *Publizist und Publikum in Afrika*. Cologne: Verlag Deutscher Wirtschaftsdienst, 1962. 312pp.
    An overview of communication and the media in Africa, including propaganda and political rhetoric. 26 pages of photographs and facsimiles of newspaper articles. 14 page bibliography. Index.

1597

Pratt, Cornelius B. "Communication Research for Development in Sub-Saharan Africa." *Communication Research in Africa: Issues and Perspectives*, 135-151. Edited by S. T. Kwame Boafo, and Nancy A. George. Nairobi: African Council on Communication Education, 1992.
    An exploration of the agendas of decision makers in mass communications industries in sub-Saharan Africa. 3 page bibliography.

1598

---. "A Cross-Cultural Study of News Media Preferences: African versus White U.S. Students." *Journal of Black Studies* 23, no. 3 (March 1993): 314-331.
    A survey by questionnaire of African students resident in the U.S. and White U.S. students to determine what media they used most in obtaining local and foreign news.

1599

---. "Ethical Perspectives on Communication Research for Africa's Development: An Extension of the Agenda-Dynamics Model." *Social Science Models and Their Impact on the Third World*, 71-94. Williamsburg, VA: College of William and Mary, 1988.
    A discussion of research models in communications and their utility in Africa.

General

1600
---. "Fallacies and Failures of Communication for Development: A Commentary on Africa South of the Sahara." *Gazette* 52, no. 2 (1993): 993-107.
>An exploration of economic development in sub-Saharan Africa, with a critique of the conditions which inhibit it. 2 page bibliography.

1601
---. "Public Relations in the Third World: The African Context." *Public Relations Journal* 41, no. 2 (1985): 11-16.
>A brief but insightful overview of issues in public relations in Africa, aimed for American businessmen considering African ventures.

1602
---. "Public Relations, Industrial Peace, and Economic Development." *Communicating for Development: a New Pan-Disciplinary Perspective.*, 167-187. Edited by Andrew A. Moemeka. Albany, NY: State University of New York Press, 1994.
>A study of the role of public relations in development, with African examples.

1603
---. "Research Priorities for Development in Sub-Saharan Africa: Breaking More Communication Bottlenecks Than Creating Them." *Africa Media Review* 1, no. 2 (1987): 32-51.
>Proposals for media research and development agendas for Africa that will ensure rather than impede progress.

1604
Pratt, Cornelius B., and Jarol B. Manheim. "Communication Research and Development Policy: Agenda Dynamics in an African Setting." *Journal of Communication* 38, no. 3 (June 1988): 75-95.
>An overview of media agenda-setting models as frameworks for communications research in Africa that will contribute to economic development.

1605
Media Matters in South Africa, edited by Jeanne Prinsloo and Costas Criticos. Durban: University of Natal, 1991. 301pp.
>A collection of essays dealing with "media education", which is here defined as dealing with "questions of language, interpretation and meaning", with the aim of increasing "students' critical understanding of the media." The essays include works on creation of effective media products as well as interpretation and understanding of media messages.

1606
Quenum, Alphonse. "Leisure in a Developing Country: the Case of Lower-Dahomey." *Cultures* 1, no. 2 (1973): 67-86.

General

Poses the concept of leisure as essential to cultural expression, particularly for modern forms such as cinema.

1607

Rachty, Gehan, and Khalil Sabat. *Importation of Films for Cinema and Television in Egypt*. Paris: Unesco, 1980. 78pp.

A study of the foreign films broadcast or screened in Egypt, outlining government regulations and discussing their effects on viewers.

1608

The Referendum in Malawi - Free Expression Denied. London: Article 19, 1993. *Censorship News* #22. 28pp.

An overview of freedom of the press and of expression in Malawi since 1964 and conditions during the 1993 referendum campaign.

1609

Rhoodie, Eschel M. *The Paper Curtain*. Johannesburg: Voortrekkerpers, 1969. 212pp.

The author, a major propagandist for South Africa later to be implicated in the Muldergate scandal, outlines his assessment of the propaganda campaign waged against South Africa.

1610

---. *PW Botha: the Last Betrayal*. Melville, South Africa: S.A. Politics, 1989. 299pp.

An examination of the former Prime Minister of South Africa and the role that the Afrikaans press played in his rise to power and the conduct of his administration. The author was a major propagandist for South Africa and principal actor in the Muldergate scandal.

1611

---. *The Real Information Scandal*. Pretoria: Orbis, 1983. 927pp.

A lengthy disposition on Muldergate by one of its principal actors. The author attempts to demonstrate that the others involved were actually more culpable than himself, although he was the only one prosecuted.

1612

Ricard, Alain. *Livre et Communication au Nigéria*. Paris: Présence Africaine, 1975. 136pp.

While principally dealing with literature and publishing in Nigeria, this book also touches on the press and broadcasting. The author raises the interesting point that governments can control broadcast media more easily than they can control the press.

1613

Riddle, Charles. "A Profile of Namibian Media: The Censored Debate." *Gazette* 44, no. 1 (1989): 45--55.

A survey of Namibian newspapers and broadcasting services, both within the country and in exile, with discussion of the government's restrictions on political information and news.

1614

Ripley, J. M. *Communication Strategies to Aid National Development.* Accra, Ghana: Ghana Universities Press, 1978. 20pp.
    The text of an address at the University of Ghana outlining the philosophical framework of communication strategies for development.

1615

Riverson, L. Kwabena. *Telecommunication Development: the Case of Africa.* Lanham, MD.: University Press of America, 1993. 115pp.

1616

Roberts, Alun R. "Namibia: What They Didn't Tell Us." *Africa Report* 34, no. 4 (July 1989): 61-62.
    A brief description of an expose by London's *Sunday Telegraph* and the New York based weekly television news magazine *South Africa Now* of South Africa's misrepresentation as SWAPO aggression the execution of hundreds of SWAPO soldiers in Namibia by Koevoet, a South African commando unit.

1617

Rockson, Kweku. "Some Perspectives on the Mass Media Under a Military Government: A Case of the Mass Media Under Ghana's PNDC." *Africa Media Review* 4, no. 3 (1990): 36-48.
    A discussion of mass media under the Provisional National Defense Council (PNDC) in Ghana, concluding that the government exercised strong control.

1618

Roelfse, J. L. *Toward Rational Discourse: an Analysis of the Report of the Steyn Commission of Inquiry into the Media.* Pretoria: J. L. Van Schaik, 1983.

1619

Role of Communication Media and Information Services in Population-Related Development Programmes in Africa. A Report of Expert Meeting. Nairobi: UNESCO Regional Population Communication for Africa, 1979. 12pp.
    Report from a meeting of media experts from eleven African countries to discuss the use of radio, newspapers, film, and television in disseminating information for family planning in Africa.

1620

The Role of Mass Media in Promoting Primary Health Care: Report of the First Working Group. Brazzaville: Regional Office for Africa, World Health Organization, 1981. 40pp.

General

1621
Ronning, Helge. *Media and Democracy: Theories and Principles with Reference to an African Context*. Harare, Zimbabwe: SAPES Books, 1994. 20pp.
> A review of freedom of the press issues and events in southern Africa.

1622
Rugaimukamu, Fabian M. "AIDS Control Campaign Programme in Tanzania: the Role of Mass Media." *Communicating Health in Africa: Research Papers of the Second Training Course of African Communicators.*, 235-250. Edited by Osmo Apunen and Pirjo Huida. Tampere, Finland: University of Tampere, Unit of Peace Research and Development Studies, 1988.
> A study of the interaction between the National AIDS Control Program (NACP) and Tanzania's newspapers and broadcast media.

1623
Ruijter, Jose M. "The Mass Media Alone Are Not Effective Change Agents." *Africa Media Review* 5, no. 1 37-48.
> A discussion of the success of the mass media in promoting the social mobilization that characterized Africa in the 1980s.

1624
---. "State and Media in Africa: A Quarrelsome Though Faithful Marriage." *Gazette* 44, no. 1 (1989): 57-69.
> A brief discussion of the lack of press freedom, coupled with a lack of professionalism among journalists in Africa.

1625
Rural Communications, Management and Media: Report on a Seminar for Managers/Planners/Policy-Makers at Kericho Tea Hotel April 10-14, 1978 and a Workshop for Production/Research/Field Officers at Egerton College, Njoro, April 17-21, 1978. Nairobi: British Council, 1978. 75pp.
> Notes and proceedings from the two conferences covering newspapers, radio, television and film for rural areas.

1626
Rusike, Elias T. M. *The Politics of the Mass Media: A Personal Experience*. Harare: Roblaw Publishers, 1990. 111pp.
> A Zimbabwean journalist discusses his personal experiences in the field, with commentary on ownership, control and corruption. Numerous photographs.

1627
Rwomire, Apollo. "The Mass Media and Cultural Imperialism in Southern Africa." *Peace Research* 24, no. 3 (August 1992): 33-50.

General

A critical assessment of the impact of Western and South African influences on media in Southern Africa, with a five point recommendation: regional cooperation; internal development; increased literacy; government support of media professionals; research.

1628
Sayah, Lahouari. "L'Information en Algérie (1962-1975)." Ph.D. diss., Université de Droit, d'Économie et de Sciences Sociales de Paris, 1976. 296pp.
A study of the laws governing the right to information in Algeria with an overview of dissemination of information through radio and the press, both French and Algerian. Appendix includes foreign periodicals (mostly French) distributed in Algeria. 40 page bibliography of laws, 27 page bibliography of articles and books.

1629
Schaar, Stuart. *The Mass Media in Morocco: In Morocco Information Still Travels Best by Word of Mouth.* New York: American Universities Field Staff, 1968. *AUFS Reports, North Africa Series*: v. 14, no. 2. 14pp.
An overview of policies controlling access to news in Morocco as well as means of distributing it.

1630
Schechter, Danny. "Covering South Africa: Issues Facing Journalists." *Nieman Reports* 43, no. 4 (December 1989): 36-38, 40, 60.
The producer of the weekly television news magazine, *South Africa Now*, lists some of the pitfalls reporters may encounter through misdirection or ignorance of the South African situation.

1631
---. "How We Cover Southern Africa." *Africa Report* 32, no. 2 (March 1987): 4-8.
A frank assessment of the problems encountered in providing news from southern Africa and how they contribute to the inadequate coverage of that area.

1632
---. "South Africa: Where Did the Story Go?" *Africa Report* 33, no. 2 (March 1988): 27-31.
Examination of the effects on American media of South African press restrictions and a discussion of what journalists can do to provide responsible coverage despite them.

1633
Schramm, Wilber Lang. *Mass Media and National Development: The Role of Information in the Developing Countries.* Stanford, CA: Stanford University Press: 1964. 333pp.
An international overview of the status and potential of mass media with numerous African examples. 17 page bibliography. Index.

General

1634
Scott, Christina. *Electronic Media in Natal, 1991: Opportunities for Development*. Durban: University of Natal, Centre for Cultural and Media Studies, 1991. 15pp.
> A survey of ownership and access to radio and television in Natal and of radio's effectiveness as means of communication compared with print media such as newspapers.

1635
The Second World Black and African Festival of Arts and Culture, 15 January-15 February, 1977, Lagos Nigeria. Pleasant Hill, CA: Pacific Coast Africanist Association, 1977. PCAA Occasional Paper No. 2. 7pp.
> A brief report on Festac.

1636
Segal, Aaron. "Africa and the United States Media." *Issue* 6, no. 2/3 (June 1976): 49-56.
> A critical overview of coverage of Africa in the U.S. press and broadcast media, detailing particularly bad examples as well as those which the author describes as "quiet triumphs" of good reporting.

1637
Seiler, John. "The World Perspectives of South African Media." *Communications in Africa* (January 1973): 26-30.
> A content analysis of a South African news magazine, *To The Point*, and the South African Broadcasting Company (SABC) for the three month period, January - March 1973 to determine extent of coverage of African and South African news, and bias expressed in the selection of stories and vocabulary used.

1638
Selmont, Aristotle, and Verity Selmont. "In Search of Seraphina." *Africa Report* 12, no. 7 (October 1967): 62-66.
> In a send-up of academic conferences on African and Third World affairs, the authors offer an analysis of *Seraphina*, a comic strip in *Jeune Afrique* during the 1960s, featuring the Third World super-heroine, Seraphina, who, aided by a telepathic squirrel, battles the forces of evil.

1639
Shaw, Tony. *Eden, Suez and the Mass Media: Propaganda and Persuasion During the Suez Crisis*. London: I. B. Tauris, 1996. 268pp.
> An examination of the way the media in Britain can be used as an instrument of propaganda, focusing on the Eden government's efforts to build public support for military action against Egypt. 9 page bibliography. Index.

1640
Shohat, Ella Stam , Robert. *Unthinking Eurocentrism: Multiculturalism and the Media*. London: Routledge, 1994. 405pp.

A wide ranging discussion of colonialism, stereotypes, themes, and aesthetics of media worldwide, focusing on the relationship of Western and Third World media. Numerous sections deal with Africa, although no sections are devoted exclusively to Africa. 18 page bibliography. Index.

1641

Showers, Kate B. "The Ivory Story, Africans and Africanists." *Issue* 22, no. 1 (March 1994): 41-46.
A discussion of the ways in which popular conceptions of Africa, which are formed and promulgated by the media, distort the environmental priorities of international organizations and African governmental agencies.

1642

Sine, Babacar. "Cultural Dynamics and New Communication Techniques in Black Africa." *Cultures* 6, no. 3 (1979): 74-88.
Examines the interplay between technologies such as radio and film versus traditional styles of communication.

1643

Slabbert, Mana. "Violence on Cinema and Television and in the Streets." *Crime and Power in South Africa*, 90-96. Edited by D. Davis, and Mana Slabbert. Cape Town: David Philip, 1985.
Report on a survey correlating film and television viewing habits with statistics on violent crime in South Africa.

1644

Smiley, Xan. "Misunderstanding Africa." *Atlantic Monthly* (September 1982): 70-79.

1645

Smith, Anthony. *The Geopolitics of Information: How Western Culture Dominates the World*. New York: Oxford University Press, 1980. 192pp.

1646

Smythe, Hugh H. "Problems of Public Opinion Research in Africa." *Gazette* 10, no. 1 (1964): 144-154.
An assessment of the factors essential to public opinion research and how difficulties with those factors contribute to the lack of such studies in Africa.

1647

Solomon, Joel A. *Failing the Democratic Challenge: Freedom of Expression in Multi-Party Kenya -- 1993*. Washington: Robert F. Kennedy Memorial Center for Human Rights, 1994. 76pp.
Contains discussion of news media censorship as well as other aspects of freedom of speech.

General

1648
Somalia, Rwanda, and Beyond: the Role of the International Media in Wars and Humanitarian Crises. Dublin: Crosslines Global Report, 1995. 218pp.

1649
Soola, E. O. "Agricultural Communication and the African Non-Literate Farmer: The Nigerian Experience." *Africa Media Review* 2, no. 3 (1988): 75-91.
> Examination of the need to bring agricultural information to rural farmers and notes on successful media campaigns.

1650
---. "Communication and Education as Vaccine Against the Spread of Acquired Immune Deficiency Syndrome (AIDS) in Africa." *Africa Media Review* 5, no. 3 (1991): 33-.
> An examination of the role of education and communication in the crusade against the spread of AIDS in Africa, with suggestions for specific courses of action for more effective communication.

1651
---. "De-Mystifying the Development Process: The Role of Communication in Community Participation for Sustainable Development." *Africa Media Journal* 9, no. 2 (1995): 16-37.
> The author concludes that a combination of communication techniques, both traditional and modern, is most effective for long-term development in Africa.

1652
---. "A Systematic Approach to Information Management at the Grassroots." *Africa Media Review* 7, no. 2 (1993): 44-51.
> A brief overview of traditional and modern means of disseminating information in African communities. 1 page bibliography.

1653
Sorenson, John. *Imagining Ethiopia: Struggles for History and Identity in the Horn of Africa.* New Brunswick, NJ: Rutgers University Press, 1993. 216p.
> The Introduction, "Images of Disaster", and Chapter 4, "Media, Famine, War", focus on images of Ethiopia in the media. Overall the book examines broader issues of the image and perception of disaster and Ethiopia. 14 page bibliography. Index.

1654
---. "Mass Media and Discourse on Famine." *Discourse and Society* 2, no. 2 (April 1991): 223-242.
> A discussion of the ways in which U.S. media represent and mis-represent events in Africa. Focusing on famine, quotations from leading U.S. newsmagazines and vignettes from documentary films show a pattern of blaming the victim and of

General

couching reports in Cold War terms, while depicting American efforts as altruistic philanthropy.

1655

South Africa. *Independent Media Commission Act 1993*. Cape Town: Govt. Printer, 1993. 28pp.

1656

South Africa. Commission of Enquiry in Regard to Undesirable Publications. *Report*. Pretoria: Govt. Printer, 1957. 285pp.
  Report of an investigation into the nature and extent of "undesirable" publications published in or imported to South Africa, with recommendations for their control. "Undesirable" covered material deemed obscene or offensive in newspapers and magazines as well as books.

1657

South Africa. Commission of Inquiry into Alleged Irregularities in the Former Department of Information. *Interim Report*. Pretoria: Govt. Printer, 1979. Rudolf P. B. Erasmus, Chair. 65pp.
  Initial investigation into Muldergate, the misuse of government funds by the South African Department of Information to conduct a propaganda campaign in South Africa and abroad.

1658

South Africa. Commission of Inquiry into Alleged Irregularities in the Former Department of Information. *Report*. Pretoria: Govt. Printer, 1978. Rudolf P. B. Erasmus, Chair. 101pp.
  The full report on the Muldergate investigation.

1659

South Africa. Commission of Inquiry into Alleged Irregularities in the Former Department of Information. *Supplementary Report*. Pretoria: Govt. Printer, 1979. Rudolf P. B. Erasmus, Chair. 72pp.
  The final report on Muldergate.

1660

South Africa. Commission of Inquiry into South African Council of Churches. *Report*. Pretoria: Govt. Printer, 1983. C. F. Eloff, Chair. 451pp.
  An investigation of alleged improper activities of the South African Council of Churches, including media campaigns against apartheid.

1661

South Africa. Commission of Inquiry into the Mass Media. *Report*. Pretoria: Govt. Printer, 1981. M. T. Steyn, Chair. 1367pp.
  The report calls for extensive government control of the media.

General

1662
South Africa. Commission of Inquiry into the Mass Media. *Supplementary Report of the Commission of Inquiry into the Mass Media: Proposed Legislation*. Pretoria: Government Printer, 1982. M. T. Steyn, Chair. 25pp.
    Text of legislation to address concerns of the earlier Commission of Inquiry, in particular, professionalising the mass media and preventing monopolies in the private sector.

1663
South Africa. Commission of Inquiry into the Publications and Entertainments Amendment Bill. *Report*. Pretoria: Govt. Printer, 1974. 69pp.
    Report of study of the 1963 Publications Bill and proposals for change. This act covers film as well as books and the press.

1664
"South Africa: Controlling the News. Report of the Media Conference." *Nieman Reports* 42, no. 3 (1988): 38-49.
    A report of a conference sponsored by the Commonwealth Society, the Association of British Editors, the Nieman Foundation and the African-American Institute on the difficulties confronting journalists covering South Africa.

1665
"South Africa Cultural Boycott -- Yes or No." *Index on Censorship* 4, no. 2 (June 1975): 5-44.
    A summary of replies to a questionnaire sent by the journal to a large list of international writers and journalists, review of South African legislation curtailing press and artistic freedom, and a critical appraisal of the South African Publications Act of 1974.

1666
"South Africa/Southern Africa: The Future of the Media." *Nieman Reports* 46, no. 4 (1992): 1-63.
    A special issue of *Nieman Reports* reporting on a conference held in Johannesburg on the media in southern and South Africa.

1667
South Africa: the Way Ahead. Bastion of the West, Treasure House of the World, Supermarket of Africa. London: Club of Ten, n.d. *Club of Ten Fact Paper* No. 1. 16pp.
    A booklet produced by the organization created by South Africa's Ministry of Information to promulgate its propaganda while posing as an independent group of international businessmen. Exposure of that fraud precipitated the Muldergate scandal.

1668
Soyinka, Wole. "Triple Tropes of Trickery." *Transition* , no. 54 (1991): 178-183.

General

The Nobel Laureate's response to Ali Mazrui's rebuttal of Soyinka's earlier review of Mazrui's television series *The Africans*. Soyinka also responds to accusations of bias in the editing of *Transition*. See Item #1490.

1669

Getting the Real Story: Censorship and Propaganda in South Africa, edited by Gerald B. Sperling and James E. McKensie. Calgary: Detselig Enterprises, 1990. 168pp.
>   Papers from a conference entitled "South Africa: Getting the Real Story", held by the School of Journalism and Communications, University of Regina (Canada), in March 1989. Participants spoke on censorship, personal experiences as journalists, the power of photographs and television images, Muldergate, and government distortion.

1670

Starving in Silence: A Report on Famine and Censorship. London: Article 19, 1990. 146pp.
>   Part II, "The Politics of Information: Famine in Ethiopia and Sudan in the 1980s", page 91-140, deals with the political factors which govern official and media response to famine. 2 page bibliography.

1671

Steeves, H. Leslie. *Women, Rural Information Delivery and Development in SubSaharan Africa*. East Lansing, MI: Michigan State University, Women in Development, 1990. *Working Paper #2*. 35pp.
>   A critical overview of the role of women in mass media in Africa, the content of mass media intended for women, and the ways in which essential development information is distributed to rural women. 9 page bibliography.

1672

Stevenson, Robert L. *Communication, Development and the Third World*. New York: Longman, 1988. 223pp.
>   Overview of the status and problems of media in the Third World with numerous African examples. 22 page bibliography. Index.

1673

Stewart, Gavin. "Intimidation and Prosecution of Journalists." *Index on Censorship* 15, no. 7 (July 1986): 24-40.
>   A checklist of cases of intimidation or arrest of South African and foreign journalists between September 1984 and June 1986, preceding the State of Emergency declared in June 1986.

1674

Reporting Africa, edited by Olaf Stokke. New York: Africana, 1971. 224pp.
>   A collection of essays on the media in Africa, focusing mostly on newspapers, and coverage of Africa in international media, focusing mainly on broadcast media.

General

1675
Switzer, Les. "Mass Communication in a Transitional Society." *Ciskei: Economics and Politics of Dependence in a South African Homeland*, 185-213. Edited by Nancy Charton. London: Croom Helm, 1980.
> A study of mass media in the Ciskei, based on four surveys conducted in two villages, the largest urban area, and the Ciskei Legislative Assembly, between 1975 and 1976. The survey measured mass media exposure and attitudes toward mass media news compared to news received orally.

1676
---. *Media Studies and the Critique of Development*. Durban: University of Natal, 1987. 58pp.
> A discussion of the role of media in development, emphasizing that use of media must be a part of development strategies. 10 page bibliography.

1677
---. "Steyn Commission I: The Press and Total Strategy." *Critical Arts* 1, no. 4 (1981): 41-45.
> A commentary on the report of the first Steyn Commission pointing out its inconsistencies.

1678
Takirambudde, Peter Nanyenya. "Media Freedom and the Transition to Democracy in Africa." *African Journal of International and Comparative Law* 7, no. 1 (March 1995): 18.
> An examination of media freedom in the context of the volatile and uncertain democratization movements in Africa.

1679
Tchienehom, Jean-Vincent. "Des Mass Média pour Promouvoir la Personnalité Africaine." *Présence Africaine*, no. 88 (1973): 70-79. Special Issue: *Mass Media and Black Civilization*.
> A brief commentary on the undeveloped state of mass media in Cameroon, observing with some alarm that a "global culture" is replacing traditional African culture and noting efforts in Zaire, Gabon, Togo and Chad to counteract this trend.

1680
Teer-Tomaselli, Ruth. "Militancy and Pragmatism: the Genesis of the ANC's Media Policy." *Africa Media Review* 8, no. 2 (1994): 73-87.
> A discussion of the factors in the development of the draft ANC media policy, emphasizing the debate over state versus private control of broadcasting.

1681
They Shoot Writers, Don't They?, edited by George Theiner. London: Faber and Faber, 1984. 199pp.
> Collection of essays by authors who, because of their experience with censorship and oppression, have appeared in the journal *Index on Censorship*. African writers

represented are Ngugi Wa Thiong'o, Camara Laye, Sipho Sepamla, Nadine Gordimer, Don Mattera, and André Brink.

1682

Theroux, Paul. "Tarzan is an Expatriate." *Transition* 7, no. 32 (August 1967): 13-19.
>The author uses Tarzan comic books as the basis of an analysis of the attitudes of White expatriates in independent African countries.

1683

Tomaselli, Keyan G.. "Intimidation of the South African Media: A Response to Arnold de Beer's 'Censorship of Terror'." *Journal of Communication Inquiry* 18, no. 1 (1994): 135-143. See Item #1328.

1684

---. "Myths, Racism and Opportunism: Film and TV Representations of the San." *Film as Ethnography*, 205-221. Edited by Peter Ian Crawford, and David Turton. Manchester: Manchester University Press, 1992.
>A discussion of the films, both documentary and feature-length, which have portrayed the San people of Namibia and Botswana, along with critical and popular responses to those works.

1685

---. "The Teaching of Film and Television Production in a Third World Context: The Case of South Africa." *Journal of the University Film and Video Association* 34, no. 4 (1982): 3-12.

1686

Tomaselli, Keyan G., and P. Eric Louw. "Communication Models and Struggle: From Authoritarian Determinism to a Theory of Communication as Social Relations in South Africa." *Journal of African Communications* 1, no. 1 (March 1996): 18-41.
>A discussion of models of communication theory and their relevancy in South Africa after apartheid.

1687

---. "Disinformation and the South African Defense Force's Theory of War." *Social Justice* 18, no. 1/2 (1991): 124-140.
>A critical analysis of the use of disinformation by the SADF during the apartheid period.

1688

---. "Militarization, Hegemony and the South African Media, 1976-1986." *Con-Text* 2 (1989): 27-47.
>A discussion of the relationship of media and the military in South Africa during the apartheid regime's effort to maintain control.

General

1689
---. "Shifts Within Communication Studies: From Idealism and Functionalism to Praxis - the South African Case." *Progress in Communication Sciences 11*, 279-312. Edited by B. Dervin. New Jersey: Ablex, 1993.

1690
Tomaselli, Keyan G., and Ruth Tomaselli. "How to Set Your House in Order, Read All About it in Steyn Commission II." *Critical Arts* 2, no. 3 (1982): 1-22.
> An analysis of the *Supplementary Report of the Steyn Commission of Inquiry into the Mass Media*, which advocated suppression of press freedom in South Africa, and subsequent legislation to that end.

1691
---. "Ideology/Culture/Hegemony and Mass Media in South Africa: A Literature Survey." *Critical Arts* 2, no. 2 (1981): 1-26.
> An overview of theoretical and philosophical issues for mass media in South Africa as reflected in scholarly writing.

1692
---. *Media Reflections of Ideology*. Durban: Contemporary Cultural Studies Unit, University of Natal, 1985. 20pp.
> An examination of the theoretical basis of "meaning" in communication, and the ways that opinion and thought could be shaped by media control in South Africa during apartheid.

1693
---. "Mediating Mandela, Modifying Apartheid." *African Commentary* (June 1990): 16-20.
> A critical analysis of U.S. coverage of events in South Africa following the release of Mandela.

1694
---. "Steyn Commission II: How to Separate Out Truth from Fact." *Reality* (May 1982): 11-15.
> A critical examination of the Steyn Commission's recommendations for the press in South Africa with emphasis on their ramifications.

1695
Tomaselli, Keyan G., and M. Van Zyl. "The Structuring of Popular Memory in South African Cinema and Television Texts." *The Struggle for Social and Economic Space: Urbanization in Twentieth Century South Africa*, 191-269. Edited by R. Haines, and G. Buijs. Durban: University of Durban-Westville, 1985.

An analysis of the ways that themes in popular South African films and television express mythic themes in Afrikaner culture: the Eden myth, the urban trek and the outsider or *uitlander*.

1696
Tomaselli, Ruth. "Inkathagate: Covert Funding - Overt Violence." *Covert Action*, no. 38 (September 1991): 39-43.
A critique of media coverage of Inkatha violence, with evidence that it was support and funded by the South African Government.

1697
---. "Media Images of Violence: South Africa's Hidden Hand." *Covert Action*, no. 36 (March 1991): 22-26.
Analysis of coverage of Inkatha/ANC clashes and their portrayal as "Black on Black" violence in South Africa and elsewhere.

1698
---. "A Pressing Emergency: The Commercial Media Under the Bureau (for Information)." *Indicator SA* 4, no. 3 (June 1987): 19-22.
Commentary on government control of the media in South Africa, focusing on the period prior to the 1987 election.

1699
Tomaselli, Ruth, and Keyan G. Tomaselli. "The Media and Mandela." *TransAfrica Forum* 7, no. 2 (June 1990): 55-66.
A critical assessment of media coverage of Mandela's release and subsequent events in South Africa.

1700
Tomaselli, Ruth, Keyan G. Tomaselli, and Johan Muller. "A Conceptual Framework for Media Analysis." *Narrating the Crisis: Hegemony and the South African Press*, 5-21. Edited by Keyan G. Tomaselli, Ruth Tomaselli, and Johan Muller. Johannesburg: Richard Lyon & Co., 1987.
A theoretical and philosophical discussion of media in South Africa.

1701
Tomaselli, Ruth, Keyan G. Tomaselli, and L. Steenveld. "Myth, Media and Apartheid." *Media Development* 34, no. 1/2 (1987): 1-20.

1702
Toumi, Mohsen. "La Presse en Tunisie." *Revue Française d'Etudes Politiques Africaine*, no. 84 (December 1972): 38-71.
An overview of the press and news media in Tunisia with reviews of the major newspapers and broadcasting services.

General

1703

Traber, Michael. "The Marginalisation of Africa by the International Media." *Africans on Africa* #1, Supplement to *IDOC Internazionale* 26, no. 1 (January 1995): 7-10.

1704

---. "Towards the Democratization of Public Communication: A Critique of the Current Criteria of News." *Africa Media Review* 2, no. 1 (1987): 66-75.
   An assessment of development journalism and the idea that some news is detrimental to development and should be repressed.

1705

Tudesq, André-Jean. "Information Média en Afrique Noire." *Mondes en Développement* 19, no. 73 (1991): 3-95.
   A collection of articles on media and development in Africa.

1706

---. "Média et Développement en Afrique Noire. Enjeux et Realités." *Mondes en Développement* 19, no. 73 (1991): 11-20.
   A critical assessment of the relationship between the media and development in Africa, concluding that radio and the rural press promise to be most effective.

1707

---. "Nouvelles Technologies de la Communication et Dépendance Renforcée de l'Afrique Noire." *Mondes en Développement* 19, no. 73 (1991): 81-95.
   An assessment of new communication technologies, which the author feels are making African countries more dependent on the West than ever before.

1708

Twumasi, Yaw. "Media of Mass Communication and the Third Republican Constitution of Ghana." *African Affairs* 80, no. 318 (January 1981): 13-27.
   A discussion of the rationale and background for inclusion of specific statements on press freedom in Ghana's Third Republican Constitution.

1709

Uche, Luke Uka. "Democratization of Communication in Africa and "History Repeats Itself" Syndrome." *Gazette* 44, no. 2 (1989): 93-106.
   The author puts examples of suppression of the press into a global historical context.

1710

---. "How the Media Reacted to Toxic Dumping in Nigeria." *Media Development* 37, no. 2 (1990):

1711
---. "Ideology, Theory and Professionalism in the African Mass Media." *Africa Media Review* 5, no. 1 (1991): 1-16.
    A discussion of the lack of articulated policy for African communication systems, and the remaining influence of former colonial powers.

1712
---. "Mass Communication and Cultural Identity: The Unresolved Issue of National Sovereignty and Cultural Autonomy in the Wake of New Communication Technologies." *Africa Media Review* 3, no. 1 (1988): 83-105.
    A study of the ways that ownership of the mass media can affect national and cultural identity.

1713
---. *Mass Media, People and Politics in Nigeria*. New Delhi: Concept Publishing Co., 1989. 225pp.
    A study of radio, television and press in Nigeria, covering their history and emphasizing their role in national politics, culture and identity as well as issues of censorship and freedom of the press. Appendices include acts and decrees relevant to the press and media and the text of a paper on media policy. 8 page bibliography. Index.

1714
Udoakah, Nkereuwem. *Government and the Media in Nigeria*. Calabar, Nigeria: Centaur Publications, 1988. 98pp.
    A discussion of press freedom under several political regimes in Nigeria.

1715
Ugboajah, Frank Okwu. *Communication Policies in Nigeria*. Paris: Unesco, 1980. 67pp.
    An overview of the status and policies of mass communications in Nigeria, focusing on the legal framework, coverage of major events and issues, and training of manpower.

1716
---. "Current Debates in the Field of Mass Communication Research: An African Viewpoint." *Africa Media Review* 1, no. 2 (1987): 1-17.
    Discussion of NWICO, communication for development and other broad issues, from a African perspective.

1717
Mass Communication, Culture and Society in West Africa, edited by Frank Okwu Ugboajah. London: Hans Zell, 1985. 329pp.
    A collection of essays on the history and development of mass communications in Africa, cultural programs and language use, professionalism, the role of media in society, and trends in communications research.

General

1718
Ugboajah, Frank Okwu. "Mobilising African Resource for National Communication Strategies." *Media Development* 32, no. 4 (1985): 31-33.

1719
---. "Nigerian Mass Communication Trends in the African Context." *Gazette* 22, no. 3 (1976): 156-168.
> Analysis of the press in Nigeria as compared to similar and different African countries.

1720
---. "Traditional-Urban Media Model: Stocktaking for African Development." *Gazette* 18, no. 2 (1972): 76-95.
> A critique of development projects which do not take into account traditional forms of communication and adapt these to modern media formats.

1721
Ugboajah, Frank Okwu, and Idowu Sobowale. "The Press in West Africa: A Comparative Analysis of Mass Media Trends." *Studies in Third World Societies* 10 (December 1979): 133-151.
> A discussion of the press, with some commentary on other media, in West Africa, focusing on issues of censorship, ownership and professional training.

1722
Ukadike, N. Frank. "Anglophone African Media." *Jump Cut*, no. 36 (1991): 74-80.
> In a few pages the author touches on aspects of the development of film and television in Nigeria, Ghana and Kenya, focusing on popular TV shows.

1723
---. "Theatre on the Screen: A Filmmaker's View on Nigerian Television." *Nigerian Theatre Journal* 2 (1985): 191-197.
> A critical assessment of Nigerian film and television, blaming poor training, lack of professionalism, and reluctance to respond to criticism for the low quality of Nigerian productions.

1724
Ungar, Sanford J.. "South Africa in the American Media." *The American People and South Africa: Publics, Elites, and the Policy Making Processes*, 25-46. Edited by Alfred O. Hero, and John Barratt. Lexington, MA: Lexington Books, 1981.
> An American journalist surveys the flow of information about South Africa and manipulations of coverage by the South African government during apartheid.

General

1725
Ungar, Sanford J., and David Gergen. *Africa and the American Media*. New York: Freedom Form Media Studies Center, 1991. 16pp.

1726
Van Rooyen, J. C. W. *Censorship in South Africa: Being a Commentary on the Application of the Publications Act*. Cape Town: Juta, 1987. 152pp.
 The Chairman of the Publications Appeal Board discusses and clarifies the South African Publications Act of 1986. This act codifies censorship of films and publications.

1727
---. "State Control of the Arts in South Africa." *Journal of Media Law and Practice* 11, no. 4 (December 1990): 136-139.
 A general discussion of censorship in South Africa under the Publications Act, the Internal Security Act, and the State of Emergency declared in 1985.

1728
van Zyl, J. A. F., and Keyan Tomaselli. *Media and Change*. Johannesburg: McGraw Hill, 1977. 168pp.
 A collection of essays on theoretical issues of communication. Although not specifically focused on Africa, most of the authors are South African.

1729
Vandi, Abdulai S. *A Model of Mass Communications and National Development: a Liberian Perspective*. Washington: University Press of America, 1979. 184pp.
 Although the focus is Liberia, most of the book is occupied with more generalized studies, with some suggestions as to how these studies of other areas could be applied to Liberia. 13 page bibliography.

1730
Vieler-Porter, Chris. *Black and Third Cinema: A Film and Television Bibliography*. London: British Film Institute, 1991. 247pp.
 A 1513 item bibliography with substantial African content. Indexes.

1731
Walsh, Gretchen. *Africa and the Media: Changing Aspects of Communication*. Boston: Boston University African Studies Center, 1979. Working Paper No. 17. 17pp.
 A working bibliography on the theme of the 1979 annual meeting of the African Studies Association.

1732
Wanyande, Peter. "Mass Media - State Relations in Post-Colonial Kenya." *Africa Media Review* 9, no. 3 (1995): 54-75.
 An examination of the relationship of Kenya's one-party state and the media.

General

1733
Waritay, Lamini A. "Problems and Possibilities for the Formulation of a Comprehensive Communication Policy for Liberia." *Africa Media Review* 4, no. 2 (1990): 11-25.
   A discussion of the factors involved in developing a communication policy for Liberia.

1734
Wark, McKenzie. "Fresh Maimed Babies: the Uses of Innocence." *Transition* 65 36-47.
   A discussion of the use of images of children of the Third World in news media.

1735
Wauthier, Claude. "Not a Rosy Picture." *Index on Censorship* 15, no. 5 (May 1986): 34-37.
   An assessment of the state of the press and news media throughout Africa.

1736
Webb, Maxine W. *Feedback in Media Production in Botswana: An Annotated Bibliography*. Gaborone: National Institute of Development and Cultural Research, 1981. Working Bibliography No. 6. 26pp.
   Compiled at the request of media producers and the Institute of Adult Education in Botswana, this bibliography lists reports and commentary useful in planning media for education.

1737
West, Harry G., and Jo Ellen Fair. "Development Communication and Popular Resistance in Africa: an Examination of the Struggle over Tradition and Modernity through Media." *African Studies Review* 36, no. 1 (April 1993): 91-114.
   A discussion of radio in Africa as a possible modern medium for a range of more traditional "folk" media, and some of the inhibiting effects of government agendas in control of radio as a news medium.

1738
Wete, Francis N. "Mass Communication and Development: Impact Depends on Strategies." *Africa Media Review* 3, no. 1 (1988): 34-45.
   A discussion of the impact of mass communications on development.

1739
---. "Mass Communication Research in Africa: Problems and Promises." *Communication Research in Africa: Issues and Perspectives*, 1-10. Edited by S. T. Kwame Boafo, and Nancy A. George. Nairobi: African Council on Communication Education, 1992.
   An overview of research in mass communications in Africa to 1992, with suggestions for areas needing further research. 2 page bibliography.

1740

What Happened to "Burger's Daughter " or How South African Censorship Works. Emmarentia, South Africa: Taurus, 1980.
    A detailed account of the banning of a novel by Nobel prize-winning Nadine Gordimer, with transcripts of official correspondence and documents interspersed with commentary by Gordimer and others. While focusing on the novel, the description of the process of banning is relevant to the media of mass communication in general.

1741

Whitten, Leslie H. "South Africa on Madison Avenue." *Progressive* 33, no. 10 (October 1969): 30-32.
    The author's son's school assignment to write about apartheid, and the information packet received from the South African embassy, led the author to investigate the pervasiveness of South African government propaganda and its lavish financing in the decade before the Muldergate scandal.

1742

Wilcox, Dennis L. "Black African States." *Press Control Around the World*, 209-232. Edited by Jane Leftwich Curry, and Joan R. Dassin. New York: Praeger, 1982.
    Overview of the constraints placed on the media in Sub-Saharan Africa, covering such issues as government ownership of media infrastructure, control of funds and access to imported materials including newsprint; the legal framework protecting or restraining journalists; the position of foreign news media and journalists.

1743

---. *Mass Media in Black Africa: Philosophy and Control*. New York: Praeger, 1975. 170pp.
    An overview of the press and broadcasting throughout Africa, with emphasis on ownership and control of the media and restraints on local and foreign journalists. Appendices compare Africa's media resources with those of the rest of the world, and list daily newspapers in Sub-Saharan Africa. 29 page bibliography. Index.

1744

Wilson, Des. "Towards a Diachronic-Synchronic View of Future Communication Policies in Africa." *Africa Media Review* 3, no. 2 (1989): 26-39.

1745

Windrich, Elaine. *The Cold War Guerrilla: Jonas Savimbi, the U.S. Media, and the Angolan War*. Westport, CT: Greenwood Press, 1992. 183pp.
    An account of the ways that Cold War agendas and propaganda, rather than objective reporting, shaped media coverage of Savimbi and the civil war in Angola. Bibliographic essay. Index.

General

1746

---. "The Johannesburg Massacre: Media Images of the South African Transition." *Africa Today* 43, no. 1 (January 1996): 77-94.
>A discussion of media coverage of violence erupting during an Inkatha demonstration in March 1994 during the South African election campaign. The reports varied in tone according to the affiliation of the media source.

1747

---. *The Mass Media in the Struggle for Zimbabwe: Censorship and Propaganda Under Rhodesian Front Rule*. Gweru, Zimbabwe: Mambo Press, 1981. *Mambo Occasional Papers, Socio-Economic Series*, no. 15. 112pp.
>A study of Rhodesia's Ministry of Information and its propaganda efforts during the Unilateral Declaration of Independence, when broadcasting and the press were severely censored. Index.

1748

---. "Media Coverage of the Angolan Elections." *Issue* 22, no. 1 (March 1994): 19-23.
>Discussion of U.S. coverage of the September 1992 elections in Angola, highlighting misconceptions in both U.S. foreign policy and media concerning events and the motives of the two parties, MPLA and UNITA.

1749

---. "South Africa's Propaganda War." *Africa Today* 36, no. 1 (1989): 51-60.
>A discussion of South Africa's propaganda campaign in the U.S., covering Muldergate and the ties of the American political and religious right wing to South Africa, with emphasis on purchase and control of a number of U.S. newspapers.

1750

Woll, Allen L., and Randall M. Miller. *Ethnic and Racial Images in American Film and Television: Historical Essays and Bibliography*. New York: Garland, 1987.
>While the focus is on ethnic groups, including African Americans, in the U.S., there is a short section of books and articles dealing with Africa's image in film and television.

1751

Woods, Bernard. *Communication, Technology and the Development of People*. London: Routledge, 1993. 158pp.
>A theoretical approach, with some practical applications, to the use of mass communication and information technology in global development. Index. Bibliographic notes.

1752

Yambo-Odotte, Dommie. "Women, Media, and Democracy." *Passages: A Chronicle of the Humanities*, no. 8 (1994): 21,24. Supplement to *Program of African Studies News and Events* (Northwestern University) Fall 1994, Vol. 5, no. 1.

General

Observations on women candidates in the Kenyan elections of 1992, and their use of the media.

1753
Zaffiro, James J. "Mass Media, Politics and Society in Botswana: the 1990s and Beyond." *Africa Today* 40, no. 1 (1993): 7-25.
    An examination of patterns and trends in governmental relations with the media in Botswana, with emphasis on the influence of South Africa, coverage of government scandals and the role of the media in development.

1754
---. "Regional Pressure and the Erosion of Media Freedom in an African Democracy: The Case of Botswana." *Journal of Communication* 38, no. 3 (June 1988): 108-120.
    An analysis of South Africa's effect on media in Botswana.

1755
Ziegler, Dhyana, and Molefe Kete Asante. *Thunder and Silence: The Mass Media in Africa*. Trenton: Africa World Press, 1992. 205pp.
    An overview and review of the literature on mass media in Africa, calling for journalists to work more vigorously to develop an authentic African voice and message. Appendices list newspapers and media facilities by country. 5 page bibliography. Index.

Author Index

Abdel Rahman, Awatef 1, 1230
Abell, Helen C. 614
Aborampah, Osei-Mensah 1231, 1254
Abu-Lughod, Ibrahim 1232
Abu-Lughod, Lila 580
Abuoga, John Baptist 2
Achile, Yves 1233
Acker, Vincent 3
Adagala, Esther K. 1234
Adam, Hussein M. 866
Adebayo, Lanre 1589
Adefela, V. Olufemi 710
Adelman, Larry 849
Adeyemi, Adeyinka 4
Adi, Isabella E 1235
Adoni, Hanna 613
Afrani, Mike 581
African Conference on Radio Education 582
Agbaje, Adigun 7, 8, 9
Agbese, Pius Ogbaba 10
Agbu, Chike 11
Agonafer, Mulugeta 1463
Ahcene-Djaballah, Belkacem 1239
Ahmed, Osman Hassan 853
Aig-Imoukhuede, Frank 854, 1240
Ainslie, Rosalynde 12
Ajia, Olalekan 584
Ajibola, William A. 1241
Akahenda, Elijah F. 13
Akam, Noble 585
Akene, Emman 1242
Akhalwaya, Ameen 14, 15, 16
Akigbo, Charles 1243
Akinfeleye, Ralph A. 17, 1244, 1245
Akinjide, Olajumoke 18
Akinyemi, A. Bolaji 19, 20, 21
Akiwowo, Akinsola A. 586
Ali, Ibrahim Abukar 1246
Allison-Broomhead, Mark 1247
Almaney, Adnan 22

Alot, Magaga 23
Amapula, Johannes Ndeshihala 587
Amatokwu, F. Nwaokedi 24, 1248
Amienyi, Osabuohien P. 588, 1249, 1250, 1251
Amin, Mustafa 25
Amosu, Akwe 589
Anamaleze, John 27
Anani, Elma Lititia 1252
Anderson, P. 855
Andrade, Mario de 1253
Andrade-Watkins, Claire 856, 857, 858, 913, 942
Andrzejewski, B. W. 590
Ankomah, Baffour 28, 29, 30
Anokwa, Kwadwo 31, 1231, 1254
Anonymous 32
Ansah, Paul A. V. 33, 34, 591, 592, 1255, 1256
Ansu-Kyeremeh, Kwasi 593
Anyadike, Nnamdi 35
Anyanwu, A. V. 758
Aouchar, Amina 36
Apunen, Osmo 1246, 1257, 1258, 1378, 1445, 1473, 1525, 1526, 1622
Armes, Roy 859, 860, 1045
Armour, Charles 594, 595
Armstrong, A. 1259
Arulogun, Adegboyega 861
Asaju, Michael 37
Asante, Clement E. 38
Asante, Molefe Kete 1755
Asch, Patsy 862
Asch, Timothy 862
Association des Trois Mondes 863
Attenborough, Richard 864
Atwood, L. Erwin 1260
Auge, Marc 865
Austin, Sydney Bryn 1261
Awa, Njoku E. 1262, 1263
Awed, Ibrahim M. 866
Ayish, Muhammad I. 1264

Author Index

Ayodele, Olumuyiwa 41, 1265
Ayu, Iyorchia D. 867
Azikiwe, Nnamdi 42

Babiker, Mahjoub Abd al-Malik 43
Bachy, Victor 868, 869, 870, 871, 872, 873
Badday, Moncef. S. 874
Badibanga, Andre 44
Baesjou, Rene 45, 77
Bagdley, Christine 1266
Baker, Raymond William 875
Baldwin, Fletcher N. 46
Balikowa, David Ouma 47
Balogun, Francoise 876, 877
Balogun, Olu 878, 1267
Balon, R. E. 596
Bamisaiye, Adepitan 48
Bamouni, Babou Paulin 1268
Barbash, Ilisa 879
Barkas, N. 880
Barnes, John 881
Barratt, John 1724
Barrett, Lindsay 882
Barrett, Mike 1269
Barton, Frank 49, 50, 51
Bassori, Timite 883
Bayart, Jean-Francois 52
Bayemi, Jean Paul 53
Bebey, Francis 597
Becker, Jorg 1270
Becker, Lee B. 1523
Beckett, Denis 55
Behn, Hans Ulrich 56
Belik, Helio 799
Bellman, Beryl L. 884
Beltran, Luis 1271
ben Ammar, Abdellatif 885
ben Barka, Souhail 886
Benassir, Smail 966
Benson, E. 1170
Benson, Ivor 57

Bensusan, A. D. 1272
Bensusan, David 887
Bentsi-Enchill, Nii K. 888
Berger, Guy 58
Bernstein, Peter 59
Bertelsen, Eve 60, 1273
Biella, Peter 889
Biesele, Megan 862
Binet, Jacques 890, 891, 892, 893
Birck, Danielle 598, 599
Blackwell, Leslie 61
Blake, Cecil A. 1275, 1276
Blay-Amihere, Kabral 62, 1277, 1278
Bled, Cynthia A. 1279
Blignault, Johan. 894
Boadu, Samuel Osei 1280
Boafo, S. T. Kwame 1, 63, 64, 262, 407, 772, 1281, 1282, 1283, 1284, 1285, 1286, 1287, 1288, 1289, 1290, 1410, 1500, 1510, 1597, 1739
Bodie, Charles Alvis 65
Boisserie, Philippe 599
Bojuwade, Dokun 66, 1291, 1292
Bolela, Albert Oscar 67
Bosompra, Kwadwo 68, 600, 1291, 1292, 1293
Bosseno, Christian 895
Boster, B. 808
Botha, Martin. 894
Botombele Ekanga Bokonga 1294
Boudjedra, Rachid 896
Boughedir, Ferid 897, 898
Boulanger, Pierre 899
Boulegue, Marguerite 69
Bourgault, Louise M. 70, 601 1295, 1296, 1297, 1298
Bourges, Herve 1299
Bouteba, P. M. 900
Bowman, Philip 645
Boyd, Douglas A. 602, 603, 604, 1300

Author Index

Braimoh, Dele 1301
Bredin, Andrew 605
Brice, K. 71
Brookes, Heather Jean 72
Brossard, Jean-Pierre 901
Broughton, Morris 73
Brown, Lee 450
Brown, Trevor 74, 75, 1302
Browne, Donald R. 607
Bruck, Peter A. 527
Brush, Michael 76
Budlender, Debbie 1303
Buijs, G. 1695
Buijtenhuijs, Rob 45, 77
Bullion, Stuart J. 1260
Bunting, Brian 78
Buntman, Barbara 1304
Burchell, Jonathan 79
Burgess, Julian 1305
Burkhart, Ford 80
Burns, Gary 707
Burton, Julianne 902
Burton, Simon 1306
Byrne, Eileen 81

Cameron, Kenneth M. 904, 905
Cameron-Dow, Joy 692
Campion-Vincent, Véronique 83
Cancel, Robert 608, 906
Carchidi, Victoria 907
Carruthers, Susan L. 1308
Carter, Felice 84, 85
Carver, Richard 86
Cassirer, Henry 609
Celarie, Andre 610, 611, 612
Cerullo, Margaret 87
Chakaodza, Bornwell 1310
Cham, Mbye Baboucar 908, 909, 910, 911, 912, 913, 942
Charles, Jeff 88
Charton, N. 1675
Cheh, Mary M. 1311
Cheminais, Gaby 1333

Cheney-Coker, Syl 1312
Cheriaa, Tahar 914
Chevaldonne, Francois 1313
Chick, John D. 89, 90
Chimutengwende, Chenhamo C. 1314, 1315, 1316
Chinje, Eric 91
Chirol, Marie-Magdeleine 915
Christensen, Philip R. 687
Christians, C. 1572
Clarke, L. J. 1317
Club of Ten 1318, 1319
Cohen, Akiba A. 613
Cohen, Lisa 657, 658
Cohen, Roberta 92
Coker, Increase H. E. 93
Coldevin, Gary 1353
Coleman, William 614
Colleyn, Jean-Paul 865, 920
Collinge, Jo-Anne 921, 1320
Collins, Richard 615, 616
Coltart, James M. 1321
Committee on Inter-African Relations 94, 95
Condon, John C. 97, 323
Connell, Dan 98
Conolly, L. W. 1170
Convents, Guido 922
Cook, David 617
Coombes, Annie E. 1324
Cooper, T. 1572
Cordeaux, Shirley 618
Coriell, Vernell 1034
Cornelius, Margo 1038
Corrigan, Edward C. 619
Cotlow, Lewis 923
Coulson, Anita 1325, 1326
Couzens, Tim 99, 100
Crawford, Peter Ian 1040, 1079, 1684
Cripwell, Kenneth K. R. 620
Criticos, Costas 1605
Cross River State, Nigeria 101

Author Index

Crowdus, Gary 924
Crowley, David 621
Cruise O'Brien, Rita 622
Cuddy, Robert 102
Curran, James 1132
Curry, Jane Leftwich 1742
Cutten, Theo E. G. 103
Cutter, Charles Hickman 623
Cyr, Helen W. 925, 926, 927

Dadci, Younes 928
Dagenais, Bernard 1484
Daoud, Zayka 624
Dare, Olatunji 104
Dassin, Joan R. 1742
Davidson, Joe 105
Davis, D. 1643
Davis, Peter 929, 930
Day, Chris 441
De Beer, Arnold S. 1328, 1329, 1330
de Fossard, Esta 625
de Kock, Wessel 106
de Koning, T. L. 626
de St. Jorre, John 107
De Villiers, Les 1331, 1332
de Villiers, R. M. 218
de Villiers, Trish 1333
DeBona, Guerric 931
Debrix, Jean-Rene 932, 933
Decker, Thomas 627
Defever, Armand 628
Deguine, Herve 108
Dekou, Abotsi 109
Delarbre, Anne 110
DeLuca, Laura 934
Demafouth, Jean-Jacques 1334
Dervin, B. 1689
Deutsche Afrika-Gesellschaft 629
Deveneaux, Gustav Kashope 111
Dexter, Gerry L. 630
Dia, Saidou 1335

Diakite, Madubuko 936, 937
Dias, Raul Neves 112
Diawara, Mamadou 631
Diawara, Manthia 938, 939, 940, 941, 942, 943, 944, 945, 946
Dickerson, Bette J. 848
Dickson, W. K-L 947
Dikshit, Kiranmani A. 634
Dine, Philip 948
Dingamsangde, Ocsar Valentin 1336
Diop, Babacar 113
Ditmars, Hadani 949
Dodds, Tony 667
Dodson, Don 1339
Doherty, Christo 114
Domatob, Jerry Komia 115, 633, 1340, 1341, 1342, 1343, 1344, 1345, 1346, 1347, 1348, 1349
Domisse, Ebbe 116
Donkor, Clifford 634
Dosse Placca, Jean-Baptiste 635
Dosumu, Sanya 950
Downer, Monica 636
Downing, John D. H. 885, 886, 911, 951, 975, 1014, 1059, 1064, 1127, 1212, 1350
Dseagu, Njoroge 1351
Dumbia, Therese 117
Dunn, Kevin 952
Duodu, Cameron 118
Durieux, A. 119
Duyile, Dayo 120, 1352
Dyck, Evellyne J. 1353

Eapen, K. E. 121
Eaton, Mick 953
Ebeogu, Afam 637
Ebo, Boshah L. 122
Edeani, David O. 123, 124, 125, 1354, 1355, 1356, 1357
Edoga-Ugwuoju, Dympna 126, 136
Edwards, Peter 127

Egbe, Edison 955
Egbon, Mike 638
Egypt. Ministry of Information 128
Egyptian Organization for Human Rights 129, 1358
Eichenberger, Ambros 956
Eilers, Franz-Josef 130, 1359
Ekaney, Nkwelle 639
Eke, Maureen 1184, 1186
Ekman, Paul 668, 669
Ekpu, Ray 131
Ekwelie, Sylvanus A. 132, 133, 134, 135, 136
Ekwuazi, Hyginus 957, 958, 959, 960, 961, 962
Ekwuene, Laz 963
Elaturoti, D. F. 640
Elias, T. O. 1360
Elion, Leandra 830
Emenyeonu, Bernard Nnamdi 137, 1361, 1362
Enahoro, Augustine-Ufua 964, 965
Enckell, Monique 966
Engelbrecht, Johannes Cornelius Rudolph 138
Eone, Tjade 641
Epule, Kome 139
Eribo, Festus 140, 141, 1363, 1364
Essoe, Gabe 967
Essoulami, Said 142, 143
Eswara, H. S. 144
Etherington, Alan 621
Etukudo, Nelson 1365
Everett, Anna 642
Evert, J. B. 145, 146
Ewane, F. Kange 1366
Ewumbue-Monono, Churchill 147, 148, 1367
Eyoh, Hansel Ndumbe 643
Ezeh, Peter 150

Fahim, Fawzia 644

Fair, Jo Ellen 372, 1368, 1369, 1737
Fairchild, Halford H. 645
Faringer, Gunilla L. 151
Faris, James C. 968
Farounbi, Yemi 646, 647, 648
Fawehinmi, Gani 152, 153
Fell, John L. 1143
Feltoe, Graham 155
Feuereisen, Fritz 156
Finn, Stephen M 157
Finnegan, William 158
Fiofori, Ferdinand O. 1370
Fitzgerald, Mary Anne 159
Flaes, Robert M. Boonzajer 1039, 1175
Flather, Horace 160
Fletcher, Richard 161
Foisie, Jack 163
Fontaine, Arlette 164
Fougeyrollas, Pierre 650
Fraenkel, Pierre 651
Frederikse, Julie 1371
Freeman, David K. 1372
Friedenberg, Daniel M. 1373
Friedgut, A. J. 165
Friedmann, Michelle 1494
Frondorf, Margaret Hardt 487, 1519
Frost, R. 213
Fuglesang, Minou 1374
Fussell, Paul 166, 1375
Fyfe, C. H. 167

Gaddy, Gary D. 515
Gadjigo, Samba 970, 1067
Gadsden, Fay 168
Gaillard, Phillippe 169
Gakosso, Jean 170
Gallay, Pierre 171
Gambia 652
Ganda, Oumarou 1107
Gardies, Andre 971, 972
Gartley, John 653

Author Index

Gathu, Faith W. 172
Gatura, Rahab 1288
Gaudio, A. 654
Gavshon, Harriet 973
Gboyega, Bade 173
Gendzier, Irene L. 174
George, Nancy A. 1, 407, 655, 772, 1289, 1290, 1410, 1500, 1597, 1739
Gerbner, George 669, 823, 1377, 1402
Gergen, David 1725
Gerogakas, Dan 974
Gerold-Scheepers, Therese 175
Getachew Tadesse Azmera 1378
Gettino, Octavio 1134
Ghali, Noureddine 975
Ghana Journalists Association 1379
Ghejam, Ali M. 1380
Gibbs, James 656
Gibson, Rex 177
Giffard, C. Anthony 178, 195, 196, 657, 658, 1381, 1382, 1383
Gikaru, Lawrence 179
Gill, Peter 1384
Gilwald, Alison 1385
Ginwala, Frene 180
Gordon, Robert 862
Gorelick, Nahum J. 659
Gorman, T. P. 790
Govea, R. 181
Graaf, Michael 182
Grant, Marcia A. 183
Grant, Stephen 660
Gray, John 976
Green, George A. L. 184
Green, Nick 1386
Green, Pippa 1387
Greig, G. 185
Grella, George 977
Grenholm, Lennart H. 661
Griffin, Michael 1388

Grogan, John 186
Guback, Thomas 978
Gueye, Amadou Mactar 187, 1389
Guiochet, Sylvie 188
Gultig, John 1306
Gupta, Anirudha 189
Gupta, Udayan 924
Gutsche, Thelma 979
Guyot, Michel 663

Hachten, William A. 190, 191, 192, 193, 194, 195, 196, 664, 13391390, 1391, 1392, 1393, 1394,
Haffner, Pierre 972, 980, 981, 982
Haile Gerima 983
Haines, Richard J. 1185, 1695
Hakimzadeh, Farhad 628
Hall, Budd L. 665, 666, 667
Hall, Stephen William 1348
Hall, Susan 984
Hallis, Ron 985
Ham, Melinda 197
Hamdane, Mohamed 1395
Hamdani, Mariam Mohamed Abudrahman 198
Hamelink, Cees. J. 1396
Hammonds, Evelynn 87
Hanna, Judith Lynne 986
Harber, Anton 199
Harding, Jeremy 200
Hardy, Pauline 1397
Harper, Douglas 1039, 1175
Harrell-Bond, Barbara E. 201
Harris, Phil 202
Harrison, Paul 1398
Harrison, Randall 668, 669
Harrow, Kenneth 987
Hartog, Simon 1109
Haule, John James 203
Hawk, Beverly G. 1399
Hayase, Yasuko 704
Hayatu, Husaini 204

Hayman, Graham 670
Haynes, Jonathan 988
Haysom, Nicholas 1400
Hazoume, Guy-Landry 205
Head, Sydney W. 206, 671, 672, 673, 1401, 1402
Heard, Anthony H. 207, 208
Heath, Carla W. 674, 675, 676
Heikal, Mohamed H. 209, 210
Hein, Charles T. 677
Hein, Kurt 687
Hellmen, Ellen 165
Hennebelle, Guy 989, 990, 991, 992, 993, 994, 995, 996, 997, 998, 999, 1000, 1001, 1002, 1003, 1004, 1005, 1006, 1007, 1403
Hennebelle, Monique 1008, 1009, 1010, 1011, 1012
Hepburn, Katherine 1013
Hepple, Alexander 211, 212
Herbert, Boh 678
Herbstein, Denis 1404
Hero, Alfred O. 1724
Hiebert, Ray Eldon 450, 657, 675, 1302
Hilke Meyer-Bahlburg 1496
Hobbs, Mary Kay 1585
Hobbs, R. 213
Hoben, Susan J 1405
Hondo, Abid Med 1014
Hopkinson, Tom 214, 215, 216
Horatio-Jones, Edward B. 1015
Horton, Philip C. 217, 349, 389, 440
Hortop, Stella 1406
Hotz, L. 218
Howard, J. 679
Howson-Wright, A. E. 220
Hughes, Anthony J. 221
Hughes, Langston 1206
Huida, Pirjo 222, 1246, 1258, 1378, 1445, 1473, 1525, 1526, 1622
Hull, Galen 1407

Hunt, Gary T. 223, 476
Hur, K. Kyoon 680, 681

Ibelema, Minabere 224, 682
Ibie, Nosa Owens 225, 1408, 1409, 1410, 1411
Ibrahim, Mohammed 683
Ibrahim, Salah M. 1412
Igbarumah, Matthias 226
Ihaddaden, Zahir 227, 228, 684
Ijere, M. O. 1413
Ikime, Obaro 685
Ilbo, Ousmane 1016
Imhoof, Maurice 686, 687
International Organization of Journalists 230, 231
International Workshop on the Radio Learning Group 688
Irving, James 232
Isaacs, Gayla Cook 1420
Isoba, J. C. G. 233
Israel, Adrienne M. 234
Iyam, David Uru 1017

Jack, Abner 1421
Jackson, Gordon S. 235, 236, 690
Jaidi, Moulay Driss 1018
Jaja, Emmanuel Adagogo 333
Jakande, Lateef Kayode 237
James, Sybil L. 1422, 1423
Jamison, Dean T. 1593
Jasper, William F. 238
Jefkins, Frank William 1424
Jell-Bahlsen, Sabine 1019
Jere, Annette 691
Jika, A 1349
Jimada, Usman 1425, 1426
John-Kanem, Anthony V. 1427
Johnson, Shaun 239, 1428
Jones, Barry 692
Jones, Elizabeth Ceirog 513
Jones-Quartey, K. A. B. 240, 241, 242

Author Index

Jose, Isma'il Babatunde 243, 244
Jules-Rosette, Bennetta 884, 1429
Julien, Eileen 1082
July, Robert W. 245
Jutras, Dominique 1020

Kabetesi, Kibisu 246, 247
Kagan, Rachael 248
Kahn, Ellison 1430
Kalemba, Robert 249
Kalter, Joanmarie 250, 693
Kalu, Onuka 251
Kamara, Musa S. 1431
Kamara, Sylviane 252
Kamara, Tom 253
Kamenya, Shadrack 934
Kamphausen, Hannes 1021
Kamuhanda, Sethi 1432
Kandaki, D. E. S. 1433
Kaplan, David 1434, 1435
Kapuscinski, Ryszard 254
Kareithi, Peter 255
Kariithi, Nixon K. 256
Karikari, Kwame 257, 258, 694, 695, 696, 1436
Kasoma, Francis P. 259, 260, 261, 262, 263, 1437, 1438
Kasongo Ibanda Ngozulu 1022
Katz, Elihu 697,. 1439
Kaufman, Michael 264
Kayyem, Juliette 265
Keane, Fergal 698
Keekeh, Florida 699
Keene-Young, Bronwyn 700
Keita, Alkaly Miriama 1252
Kenney, Keith R. 266
Kern-Foxworth, Marilyn 1442
Kerr, David 1023, 1443
Kershaw, Richard 270
Khan, M. 1024
Khelil, Hedi 1444
Khlifi, Omar 1025
Kiai, Wambu 1234

Kidd, Ross 621
Kifle Sede 1445
Kilongson, Mike 1446
Kindem, Gorham H. 1026
Kirat, M. 271
Kitchen, Helen 272, 273, 1591
Kivikuru, Ullamaija 274, 1447, 1448, 1449
Kiwanuka-Tondo, James 701
Kizito, Robert N. 1450
Klee, Hans Dieter 702, 1451
Kleu, Sebastiaan J. 275
Klotman, Phyllis Rauch 1027
Koffi, Atta 703
Kojima, Hiroshi 704
Konde, Hadji 1452
Koné, Hugues 276, 570, 705, 1453, 1454, 1455
Kono, Shigemi 704
Korzenny, F. 213
Kotane, Solomon 706
Kovach, Bill 277
Kozol, Wendy 707
Kramer, Jane 1456
Kramer, Reed 1457
Kugblenu, John 673
Kulakow, Allan 708
Kumbula, Tendayi S. 1458
Kushner, James M. 709, 1300

Lacob, Miriam 279, 280
Ladele, Olu 710
Land, Mitchell 711
Landy, Marcia 1028, 1029
Lantz, Charles R. 613
Lardner, Tunji 1459
Larson, Charles R. 1030
Lasekan, Olu 710
Lasode, Obafemi 712
Latham, G. C. 1069
Laurence, John 281, 1460
Le Pape, Marc 282
Le Roy, Marie Claire 1031

Leahy, James 1032
Lederbogen, Utz 1461
Lee, Philip 1255
Lee, R. B. 1033
Lee, Raymond 1034
Lee, Richard 862
Lehman, C. 1185
Lems-Dworkin, Carol 713
Lepine, Richard M. 283, 284, 1462
Leprohon, Pierre 1035
Leslie, Michael 263
Lester, Julius 1036
Levi, Antonia 1463
Lewin Robinson, A. M. 285
Lewin, Hugh 453
Leymarie, Philippe 286
Liberia Broadcasting System 714
Lobulu, William 288
Lodge, Tom 1464
Loizos, Peter 1037
Lopo, Julio de Castro 289
Lorber, Howard Z. 1038
Louw, Louis 290
Louw, P. Eric 527, 528, 616, 716, 1465, 1466, 1467, 1468, 1469, 1686, 1687, 1688, 1689
Louw, Raymond 1470, 1471
Luc, Jean-Claude 717
Lundeen, Alisa 800
Lungwangwa, G. 750
Luthi, Jean-Jeacques 291
Lydall, Jean 1039, 1040
Lyons, Andrew P. 718
Lyons, Louis M. 292

M'Bayo, Ritchard 1491, 1492
M'inoti, Kathurima 1509
MacKay, Ian K. 719
MacRae, Suzanne H. 1041
Madjri, John 293
Magnate, Joseph 294
Magubane, Peter 295
Maillot, Dominique 1042

Maina, Wachira 1509
Maingard, Jacqueline 1472
Maissara, Neema Mussa 1473
Maja-Pearce, Adewale 296, 297, 298, 299, 300, 301, 302, 1474, 1475, 1476
Majerzi, Lotfi 1043
Makedonsky, Erik 1044
Malden, Sue 720
Malkmus, Lizbeth 1045
Manheim, Jarol B. 1604
Manoim, Irwin 303
Mantoux, Thierry 1046
Maqetuka, Sello 1480
Marchand, Jacques 1481
Marcus, Gilbert 1400, 1482
Marcus, Harold G. 206
Maren, Michael 721
Maron, Claude 304
Marshall, John 1047
Marsot, Afaf Lutfi Al-Sayyid 305
Martin, Angela 1048
Martin, L. John 450, 657, 675, 1302
Martin, Louis E. 306
Martin, Michael T. 857, 898, 941, 1049, 1086, 1181, 1199
Martin, Robert 1483
Masilela, Ntongela 1050, 1188
Masmoudi, Mustapha 1484, 1485
Matabane, Paula W. 722
Mathane, Nomavenda 307
Matheson, Alastair 308
Matheson, H. 723
Mathews, Anthony S. 1486
Mativo, Kyalo 1051
Mativo, Wilson 1052
Matloff, Judith 309
Matovu, Jacob 1487
Mayer, Doe 1489
Maynard, Richard A. 1053
Mazrui, Ali A. 724, 1490
Mbachu, Dulue 302
Mbejume, Onyero 1493

Author Index

McAnany, Emile 725
McCaffrey, Kathleen 1054
McCarthy, Jeffrey 1494
McCarthy, Michael 1495
McCavitt, William E. 626
McGarry, Georgia 310
McGarry, Richard G. 311
McIntyre, Joseph 1496
McKay, Vernon 1497, 1498, 1499
McKensie, James E. 1669
McLaughlin, Gerald W. 429
McLean, Polly E. 726, 1500
McLellan, Iain 727
McLeod, W. Edward 46
McLoughlin, T. O. 312
McParland, Kelly 313
Media Institute of Southern Africa 1502, 1503
Megherbi, Abdelghani 1055
Megwa, Eronini 1554
Mehra, Achal 314
Meldrum, Andrew 315
Mellen, Joan 1056
Menard Robert 108
Menga, Guy 1504
Mercer, Kobena 1057
Mermin, Elizabeth 1058
Merrett, Christopher 1505
Mersham, Gary M. 728
Merzak, Allouache 1059
Meurant, L. H. 316
Meyer, William H. 1506
Mhlaba, L. 317
Miller, Randall M. 1750
Miller, Seumas 1507, 1508
Minot, Gilbert 1060
Misser, Francois 729
Miyouna, Ludovic-Robert 730
Mkhondo, Rich 318
Mlama, Penina M. 1510
Modisane, Bloke 319
Mody, Bella 1511

Moemeka, Andrew A. 362, 731, 732, 1512, 1513, 1514, 1569, 1602
Moffett, Martha Roadstrum 320
Moghalu, Kingsley Chiedu 321
Mohamed, Ali N. 322
Mohammed, Jubril Bala 733, 1515, 1516
Mollard, Pierre Jose 323
Momoh, John 1517
Moolmam, H. M. 324
Moore, R. M. 1185
Moore, Robert C. 325
Morgenthau, Henry 1061
Moroney, Sean 326
Morris, Roger 327
Mortimer, Mildred 1082
Mortimer, Robert A. 1062
Morton-Williams, P. 1063
Moseki, Mojalefa 328
Moshiro, G. 734
Mosia, Lebona 735
Mostefaoui, Belkacem 736
Motlomelo, Samuel 1518
Moundolock, Ignace Bertrand 329
Mowlana, Hamid 487, 1519
Mpanya, Motombo 1266
Mphahlele, Ezekiel 1521
Mphahlele, Teresa K. 1551
Mpoyi-Buatu, Th. 1064
Mthombothi, Barney 737
Muddathir, Ahmed 330
Mueller, Claus 738
Mugerwa, P. J. Nkambo 331
Mukamba Longesha 1522
Mukasa, Stanford G. 1523
Mukela, John 1524
Mukenge, Mauadi 332
Mukupo, Titus 333
Muller, Johan 334, 529, 530, 531, 670, 807, 809, 813, 830, 1700
Mulu, John 1525
Munanga, Jonathan 1526
Munger, Edwin S. 116, 739

Muoria, Henry 335
Murphy, Sharon M. 336, 1260
Mutere, Absalom Aggrey 2, 1527
Muzavazi, Christopher 1528
Mwaffisi, M. Samwilu 337, 740, 741
Mwase, Ngila R. L. 338
Mwaura, Peter 1529
Mwendamseke, Nancy 1530
Mytton, Graham L. 1531, 1532, 1533, 1534

N'Gosso, Gaston Same 1541
Nabwa, Ali 1535
Nakasa, Nathaniel 339
Nasidi, Yakubu 961, 962
Nasser, Munir K. 340
National Symposium on Broadcasting in Nigeria 742
Natsoulas, Theodore 341
Nazareth, Peter 743
Ndiaye, A. Raphael 1536
Ndifang, David 1537
Ndovi, Victor 342
Nduru, Moyiga 343
Nederveen Pieterse, Jan 1538
Negash, Ghirmai 344
Neier, Aryeh 345
Nelson, Daniel 346
Newman, Johanna 1539
Newsinger, John 1540
Ng'wanakilala, Nkwabi 1544
Ng'weno, Hilary B. 349, 350
Nga Ndongo, Valentin 348
Ngakane, Lionel 866, 1065
Ngansop, Guy Jeremie 1066
Ngomba, Mbella M. 744
Ngure wa Mwachofi 1542
Ngwainmbi, Emmanuel Komben 1543
Ngwenya, Sindiso 1545
Niambele, Abdramne 745
Niang, Sada 1067

Nichols, Lee 746
Nichols, Bill 1134
Niemeijer, Rudo 45
Nienaber, G. S. 351
Nixon, Rob 747, 1068
Njawé, Pius 352
Nkrumah, Kwame 353
Nkwabi Ng'Wanakilala 1547
Nnaemeka, Tony Ike 1546
Nolot, P. 354
Nordenstreng, Kaarle 1547, 1548
Notcutt, L. A. 1069
Novicki, Margaret A. 1070, 1071
Nowrojee, Binaifer 1549
Nse, Alberto Elo 1550
Ntemfac, Ofege 678
Nwabughuogu, Anthony I. 355
Nwankwo, Clement 356
Nwankwo, Robert L. Nwafo 149, 357, 358, 359, 744, 1551
Nwokeafor, Cosmas 359, 1492
Nwosu, Ikechukwu E. 360, 361, 362, 1349, 1552, 1553
Nwosu, Peter O. 1554
Nwuneli, Onuora E. 363, 854, 861, 950, 955, 963, 1015, 1075, 1076, 1136, 1555, 1556
Nyamnjoh, Francis B. 364, 748, 749, 1557
Nyika, Tambayi 365
Nyirenda, J. E. 750
Nyirenda, Kambona 1558
Nyong'o, Dorothy 1559

O'Brien, Sue 368
O'Meara, D. 1582
O'Meara, Patrick 1583
Obadina, Tunde 366
Obaze, Abraham I. 367
Obeng-Quaidoo, Isaac 1560, 1561, 1562, 1563
Ochieng, Mark 1564
Ochieng, Philip 369

Author Index

Ochilo, Polycarp J. Omolo 1565
Ochola, Francis W. 1566, 1567
Ochs, Martin 370
Odhiambo, L 371
Oduko, Segun 751
Ogan, Christine L. 372
Ogbondah, Chris W. 10, 373, 374, 375, 376, 377, 378, 379, 380, 381, 382, 1568
Ogunbi, Adebayo 752, 1077
Ogundimu, Folu 753, 1569
Ogundipe-Leslie, Molara 1570
Ohrn, Steven G. 1072
Okeowo, Kunle 383
Okere, Linus C. 384
Okigbo, Charles 385, 386, 387, 754, 1571, 1572, 1573, 1574
Okomba Wetshisambi 1073
Okome, Onookome 1074
Okonkwo, Jerome Ikechukwu 755
Okonkwor, R. Chude 388
Okoth-Owiro, A. 1575
Okoye, Felix N. 1576
Okoye, Innocent 756
Okunna, Chinyere Stella 757, 1577, 1578, 1579
Okwudishu, Chris 1580
Olasope, Biola 389
Olayiwola, Rahman Olalekan 390
Olkes, Cheryl 1581
Omari, I. M. 391
Omu, Fred I. A. 392, 393, 394
Onagoruwa, G. Olu 395
Onah, J. O. 758
Onu, P. Eze 396, 397
Onwudiwe, Ebere 682
Onwumechili, Chuka 1492
Onyango-Obbo, Charles 1584
Onyedike, Emmanuel U. 382, 398, 399
Opoku, Andrew A. 614
Oppenheimer, Harry 400

Opubor, Alfred E. 854, 861, 950, 955, 963, 1015, 1075, 1076, 1077, 1136, 1585
Oreh, Onuma O. 401, 1076
Orewere, Ben 1586
Orivel, François 759, 1593
Orlik, Peter B. 402, 760
Osakue, John 1587
Osinbajo, Yemi 1588
Oso, Lai 403, 761, 1589
Ossman, Susan 762
Otieno, Barrack 581
Oton, Esuakema U. 404, 405
Otten, Rik 1078
Oudes, Bruce 406
Overballe, Henrik 1079
Oyediran, Oyeleye 237, 1363
Ozoh, Hilary C. 407, 408, 763

Pachai, B. 409
Page, Melvin E. 410
Palmer, Robin 1398, 1590
PanAfrican Federation of Filmmakers/FEPACI 1080
Pasquier, Roger 411
Pate, Umaru A. 412, 764
Paterson, Adolphus A. 413
Paterson, Christopher 765
Pather, Dennis 414
Patterson, James 1081
Pawlouschek, Andreas 766
Payne, Les 16
Payne, W. A. J. 1591
Payne, William A. 333
PEN American Center 415
Pennell, Richard 416
Perkins, Kenneth J. 418
Perraton, H. D. 1593
Peters, Jonathan 1082
Petley, Dexter 419
Petty, Sheila 767, 1083
Pfaff, Françoise 1084, 1085, 1086, 1087, 1088

Phelan, John M. 1594
Pige, François 768
Pike, Charles Ben 1089, 1090, 1091
Pines, Jim 944, 983, 1092, 1152, 1154, 1207
Pinnock, Don 1595
Platzbecker, Toni 769
Plude, F. F. 1572
Pogrund, Benjamin 420, 421
Poirer, Leon 1093
Pollak, Richard 422
Pollock, Francis 423
Pommier, Pierre 1094
Porter, Vincent 1132
Potter, Elaine 424
Poussaint, Renée 1095
Prakke, Heinrichus Johannes 1596
Pratt, Cornelius B. 425, 426, 427, 428, 429, 1597, 1598, 1599, 1600, 1601, 1602, 1603, 1604
Predal, René 1096
Pretorius, William 1097
Prince, Bill 771
Prince, Viv 436
Prinsloo, Jeanne 1605
Prior, M. 437
Puri, Shamlal 438

Qoboza, Percy 440
Quarmyne, Wilna W. 772
Quaye, Paa Keow 773
Quenum, Alphonse 1606

Raboy, Marc 527, 1484
Rachty, Gehan 1607
Raeburn, Michael 1098
Rahman, Awatef Abdel 1252
Rattley, Sandra 774
Raya, Gamal Abu 775
Rayfield, F. R. 1099
Rayfield, J. R. 1100
Reda, Adly Sayed Mohamed 776

Rees, Mervyn 441
Reg Lascaris 1386
Reid, Mark A. 1101, 1102
Revill, Stuart 778
Rhoodie, Eschel M. 1609, 1610, 1611
Ricard, Alain 779, 1612
Riddle, Charles 186, 735, 780, 1613
Ridore, Charles 781
Riesenfeld, Daniel 930
Riggins, S. H. 684
Righter, Rosemary 445
Riley, Rebecca 1072
Ripley, J. M. 1614
Riverson, L. Kwabena 1615
Robert, Guy 782
Roberts, Alun R. 1616
Roberts, Andrew 1103
Roberts, John Storm 446
Robinson, Cedric 1104
Robinson, Elizabeth 946
Robinson, J.P. 681
Rockson, Kweku 1617
Roelfse, J. L. 1618
Rogerson, C. M. 783
Rollwagen, Jack R. 889, 968, 1019, 1105
Ronan, Barry 447
Ronen, Dov 480
Ronning, Helge 1621
Rosenthal, Eric 448, 449, 784
Roser, Connie 450
Rothbart, G. 679
Rothmeyer, Karen 451, 452
Rouch, Jean 1106, 1107
Rowlands, Don 453
Rubenstein, Lenny 974
Rubin, Barry 454
Ruby, Jay 1108
Ruelle, Catherine 1541
Rugaimukamu, Fabian M. 1622
Ruijter, Jose M. 1623, 1624

Author Index

Rukuni, Charles 455
Rusike, E. T. M. 1626
Rwomire, Apollo 1627

Sabat, Khalil 1607
St. Leger, Fred 232, 456
Salama, Jirgis 786
Salinas, Raquel 1283
Salmane, Hala 1109
Salwen, Michael B. 31
Sam, Albert 457
Sambe, John A. 787
Sampson, Anthony 458
Sanger, Clyde 333
Sauer, Matthew E. 1110
Sauldie, Madan M. 459
Sayah, Lahouari 1628
Schaar, Stuart 1629
Schade, Curtis 1082
Schechter, Danny 1630, 1631, 1632
Schiller, Herbert I. 1548
Schmacke, Ernst 156
Schmidt, Nancy J. 460, 1111, 1112, 1113, 1114, 1115, 1116, 1117, 1118, 1119
Schneider, William 461
Schramm, Wilber Lang 1633
Scott, Christina 462, 1634
Scott, Chuck 1120
Scotton, James F. 336, 463, 464, 65, 466
Segal, Aaron 1636
Seiler, John 1637
Sekalala, Aga 467
Selmont, Aristotle 1638
Selmont, Verity 1638
Senekal, J. E. 789
Senghor, Blaise 1122
Serceau, Daniel 1123
Serfontein, J. H. P. 468
Shaka, Femi Okiremuete 1124
Shaloff, Stanley 469
Shaw, Gerald 470, 471

Shaw, Tony 1639
Sheehan, Edward R. F. 472
Shepperson, Arnold 1186
Sherrington, R. W. 790
Shija, William M. F. 358
Shiri, Keith 1125
Shohat, Ella 1126, 1640
Shore, Larry 88
Showers, Kate B. 1641
Sicherman, Carol 473
Sienaert, Edgard 1187
Sikakane, Joyce 474
Silla, Mactar 791
Silver, Louise 475
Silverman, Theresa 792
Simonsen, Jan Ketil 1040, 1079
Sine, Babacar 1642
Sing, Michael 476
Skurnik, W. A. E. 477, 478, 479, 480
Slabbert, Mana 1643
Sloan, L. 679
Sly, Liz 481
Smart, M. Neff 482, 483
Smart, Tony 161
Smihi, Moumen 1127
Smiley, Xan 1644
Smith de Sherif, Teresa K. 487
Smith, Anthony 1645
Smith, H. Lindsay 484
Smith, Howard 793
Smith, Jasper K. 485
Smith, Richard L. 486
Smyth, Rosaleen 1128, 1129, 1130, 1131, 1132, 1133
Smythe, Hugh H. 1646
Sobowale, Idowu 488, 540, 1721
Sock, Boubacar 794
Solanas, Fernando E. 1134
Solinas, PierNico 1135
Solomon, Joel A. 1647
Sommerlad, Lloyd E. 489
Soola, E. O. 1649, 1650, 1651, 1652

Sorenson, John 1653, 1654
Souriau-Hoebrechts, Christiane 490
South Africa 1655
South Africa. Commission of Enquiry 1656
South Africa. Commission of Inquiry .... (Erasmus)1657, 1658, 1659,
South Africa. Commission of Inquiry 795
South Africa. Commission of Inquiry 491
South Africa. Commission of Inquiry .... (Eloff) 1660
South Africa. Commission of Inquiry .... (Steyn)1661, 1662
South Africa. Commission of Inquiry 1663
South Africa. Task Group on Broadcasting 796
Sow, Mamadou Aliou 797
Soyinka, Wole 495, 496, 1136, 1668
Sparks, Allister 177, 497, 498
Spass, Lieve 1137
Spence, Louise 1138, 1140
Sperling, Gerald B. 1669
Spitulnik, Debra 798
Sreberny-Mohammadi, Annabelle 799
Ssali, Ndugu Mike 499, 1139
Staff of NTV 685
Stam, Robert 1140, 1640
Stanley, Joyce 800
Startt, James D. 500
Steele, Martha 1026
Steenveld, Lynette 1141, 1701
Steeves, H. Leslie 1671
Stein, M. L. 501
Stevenson, Robert 502
Stevenson, Robert L. 1672
Stewart, Desmond 503

Stewart, Gavin 504, 1673
Stockard, Russell 645
Stokke, Olaf 1674
Stoller, Paul 1142
Storm, Roeland 505
Strebel, Elizabeth Grottle 1143, 1144, 1145
Strong, John A. 1146
Stuart, Kelsey William 506
Sumaili, F. K. M. 750
Sumo, Honore de 1147
Surlin, S. H. 801, 802
Sussman, Leonard R. 509, 510
Switzer, Donna 514
Switzer, Les 511, 512, 513, 514, 1675, 1676, 1677

Tagama, Herald 581
Takirambudde, Peter Nanyenya 1678
Tamzali, Wassyla 1148
Tanjong, Enoh 515
Tanner, Henry 516
Tanzania. Ministry of Information and Tourism. 517
Taylor, Elyseo J. 1149
Taylor, Lucien 879
Tchienehom, Jean-Vincent 1679
Teboho, Moja 804
Teer-Tomaselli, Ruth 805, 1680 (See also Tomaselli, Ruth)
Tegambwage, Ndimara 518
Teheranian, Majid 628
Terrell, R. L. 519
Teshome H. Gabriel 1150, 1151, 1152, 1153, 1154, 1155, 1156, 1188
Theiner, George 1681
Theroux, Paul 806, 1682
Thompson, J. S. T. 520
Thompson, James C. 521
Thompson, Robert J. 707
Thoraval, Yves 1157

Author Index

Timothy, Bankole 522
Todd, Judith 523
Todd, Rusty 88
Tomaselli, Keyan G. 334, 524, 525, 526, 527, 528, 529, 530, 531, 670, 807, 808, 809, 810, 813, 830, 887, 929, 1097, 1141, 1158, 1159, 1160, 1161, 1162, 1163, 1164, 1165, 1166, 1167, 1168, 1169, 1170, 1171, 1172, 1173, 1174, 1175, 1176, 1177, 1178, 1181, 1180, 1179, 1182, 1183, 1184, 1185, 1186, 1187, 1188, 1205, 1469, 1683, 1684, 1685, 1686, 1687, 1688, 1689, 1690, 1691, 1692, 1693, 1694, 1695, 1699, 1700, 1701. 1728
Tomaselli, Ruth 334, 529, 530, 531, 670, 807, 809, 810, 811, 812, 813, 830, 690, 1691, 1692, 1693, 1694, 1696, 1697, 1698, 1699, 1700, 1701 (See also Teer-Tomaselli, Ruth)
Torchia, Andrew 532
Toumi, Mohsen 1702
Traber, Michael 1703, 1704
Trichet, P. 654
Tudesq, André Jean 534, 814, 815, 816, 1705, 1706, 1707
Turecamo, David 1189
Turki, Mohamed 535
Turner, Patricia A. 1190
Turton, David 1684
Turvey, Gerry 1191
Tusa, John 817
Twumasi, Yaw 536, 1708
Tyson, Harvey 537, 538

Uche, Luke Uka 819, 1709, 1710, 1711, 1712, 1713
Udoakah, Nkereuwem 1714
Udofia, Callix 539
Udoh, Effiong 363
Uganda 820
Ugboajah, Frank Okwu 540, 821, 822, 823, 1424, 1715, 1716, 1717, 1718, 1719, 1720, 1721
Ugochukwu, F. 824
Ukadike, N. Frank 1192, 1193, 1194, 1195, 1196, 1197, 1198, 1199, 1200, 1722, 1723
Ume-Nwagbo, Ebele N. E. 541, 825
Umexh, Charles C. 826
Ungar, Sanford J. 1724, 1725
United Nations. Economic Commission for Africa 542, 827
Utomi, Patrick 543
Uwazurike, Chudi 544
Uys, Stanley 545

Van Amelsvoort, Vincent 546
Van Bever, L. 1201
Van Bol, Jean-Marie 547
Van Den Heuvel, Alex 1202
van den Wijngaard, Rian 548
van Deventer, Hennie 549
Van Rooyen, J. C. W. 1726, 1727
Van Tonder, J. W. 828
Van Wert, William 1203
van Zyl, Hannes 1204
Van Zyl, J. A. F. 829, 1728
van Zyl, John 1180, 1205
Van Zyl, M. 1695
van Zyl, Mikki 830
Vandi, Abdulai S. 1729
Vaughn, J. Koyinde 1206
Vaughn, Stephen 1364
Venkatasamy, Coll 550
Verbaan, Mark 551
Vergeldt, Vicki 831
Versi, Anver 552, 832
Vidale, Marcello L. 628
Vieler-Porter, Chris 1730

Vieyra, Paulin Soumanou 1207, 1208, 1209, 1210, 1211, 1212, 1213, 1214
Visser, Rud. P. 553
Vittin, Thophile 833

Walling, William 1215
Walsh, Gretchen 1731
Wander, Philip 834
Wanyande, Peter 1732
Waritay, Lamini A. 1733
Wark, McKenzie 1734
Wasburn, Philo C. 835, 836
Wason, Eugene 554
Waterman, Christopher A. 837
Watling, Cyril 555
Wauthier, Claude 556, 1735
Weaver, Harold D. Jr. 1216, 1217
Webb, Maxine W. 1736
Wedell, George 697, 838
Weinberger, Eliot 1218
Weiss, Ruth 557
Weissman, Steve 558
Wellington, Nicholas 1219
Wells, Alan 1392
Welsh, B. W. W. 839
Wendland, Wend 840
Werman, Marco 1220
West, Harry G. 1737
Wete, Francis N. 1738, 1739
White, Luise 559
White, R. 1572
Whiteley, W. H. 590
Whitten, Leslie H. 1741
Wilcox, Dennis L. 1742, 1743
Wilhelm Herzog 1359
Wilkinson, J. F. 842
Willan, Brian 560
Willemen, Paul 944, 983, 1092, 1152, 1154, 1207, 1221
Williams, Amie. 1188, 1222
Wilmsen, Edwin M. 1223
Wilson, David 1109
Wilson, Des 843, 1744
Windrich, Elaine 561
Windrich, Elaine 1745, 1746, 1747, 1748, 1749
Winks, Robin W. 1077
Wisselmann, Rene 663
Witherell, Julian W. 567, 1119
Woll, Allen L. 1750
Woods, Bernard 1751
Woods, Donald 562, 563, 564, 1224
Woodson, Dorothy C. 565, 566, 567
Woolford, Pamela 1225
Wright, Rob 1226
Wubneh, M. 1363

Yakir, Dan 1227
Yambo-Odotte, Dommie 1752
Yankah, Kojo 568, 569
Yao, Faustin K. 570
Yata, Ali 571
Yearwood, Gladstone L. 1217

Zacks, Stephen A. 1228
Zaffiro, James J. 735, 844, 845, 846, 1753, 1754
Zamparoni, Valdemir D. 572
Zaremba, Alan 573
Zaring, D. T. 574
Zeff, Eleanor E. 575, 576
Zemoniaco, Patrice 847
Zerbst, Jeff 577
Ziegler, Dhyana 848, 1755
Zimmermann, Patricia R. 1229
Zindela, Theo 579
Zonn, L. 1363

Subject and Geographical Index

Abacha, Sani 300
Accident 1046
Achebe, Chinua 1030
Achkar, David 1192
Acting 960
Addis Zeman 206
Adult Education 467, 620, 661, 806, 1344
Advertising 397, 763, 1266,1273, 1304, 1386, 1420,1424, 1442, 1538
Africa: Broadcasting 582, 583, 594, 595, 596, 597, 605, 608, 612, 618, 621, 629, 630, 642, 643, 645, 662, 672, 679, 680, 681, 682, 688, 693, 696, 697, 702, 703, 704, 705, 709, 713, 715, 722, 723, 724, 727, 729, 732, 738, 739, 746, 748, 752, 753, 765, 773, 774, 788, 801, 802, 814, 815, 816, 817, 818, 827, 831, 833, 834, 836, 838, 841, 842, 847
Africa: Film 850, 851, 852, 854, 859, 860, 863, 866, 867, 873, 878, 879, 883, 890, 891, 892, 893, 897, 898, 900, 903, 904, 905, 913, 914, 916, 917, 918, 920, 922, 923, 926, 927, 932, 933, 937, 938, 940, 941, 944, 945, 949, 951, 952, 956, 958, 965, 967, 969, 976, 978, 981, 982, 986, 991, 992, 994, 1003, 1013, 1014, 1021, 1022, 1027, 1034, 1035, 1037, 1048, 1049, 1051, 1052, 1053, 1060, 1061, 1069, 1072, 1077, 1080, 1081, 1083, 1091, 1093, 1095, 1096, 1099, 1101, 1102, 1105, 1106, 1111, 1112, 1113, 1116, 1117, 1118, 1119, 1121, 1122, 1128, 1132, 1133, 1140, 1142, 1149, 1158, 1183, 1186, 1190, 1192, 1193, 1194, 1195, 1200, 1206, 1207, 1208, 1210, 1214, 1217, 1221, 1222, 1228, 1229

Africa: General 1230, 1233, 1234, 1236, 1237, 1238, 1256, 1258, 1261, 1262, 1263, 1266, 1267, 1268, 1269, 1270, 1274, 1275, 1276, 1279, 1280, 1281, 1282, 1283, 1286, 1287, 1288, 1289, 1290, 1295, 1296, 1297, 1298, 1299, 1307, 1310, 1312, 1315, 1321, 1322, 1324, 1335, 1339, 1348, 1349, 1351, 1354, 1355, 1359, 1363, 1364, 1366, 1367, 1368, 1369, 1373, 1377, 1386, 1389, 1390, 1391, 1392, 1394, 1398, 1399, 1401, 1402, 1405, 1414, 1415, 1416, 1418, 1420, 1424, 1425, 1427, 1429, 1442, 1443, 1450, 1451, 1453, 1454, 1457, 1458, 1459, 1463, 1475, 1476, 1483, 1491, 1495, 1506, 1510, 1511, 1512, 1513, 1514, 1519, 1523, 1532, 1537, 1538, 1539, 1541, 1546, 1548, 1552, 1553, 1559, 1561, 1562, 1566, 1567, 1571, 1573, 1576, 1585, 1590, 1591, 1596, 1597, 1598, 1599, 1600, 1601, 1602, 1603, 1604, 1615, 1619, 1620, 1623, 1624, 1625, 1633, 1635, 1636, 1638, 1641, 1642, 1644, 1646, 1650, 1651, 1652, 1654, 1671, 1672, 1674, 1678, 1681, 1682, 1703, 1704, 1705, 1706, 1707, 1709, 1711, 1712, 1716, 1718, 1719, 1720, 1725, 1730, 1731, 1735, 1737, 1738, 1739, 1742, 1743, 1744, 1750, 1755
Africa : Press 5, 6, 12, 17, 26, 33, 34, 40, 45, 49, 50, 51, 54, 65, 68, 71, 72, 87, 88, 91, 98, 105, 109, 115, 124, 130, 139, 140, 144, 145, 146, 147, 151, 156, 159, 161, 169, 170, 175, 181, 187, 188, 189, 192, 194, 203, 217, 219, 222, 223, 224,

Subject and Geographical Index

225, 230, 243, 250, 251, 256, 257, 259, 261, 262, 264, 266, 270, 272, 273, 276, 279, 287, 288, 292, 306, 315, 326, 333, 336, 349, 353, 358, 362, 370, 371, 378, 389, 396, 398, 401, 407, 410, 413, 427, 432, 433, 434, 437, 438, 445, 450, 452, 453, 457, 459, 460, 461, 477, 480, 481, 486, 502, 509, 510, 519, 522, 532, 533, 534, 539, 541, 542, 552, 569
Africa News Service 1457
African Daily News 554
The African Queen 1013
The Africans 722, 1490, 1668
Africasat TV 729
Afrikaans Films 1204
Afrikaans Press 116, 275, 334, 549, 553, 1610
Afrikaner Culture 1695
Afrique, Je Te Plumerai 1184, 1192
Agence France Presse 110, 169
Agriculture 614, 628, 634, 761, 1554, 1593, 1649
AIDS 87, 600, 1261, 1526, 1622, 1650
Akhbar al-Youm 25
Al Ahram 271, 340, 503
Al Ikhtyar 1005
Algeria 81, 142, 227, 228, 271, 622, 684, 768, 896, 901, 919, 928, 948, 966, 997, 999, 1000, 1008, 1009, 1043, 1055, 1056, 1059, 1109, 1135, 1140, 1148, 1215, 1239, 1313, 1403, 1417, 1628
Algerian War of Independence 896, 948
Allah Tantou 1192
Alternative Press 14, 15, 154, 528, 1428
Amakiri Case 237, 377, 395
Ampaw, King 1071
ANC 118, 238, 462, 700, 706, 735, 1480, 1680, 1697

Anglophone Africa 942, 1089, 1243
Angola 102, 254, 289, 360, 1012, 1090, 1146, 1325, 1745, 1748
Animated Films 1202
Ansah, Kwaw 1085
Anthropology 862
Apartheid 195, 212, 318, 328, 345, 415, 422, 500, 524, 527, 615, 616, 735, 778, 808, 887, 907, 921, 930, 1032, 1139, 1141, 1161, 1162, 1163, 1164, 1219, 1305, 1306, 1316, 1330, 1382, 1460, 1464, 1480, 1594, 1595, 1660, 1692, 1701
Arabic 604
Arabvision 766
Archives 1081
Argus Company 449
Ashanti Pioneer 234
Ashanti Times 89
Asia 1390
Asian Press 84
Asking for Trouble 1224
Associated Press 223
Atlas 460
Atria Film Company 1102
Attenborough, Richard 864
Audience Surveys 586, 596, 645, 679, 680, 722, 758, 801, 1232, 1250, 1279, 1531, 1556, 1598, 1634, 1675
Audiences 1044
Australia 1180
Authoritarian Regimes 1425

Balogun, Olu 882, 888
Banda, Hastings 127, 249
Bassori, Timité 995, 1003
Battle of Algiers 1056, 1135, 1140
BBC 583, 594, 595, 618, 720, 793, 817, 842
Beeld 334
ben Ammar, Abdellatif 885, 989

ben Barka, Souhail 886
Benin 83, 205, 628, 725, 1606
Bennani, Hamid 1004
Bensusan, David 887
Berkani, Derri 1000
Beyond the Plains Where Man Was Born 996
Biafra 19, 20, 21, 48, 107, 406, 787, 824, 1241
Bias 19, 125, 248
Bibliographies 69, 164, 175, 287, 376, 380, 417, 475, 486, 507, 514, 565, 566, 640, 752, 976, 1115, 1117, 1118, 1119, 1271, 1281, 1288, 1391, 1401, 1407, 1421, 1585, 1730, 1731, 1736
Biko 1224
Biko, Steve 74, 562, 563
Biograph 947
Biographies 11, 99, 160, 174, 184, 205, 214, 216, 218, 244, 245, 254, 295, 316, 319, 335, 351, 436, 437, 447, 458, 474, 520, 535, 555, 560, 562, 563, 579, 771, 895, 1084, 1088, 1123, 1142, 1213
Birth of a Nation 1145
Black Girl (La Noire de...) 1029, 1137, 1212
Blue Eyes of Yonta 1197
Boer War 500, 881, 947, 1143, 1144, 1174
Bongo, Omar 868
Botha, P. W. 1610
Botswana 299, 691, 725, 844, 1047, 1177, 1188, 1437, 1684, 1736, 1753, 1754
Bottle Babies 1038
Brazil 1203
Broadcasting 704, 1271, 1274, 1295, 1299, 1352, 1394, 1402, 1405, 1452, 1474, 1480, 1487, 1494, 1532, 1535, 1544, 1560, 1612, 1613, 1622, 1636, 1674, 1702

Broke Time Bar 656
Die Burger 114
Burkina Faso 293, 872, 915, 1070, 1115, 1278
Burroughs, Edgar Rice 967
Burundi 119, 1078

Cabascabo 1107
Cabral, Amilcar 1029
Cameroon 28, 32, 52, 53, 82, 96, 148, 329, 348, 352, 354, 364, 365, 570, 611, 633, 639, 641, 678, 744, 749, 767, 911, 1066, 1147, 1192, 1543, 1557, 1679
Cameroon Calling 678
Cameroon Tribune 570
Camp de Thiaroye 1124
Campaign for Open Media 700
Canada 96, 396, 1020
Cape Times 114, 118, 144, 207, 470, 471
Cape Verde 1253
Carcase for Hounds 882
Caribbean 1263
Carter, Kevin 309
Cartoons 305, 312, 410, 538, 1403, 1538, 1638
Casablanca 762
Ceddo 1017, 1064, 1212
Censorship 28, 91, 92, 118, 150, 166, 180, 199, 211, 231, 249, 352, 378, 415, 419, 421, 424, 440, 492, 504, 540, 551, 561, 564, 577, 605, 635, 657, 658, 695, 747, 979, 1001, 1050, 1065, 1160, 1163, 1172, 1309, 1314, 1328, 1375, 1400, 1404, 1430, 1446, 1474, 1476, 1482, 1488, 1504, 1505, 1521, 1524, 1565, 1592, 1612, 1632, 1656, 1663, 1665, 1670, 1681, 1683, 1713, 1721, 1726, 1727, 1740, 1747
Central Africa 171, 1130

Central African Film Unit 1129
Central African Republic 1334
Chad 1336, 1679
Chahine, Youssef 895, 1003, 1005
Change 1382
Children 206, 644, 745, 756, 775, 1734
Chiluba, Frederick 298
Christian Science Monitor 19
Chronicle 86
Cinema *Djidid* 966, 997, 1009
Circulation 178
Ciskei 512, 700, 1675
Cisse, Souleymane 1041
Clandestine Broadcasting 636, 828
Classroom use of films 862, 1099
Club of Ten 1318, 1319
Cock Crow at Dawn 825
Colonial Film Unit 1063, 1089, 1091, 1128
Colonialism 977, 1140, 1540
Come Back Africa 1050
Comedy 637, 656, 1097
Comic Books 1682
Committee to Protect Journalists 71
Communications 1258, 1263, 1516
Comoros 1535
Computers 1429, 1751
Conferences 852, 866, 956, 970, 1057, 1528
Conflict 108, 123, 141, 200, 282, 343, 516, 574, 1146
Congo 730, 1504
Conrad, Joseph 931
Conscription 182
Constitution 172, 1379, 1708
Content Analysis 45, 68, 76, 88, 97, 115, 125, 137, 140, 141, 144, 206, 223, 229, 271, 322, 358, 359, 360, 363, 386, 396, 427, 428, 456, 459, 477, 478, 479, 488, 512, 513, 515, 541, 568, 570, 573, 574, 835, 836, 1637
Côte d'Ivoire 478, 479, 570, 660, 711, 865, 871, 911, 935, 993, 995, 1003, 1107, 1394, 1429, 1455
Court Cases 79
Credibility 480
Crises 1484, 1648
Criticism 902, 929, 945, 988, 1041, 1084, 1088, 1116, 1150, 1151, 1153, 1154, 1155, 1213
Cry Freedom 864, 882, 907, 1224
Cultural Boycott 60, 921, 1665
Cultural Change 1051, 1052
Cultural Identity 900, 965, 1155, 1121

Daily Comet 42
Daily Dispatch 232, 512
Daily Graphic 258, 568, 573
Daily Nation 77, 479, 574
Daily Times 137, 244, 359, 372, 397, 570
Dance 986
Daventure, Andrée 1102
de Klerk, F. W. 1542
Debrix, Jean-Rene 994
Democracy 1709
Densu Times 483
Destablization 1497
Development 52, 223, 359, 362, 372, 425, 587, 601, 612, 639, 699, 725, 727, 734, 750, 757, 794, 1110, 1231, 1256, 1262, 1276, 1280, 1289, 1298, 1303, 1335, 1339, 1354, 1361, 1370, 1415, 1433, 1450, 1483, 1510, 1512, 1514, 1516, 1519, 1523, 1534, 1536, 1543, 1579, 1585, 1589, 1599, 1600, 1603, 1604, 1614, 1623, 1633, 1651, 1671, 1672, 1676, 1705, 1706, 1720, 1738, 1751, 1753
Development Journalism 256, 337,

371, 401, 476, 1287, 1348, 1356, 1704
Dhlomo, H. I. E. 99
Diaspora 1049
Dictionaries 1496
Diop-Mambety, Djibril 1100
Directories 156, 629, 773, 863, 897, 1125, 1274, 1359, 1461, 1475
Disinformation 1616, 1687
Distribution 738, 914, 1018, 1196, 1220
Divestment 849
Documentaries 642, 855, 862, 984, 985, 1039, 1047, 1093, 1103, 1108, 1120, 1141, 1146, 1173, 1175, 1187, 1188, 1195, 1198, 1223, 1472, 1684
Doe, Samuel 253
Drama 825
Drought 229, 570
Drum 54, 214, 216, 295, 458, 566, 567
A Dry White Season 907
Dürrenmatt 1100
Deutsche Welle 583

East Africa 171, 274, 350, 489, 790, 130, 1257, 1323, 1462
East African Standard 144
Ecare, Desiré 993
Economic Status 1313
Editorials 425
Education 1406
Educational Broadcasting 701, 7 50, 757, 804, 839, 1301
Educational Films 849,, 862, 954, 969, 1023, 1063, 1069, 1129, 1130, 1131, 1133, 1206, 1593
Educational Media 1343, 1344, 1518
Educational Radio 582, 593, 609, 611, 614, 621, 625, 628, 634, 640, 661, 665, 666, 667, 686, 687, 688,

726, 731, 732, 782, 785, 788, 797, 800, 803, 806, 816, 831, 1593
Educational Television 585, 609, 620, 650, 660, 663, 717, 759, 781, 790, 792, 816, 826
Egypt 1, 22, 25, 128, 129, 174, 209, 210, 291, 305, 314, 340, 472, 503, 580, 603, 644, 775, 776, 875, 895, 954, 1002, 1003, 1005, 1010, 1024, 1126, 1157, 1232, 1252, 1260, 1300, 1358, 1412, 1607, 1639
Elections 157, 179, 311, 495, 662, 805, 829, 1273, 1291, 1477, 1478, 1520, 1574, 1698, 1748
Electronic Media 1467
Eloff Commission 1594, 1660
Emerge 266
Emitai 975, 1017, 1082, 1212, 1216
Employment 1234
English in Action 687
ENTV 1240
Environment 568, 1286, 1641
Equatorial Guinea 416, 1550
Erasmus Commission 1657, 1658, 1659
Eritrea 344, 636
Eritrean People's Liberation Front 636
Ethics 122, 225, 226, 259, 282, 309, 315, 361, 367, 368, 426, 428, 429, 443, 454, 467, 496, 518, 1265, 1572
Ethiopia 76, 92, 206, 636, 653, 1039, 1040, 1225, 1378, 1384, 1445, 1653, 1670
Ethnicity 728, 1083
Ethnographic Films 865, 879, 884, 889, 920, 953, 968, 1019, 1037, 1040, 1105, 1106, 1173, 1206, 1218, 1229
Europe 893, 1305, 1366
Exile 1014
Eyadéma, Gnassingbé 635

Subject and Geographical Index

Family Planning 1455, 1559, 1619
Famine 92, 200, 358, 1369, 1384, 1446, 1654, 1670
Fanon, Frantz 1029
FAO 628
Feature Films 859, 888, 942, 984
Female Genital Mutilation 1246, 1463
FESPACI 941
FESPACO 857, 939, 972, 1006, 1031, 1070, 1080, 1189, 1196, 1211, 1220, 1226
FESTAC 1635
Fiction 283, 1462
Fighting Talk 565
Film 1253, 1267, 1269, 1271, 1272, 1416, 1443, 1444, 1452, 1472, 1489, 1522, 1538, 1541, 1544, 1606, 1607, 1619, 1625, 1642, 1643, 1695, 1722, 1723, 1730, 1750
Film Industry 856, 858, 859, 874, 883, 898, 910, 933, 938, 949, 950, 959, 962, 964, 994, 1044, 1058, 1094, 1114, 1122, 1138, 1181, 1180, 1179, 1185, 1207
Filmmaking 916, 991, 1060, 1089, 1091, 1095, 1106, 1121, 1193, 1208, 1209
Filmographies 850, 851, 853, 863, 918, 925, 926, 927, 954, 969, 992, 1020, 1027, 1072, 1077, 1088, 1113, 1123, 1125, 1164
Finances 1185
Finland 1449
Finzan 934
First, Ruth 565
Focus Groups 1562, 1563
Foreign Broadcasts 1342
Foreign Coverage 20, 21, 39, 45, 48, 68, 98, 102, 115, 159, 169, 179, 202, 203, 223, 238, 264, 270, 271, 273, 279, 290, 314, 327, 333, 358, 374, 396, 398, 406, 423, 427, 452, 459, 479, 481, 493, 502, 509, 516, 519, 532, 693, 707, 787, 1398, 1590, 1630
Foreign Influence 234, 286, 353, 624, 740, 860, 958, 1068, 1095, 1201, 1233, 1413, 1439, 1523, 1679
Foreign Policy 412, 1432
France 83, 96, 169, 188, 271, 286, 461, 486, 748, 776, 779, 833, 852, 856, 918, 978, 991, 995, 999, 1008, 1089, 1093, 1102, 1142
Francophone Africa 44, 252, 779, 791, 856, 910, 971, 1089, 1094
Fraternité Matin 372, 478, 479, 570
Free Press 62
Freedom of Speech 269, 840, 1549

Gabon 610, 868, 1679
Gambia 301, 652, 1376
Ganda, Oumarou 1107
Gandhi, Mahatma 409
Gaskiya ta fi Kobo 204
Gatekeepers 385, 765, 1300
Genocide 598
Germany 956
Ghana 3, 29, 30, 31, 38, 62, 63, 64, 89, 95, 132, 136, 151, 176, 191, 234, 240, 241, 242, 258, 278, 301, 365, 397, 443, 469, 482, 483, 485, 536, 546, 568, 573, 575, 576, 581, 591, 592, 593, 606, 614, 634, 649, 671, 673, 694, 695, 910, 911, 1071, 1085, 1098, 1231, 1254, 1284, 1285, 1293, 1379, 1394, 1436, 1560, 1563, 1614, 1617, 1708, 1722
Ghana Broadcasting Corporation 591, 673, 695
Ghanaian Times 397, 568
Giwa, Dele 294
Global 1396
The Gods Must Be Crazy 929, 1033, 1178

Gomes, Flora 1197
Gordimer, Nadine 906
Government Control 4, 7, 22, 32, 42, 62, 63, 66, 75, 81, 86, 91, 104, 127, 132, 134, 135, 161, 176, 186, 191, 192, 193, 196, 207, 210, 221, 231, 236, 237, 253, 258, 267, 268, 277, 296, 297, 302, 313, 314, 320, 331, 340, 342, 343, 348, 349, 352, 364, 375, 377, 381, 383, 399, 406, 416, 420, 422, 423, 434, 435, 444, 454, 455, 457, 468, 469, 473, 480, 484, 491, 496, 497, 503, 508, 520, 523, 531, 545, 571, 578, 641, 675, 703, 780, 795, 973, 1018, 1042, 1165, 1171, 1247, 1248, 1251, 1259, 1292, 1322, 1328, 1334, 1338, 1388, 1425, 1436, 1440, 1441, 1474, 1479, 1509, 1557, 1564, 1575, 1591, 1613, 1617, 1660, 1661, 1662, 1673, 1688, 1690, 1694, 1698, 1724
Griots 1079
Guardian (Lagos) 137, 520
Guardian (Manchester) 179
Guelwaar 1067
Guinea 797, 1192, 1277
Guinea Bissau 1197, 1253

Haile Gerima 909, 943, 1225
Health 87, 222, 274, 546, 650, 665, 667, 800, 934, 1038, 1257, 1258, 1286, 1293, 1378, 1445, 1473, 1525, 1563, 1569, 1620, 1650
Heard, Anthony 118
Heart of Darkness 931
Heikal, Mohamed H. 340, 472, 503
Herald 372
History: Broadcasting 591, 594, 595, 606, 649, 651, 670, 671, 685, 710, 755, 784, 814, 816, 819, 842, 844

History: Film 858, 868, 870, 873, 881, 896, 897, 898, 899, 916, 922, 928, 940, 941, 952, 957, 959, 979, 988, 1002, 1016, 1023, 1025, 1035, 1042, 1043, 1055, 1063, 1073, 1074, 1078, 1091, 1103, 1109, 1126, 1128, 1129, 1130, 1131, 1132, 1133, 1146, 1157, 1159, 1169, 1174, 1187, 1193, 1194, 1200, 1201, 1202, 1208
History: General 1241, 1295, 1392, 1427, 1452, 1541, 1568, 1709, 1747
History: Press 2, 23, 27, 38, 43, 67, 73, 83, 89, 93, 103, 106, 111, 112, 119, 120, 136, 167, 185, 198, 204, 209, 227, 228, 233, 235, 240, 241, 242, 258, 260, 285, 289, 291, 305, 308, 310, 316, 323, 329, 334, 341, 354, 355, 364, 373, 393, 404, 411, 449, 461, 469, 470, 471, 484, 486, 490, 499, 511, 513, 528, 543, 547, 553, 567
Holland 45, 569
Hollywood 1219
Homelands 1141
Hondo, Med 990, 1064
Housing 1494
Human Rights 379, 1396, 1450, 1501
Hunkanrin, Louis 205
Hyenas 1100

Identity 972, 1121, 1183, 1196
Ilanga 462
Images 72, 83, 110, 137, 188, 266, 324, 332, 374, 398, 410, 461, 569, 599, 642, 753, 762, 765, 812, 854, 861, 867, 901, 904, 905, 907, 923, 931, 932, 948, 952, 967, 977, 1013, 1020, 1034, 1035, 1053, 1054, 1055, 1068, 1077, 1106, 1139, 1173, 1190, 1192, 1195, 1199, 1200, 1206, 1222, 1229, 1261,

Subject and Geographical Index

1266, 1270, 1332, 1351, 1353, 1366, 1368, 1369, 1399, 1406, 1414, 1422, 1427, 1442, 1458, 1459, 1495, 1530, 1538, 1539, 1570, 1573, 1576, 1591, 1640, 1641, 1653, 1654, 1682, 1734, 1750
Immigrants 1008
Imvo Zabantsundu 165, 511, 512
In Black and White 617
Indaba 512
Independent Broadcasting Authority 737, 840
Independent Filmmakers 921
India 144, 189, 459, 958, 1110
Indian Opinion 409
Information Technology 1429, 321, 1564, 1742
Inkatha 462, 1696, 1697
International Organization of Journalists 230
International Press Institute 215
Internet 1457
Interviews 879, 908, 974, 975, 1011, 1048, 1059, 1096, 1098, 1127, 1225, 1227
Ivory 1641
Izvestia 140, 141

Japan 893
Jeune Afrique 1638

Kabore, Gaston 915, 943
Kadoma Declaration 1397
Kenya 2, 13, 23, 77, 84, 85, 110, 144, 151, 168, 172, 179, 193, 221, 248, 255, 267, 268, 269, 277, 283, 284, 311, 332, 335, 341, 369, 446, 464, 465, 473, 479, 501, 546, 574, 581, 625, 655, 674, 675, 676, 686, 687, 702, 785, 821, 908, 1198, 308, 1309, 1374, 1394, 1429, 1440, 1441, 1489, 1509, 1525, 1527,
1529, 1549, 1564, 1565, 1575, 1584, 1647, 1722, 1732, 1752
Kenya Broadcasting Corporation 676
Kenya Times 574
Kilongson, Mike 1388, 1446
King, Cecil 244
Koevoet 1616
Koranta ea Becoana 560
Krieg, Peter 1038

Lagos 756
Language 41, 109, 113, 168, 204, 263, 278, 283, 284, 291, 304, 311, 330, 335, 391, 560, 590, 592, 626, 650, 663, 673, 684, 717, 794, 799, 837, 870, 885, 891, 903, 1196, 1405, 1445, 1462, 1496
Laroui, Abdelaziz 535
Laws 9, 33, 35, 43, 61, 119, 128, 148, 152, 153, 155, 180, 246, 247, 317, 323, 361, 373, 375, 393, 382, 399, 402, 433, 435, 440, 443, 475, 506, 841, 1235, 1311, 1320, 1325, 1360, 1379, 1395, 1400, 1430, 1437, 1438, 1482, 1509, 1521, 1568, 1575, 1588, 1628, 1655, 1662, 1665, 1678, 1708, 1715, 1726, 1727
Leisure 1606
Lesotho 514, 1120, 1437, 1518, 1524
Liberation 338, 709, 858, 867, 924, 1422
Liberia 95, 253, 405, 601, 699, 714, 884, 1433, 1517, 1729, 1733
Liberian Age 253
Liberian Broadcasting System 714
Liberian Rural Communications Network 1433
Libya 1380
Literacy 252, 483, 1301
Literature 284, 617, 743, 746, 779, 1111

Lorang's Way 1198
Los Angeles Times 102
Lumière 304
Lusophone Africa 799, 858, 924
A Luta Continua 924

M'Membe, Fred 298
MacDougall, David 1198
MacDougall, Judith 1198
Mackenzie, Thomas William 218
Madagascar 304, 1046
Magazines 54, 285, 567, 1495
Malaria 1473, 1525
Malawi 127, 249, 297, 299, 342, 442, 651, 1023, 1129, 1477, 1478, 1479, 1558, 1593, 1608
Maldoror, Sarah 1003, 1012, 1054
Mali 117, 365, 623, 631, 745, 869, 934, 946
Mambety, Djibril Diop 935
MAMSER 125
Mandabi 1036, 1212
Mandela, Nelson 374, 808, 1699
Marinovich, Gregory 368
Marketing 47
Marshall, John 1108
Masarurwa, Willie 313
Masri, Samir 1003
Mass Communications 1239, 1282, 1329, 1371, 1566, 1567, 1717, 1729, 1751, 1395, 1501, 1512, 1546, 1547, 1550, 1555, 1569, 1581, 1596, 1620, 1629, 1640, 1692, 1700, 1728
Mau Mau 332, 335, 882, 1308
Mauritania 990, 1417
Mauritius 286, 550
Mazrui, Ali 722, 1490, 1668
Media Council Decree 24, 173, 1251, 1292
Media Education 1243, 1343
Merabtene, Menouar 1403
Merzak, Allouache 1059

Middle East 573
Military 1688
Missions 980
Moati, Serge 1007
Moi, Daniel Arap 277
Moi, un Noir 1107
Momie 1002
Le Monde 271
Money Power 888
Morocco 36, 323, 571, 762, 768, 886, 919, 1004, 1018, 1042, 1127, 1393, 1417, 1629
Mozambique 112, 200, 322, 572, 985, 1326, 1470, 1520
MPLA 1748
Mubarak, Hosni 128
Muldergate 177, 195, 196, 236, 422, 441, 451, 973, 1318, 1319, 1331, 1337, 1407, 1419, 1481, 1582, 1583, 1592, 1609, 1610, 1611, 1657, 1658, 1659, 1667, 1669, 1724, 1749
Mulee Ngea 354
Mumenyereri 335
Mungai, Anne 908
Munnansi 419
Murder 294
Murphy, Eddie 905
Museums 1324
Music 837, 963
Mwangi, Meja 882
MWASA 55
My Country, My Hat 887

Nairobi Law Monthly 267, 277
Nakasa, Nat 579
Namibia 299, 338, 551, 587, 659, 780, 1047, 1108, 1177, 1188, 1404, 1470, 1499, 1613, 1616, 1684
The Namibian 551
Nasser, Gamel Abdel 209, 603, 1126
The Nation 427

Subject and Geographical Index

National Concord 137
National Identity 1083, 1112, 1214, 1431, 1712
National Integration 90, 1249
National Press Union 303
National Review 427
National Security 1311
National Unity 13, 588, 638, 1487
Nationalist 97
Nazi Germany 1317
New Age 78
New Nation 154
New Nigerian 372, 570
New Republic 27
New World Information Order (NWICO) 387, 450, 502, 1239, 1255, 1264, 1270, 1342, 1431, 1485, 1716
New York Times 19, 88, 179, 223, 314, 358, 374, 396, 479
News 39, 44, 97, 98, 114, 121, 159, 189, 202, 234, 270, 363, 386, 389, 445, 477, 478, 479, 486, 493, 505, 515, 541, 557, 613, 657, 658, 707, 754, 787, 811, 817, 829, 841, 881, 1103, 1232, 1260, 1277, 1300, 1326, 1336, 1343, 1394, 1399, 1534, 1535, 1590, 1702
News Agencies 347, 1268, 1412, 1457
News Coverage 10, 76, 181, 187, 224, 248, 288, 332, 360, 412, 488, 518, 573, 1248, 1302, 1307, 1364, 1369, 1384, 1387, 1389, 1422, 1459, 1494, 1539, 1552, 1631, 1632, 1636, 1644, 1654, 1664, 1666, 1669, 1674, 1693, 1696, 1699, 1703, 1725, 1746
Newspapers 1250, 1254, 1289, 1381, 1445, 1447, 1455, 1471, 1473, 1494, 1518, 1525, 1533, 1554, 1560, 1613, 1619, 1622, 1625, 1702

Newsweek 115, 181, 224, 266, 427, 515, 1350
Ng'weno, Hilary 446
Ngakane, Lionel 1164
Ngugi wa Thiongo 906
Ngurumo 97
Nieman Foundation 292, 492, 493, 1236, 1237, 1238, 1664
Niger 585, 717, 725, 781, 782, 792,
Nigeria: Broadcasting 584, 586, 588, 600, 637, 638, 640, 646, 647, 648, 656, 683, 685, 710, 712, 718, 719, 731, 733, 742, 751, 754, 756, 757, 758, 761, 763, 764, 786, 787, 819, 823, 824, 825, 826
Nigeria: Film 854, 861, 876, 877, 888, 910, 911, 950, 955, 957, 959, 960, 961, 962, 963, 964, 988, 1015, 1019, 1030, 1063, 1074, 1075, 1076, 1110, 1114, 1115, 1136, 1199
Nigeria: General 1235, 1240, 1241, 1242, 1244, 1245, 1248, 1249, 1250, 1251, 1260, 1265, 1291, 1292, 1301, 1352, 1356, 1360, 1361, 1362, 1365, 1370, 1394, 1408, 1409, 1410, 1411, 1413, 1426, 1489, 1492, 1493, 1515, 1516, 1532, 1556, 1568, 1569, 1570, 1572, 1574, 1577, 1578, 1579, 1580, 1586, 1587, 1588, 1589, 1612, 1649, 1710, 1713, 1714, 1715, 1719, 1722, 1723
1006, 1007, 1016, 1107, 1252, 1581
Nigeria: Press 3, 4, 7, 8, 9, 10, 11, 18, 19, 20, 21, 24, 27, 35, 37, 41, 42, 48, 66, 70, 80, 90, 93, 95, 104, 107, 120, 122, 123, 125, 126, 131, 133, 134, 135, 137, 144, 150, 151, 152, 153, 173, 183, 201, 204, 220, 226, 237, 244, 294, 296, 300, 302, 321, 347, 355, 356, 357, 359, 361, 363, 365, 366, 367, 373, 375, 376, 377, 379, 380, 381, 382, 383, 384,

385, 386, 387, 388, 390, 394, 395, 397, 399, 403, 404, 406, 408, 412, 425, 426, 428, 429, 476, 488, 495, 496, 515, 520, 543, 544, 546, 570
Nigeria-Anambra State 755
Nigeria-Cross River State 101
Nigerian Broadcasting Corporation 710, 719
Nigerian Film Corporation 961
Nigerian Tribune 359
Nightline 721
Nkomati Peace Treaty 322
Nkrumah, Kwame 89
No Longer at Ease 1030
La Noire de... See *Black Girl*
North Africa 330, 418, 490, 602, 604, 624, 736, 766, 899, 1045, 1417
North America 835
Nous Deux, France 993
Nyamanton 946
Nyerere, Julius 203

O Africano 572
O Povo Organizado 924
OAU 221
Observer 150
Oral Tradition 70, 608, 631, 906, 912, 943, 944, 945, 1079, 1086, 1090, 1152
Orality 1184, 1186
Ownership 58, 85, 124, 126, 136, 183, 265, 390, 403, 489, 540, 543, 674, 676, 689, 694, 733, 1245, 1276, 1408, 1580, 1587, 1721, 1742, 1743

Pan African News Agency (PANA) 147, 187, 223, 552, 1255, 1389
Passagers 999
Public Broadcasting Service 1030
People of the Great Sandface 1047, 1223

Photographs 295, 309, 368, 1272
Pioneer 29
Plaatje, Sol 560
Poland 254
Policies 385, 557, 615, 632, 648, 652, 659, 664, 671, 705, 714, 716, 809, 810, 820, 914, 962, 1089, 1131, 1230, 1249, 1253, 1283, 1292, 1294, 1310, 1347, 1349, 1396, 1436, 1437, 1438, 1484, 1468, 1493, 1527, 1529, 1534, 1537, 1548, 1597, 1604, 1627, 1711, 1680, 1715, 1718, 1733, 1744
Politics 10, 36, 52, 73, 117, 139, 157, 168, 229, 261, 276, 296, 312, 334, 340, 369, 384, 388, 390, 391, 394, 409, 424, 463, 466, 498, 511, 526, 536, 556, 572, 575, 576, 603, 666, 667, 715, 770, 783, 798, 805, 819, 845, 875, 940, 983, 987, 998, 1003, 1009, 1041, 1062, 1070, 1082, 1159, 1254, 1256, 1273, 1284, 1291, 1314, 1315, 1322, 1347, 1363, 1364, 1380, 1451, 1453, 1454, 1492, 1544, 1546, 1549, 1595, 1610, 1626, 1645, 1647, 1713, 1732, 1748, 1752
Pontecorvo, Gillo 1135
Popular Music 837
Population 1286
Pornography 577
Portugal 1373
Post 298
Poulou le Magnifique 1000
Pravda 140, 141
Press 530, 554, 1246, 1269, 1271, 1274, 1295, 1299, 1309, 1336, 1352, 1359, 1378, 1390, 1394, 1402, 1405, 1416, 1444, 1452, 1474, 1481, 1484, 1487, 1497, 1522, 1526, 1532, 1536, 1544, 1551, 1558, 1566, 1567, 1594, 1612, 1628, 1634, 1636, 1713, 1719

Press Freedom 5, 8, 13, 25, 29, 30, 33, 35, 40, 46, 51, 53, 56, 59, 66, 71, 79, 80, 82, 105, 119, 128, 129, 145, 146, 149, 151, 170, 172, 177, 195, 201, 208, 217, 219, 220, 243250, 255, 257, 261, 280, 287, 298, 299, 300, 301, 302, 315, 321, 325, 329, 346, 350, 356, 365, 366, 367, 377, 378, 379, 382, 392, 395, 400, 402, 405, 413, 430, 431, 432, 442, 446, 494, 498, 506, 509, 510, 521, 522, 537, 538, 578, 841, 1235, 1245, 1278, 1296, 1325, 1326, 1338, 1358, 1417, 1425, 1452, 1492, 1503, 1506, 1507, 1508, 1557, 1565, 1568, 1580, 1584, 1608, 1621, 1624, 1628, 1647, 1678, 1708, 1714, 1735, 1743

Prison 11, 249, 342, 420, 520, 523, 678

Production 1736

Professionalism 251, 622, 1624

Propaganda 57, 195, 355, 406, 418, 423, 558, 671, 740, 822, 835, 861, 922, 948, 1023, 1129, 1130, 1132, 1141, 1144, 1168, 1305, 1317, 1331, 1345, 1373, 1397, 1407, 1460, 1481, 1498, 1499, 1583, 1596, 1609, 1639, 1667, 1724, 1741, 1745, 1749

Public Opinion 111, 583, 829, 1022, 1410, 1646

Public Relations 1411, 1601, 1602

Qoboza, Percy 16, 414, 417, 439

Race 78, 100, 165, 190, 265, 281, 306, 328, 345, 448, 525, 707, 722, 737, 857, 904, 931, 1139, 1176, 1201, 1368

Racism 65, 1138, 1140, 1167, 1270, 1312, 1369, 1460, 1540

Radio 586, 587, 589, 592, 597, 602, 603, 605, 606, 607, 608, 610, 612, 617, 618, 623, 624, 626, 629, 630, 631, 632, 633, 636, 639, 641, 651, 655, 656, 677, 678, 683, 692, 695, 696, 699, 703, 704, 705, 708, 709, 710, 715, 719, 725, 733, 734, 735, 743, 746, 754, 768, 769, 770, 772, 779, 780, 784, 794, 798, 805, 815, 819, 821, 822, 824, 827, 828, 830, 833, 835, 836, 838, 847, 1246, 1250, 1253, 1289, 1335, 1336, 1378, 1388, 1443, 1445, 1446, 1447, 1455, 1473, 1497, 1518, 1522, 1525, 1526, 1533, 1536, 1554, 1558, 1619, 1625, 1628, 1634, 1642, 1713, 1737

Radio Language Arts Project 687

Radio Moscow 836

Raeburn, Michael 996, 1001

Ramampy, Benoit 1046

Ramparts d'Argile 990

Rand Daily Mail 95, 322, 372, 456, 497, 545

Rawlings, Jerry 29, 63, 695

Reader Surveys 31, 232, 288, 515

Refugees 487

Regional Integration 1367

Religion 130, 142, 171, 228, 580, 604, 677, 773, 789, 580, 604, 677, 773, 789, 870, 1282, 1415, 1660

Research 1, 407, 1103, 1276, 1279, 1290, 1323, 1355, 1357, 1410, 1449, 1491, 1500, 1553, 1561, 1562, 1571, 1597, 1599, 1603, 1604, 1646, 1689, 1691, 1716, 1739

Réunion 286

Reuters 110, 161

Rhetoric 1542

Rhodes of Africa 880

Rhodesia 57

Rhodesia Count Down 1001

Robeson, Paul 905

Rocha, Glauber 1203

Subject and Geographical Index

Rogol, Marty 1327
Roots 596, 645, 679, 680, 681, 724, 774, 801, 802, 834
Rouch, Jean 918, 953, 995, 1096, 1123, 1142, 1227
Rural Areas 34, 262, 278, 293, 408, 482, 487, 601, 633, 673, 708, 821, 827, 843, 285, 1269, 1303, 1448, 1519, 1552, 1560, 1586, 1625, 1652, 1671, 1720
Rural Newspapers 252
Russia 76, 140, 141, 836, 1364, 1380
Rwanda 108, 119, 282, 598, 599, 698, 769, 1078, 1648

Sadat, Anwar 314, 503
Salah, Tewfik 1010
Salam, Chadi Abdel 1002
Samara, Noah 832
Sambizanga 1012
San 1047, 1108, 1175, 1177, 1188, 1223, 1304, 1684
Sankara, Thomas 1278
Sankofa 1225
Satellites 729, 766, 832
Savage Splendor 923
Savimbi, Jonas 1745
Script Writing 625, 743, 1511
Self-Reliance 1340, 1341
Selskaya Zhizn 140
Sembene, Ousmane 860, 909, 912, 937, 970, 974, 975, 987, 995, 998, 1003, 1017, 1026, 1028, 1029, 1031, 1064, 1067, 1082, 1084, 1086, 1087, 1104, 1123, 1124, 1137, 1155, 1156, 1203, 1212, 1213, 1216
Semiotics 1186
Senegal 69, 77, 96, 110, 113, 164, 229, 411, 505, 548, 570, 609, 622, 650, 663, 725, 759, 794, 848, 911, 995, 998, 1003, 1044, 1058, 1062, 1100, 1123, 1203, 1209, 1212, 1394

Sensationalism 559
Seraphina 1638
Sex 600
Shaba(Katanga) 102
Shaka Zulu 728
Sharpeville 793
Shehu, Brendan 961
Sierra Leone 111, 167, 241, 301, 393, 627, 1252, 1492
Sissoko, Cheik Oumar 934, 946
Smihi, Moumen 1127
Soap Operas 581, 830
Social Conflict 613
Soldiers Three 880
Le Soleil 77, 229, 505, 570
Soleil O 990
Somalia 141, 590, 642, 1246, 1648
Sophiatown 319
South 154
South Africa: Broadcasting 589, 607, 615, 616, 619, 626, 632, 657, 658, 664, 668, 669, 670, 689, 690, 692, 700, 706, 707, 716, 721, 728, 735, 737, 747, 760, 771, 777, 778, 780, 783, 784, 793, 795, 796, 804, 805, 807, 808, 809, 811, 812, 813, 822, 828, 829, 830, 835, 840, 846
South Africa: Film 849, 855, 864, 880, 881, 887, 894, 906, 907, 921, 930, 947, 973, 979, 1032, 1033, 1050, 1065, 1068, 1097, 1098, 1139, 1141, 1143, 1145, 1158, 1159, 1160, 1161, 1162, 1163, 1164, 1165, 1166, 1168, 1169, 1170, 1171, 1172, 1173, 1174, 1176, 1178, 1181, 1180, 1179, 1182, 1184, 1185, 1187, 1204, 1205, 1219, 1224
South Africa: General 1247, 1259, 1272, 1273, 1302, 1303, 1304, 1305, 1306, 1311, 1314, 1316, 1317, 1318, 1319, 1320, 1328, 1329, 1330, 1331, 1332, 1333,

1337, 1338, 1350, 1375, 1381,
1382, 1383, 1385, 1387, 1394,
1397, 1400, 1404, 1406, 1407,
1419, 1421, 1428, 1430, 1434,
1435, 1456, 1460, 1464, 1465,
1466, 1467, 1468, 1469, 1470,
1471, 1472, 1480, 1481, 1482,
1486, 1488, 1494, 1497, 1498,
1499, 1505, 1507, 1508, 1521,
1542, 1551, 1582, 1583, 1592,
1594, 1595, 1605, 1609, 1610,
1611, 1616, 1618, 1630, 1632,
1634, 1637, 1643, 1655, 1656,
1657, 1658, 1659, 1660, 1661,
1662, 1663, 1664, 1665, 1666,
1667, 1669, 1673, 1675, 1677,
1680, 1683, 1685, 1686, 1687,
1688, 1689, 1690, 1691, 1692,
1693, 1694, 1695, 1696, 1697,
1698, 1699, 1700, 1701, 1724,
1726, 1727, 1740, 1741, 1746,
1749, 1753, 1754
South Africa: Press 14, 15, 16, 39,
46, 55, 57, 58, 59, 60, 61, 73, 74,
75, 78, 79, 99, 100, 103, 106, 114,
116, 118, 138, 144, 149, 154, 157,
158, 160, 162, 163, 165, 166, 177,
178, 180, 182, 184, 185, 186, 190,
195, 196, 199, 207, 208, 211, 212,
214, 215, 216, 218, 231, 232, 235,
236, 238, 239, 265, 275, 280, 281,
285, 290, 295, 303, 307, 308, 316,
318, 320, 322, 324, 328, 334, 339,
345, 351, 368, 374, 400, 402, 409,
414, 415, 417, 420, 421, 422, 423,
424, 431, 435, 436, 439, 440, 441,
444, 447, 448, 449, 451, 454, 456,
458, 462, 468, 470, 471, 474, 475,
484, 491, 492, 493, 494, 497, 498,
500, 504, 506, 511, 512, 513, 514,
521, 524, 525, 527, 528, 529, 530,
531, 537, 538, 545, 549, 553, 555,
556, 558, 560, 562, 563, 564, 565,
566, 567, 577, 579
South Africa Now 1616, 1630
South Africa Telegraph 471
South African Broadcasting
   Corporation (SABC) 589, 700,
   706, 737, 778, 784, 805, 809, 810,
   846, 1637
*South African Commercial
   Advertiser* 185
South African Defense Force 1687
South Africa Television 613
Southern Africa 202, 1397, 1500,
   1501, 1502, 1503, 1545, 1621,
   1627, 1631, 1666
Sow, Theirno Faty 1124
Sowetan 265
Soweto 158, 281, 307, 368, 474
Soyinka, Wole 656, 1490, 1668
Spain 416
Sparrow, Gerald 1318
Springbok Legion 565
Staffing 696, 737
Standard 97
Star 160, 1551
State of Emergency 1673
Statesman 144
Stereotypes 861, 1206
Steyn Commission 163, 195, 196,
   303, 1338, 1421, 1464, 1618, 1661,
   1662, 1677, 1690, 1694
Student Protests 114
Sudan 43, 343, 507, 508, 853, 968,
   1388, 1412, 1446, 1670
Suez 1639
Sunday Concord 294
Sunday Mail 313
Sunday Telegraph 1616
Swamp Dwellers 900
SWAPO 735, 1616
Swaziland 726, 1437, 1500, 1554
Symbolism 972, 1087

Subject and Geographical Index

Tambo, Oliver 118
Tanzania 13, 97, 203, 337, 391, 466, 517, 518, 546, 581, 587, 661, 665, 666, 667, 702, 725, 734, 800, 839, 889, 996, 1131, 1432, 1447, 1448, 1449, 1452, 1461, 1530, 1532, 1533, 1534, 1544, 1547, 1622
Tarzan 967, 1034, 1540, 1682
Techniques 886, 1146
Technology 246, 510, 691, 783, 788, 827, 1230, 1303, 1435, 1573, 1578, 1707
Ted Koppel 721
Telecommunications 1434, 1545, 1615
Television 580, 581, 584, 598, 599, 600, 602, 605, 610, 615, 619, 624, 626, 635, 637, 638, 642, 643, 644, 647, 657, 658, 659, 664, 668, 669, 679, 680, 682, 685, 690, 693, 703, 707, 710, 711, 712, 718, 719, 720, 721, 724, 727, 729, 730, 733, 736, 738, 739, 744, 745, 747, 749, 751, 753, 755, 758, 760, 761, 762, 763, 765, 766, 767, 768, 774, 776, 783, 786, 789, 791, 793, 795, 801, 802, 805, 807, 812, 814, 818, 825, 826, 829, 834, 838, 843, 976, 1097, 1173, 1240, 1269, 1289, 1381, 1443, 1444, 1455, 1471, 1473, 1522, 1525, 1526, 1541, 1551, 1592, 1607, 1619, 1625, 1634, 1643, 1695, 1713, 1722, 1723, 1730, 1750
Teno, Jean-Marie 1184, 1192
Terminology 1351
Teshome H. Gabriel 902, 1092, 1134
Theatre 618, 643, 1136, 1199, 1443
Themes 867, 885, 887, 888, 890, 892, 893, 903, 912, 971, 1028, 1082, 1151, 1152, 1166, 1180, 1215, 1217

Theory 1275, 1513, 1686
Things Fall Apart 1030
Third Cinema 1057, 1092, 1134, 1150, 1152, 1153, 1154
Third World 936, 983, 1260, 1377, 1506, 1511, 1512, 1640, 1734
Third World Cinema 902
Tiakeni 855
Time 19, 115, 224, 427, 1350
The Times (London) 314
To the Point 1637
Today 682
Togo 109, 635, 1679
Tolbi, Abdelaziz 966
Torture 508
Touki Bouki 935
Toxic Waste 1710
Traces 1004
Trade Unions 6, 55
Traditional Communication 653, 1642
Training 17, 37, 49, 64, 96, 194, 222, 251, 274, 336, 337, 405, 434, 446, 453, 517, 539, 542, 621, 772, 878, 985, 1076, 1151, 1205, 1242, 1255, 1257, 1276, 1297, 1298, 1315, 1340, 1341, 1344, 1346, 1349, 1362, 1423, 1426, 1465, 1466, 1469, 1489, 1515, 1553, 1561, 1577, 1605, 1685, 1715, 1721
Transition 1490, 1668
Die Transvaler 334
Traore, Mahama 995
Tresgot, Annie 999
Trud 140
Tunisia 535, 768, 870, 874, 885, 919, 989, 1011, 1025, 1148, 1395, 1417, 1444, 1484, 1485, 1702
Turkana 1198
Two Rivers 1184

U.S. News and World Report 27
Uganda 13, 47, 233, 331, 346, 419,

Subject and Geographical Index

463, 467, 499, 559, 617, 701, 806, 820, 1487, 1526
Ugbomah, Eddie 1199
Uhuru 97
Ujamaa 1447
Une Si Simple Histoire 989
UNESCO 501
Unilateral Declaration of Independence. 554, 561, 1747
UNITA 1748
United Kingdom 20, 21, 72, 161, 179, 332, 333, 360, 438, 500, 618, 793, 904, 952, 1074, 1089, 1091, 1128, 1130, 1132, 1206, 1241, 1308, 1321, 1639
United States: Press 46, 65, 74, 76, 98, 102, 115, 159, 172, 179, 224, 248, 264, 266, 273, 279, 288, 306, 327, 332, 333, 360, 374, 398, 418, 423, 427, 479, 519, 532, 558
United States: Film 596, 607, 645, 657, 658, 679, 680, 681, 682, 693, 721, 722, 724, 738, 739, 753, 774, 801, 802, 834, 836, 848
United States: Broadcasting 867, 904, 905, 913, 921, 930, 937, 952, 958, 978, 1013, 1027, 1030, 1034, 1077, 1206, 1216, 1220, 1229
United States: General 1261, 1266, 1302, 1305, 1307, 1311, 1339, 1350, 1368, 1369, 1373, 1380, 1442, 1457, 1459, 1498, 1539, 1576, 1598, 1632, 1636, 1654, 1693, 1725, 1741, 1745, 1748, 1749, 1750
Urban Areas 633, 821, 1285, 1720
USA for Africa 1327
Uys, Jamie 929, 1178

Die Vaderland 553
Van den Heuvel, Alexandre 980
Van Lierop, Robert 924
Vanguard 137

Video 702, 713, 756, 837, 848, 1162, 1472, 1374, 1489
Viljoen Task Group 616, 689, 796
Viljoen, Christo 777
Violence 181, 462, 644, 700, 893, 1333, 1441, 1643, 1696, 1697, 1746
The Visit 1100
Voice of America 583, 836, 746
de Voortrekkers 1145, 1174, 1204

War 437, 698, 1371, 1517, 1745
Washington Post 314, 358
Washington Star 451
We Are the World 1327
Weekend Argus 114
Weekend World 456
Weekly Mail 79, 154, 199
Weekly Post 197
Welles, Orson 931
Wend Kuuni 900, 915, 943, 944
West Africa 56, 94, 95, 123, 245, 310, 379, 392, 540, 708, 770, 910, 1357, 1496, 1528, 1536, 1555, 1717, 1721
West African Pilot 11, 42, 144, 357
West Indies 1064
Western Sahara 487
Wild Geese 1140
Wina, Arthur 317
Western Nigeria Television (WNTV) 685,
Women 542, 548, 650, 655, 757, 764, 767, 772, 800, 848, 857, 891, 984, 1026, 1040, 1054, 1087, 1101, 1137, 1222, 1234, 1252, 1333, 1362, 1374, 1385, 1409, 1420, 1510, 1530, 1570, 1577, 1578, 1579, 1671, 1752
Women Who Smile 1039
World 100, 444, 456
A World Apart 907
World War II 1128

WorldSpace 832

Xala 975, 987, 1017, 1028, 1087, 1104, 1155, 1156, 1212

Ya'qub Sanu' 174
Yan-Diga 1007
Yaoundé Declaration 1537
Yeelen 900, 1041
Yugoslavia 141

Zaire 67, 102, 117, 119, 516, 547, 980, 1073, 1078, 1202, 1271, 1294, 1522, 1679
Zambia 121, 197, 260, 263, 298, 299, 317, 325, 620, 651, 741, 750, 798, 884, 1023, 1129, 1394, 1438, 1497, 1531, 1532, 1621
Zambia Broadcasting Service 1531
Zambia News Agency (ZANA) 121
ZANU (Zimbabwe African National Union) 735, 846
Zanzabuku 923
Zanzibar 198, 1473
ZAPU 735
Zid ya Bouzid 1403
Zimbabwe 86, 149, 155, 299, 312, 313, 327, 365, 430, 455, 494, 523, 554, 557, 561, 578, 651, 655, 682, 702, 772, 845, 846, 880, 1001, 1129, 1371, 1621, 1626, 1747
Zulus 728